Computers and the Collaborative Experience of Learning

Charles Crook takes a novel stance in considering how new technology can enhance rather than undermine the social experience of learning and instruction. He allays fears that computers must isolate the learner from peers and teachers. Through both a review of existing research and the presentation of new empirical work, he argues that computers can provide the conditions for effective collaboration and thereby enhance the social dimension of education.

With its unique blend of theory and practice, *Computers and the Collaborative Experience of Learning* locates this topic of educational technology within the contemporary movement of socio-cultural theory, thereby showing how cultural theories present radical challenges to orthodox psychological thinking. This book will be of interest to educational psychologists, as well as psychologists studying group processes, cognition and development.

Charles Crook is Reader in Psychology at Loughborough University. He is the author (with Julie Rutkowska) of *Computers, Cognition and Development* (1987).

International Library of Psychology
Editorial adviser,
Developmental psychology:
Peter K. Smith
University of Sheffield

Computers and the Collaborative Experience of Learning

Charles Crook

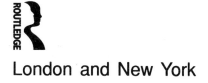

London and New York

First published 1994
by Routledge
11 New Fetter Lane, London EC4P 4EE

First published in paperback 1996

Simultaneously published in the USA and Canada
by Routledge
29 West 35th Street, New York, NY 10001

Typeset in Times by
Florencetype, Stoodleigh, Devon
Printed and bound in Great Britain by
Mackays of Chatham PLC, Chatham, Kent

British Library Cataloguing in Publication data
A catalogue record for this book is available from the British Library

Library of Congress Cataloguing in Publication Data
A catalogue record for this book has been requested

ISBN 0–415–05360–9 (pbk)

Contents

Illustrations

FIGURES

TABLE

Preface

Durham is a small town in the north of England: it is dominated by a large Norman cathedral. The prominance of this building has reminded me of Schelling's famous study in which people were asked how they would set about meeting an unknown person in Manhattan on a specified particular date. No instructions were given: all that Schelling's subjects were told about this stranger was that he or she knew about the world the same things that they knew. The inhabitants of Durham are likely to be in good agreement about what to do in a comparable situation – I suspect that many of them would stand outside the northerly entrance to their cathedral, beneath the Sanctuary knocker no doubt. Perhaps they would stand there at mid-day. Just as with Schelling's subjects heading for the clock at Grand Central Station, this harmony of action tells us something very important about living in human cultures; something that it is easy to lose sight of. We all know a great deal about what others around us expect about our expectations. More generally, we are all in possession of a great deal of common understanding, and we deploy this mutual knowledge most effectively in the coordination of social action.

The example highlights a distinctively human capacity for intersubjectivity – for projecting beliefs, expectations and other psychological states into others. It does so in relation to mutual knowledge of a very general kind: knowledge about local geography and culture. However, such intersubjective attitudes also are adopted in situations where common ground between us is much more intimate. In particular, this human capacity is what gets mobilised in situations that typically we describe as 'collaborative'. Moreover, I believe it is at the core of our achievements within the various settings of organised learning. The communications of learning are most effective when they occur against a rich background of shared understanding. Much of what must go on in education can be described as an investment in constructing such a resource and deploying it as a platform from which to explore further.

In the present book, I shall develop this orientation to educational practice and consider how it is best supported – rather than undermined – by new technology. I believe the relationship of new technology to education now is a matter of some concern. In Chapter 1, I review the progress that has been made during the recent period, as computers have been applied to teaching and learning. I sense that there is an unease regarding the threat that this technology presents to the social quality of educational practice. Consequently, I summarise in Chapter 2 a theoretical perspective that does pay serious attention to this social dimension. It is a perspective that I believe helps us frame the place of technology in education more effectively: we may refer to it as a socio-cultural perspective. In Chapter 3, it is contrasted with more familiar psychological theorising. There I discuss computational and constructivist models of cognition, and contrast them with socio-cultural theories – particularly in terms of their implications for the development of new educational technology.

Chapter 4 presents a discussion of the most controversial metaphor for characterising the possible relation of computers to teaching: the metaphor of a computer-based 'tutor'. The nature of such learning interactions *with* the technology is compared with those interactions that we enjoy with more traditional tutors. One of the problems arising from the experience of computer tutoring is that the experience of learning can easily become dislocated from a broader community structure that characterises classroom life. In Chapter 5, I consider this context by discussing the senses in which a collaborative culture of learning has to be developed *in relation to* this technology.

A more traditional sense of collaborative learning is introduced in Chapter 6. Here the findings of research on peer-based structures are discussed and a framework for systematising this research presented. In Chapter 7, this is pursued in relation to some empirical observations in primary school settings: children interacting *at* computers. The observations happen to involve young children and they happen to involve modest computer resources. However, it is intended that they illustrate very general points about the nature of collaborative discourse and about how it is effectively resourced by technologies. Further case study material is presented in Chapter 8, where I discuss the circumstances of interacting *around* computers and interacting *through* them. In both cases, it is possible to see the supportive role of new technology within collaborative structures that are more loosely-coupled rather than in the more usual sense of collaboration as focused, localised joint activity.

There are three principal motives for writing this book. One arises from a belief that psychological thinking should more actively address practitioner concerns. At the moment, I perceive an uneasy relation between teachers and new technology. Yet, I do not find within cognitive psychology a great deal of helpful theorising or research to guide the effective appropriation of computers into educational practice. Second, I am motivated by a concern to demonstrate that socio-cultural theory provides a persuasive framework for thinking about teaching and learning. In particular, it may offer a distinctive perspective on the relation of technologies to education. Finally, I believe that the experience of collaboration is a neglected topic within psychology. Certainly, there is some tradition of researching collaborative learning within developmental psychology, but I believe that tradition is limited in its scope.

In the past, psychologists interested in children and their development have not been greatly interested in computers. Equally, psychologists interested in computers have not been greatly interested in development. I risk by-passing many people by working at the intersection of these topics. Yet, I feel there is a fascinating challenge arising from the task of integrating new technology with the practice of teaching, the experience of learning and with psychological theories of cognition very generally.

Acknowledgements

I am grateful to the Laboratory of Comparative Human Cognition (LCHC) for twice welcoming me into their community at San Diego and, subsequently, welcoming me into the more virtual community of XLCHC – an international discussion forum for socio-cultural ideas that is sustained over computer networks. I am particularly grateful to Michael Cole for his encouragement and advice. Rhona, Katherine and Richard generously tolerated my long preoccupation with this project: the product of which is dedicated to them. I am particularly grateful to Rhona Nicol who patiently read many drafts of the material presented here, making persistent and insightful comments about it. It would be a far less adequate document without that criticism although its flaws remain entirely my own responsibility.

Chapter 1

Computers in education: some issues

From some point in the early 1980s, the microcomputer became an increasingly conspicuous object: a potent symbol of 'new technology'. In Britain, for example, 1980 was the year that Clive Sinclair launched the first mass-produced micro – the ZX80. Since then, other manufacturers have marketed ever cheaper, smaller and more powerful versions of this instrument. It has penetrated and occupied the offices, shops, factories and spare bedrooms of our culture. Moreover, within these various niches it supports a curious variety of human activity: a situation that has been of some interest to social scientists. Perhaps their research may help us appreciate just how this pervasive technology is affecting our experiences of work, recreation and social relations. Certainly, that is the very area to be explored in the present book. We shall consider one particular niche occupied by computers – classrooms or, more generally, those places where teaching and learning get deliberately organised.

I shall concentrate on the British experience of this educational innovation; although I am sure circumstances in many other countries will reflect that experience quite closely (see Eraut, 1991a; Gywn, 1988; Plomp and Pelgrum, 1991). In the past ten years, rapid evolution of the microcomputer has made it possible for British schools to contemplate substantial investment in this technology. Political pressure has encouraged them to do so and targeted financial support (via the Department of Trade and Industry) allowed schools to cope with the strain that this sudden financial commitment entailed. Moreover, institutional structures were created to support the curriculum development and staff training that would necessarily follow. For example, the Microelectronics in Education Program was launched for schools and the Computers in Teaching Initiative for Higher Education.

Ten years on, much of this priming activity has ended. Recent National Curriculum documents indicate that pressure to assimilate new technology has now been applied to most subject teaching. The majority of teachers will have enjoyed some form of in-service training for tackling the management and application of computers. Most British classrooms will have reliable access to at least one machine. So, at the time of writing, there is some sense of stability in terms of staff development and infrastructure investment. This is not to imply that the technology itself is not evolving: far from it, recent developments (notably in multimedia) are impressive and hold a special promise for educational applications. In any case, it seems a good time to be taking stock of what has been achieved.

The first question an observer of this scene might ask is: 'Have computers been any use to education?' Has this substantial commitment allowed teachers and learners to reach their goals more efficiently, more creatively, more agreeably – or however it is we want to express progress?

In the next section, I offer a summary of evaluative research concerned with such questions. Evaluation defines the first of three central 'issues' arising from computer-based learning that will be reviewed in this chapter. Discussion of the evaluative research will be organised under two sub-headings below, but the discussion in each case will be quite brief. This is because I am not convinced that judging the outcomes of disparate current practice is necessarily the only, or the most urgent, kind of enterprise to be tackled. The situation is in a great flux and we find a good deal of educational computing has an improvised and volatile quality. Evaluation makes sense when we are comfortable with our general aims as practitioners, and have done some conceptual work to help understand how technology can relate to them. Without a preliminary analysis of just what kind of educational environment we want pupils to experience, formal evaluations of particular computer-based ventures are unlikely to have very much impact. These more overarching concerns motivate a good deal of the discussion in this book.

The second of the three broad issues to be considered in the present chapter concerns prevailing models of what an educational computer activity might 'do' for a learner: what kind of learning resource does this technology provide? I shall review contemporary models of computer-based learning by reference to four metaphors that are suggested by them. Given my declared interest in the social dimension of education, the frameworks for practice that emerge from this review will prove somewhat discouraging: none of them defines a clear priority for processes of social exchange.

This problem will be defined and explored as the final issue to be addressed in this chapter. My remarks there set the scene for all the discussion that then follows. Typically, computers are not regarded as objects that contribute to the 'social' quality of our lives. Yet, I shall argue, effective educational environments are necessarily rich in socially organised experiences. The notion of learning as a 'collaborative' activity will be central to the present analysis. I shall principally be concerned with defining how new technology can support the collaborations that should flourish within educational settings.

EVALUATION OF COMPUTER-BASED PRACTICE

Now, I would like to turn to the first issue referred to above: the educational evaluation of computer-based practice. Because of my concern with social psychological themes, it is natural to begin with some observations focusing on the *people* caught up in this innovation. In the first of the following two sections, I will summarise difficulties associated with the reaction of practitioners to the implementation of new technology in education. In the second section, I shall summarise evaluative research on learning outcomes associated with computer-based instruction where it has been implemented.

Evaluation of implementation strategies

When we reflect on experience within schools and colleges over the past ten years, it is inevitable that our judgements about progress will be influenced by what was *expected* when investment and training began. These expectations were often extravagant. As Maddux (1989) observed in this context, pessimism is the familiar enemy of innovators, so a degree of vigorous optimism was natural enough in the early period of computer diffusion. Even commentary on the very first, and most modest, examples of such educational intervention could be fired with enthusiasm (the title of a review by Feldhusen and Szabo (1969) refers to computer-assisted instruction as the 'educational heart transplant'). A more recent judgement that is often cited occurs in an article by Bork (1980). He comments:

> We are at the outset of a major revolution in education, a revolution unparalleled since the invention of the printing press. The computer will be the instrument of this revolution.... By the year 2000, the major way of learning at all levels, and in almost all subject areas, will be through the interactive use of computers. (p. 53)

This prediction has more time to run but, in my view, it now looks to have misjudged something significant in the relation between education and new technology. It seems that the diffusion of this technology has not been as dramatic as was expected in the early period of microcomputer development. Certainly, within recent years, a number of commentators (themselves sympathetic to computer-based learning) have felt obliged to remark on the problems associated with getting computers into active use within education (e.g. Bliss, Chandra and Cox, 1986; Collis, 1987; Cox, Rhodes and Hall, 1988; Cuban, 1986; Hanson, 1985; Heywood and Norman, 1988; Holden, 1989; Lepper and Gurtner, 1989; McCormick, 1992; Plomp, Pelgrum and Steerneman, 1990).

Consequently, actual classroom usage remains limited. A recent British government report suggests that only about 20 per cent of teaching time is making use of computers (DES, 1989b). Similar limits on uptake are apparent in other countries (Dillon, 1985; Plomp and Pelgrum, 1991). Becker comments on the findings of one large-scale US survey: 'in spite of the changes that computers have brought to schools, only a small minority of teachers and students can be said to yet be major computer users' (Becker, 1991).

What are the obstacles? It is natural to seek them within the attitudes or strategies adopted by the teachers who manage this technology – by looking in a focused way at what is being done at the classroom chalk-face. However, this would be too narrow a view. McCormick (1992) characterises problems arising from a widespread failure to develop a whole-school strategy. McInerney (1989), Plomp *et al.* (1990) and Wild (1991) identify a whole range of issues at the institutional level that need to be confronted to make this innovation work.

So, progress may depend, to an important extent, upon action organised at the level of institutional practices. Research that is directed more at the classroom level tends to dwell on teachers' lack of self-assurance when using this technology. For example, Heywood and Norman (1988) highlight obstacles to good practice arising from a shortfall in (primary) teachers' self-confidence. In Britain at least, there was limited anticipation of how difficult it might prove for staff unfamiliar with computers to assimilate them into their practices. On reflection, the combination of circumstances characterising many teachers' first encounters with this technology should have been fairly explosive. Early configurations of classroom microtechnology were tedious and time-consuming to prepare (often requiring the loading of programs off small audio cassettes). Educational software could be of very dubious quality. All sorts of occasions were possible where the computer would appear to fail – leaving the teacher exposed as having lost control (the children's more spontaneous enthusiasm having been undermined in the process).

Politicians and educational administrators were sensitive to this problem – if not to its scale. Certainly, some of the extra financial support for priming this innovation was given over to staff development. Many formal courses of in-service training (Inset) were offered. Yet the feeling often expressed within the profession (in Britain, at least) is that it was not enough and, often, not of the right character. It is now popular to challenge the faith of early policy makers (e.g. Fothergill, 1984) that in-service provision was the quickest way to create an impact. A cascade model underpinned much of this thinking: the hope was that those who received training on intensive short courses would go back to their institution and pass on their expertise. For one reason or another, if they gained any expertise, it looks as if they often kept it to themselves (Boyd-Barrett, 1990).

The contemporary view is that a better strategy would have been to concentrate more effort on initial training (Davis, 1992). We are still in a situation where new teachers can be awkwardly unfamiliar with this technology – possibly seeing it only as threatening (Bracey, 1988; Wellington, 1990). It remains true that many teachers will have had only superficial pre-service exposure to new technology; few will yet have enjoyed the experience of growing up themselves within an established culture of computer use. At the moment, the opportunities for teachers to gain confidence with new technology across the period of initial training are often limited. One survey in 1986 suggested that only 10 per cent of students would use IT on teaching practice (ITTE, 1987). The situation has improved recently, although most students report they are still encountering the technology as an isolated activity (Dunn and Ridgeway, 1991).

The urgency of this problem is hinted at by one extensive review of the effectiveness of microcomputer work (in primary classrooms). In a meta-analysis of recent evaluative research, Ryan (1991) documented the effects of forty variables on the impact of computer-based learning experiences. Only one external variable was found to exert any moderating effect of computer activity on pupil achievement: the extent of teacher pre-training on the activity under study. This draws attention to the fact that effective preparation involves more than instilling the confidence to *motivate* implementation. The success of computer-supported learning also depends upon teacher contact with pedagogic ideas concerning good practice with this technology: the enthusiastic teacher needs to be prepared in this sense also.

Of course, any present initiative for acting at the point of initial training is of little relevance to teachers already in post. Thus, attention to the format of Inset experiences remains important. At present, there is evidence that these experiences are not always ideal. The problems are not merely a limited cascade of expertise: the experience of course participants themselves is often one of disappointment. The problems are illustrated in an extensive study of in-service provision carried out by Rhodes and Cox (1990a, b). They were able to witness the management of training programs and to visit the schools of staff who had attended them, so they could observe classroom practice as well as interview participating teachers. A somewhat gloomy picture emerges from this comprehensive survey. The training regimes did not appear well matched to the experience or needs of these teachers. Consequently, they were not as effective as the tutors had expected or hoped. Much of what was achieved related to problems of using the technology itself, at the expense of tackling real educational issues. Half of the sample of teachers believed the computer resulted in an increase in their workloads and that it made no fundamental change to the way in which they worked – merely reinforcing existing patterns of activity.

This snapshot of practitioner experience is sobering – particularly to those of us researchers whose (possibly selective) contact with classroom practice may create a rosy picture of innovative possibilities. The situation is well summarised in one survey that revealed only 14 per cent of primary school teachers felt competent to use a range of IT applications without assistance (Davis, 1992). Yet how might the general picture be made more heartening? Rhodes and Cox identify the commitment of the head teacher as significant in determining attitudes within a school more generally. But they also urge more effective experiences for preparing and supporting teachers in their use of this relatively unfamiliar resource. Thus, at present, there may be few sites where a culture of computer use is comfortably established – where the potential impact of particular computer-based activities can be evaluated in a convincing manner.

Nevertheless, my colleague Geoff Alred and I have recently had the opportunity to study one initiative where an effective context for innovation was carefully cultivated and thus where circumstances seemed more favourable to effective implementation of the kind that policy-makers hope for. A local education authority invited primary schools to volunteer staff for participation in a project to evaluate Turtle Logo. This is an activity that will be described in more detail in a later section. Suffice to say it is a challenging exercise in computer programming based upon controlling the movements of either a floor robot or a screen icon ('turtle'). New equipment was supplied; the project ran over a generous time period (at least four terms), and it incorporated specialised in-service support (with suitable teaching cover). In short, the conditions of the venture would seem to be very favourable: the focal activity (Logo) is widely endorsed in early education and the project was well supported by specialised training opportunities. Moreover, the participants were motivated (if not highly experienced) and could enjoy the advantage of being part of a community of innovators. In summary, this situation seemed to us to approximate what elsewhere has been described as the 'ideal' circumstance of an IT-related in-service provision (Owen, 1992, p. 130).

These teachers kept diaries summarising their experience and Alred and I were able to interview them at some length towards the end of the formal project. The emerging picture is a mixed one. Although it was not part of our purpose to observe the classroom activity directly, it was apparent that the children had enjoyed the Logo work: most of the teachers had been impressed by their engagement with it. Yet, on balance, the implementation project as a whole cannot be regarded as a great success. One measure of success would be how far the activity remained in use to become part of classroom routine for subsequent generations of pupils to enjoy. One year after the official end of the project, less than a quarter of the teachers were found to be still using Logo with their new classes. As it happens, our conversations with them had led us to expect this.

Although they recognised the innovative nature of the activity – as well as the children's enthusiasm for it – they were also keen to identify the practical difficulties associated with managing it on a routine basis. Mundane problems of unreliable turtles were a major source of disappointment. But as the activity can be supported on the screen alone (i.e. it does not depend on a working floor robot), this cannot explain the widespread failure to consolidate the experience beyond the life of the project. Other problems mentioned related to the time and effort involved in preparing the computer and ensuring its security. The teachers also remarked on the difficulty of monitoring and supporting the activity while classroom life continued as normal around it. Finally, taking such necessary effort into account, there was some doubt as to whether comparable academic achievements could not be reached in simpler ways.

To some extent the adequacy of the in-service provision arises again here: certainly, this was another source of some dissatisfaction among the participants. Many of the problems experienced *seem* as if they should have been tractable with experienced advice and encouragement; however, there is a danger in continually laying the blame at this door. At some point we may have to acknowledge that the creative deployment of this technology puts a lot more strain on the status quo of classroom life than has been recognised. More sensitive preparation and training might be some part of a solution to this problem but there is clearly an invitation to reflect more carefully on defining the optimal computer *environment* for supporting innovation as effortlessly as we can. That is an issue to which I shall return later in this book.

Evaluation of learning outcomes

Evaluation of what gets learned from such a multi-faceted innovation is not easy. For one thing, its use has not been planned in programatic terms. In so far as pressure for innovation has largely been applied from above, practitioners may have felt little sense of dealing in *options* for change: options that might be catalogued and approached in a spirit of formal evaluation. The atmosphere has been more one of seizing opportunities and improvising a way forward. However, if we persist in seeking evaluative data, it can be sought in respect of two broad questions. First, has there been progress in imparting to young learners some fluency in simply using new technology? The phrase 'computer literate' has evolved to capture what this might mean. Second, can computers assist mastery of those particular curriculum areas where they have been used to support teaching: geography, maths, music or whatever? This is a more subject-based question.

Simply in terms of whether pupils now have the chance to encounter new technology in schools, we can say that things have worked. Most school children will enjoy some hands-on experience of computers. Whether the experience leaves them adequately comfortable and confident is another matter; it may yet be too modest in scope. This may be a matter of some concern, given what is known about attitudes to new technology among the current generation of adults. For that generation, a clinical vocabulary has been felt necessary to capture the extremes of feeling: computers are capable of inducing 'phobic' responses in some (Meier, 1985) while in others they can acquire the status of an 'addiction' (Shotton, 1989).

What can be said about the rising generation of computer users is that such extremes of attitude are not apparent at the earlier stages of using computers in school. Numerous reports endorse the view that children's early experience with computers in classrooms today is a positive one – as they themselves judge it (Hughes, Brackenridge and Macleod, 1987). It is perhaps still too soon to decide whether such favourable early reactions predict greater confidence (and less aversion) on completion of school. Data to be presented later in this book suggest that some of the most academically successful of school leavers (undergraduates) still include significant numbers who remain (1) relative novices in terms of experience and (2) have very uncertain attitudes regarding the appeal of using computers. Perhaps ten years of gradual development is still too short a period to assess whether educational practice is creating a natural culture of computer use.

However, we are not just concerned with learning to use computers: we are also interested in using computers to learn. A second evaluation question concerns impacts associated with deploying computers to support teaching in the traditional curriculum areas. Can this technology help pupils learn about, say, mathematics, geography, design and so on? The more circumscribed nature of such questions suggests that they might allow more confident answers. Unfortunately, the resulting picture is not as clear as we might like it to be.

For one thing, research in the relevant settings and under the prevailing conditions of innovation is not easy to manage (Bork, 1991). We will usually wish to conduct studies in which different conditions of learning are created and compared. However, explicitly tinkering with resource allocation may be both unwelcome and impractical. Institutions may be open to participation in research but not if the research procedures undermine equity of opportunity for their pupils. They will also resist being deprived of access to leading-edge technologies where this is simply in the interest of comparative research exercises. Thus, true *experiments* are not easy to conduct. Moreover, 'natural experiments' (in which we compare spontaneously differing educational circumstances) bring their own problems: the differences found in these cases may conceal other differing population characteristics that also contribute to the outcomes compared. These problems were identified by reviewers of early initiatives (e.g. Jamison, Suppes and Wells, 1974) and they still remain an obstacle to confident evaluation.

Moreover, it is surely fanciful to suppose singular generalisations will be found that can make sense of such diverse educational activities. Computers support a very wide variety of learning encounters in a very wide range of curriculum areas. We must be wary of sweeping rulings on the success (or failure) of new technology.

However, if some feeling for the state of an evaluation balance sheet is still felt valuable, summaries of such research have been reported. Kulick, Kulick and Bangert-Drowns (1985) have conducted a meta-analysis over a large number of published studies evaluating computer-based teaching projects in early education. They find reliable and recurring positive impacts – amounting, on average, to improvements of around 0.48 standard deviations on outcome test scores, or student movement from the 50th to the 68th percentile. These effects seem strongest in early educational settings. More recently, a further meta-analysis (Ryan, 1991) has focused on primary school interventions of eight weeks or longer. Similar findings are reported. The mean effect size across the studies reviewed was 0.309. This may be expressed by saying that the treatment groups, on average, exceeded the performance of 62 per cent of their matched peers in control groups.

Kulick and Kulick (1987) report comparable effect sizes beyond early education, although it is widely believed that outcome effects remain strongest for interventions within the elementary sector (Niemiec and Walberg, 1987). In a meta-analysis of such meta-reviews Niemiec and Walberg conclude: 'The average and typical effect of CAI is to place the average student using it at the 66th percentile of traditional groups – a substantial though not overwhelming advantage' (1987, p. 31).

Given the scale of the underlying educational investment and upheaval, effects of this magnitude might be judged less dramatic than we could hope for. Of course, we must be cautious in interpreting such findings. The statistics will conceal a great deal of variation associated with the sheer range of possible computer-based activity. Moreover, methodologically pure evaluation studies are more feasible with those forms of computer-based instruction that reinforce existing curricular concerns – and for which teacher-based control groups are more readily defined. Certainly, studies focused on drill-and-skill forms of software seem over-represented in reviews. The more radical and innovative applications of the technology may be less easily studied under the strict methodological requirements sought by meta-reviews of the literature. Disappointment in these findings may be premature for other reasons: many practitioners will declare that, whatever evaluation research shows, they can simply see the computer 'doing good'. If post-intervention testing is failing to endorse this then, they would argue, this may be a reflection of the short-term, piecemeal nature of the outcome measures. Our tools for assessing what is being changed may be blunt instruments. Moreover, the modest scope and duration of many formalised interventions could miss effects apparent in a truly motivated and committed classroom.

If we do wish to conduct evaluations of what is learned in computer-based contexts, we must go beyond the input–output designs that characterise much research in the area. It may not be enough only to expose a pupil to some software and, some time later, do an outcome test of understanding. The reason this is inadequate is because any such computer experience is more or less situated in some broader framework of teaching activity. In short, there is a risk of casting this educational technology in terms that suggest a medical model of how it works. Computers are unlikely to function as magic bullets – effortlessly releasing their therapeutic effects at points identified by teachers. The unfamiliarity and wizardry that surrounds them may cultivate such notions, but the real impact of learning through this technology may need to be measured with attention to how it is assimilated into the surrounding frame of educational activity. That will be one theme to be developed in what follows here. There is considerable variation possible in how researchers conceptualise the way a computer program is being 'used'. This, in turn, must influence empirical strategies favoured for evaluating the 'effects' of some computer activity.

For this reason, the research reviewed above should not encourage too hasty and definitive conclusions about how effective computers are in supporting learning. Their impact may need to be judged with careful attention being paid to broader patterns of *use*. This demands consideration of how computer-based experiences are integrated into the broader frame of activities that define an organised environment for teaching and learning. Across different settings, there may be significant variation in how radically the same technology serves to restructure the activity of learning. Thus, its influence will not always be neatly contained within events at the pupil–computer interface itself. Researchers may need to look further than this in defining the 'place' at which computers work their effects.

My discussion of evaluation has converged on this issue of understanding the broader context of computer-based learning. The same theme of integration will arise in the discussions below of more theoretical perspectives available to characterise computer-based learning. It does appear that seamless integration has been more problematic than many committed observers had hoped. I would suggest that there are three persistent problems that underlie the dislocated nature of many classroom computer experiences. First, there is a great deal of controversy over how this technology is best deployed: what *sort* of role it is supposed to play in relation to existing patterns of teaching. Second, there has been some teacher resistance to computers on grounds of limited familiarity – a circumstance that might suggest inadequate provision of pre-service preparation and in-service staff development. Finally, there may be deeply rooted concerns regarding the impact of technology on the *social* quality of educational experience. This last problem is a particular focus within what follows in this book.

These various obstacles to implementation will be explored further in the remainder of this chapter. In dealing with the first (conceptualising the computer as a learning resource), I shall evaluate four prevailing metaphors: computer-as-tutor, computer-as-pupil, computer-as-simulation and computer-as-tool. The second problem (that of teacher preparation), I have discussed above. The final obstacle to a seamless integration will be introduced and defined in the last section of the chapter. There I shall consider how an (apparently) impersonal technology relates to what is traditionally a most socially organised activity: classroom learning.

CONCEPTUALISING THE NATURE OF COMPUTER-BASED LEARNING

One imbalance within the review that follows should be acknowledged. Much of the published research in this area has been focused on the concerns and practices of *early* education. To some extent this merely reflects the special interest that psychologists and educationalists have in the management of learning in the 'formative' years. It also may reflect the fact that computer use may be more pervasive (Becker, 1991) and more successful (Niemiec and Walberg, 1987) in primary education than it is in the secondary sector. However, I am confident that the substantive points arising here apply very generally to other sectors of education.

It is not possible to review all of the achievements and arguments that rightly belong under each of the sub-headings used in the present section. I merely intend to establish that there are problems to be addressed and that these are not problems that can be solved through the application of simple evaluation experiments. Here my own preference for a method of tackling the practical problems is apparent. I shall argue that what is more urgently needed is a theoretical framework to help systematise some of the tensions and uncertainties associated with the present state of computers applied to education. What will actually emerge in later chapters is one particular theoretical framework which is closely associated with certain contemporary preoccupations within developmental psychology: namely, the socio-cultural or socio-historical perspective.

In short, the following review of options for framing computer-based practice will not attempt to be comprehensive; instead, it will crystallise a number of challenges that will be recovered in later chapters for reconsideration in terms of a socio-cultural view. This will be particularly pertinent for discussion in Chapter 2, where the nature of this perspective is more fully discussed.

The tutorial metaphor: computer-as-tutor

This section concerns a form of computer software that reproduces a traditional model of teaching and learning. I shall note that such software is popular despite criticisms from educational theorists. I argue that the reasons for its popularity are complex and deserve more sympathetic reactions.

In his book *Teachers and machines*, Cuban (1986) reminds us that the enterprise of marrying educational practice with contemporary technologies has a long history. Yet it was not until the 1950s that people began to entertain the concept of a 'teaching machine' – in the sense of a mechanism that directly instructs. Such a technology would not simply be something that teachers employed to illustrate or elaborate their teaching. To a significant degree it could take over, wholesale, what a teacher does.

Efforts to create such machines arose from a species of applied psychology associated with behaviourism, a dominant theoretical paradigm within psychology at the time. Yet, whatever the former authority of behaviourism, it is fair to say that the teaching machines of this era were neither very successful nor very popular (see Skinner, 1984 for disappointed reflection on the neglect of such behaviourist enthusiasms). Certainly, the early realisation of this idea had virtually disappeared from education at the time that microcomputers made their entry. However, the spirit of machine-as-tutor has been revived: finding its modern realisation in certain controversial varieties of educational software that are in widespread current use.

It seems that the ambition to simulate tutorial instruction does retain a seductive quality. So, when school micros began to appear in Britain, the education correspondent of *The Times* was able to headline his copy 'A teacher on every desk' (*The Times*, 1984). Yet, if we are amused by this ten years on, it is surely for the sheer scale of computerisation implied by such a vision. The underlying principle of desktop teachers probably still carries serious credibility. Many enthusiasts suppose that the obstacle is merely limited access to adequately powerful delivery systems. Certainly, it must be granted that contemporary technology is far more versatile than that available to an earlier generation of designers. So, it may be argued, we should take seriously the mission to embody features of teacher–pupil-interaction within the design of educational software.

In fact, the appeal of computer-as-tutor may, in part, be sustained by one particular perspective on the nature of teacher–pupil dialogue. Some commentators (Dillon, 1985; Levin, Kim and Riel, 1990) have drawn a parallel between the design of much educational software and a form of classroom interaction characterised as I–R–E sequences (Mehan, 1979; Sinclair and Coulthard, 1975). That is, verbal exchanges taking the form of a (teacher) Initiation, a (pupil) Response and a (teacher) Evaluation. As in:

Teacher: ... if it's a pentagon, how many sides does it have?
Pupil: Five sides.
Teacher: That's right, well done.

Ethnographers of classroom discourse report such sequences are commonplace. It is, of course, a form of talk into which pupils become socialised and which we recognise as peculiarly characteristic of school experience. We accept its features, perhaps without much reflection: the ritualistic nature of the exchange, the idea of people asking questions to which they know the answer, the expectation of evaluative feedback, and so on. It is clearly something that happens when teaching is in progress. It might also be something that could happen within a dialogue arranged between a pupil and a computer: 'The computer initiates, the student replies, the computer evaluates, the computer initiates again, and so on' (Levin *et al.*, 1990 p. 210).

In fact, such sparse realisation of the computer-as-tutor is quite common within the so-called 'Computer-aided instruction' (CAI) tradition. This approach has involved preoccupation with two goals in the creation of effective tutorial software: (1) individualisation problems and questions tailored to the (changing) needs of particular learners, and (2) the delivery of constructive feedback. What this has often entailed is refining procedures for getting the initiating questions 'right' (matched to what the current pupil knows) and attending to the crafting of accurate and motivating feedback. At its most modest, this may merely mean saying 'No' if a pupil makes an error, supplying correct answers where appropriate, and choosing a new level of problem to match pupil progress.

The more advanced versions of such CAI are sometimes termed 'Intelligent Tutoring Systems' (e.g. Anderson, Boyle and Reiser, 1985; Burns, Parlett and Redfield, 1991; Mandl and Lesgold, 1988; Self, 1988; Sleeman and Brown, 1982). They illustrate one particular enthusiasm closely associated with computer-based education: namely, the goal of creating a strongly individualised curriculum. Thus, the 'intelligence' of an ITS system would reside not merely in its programmed expertise for the domain of knowledge. It would also be able intelligently to diagnose the learner's needs and then intelligently implement an individualised tutorial dialogue.

The ITS tradition of instructional software has been more visible in military and industrial training contexts than within formal education. This may partly reflect the sophisticated hardware platforms that are needed (usually beyond the financial reach of schools). It may also reflect the fact that implementation may be more realistic for developing skilled behaviour within fairly circumscribed domains of action. Broader educational goals may be more difficult to realise. Thus, at the time of writing, really effective examples of this format are rarely encountered in classrooms. The preoccupation of ITS enthusiasts has been with the possibility of seriously individualising the curriculum – a teaching technology sensitive to individual learners. Yet it has proved surprisingly difficult to construct algorithms that effectively diagnose a pupil's particular errors and needs. Even something as apparently straightforward as learning subtraction turns out to be a skill that supports a rich variety of pupil misunderstandings and procedural 'bugs' (Brown and Burton, 1978), so even this simple domain is not easy to 'tutor' in the automated sense we are contemplating here.

Perhaps a compromise is possible – could some of the decisions regarding customisation of problems to the learner's needs be passed over to pupils to make for themselves? For example, pupils might make their own choices in respect of the difficulty of problems they are equipped to tackle. This is evidently an option; although, when younger children confront computer-based problems, it seems we cannot necessarily assume that they will choose levels of difficulty that are challenging or well matched to their state of knowledge (Crook and Steele, 1987).

In spite of the admitted difficulty of building 'intelligence' into computer-based tutoring systems, software conceived within this broad (tutor) model of educational computing has often been that most readily adopted by teachers. This is particularly the case within early education. Moreover, the most widely employed examples are those with the least pretension to some modest 'intelligence'. Such programs – repetitively delivering discrete problems within some domain of study – are often termed 'drill-and-practice' or 'drill-and-skill' programs. Surveys of classroom practice reveal a striking preference for these more didactic forms of software (Becker, 1991; Jackson, Fletcher and Messer, 1986), particularly for children under 9 years old (DES, 1991).

Conversely, these are programs held in very poor regard among professional commentators (e.g. Papert, 1980; Self, 1985). Papert, in particular, is a vigorous critic whose slogan that the modern pupil is being controlled by the computer (rather than vice versa) is frequently cited. Thus, the most widespread practical realisation of our computer-as-tutor metaphor is widely criticised by educational theorists as constraining the learner's experience. It is judged to offer poor approximations to what is itself a rather poor model of the teaching process in the first place (didactic encounters guided by the IRE pattern of dialogue). However, simply because of their widespread use, we should reflect on these kinds of activity a little further here. Why have programs fashioned in this tradition been so widely preferred by practitioners?

To answer this, we should consider an observation made by Cuban (1986). Reviewing the history of teaching and machines, Cuban concludes that what practitioners prefer to do with computers merely reproduces the typical fate of any new technology applied to education. It tends to be assimilated to prevailing traditions of classroom practice. Cuban's documentation of this relentless pattern is convincing but the analysis is often invoked by others in a rather disparaging manner. We may agree that this inertia is unfortunate in that it reflects a failure to seize *new* opportunities – but we should attempt to make sense of it. Simply proposing that teachers have a limited vision of good practice is an ungenerous and probably inaccurate conclusion.

Thus, we may accept Cuban's claim that the popularity of drill-and-skill computer activities can serve to maintain a status quo. But I would then suggest two particular ways to make more sense of this. First, the strategy of assimilation to existing practice is a ready reaction to the unwelcome demands of an imposed innovation. Second, the strategy reflects some degree of genuine commitment to that feature of the status quo. Opportunity for structured practice is seen as something that is worth developing – and new technology is identified as one way to do this.

The first of these two observations supposes that innovative adoption of computers is more difficult to achieve than is often assumed. In an earlier section, attention was drawn to the practical problems associated with incorporating new technology into classrooms. Studies of in-service training provision suggest a mismatch between what is offered and what is needed. They draw attention to how we may overestimate the ease with which teachers can develop confidence with an unfamiliar technology. Research also highlights the hidden demands entailed in the professional support of innovative work on classroom computers. Under such pressure, teachers may well adopt the comparatively effortless solution of focusing their commitment on straightforward, self-contained programs that pupils can work through independently. These would be drill-and-skill software of the sort that is found to be widely used. There is evidence that this preference does represent a kind of holding response in an uncomfortable situation (Heywood and Norman, 1988).

This reason for the popularity of more humdrum tutorial software is a reactive one – though none the less important to uncover and understand. However, the second reason I proposed for the popularity of drill-based programs suggests a more actively positive attitude towards them. It may be rash simply to exclude drill and practice from the learning process. Teachers may feel that such experiences form an important part of achieving certain educational goals. Anyone who has, for example, attempted to cultivate musical pitch, or master the differential calculus will probably appreciate the merit in dense experience of exemplary problems from the relevant domain. Dreyfus and Dreyfus (1984, 1986) elaborate this point in the context of a psychological model describing the development of skilled expertise. So, the value of furnishing opportunities for unadorned practice may be accepted. Yet, if it is accepted, it need not presume wholesale reduction of educational activity to the rehearsal of discrete sub-skills.

Practitioners may, therefore, endorse the view that much of what they teach permits some place for such focused practice. They may also concede that furnishing the necessary opportunities is not the easiest or most rewarding part of their responsibility. That is exactly where computers may offer an easy appeal. They seem to offer some release from this problem. Computer-based versions of practice within a domain may be particularly attractive simply because they can offer this opportunity in an (apparently) engaging manner. In fact, Cuban (1986) admits some sympathy with the use of computers for drills, arguing that this is what computers are actually very good at (see also Dreyfus and Dreyfus, 1984; Marsh, 1985).

I am proposing that the preference for simple computer-as-tutor implementations needs to be made sense of rather than automatically disparaged. Part of the sense we might make of it involves acknowledging the local ecology within which computer innovation is being encouraged: those conditions may not always be favourable, and skill-type programs are a ready solution to sustain some level of computer use. But the sense we make of it might also involve an admission that the creation of practice-oriented opportunities has some legitimacy. Computers can raise the appeal of what might otherwise be a less rewarding activity. In fact, when we confront examples of the genre we may even fail to notice that their underlying format is quite mundane. An illustration from early education may help to make this point.

In a recent review, Scott, Cole and Engel (1992) are critical of the computer drill tradition. Yet, an example program they furnish for purposes of contrast – and to illustrate imaginative use of computers – seems to have typically drill-like features. The program invites pupils to assign values at positions on a number line; an activity that is embedded in a game involving the harpooning of a shark. In other words, a repetitive exercise in which the shark's position on the computer screen is an invitation to generate a numerical representation. This would count as a drill program in any survey of classroom practice: it is apparently a self-contained and repetitive exercise involving a basic mathematical skill.

Yet, Scott *et al.* may be right to cite such a program with some approval. It sounds engaging enough, and surely a teacher with the task of helping children cultivate strategies of estimation will find it attractive. Moreover, there are plenty of other examples of such circumscribed activities that could be judged equally appealing. Some of them have evolved from careful work within cognitive psychological theory (e.g. Resnick and Johnson, 1988). In the face of temptation from interesting drill-based programs such as that described above, a tolerant attitude to the genre seems possible – especially if Dreyfus and Dreyfus' caution is respected: 'the only danger in the use of the computer for drill and practice and for diagnosis arises from the temptation to overemphasise the sort of training in which the computer works, precisely because it works so well' (1986, p. 133). Coming to believe that domains of knowledge could be reduced *only* to packaged exercises is one possibility we should remain alert to. I shall mention one more before closing this section on computer-as-tutor: one that is more central to my concern here with social context.

This flirting with computer activities – incorporating them at the periphery as vehicles-for-practice – is a strategy with its own problems. In particular, marginalising certain activities in the way that can happen with computers, may serve to undermine their impact. Something of value may be lost where such activities are not knitted into a mainstream of class learning. The limit to computers functioning as tutors arises not just because tutorial dialogue is hard to simulate at the moment-to-moment level of conversation. Computers are also limited in this role because 'tutoring' talk is something that is organised at levels superordinate to that of the current moment. In other words, effective tutorial dialogues are embedded in more extensive contexts of shared classroom experience. Such dialogues are normally made possible by the history of this experience. Their effectiveness may depend on creating a natural continuity of reference with it – a richness of context that will be very hard to reproduce mechanically. This is a concern I shall elaborate further in Chapter 4, where it will be approached in terms of our current theme of collaboration.

A failure to involve activities of the kind we have been discussing within a fuller collaborative pattern is one basis for concern with the popular computer-as-tutor strategy. Another has already been alluded to: namely, that this preferred use of computers causes us to miss an opportunity for innovation. The misfortune here is more a failure to recognise that a particular technology has potential beyond that which represents its more accessible and effortless applications. More generously, and as argued above, we may grant that the potential may be recognised by teachers, but the reality of implementation may be more demanding than educational commentators appreciate.

There are grounds to feel disappointment that circumstances are apparently jeopardising opportunities to do genuinely *new* things through the mediation of computers. The technology is capable of supporting distinctively challenging and innovative activities, as well as re-formatting more familiar tasks. This is an observation commonly deployed to justify and encourage implementations conceived according to our second metaphor, the one to be considered next.

The construction metaphor: computer-as-pupil

We encountered above Papert's (1980) widely-cited concern that to regard the computer as a form of teacher was to risk a situation in which children were 'controlled' by the technology. Yet the survey statistics reveal that software in the simple tutorial tradition commands considerable appeal. Perhaps the rhetoric of 'control' is too provocative here to be fully persuasive. Teachers recognise that these computer-based activities often parallel traditional classroom activity; they conform to the purposes pursued elsewhere in the class; moreover, they may be more engaging in format. If this is to be conceptualised as 'control', then it runs deeply within educational culture and, thus, the critique is somewhat defused.

On the other hand, there may be teachers who are uneasy about that culture and impatient with the style of practice they often find themselves party to. They may then recognise in new technology a potential for subverting the status quo rather than upholding it. In particular, they may sense a possibility of shifting from more teacher-centred to more pupil-centred practices. For many, Papert's vision of the computer in education offered something of this potential. In his book *Mindstorms* (1980), Papert not only denied the tradition of computers in control of pupils, he proposed an alternative in which that relation would be reversed: pupils would control the machines. But, most importantly, the ways in which they might come to do this would entail especially potent learning experiences. The idea is captured well in his notion of a microworld. This is a setting in which learners can apply principled knowledge to effect genuinely creative activity. They *construct* new understandings through their exploratory activity.

Papert's proposal is driven by a compelling image. If you wish to learn to speak French, he argues, you go to France. This surely makes good sense to us. But if France is where you go to command French, where do you 'go' to command, say, mathematics? What must be discovered in that case is a sort of 'Mathsland'. In such a place, the learner might encounter situations where various opportunities are offered for hypothesis-testing explorations; where existing knowledge must be mobilised to solve urgent and motivated problems. It would be a versatile platform from which one's initially modest base of knowledge could be meaningfully exercised.

This describes an environment of discovery-based learning. So, it suggests an important theoretical influence: namely, the ideas of Piaget on cognitive development. First, Piaget's notion of the learner as necessarily active is strongly endorsed. A microworld is a place where things are getting *done*: in Papert's realisations, such action amounts to teaching computers to do something interesting – the computer is thus the 'pupil' in these encounters. Another important principle defining the microworld environment is that it should be somewhere that maximises the experience of discovery. So, it might be a place where teachers can more effectively respect Piaget's warning: 'Each time we prematurely teach a child something he would have discovered for himself, the child is kept from inventing it and consequently from understanding it completely' (Piaget, 1970, p. 715).

Papert furnished a particularly striking example of a microworld environment with his Turtle Logo. This is an activity that can be described from two perspectives. First, it is a vehicle for introducing certain concepts that are central to writing computer programs. Logo is a computer language that has a number of important features. In particular, it incorporates procedures (sub-units of code performing discrete functions), it is extensible (the user can define these units to be used as primitives) and it embodies recursion (such procedures can be self-referring). For Papert, these exemplify 'powerful ideas': ideas that can be mobilised very generally for problem-solving. He supposes that the opportunity to exercise them in some concrete (computer-based) activity allows them to surface sufficiently clearly that the learner can directly contemplate them. Such reflection will help these skills become more readily available in other problem-solving domains. Treating the computer as a 'pupil' in Papert's sense (by programming it) is thus taking an opportunity to cultivate general problem-solving skills.

So, Logo is about acquiring such skills via programming. It is also about controlling the particular settings which act as vehicles for the programming. The vehicle that Papert promoted most successfully was turtle geometry. Within this microworld, the learner can issue instructions (a program) that cause movement of a floor robot (turtle). The same instructions can, more simply, be used to create patterns on a computer screen. Here, then, we find something corresponding to the elusive 'Mathsland': arithmetic, algebra and geometry all encountered in the purposeful task of generating movement or creating patterns. The computer offers a meaningful and motivating environment in which principled knowledge can be applied towards creative goals. The learner is using her understanding to 'teach', the computer is acting as pupil.

Turtle maths is not the only outlet for Logo. For example, in another instantiation of the basic programming environment, some interesting possibilities can be created to support work in the language curriculum. However, it was turtle Logo that truly captured the imagination of educators. It could be said that it remains the most striking realisation of what Papert so appealingly defined as a 'microworld'. Certainly, it must be unique in the sheer energy and enthusiasm that it drew from users. Magazines and special interest groups have flourished in support of the Logo teaching community.

Ten years on, some of that energy arguably has dissipated. One important reason should be noted here. Logo attracted more focused evaluation research than any other computer-based enterprise. The strength of the claims made for it and its obvious appeal among pupils naturally invited careful assessment. On the whole, the evaluations have not been as positive as enthusiasts might have hoped for. A number of critical reviews have now appeared (e.g. Dudley-Marling and Owston, 1988; Pea and Kurland, 1987; Pea, Kurland and Hawkins, 1987; Simon, 1987). Moreover, apart from the example of Logo, studies of pupils learning other computer languages have not furnished very persuasive evidence for the generalisability of programming skills (Dalbey, Tournaire and Linn, 1986; Palumbo, 1990).

Yet the emerging picture is not one of unqualified disappointment. In fact, in terms of the arguments developed elsewhere in this book, the findings of Logo evaluations are very instructive. Pea and his colleagues, in particular, have made a useful characterisation of the circumstances under which this kind of learning environment may and may not be effective. It seems that situations where outcomes from Logo experience have been less successful are those where participants have too enthusiastically adopted Piaget's dictum (quoted above) about avoiding 'premature' teaching. These less successful ventures may illustrate too great a faith in the principle characterised by Perkins (1985) as 'the opportunity does the teaching by itself' – the idea that simply using it is enough. Except that, in this case, such faith is likely to be amplified by witnessing conspicuous engagement among the learners.

Enthusiasm for such pupil-led opportunities is complemented by natural distrust of the opposing alternative: more teacher-controlled situations. Perkins comments (sceptically) 'Often it is even urged that direct teaching may do mischief by forcing the issue in an unmotivated and a contextual manner' (1985, p. 13). In all this there may be too careless a polarisation of the options. There *is* an issue associated with inauthentic learning and we wish to remain vigilant in respect of it. But 'direct teaching' is not the exclusive alternative to a discovery-based microworld encounter. In the ideal situation, involvement of teachers may need to be very much 'indirect' in manner, nevertheless their involvement is crucial. Around Logo-learning pupils, there are important things to be done (and said) by others who are themselves more confident with the relevant concepts. The challenge is to discover more of how this supportive function is to be defined: that, in turn, may require us to consider the 'collaborations' that computers-as-pupils afford.

This section on computers-as-pupils has reached one conclusion very similar to that reached in the discussion computers-as-tutors above. In each case, the implementation of the computer activity may too easily encourage a distancing of teacher involvement; or, more generally, a dislocation from the normally rich context of class-based activity and discussion. As was remarked at the end of the previous section, this is a threat to the collaborative quality of learning experiences: one to which we shall give more attention in later chapters.

Conceptions of computers as tutors and as pupils have been important in determining the most common patterns of use. However, there are at least two further metaphors with wide appeal. I shall comment more briefly on each of these next.

Simulations

It is characteristic of Papert's microworlds that they should have an open-ended quality. A set of powerful ideas are available, the application of which will support a rich variety of creative activity. A relatively clean working surface is supplied and pupils direct action towards it. In this version of computer-based learning, the power of the computer to manage symbolic activity is harnessed to allow the pupil real control over a given domain of knowledge. However, this form of control can be realised in more circumscribed ways. Learners can interact with more closed systems and, in doing so, instructive experiences are made to occur within them.

In such cases, the symbol-manipulating power of the technology is exploited to offer simulations of real-world systems. Computers might, for example, simulate a stock exchange for students of economics; or the behaviour of cell membranes for students of biology. The promise of such scaled-down experiences lies in their capability for offering the learner control over the operating parameters of some system. In this way, a system's characteristics may be explored through experimentation. It is likely that simulation software will become more commonplace as multimedia technology develops.

An early indication of what is possible with such resources – and a theoretical context for evaluating it – is available in the work of the Cognition and Technology Group at Vanderbilt (1990). This group have employed video-disc technology to create 'macro-contexts' for learning. They encourage the idea of 'anchored instruction': a form of educational practice that is strongly oriented to exercising knowledge in rich and meaningful settings of authentic practice. The learner is invited to control some domain of interest in a manner that more resembles the experience we associate with apprenticeship modes of learning.

Exposure to simulations is seen by some as a solution to slow progress being made within the computer-as-tutor tradition. A limitation of many intelligent tutoring systems may be their approach to the representation and the communication of expert knowledge in the domain being taught. Such representation is typically guided by ideas from artificial intelligence. AI stresses the *rule*-based nature of a knowledge domain. This perspective encourages learning resources that tend to support the integration of rules describing families of 'if x then y' relationships (thought to describe some domain of knowledge). Riesbeck and Schank (1991) have argued that this form of representation may be impractical for domains of any complexity. More important, they argue (1989) that rule-based reasoning may not be a good model of everyday intelligent thinking. Instead, they propose that human reasoning can be described as 'case-based' (Schank, 1982). Expertise arises from dense experience with representative and discrete problems from particular domains of practice. Such human reasoning demands a particular kind of resource to support new learning: access to a library of concrete situations (cases) in which problem-solving can be exercised. Creative teaching would then partly be located in the effective 'indexing' (Riesbeck and Schank, 1991) of these experiences – such that they were readily retrievable for reference in dealing with novel circumstances. The principle of case-based reasoning suggests that traditions of computer-as-tutor and computer-as-simulation could move closer together. At present the relevant theoretical debates underlying this possibility are still in progress.

One worrying aspect of learning from simulations concerns the possibility of over-simplifying complex systems. This is often inevitable if a simulation must meet the finite possibilities of delivery on microcomputers. The necessary simplifications may convey a misleadingly straightforward impression of how a multivariate, open-ended system works in the real world. This is particularly problematic in situations where attempts are made to simulate systems whose real behaviour is governed by significant human agency. The microcomputer may force too rigid a representation of how typical human intervention is organised. So, it may be seriously misleading if simulations imply that systems incorporating substantive social management are, for that reason, governed by rule-like and planful processes: often it is clear that they are not (Suchman, 1987).

Finally, it is apparent that these forms of computer-based learning environments must share some of the characteristics (and attractions) noted above for microworld environments. They offer the novice a strong discovery-oriented experience and they are engagingly interactive. They have not yet attracted a great tradition of evaluative research. But, as with microworlds, we are likely to be anxious as to the necessary role of experts (teachers) in sustaining and consolidating this kind of learning and contextualising it within a broader classroom experience. Sheingold, Kane and Endreweit (1983) show that such integration does not typically happen. Moreover, Laurillard (1992) has highlighted the poor showing of simulation software in situations where it is not carefully integrated into a broader context of socially organised teaching.

The toolbox metaphor: computer-as-tool

It is common to characterise the computer as a 'general purpose' machine. We say this because it can be fashioned (programmed) to serve a wide range of human purposes. In other words, there is an important sense in which it can be said to provide a 'toolbox'. Indeed, when we now think of computers most of us are likely to think first of word processors, spreadsheets, databases, applications for graphics or design and so on. This naturally supplies a straightforward reason why we might encourage such use of computers within education. The tools they create are in widespread use within everyday contexts. Thus, quite simply, children must be helped to control and understand them within the preparatory settings of school. Surveys reveal that teachers are increasingly seeing the educational potential of the technology in terms of these tool-like characteristics (Becker, 1991).

However, strategies for fostering experience with computer-based tools will be motivated by more than just narrow vocational concerns. The falling cost of new technology has had the effect of creating a greater continuity between school and work, in that powerful tools that would previously only have been encountered in specialist settings are now accessible in classrooms. It would be disappointing if these tools were only used in ways that mirrored too literally the particular demands of the world of work. Fortunately, the *content* of problems tackled with these powerful new tools can reflect interests that are actually nearer the world of childhood. Thus it is possible to respect the widely accepted educational principle that problems posed for children should be authentic – drawn from their own experience and reflecting their own concerns. Children may well be more engaged by information-managing activities if what they discover (through summarising, systematising, communicating, etc.) describes something immediate to their own experience. The possibility of provoking such vivid discoveries means that computers offer teachers a valuable opportunity: to foster within even young children powerful skills relating to the organisation and communication of data.

However, the educational deployment of computers in this guise is more controversial than that characterisation might imply. Here, I shall identify two troublesome perspectives associated with the computer-as-tool conception. The first is a worry that pupils enjoy less direct encounters with the world they are learning about. The second is a particular theoretical perspective on learning that the tool metaphor encourages – one that I find problematic.

The arguments arising from the first of these concerns are located around the concept of 'mediated experience'. Mediation is one way to capture the multi-faceted character of this technology. The computer mediates our action – it exists between us and the world and transforms our activity upon the world. For one thing, it encourages us to act upon that more elusive quantity: information. This mediated quality of computer-based activities has attracted some critical commentary, particularly as it is realised in the contexts of early education. Thus, in a collection of sceptical essays edited by Sloan (1984), Cuffaro (1984) voices a recurrent concern that computer-using pupils are being deprived of the opportunity for 'direct' manipulative activity on their world. Interactions with computers are supposed to render their experience increasingly 'indirect'. Most worrying, perhaps, the more powerful these tools, the more they can be accessible to younger and younger children (Crook, 1992b).

Cuffaro, and other critics in this collection, make frequent reference to the Piagetian interpretation of cognitive development. Piaget's commitment to the importance of direct manipulative activity on the world is cited with approval as the foundation of discovery learning. It is this foundation that is seen as threatened by the mediational status of computer tools. Evidently, it is right to be cautious here. As noted in remarks above regarding computers furnishing full-blown simulations: access to a simulation should not undermine efforts to give pupils more direct encounters with the system modelled. Not enjoying direct interactions may create a misleading impression as to the simplicity and self-contained nature of that system.

However, the force of this critique turns on cases where computers are made to function as *alternative* tools to those traditionally used in children's exploratory activity. Certainly, if computer graphics packages became a commonplace *substitute* for work with, say, paints or charcoal, then we might feel that valuable creative opportunities were being lost to pupils. However, we should allow the possibility that these computer tools can offer a different and distinctive kind of experience in graphic media (to take the present example): an experience that will complement others. For instance, my own research (1992b) on young children using screen painting programs suggests that these tools may cultivate a more editorial attitude towards graphic creations. Thus, the opportunity to delete or 'undo' painting strokes seems to reinforce active review and revision of a developing composition – much as a word processing tool does for the editing of text. This may be just one distinctive feature of experience with graphic work in the computer medium.

Deploying computers in this way – to *extend* the experience of drawing, writing, classifying or calculating – seems an exciting enterprise. The mediating status of this technology is something we may come to terms with: we may become sensitised to its effective management. The second controversy arising from the tool metaphor concerns some of the more overarching theoretical attitudes that it encourages. It encourages a line of theorising that I find problematic: in particular, the view claiming that such experiences with computer tools have very general effects on the thinking of those who use them. We can see this possibility more clearly with respect to a working example.

In writing the present text, I am using a computer in its capacity as word processor. The tool-like character of the device allows me to engage in various useful manipulative activities. Thus, I can certainly have my spelling checked to some advantage. But I can also 'manage' the overall text in a more flexible manner. So, I might organise material into headed sections: then, by using a pointer on an index of headings at the start of a document, I can easily move around my text. Or, I can shuffle sections into a more optimal organisation. I can refer to files containing notes or references; both of which are visible in windows 'behind' my main text. I can import material between these areas. Is imparting to students fluency with this kind of tool 'merely' a preparation for employment in settings where it will be expected? Or does it create more far-reaching cognitive impacts?

One widely-acknowledged consequence of access to computer tools is the freeing up of 'space' for parallel cognitive activity. Thus, in using a word processor, I could be said to relieve myself of some of the (humdrum) burden of text management and release cognitive resources for other creative work, the idea being that I have a finite reserve of such resources. The quality of my thinking might benefit if some of it can be rescued from more routine cognitive commitments and, thereby, become focused more effectively. So far, this does not entail a particularly radical claim about the impact of experience in using such tools. It could be said merely to clarify just why experience with such technology will be prized in the world of work: the tool is effective and useful. But there is a more radical claim that can be made about the experience of coming to control it.

Suppose that expertise with certain tools leaves us equipped with new tools of *thought*. This point is made energetically in one recent book reviewing the effective application of computers to early education (Underwood and Underwood, 1990). These authors propose that an important focus of computer-based activities is 'to equip children with a toolkit of basic mental skills' (p. 29). This perspective is not without its problems. However, it is a compelling idea; one that has been argued with particular effect in a recent paper by Salomon, Perkins and Globerson (1991). They make a useful distinction relating to the 'effects' associated with computers as students use them: the various products of student activity can be seen in terms of effects achieved *with* computers or in terms of the effects *of* computers. In the first case, we note that some creative product has depended upon a working partnership with a machine; the machine has taken over lower-level activities associated with the task and allowed the student to do the whole thing more economically, more efficiently, more imaginatively, or whatever (cf. the example of text processing rehearsed above). However, the whole enterprise may generate what Salomon *et al*. (1991) refer to as a 'cognitive residue', in which case, students walk away from the experience with new (or more finely honed) tools in their cognitive toolkits (Salomon, 1988a, 1993). So, in other settings – including those that do not incorporate the computer as a prop – more powerful intellectual work can get done.

Returning to the example of using word processing technology: we might suppose that a cognitive residue is imparted by coming to control the device. This supports the subsequent manipulation of text, including work done *off* the computer, and will be to the benefit of cognitive skills associated with the general management of ideas in written form, including their effective communication. We might even consider that the experience of acting upon text in this way heightens our sensitivity to the written word as a manipulable quantity and, for example, cultivates a richer sense of audience as we compose.

In summary, the metaphor of computer-as-tool is a powerful one and provocative in at least two ways. First, it draws our attention to the mediating role of technology. Some commentators have expressed concern about this, worrying that it deflects the learner's experience from concrete exploratory activity. However, viewing this technology as a mediational means will be a useful idea to which I shall want to return later. Second, others have suggested that the consequences of experience with computer-based tools may include cognitive residues – new tools of an intellectual kind for interpreting the world. I shall also return to this idea, although with a less positive response towards it.

Both of these themes will be taken up in later chapters, along with others that have been highlighted in the present general review of implementation metaphors.

I shall conclude the present chapter by highlighting a recurring concern that integrates several problematic issues mentioned so far – namely, the relation of new technology to the social quality of educational experience.

THE SOCIAL FRAMEWORK OF COMPUTER EXPERIENCE

Under this heading we confront some of the core concerns that motivate the present book. A good number of the implementation controversies that have been reviewed above can be usefully considered in terms of tensions between new technology and the *social* quality of educational settings. Numerous commentators have cautioned against technological determinism in applying computers to education. For example, Bowers (1988) and Noble (1991) each explore within substantial monographs the non-neutrality of information technology as it has been developed within education. They argue that this technology does not 'simply' serve human interests in some benign fashion: it actively transforms human relations.

It is important to acknowledge and act upon this state of affairs. My own view is that its consequences are not inevitably to be regretted. Indeed, a significant challenge is to recognise the transformational effects of new technology and thus mobilise them towards realising goals that we regard as precious. If we miss this challenge there is some danger that the medium will be seized and used to support forms of educational practice that many may find unwelcome. In this section, I shall review some straightforward ways in which there can be said to exist a 'social' dimension to the development of computers for educational purposes.

The reproduction of inequalities

An early but recurring strand of critical commentary relating to computers in schools dwells upon the irony of equipping so many children with skills for jobs that will be scarcely available in the world beyond school (cf. Noble, 1991; Robins and Webster, 1987). Yet this is a concern that might be voiced very widely in relation to educational practice: the *special* status of information technology in this respect is no longer so obvious. For most pupils, the learning they do that involves computers is more through them than about them. That is, the technology impinges very broadly on the curriculum, its use involving more than the teaching of specialised knowledge about technology itself. However, its generic quality gives rise to another strand of criticism.

If computers really are a wide-ranging resource for learners, then we must be wary that their deployment does not serve to *amplify* existing patterns of disadvantage (Olson, 1988). Evidently, there is a straightforward way in which the technology is likely to be divisive in this sense: it demands significant financial investment and the opportunities for funding will be distributed unevenly within education systems. Surveys of the present distribution of computers in schools reveal a 10:1 ratio of variation between the best and least well equipped schools (POST, 1991).

Moreover, this is a technology that can be differentially available as a resource in children's own homes. Educational advantage arising from such domestic access is evidently a possibility. However, we should note two observations that suggest it may not be a significant source of inequality. First, ownership of home computers appears to have reached a peak – at least, for the present generation of technology. The UK General Household Survey indicates that around 20 per cent of households own a computer but that this figure has barely changed between 1985 and 1991 (OPCS, 1991). Because prices have come down across this period, these statistics are telling. They suggest that consumers have discovered that general-purpose computers do not much enrich family life. One form of such enrichment might have involved the support of educational agendas within children's home experience. Yet there is some suggestion that this is not a role the technology is currently playing. Giacquinta and Lane (1989) studied how computers were used in fifty-one (US) families with school-aged children. Of the 113 children involved, most had no access at all to educational software at home: those that did made very rare use of it. This is a provocative observation that partially allays our present concern about reproducing inequalities – although the research could usefully be replicated with wider samples and in other cultures.

In the end, however, these are all observations that are very generally true for educational resourcing at home and school; it remains to be seen whether computers emerge as a particularly telling differential. There are more subtle senses in which the technology may reproduce inequalities.

One is in respect of gender. A number of surveys reveal that girls do not perceive computers as being so much 'for them' as do boys (Durndell, 1991; Fife-Shaw, Breakwell, Lee and Spencer, 1986; Hoyles, 1988; Hughes et al., 1987). Moreover, their attitude to using the technology may become increasingly negative as they proceed through school. Various surveys show that the percentage of women pursuing computer science as an undergraduate subject is actually falling (Newton and Beck, 1993).

Scott, Cole and Engel (1992) provide a review of work on this topic and articulate a widespread concern regarding its implications. Chivers (1987) identifies the problem as present in a number of contemporary cultures and also discusses some of the possible measures that we might adopt to tackle it. There is some doubt just how early this differential perception and interest set in. Lipinski, Nida, Shade and Watson (1986) report that boys in a pre-school setting spent more time on a computer activity than girls. On the other hand, Essa (1987) finds no such distinction among pre-schoolers and Crook and Steele (1987) report no gender differences in time spent using a cafeteria-style computer activity maintained in the Reception class of a primary school. The problem invites more research. However, we may say that gender-based attitude differences are not *convincingly* present at the start of schooling: they must somehow be cultivated within the early school years.

Scott et al. (1992) consider a further sense in which the application of this technology may be socially divisive (see also LCHC, 1989). They note that there is some evidence to suggest that the type of software favoured in different educational settings can reflect the educational advantage or disadvantage of the pupils (see Becker and Sterling, 1987). They caution, in particular, against a trend whereby the less innovative software (e.g. drill-and-skill programs) are over-represented in the experience of disadvantaged communities. Both this discrimination and that associated with gender should certainly be looked at carefully and attract more comprehensive documentation. Despite its significance, however, this sense of 'social context' is not central to the more interpersonal concerns of the present book. Issues identified in the following two sub-sections however are.

Computers and social development

Whether encountered within education or elsewhere, at least two features of computers may exert unwelcome influence on children's early social development – that is, on the development of their capacities for entering into a world of social relationships. The first feature is the apparently compulsive attraction this technology can exert over many users (Kidder, 1981; Levy, 1984; Shotton, 1989; Turkle, 1984; Weizenbaum, 1976). The second arises from the quality of 'intelligence' that we tend to identify within computer interaction. Contact with this, it is feared, might encourage a mechanistic interpretation of *human* activity or, more generally, blur important distinctions between ourselves and our machines. At least two consequences arise in relation to social development: children's social cognitions (their *thinking* about the social domain) may be overly influenced by the mechanistic or computation metaphor (Boden, 1981; Brod, 1984; Papert, 1980) and, in addition, they may be drawn towards too dedicated or absorbing an engagement with this highly interactive and responsive technology. They thereby risk entering a socially reclusive world (Boden, 1977; Bontinck, 1986; Simons, 1985). I have reviewed these possibilities elsewhere (Crook, 1992b) and concluded that such fears have been overstated. First, many of them depend upon a particular conception of computer use: one that can indeed evoke self-contained and compulsive involvement, namely computer programming. It is true that absorption in the writing of programming code may have preoccupied an earlier generation of 'hollow-eyed youths' (Weizenbaum, 1976), but the present generation of users will encounter computers in a form more akin to Ivan Illich's conception of 'convivial tools' (Illich, 1973; Norman, 1986). Second, there is some question as to whether children really are so readily seduced by psychological metaphors in their thinking about computers (cf. Hughes *et al.*, 1987). Finally, Shotton (1989) has documented an intimate study of dedicated (adult) computer hobbyists and paints a picture of their involvement that is merely suggestive of very many other innocent recreational enthusiasms.

These remarks relate very generally to young people's experience of computers. However, there is a species of this general concern that is rather more focused on computers encountered in educational contexts. Murphy and Pardeck (1985), for example, dwell upon the dangers of a mechanistic model of mentality being inadvertently fostered within classroom experience. Sloan (1984) cautions the danger of 'relegating feelings to the realm of the peripheral in education' (p. 543) and regrets the mechanistic imagery that characterises computer culture. My own view is that vulnerability to these dangers has been greater among professional psychologists than among school children. Whatever may have been the curriculum emphasis in earlier educational applications, contemporary encounters with class-room technology are now much richer in their variety. Often they are encounters in which the computer is experienced as a tool, rather than an independent intelligence. This new form of relationship between pupil and technology may less readily encourage preoccupation with ontological issues.

Nevertheless, there remains a real strand of concern regarding children's social experience that does arise in the particular context of computers within education. It is more directly concerned with the process of learning itself and I will consider it in the final section of the present overview of issues.

The social quality of learning

Kreuger, Karger and Barwick (1989) identify the solitary quality of much micro-computer-based learning when they warn against the cultivation of 'thought in isolation' (p. 113). They comment: 'What is learned, then, is passivity and aliena-tion from oneself and others, and that the most fruitful relationships with people will be as passive and impersonal as the solitary interaction with the computer' (p. 114). Cuban (1986, p. 89) expresses similar concern: 'In the fervent quest for precise rationality and technical efficiency, introducing to each classroom enough computers to tutor and drill children can dry up that emotional life, resulting in withered and uncertain relationships.'

This worry over the isolation of the computer-based *learner* is commonplace in critical commentaries of how educational technology is currently deployed (e.g. Baker, 1985; Moore, 1993).

In respect of one problematic issue discussed above – the slow uptake of innovative practices based on new technology – Cuban further suggests a tension that exists for teachers confronting pressure to develop computer-based work. That tension arises from their perception of how the technology is to be used: its deployment seems at odds with a strong professional commitment to the *interper-sonal* quality of education.

Reflecting on the models of implementation reviewed above, it is apparent that such concerns are well founded. The computer-as-tutor metaphor seems quite explicit in its implication that the teacher's role might be vulnerable to substitution. In its popular representation, this is the technology of the journalist's 'desktop' teacher. It is the image that will haunt any teacher who encountered the stultifying example of the behaviourist's teaching machine. However, the perceptions of journalists are stimulated by the commentary of educationalists themselves. The often-cited view expressed by Suppes still has some appeal:

One can predict that in a few more years millions of school children will have

access to what Philip of Macedon's son Alexander enjoyed as a royal preroga-
tive: the personal services of a tutor as well-informed and responsive as Aristotle.
(Suppes, 1966, p. 207)

This is surely another misjudged prediction, but the popular interest in computers
as substitutes for the services of a tutor remains real enough. The computer-as-pupil
metaphor also leaves underspecified the place of social interaction between teachers
and learners. This style of computer use is firmly located within the discovery
learning tradition of educational theory – as has been remarked above in relation
to the ubiquitous example of Logo. The interactive opportunities of much open-
ended software of this kind may be particularly effective in sustaining pupils' task
engagement. This, in turn, may suggest less tutorial involvement on the part of a
teacher. Thus, Papert's presentation of Logo in *Mindstorms* (1980) includes sparse
consideration of how teachers do participate productively within Logo learning.
The stronger impression given by his account is of the possibilities within the
software for spontaneous discoveries on the part of the independent learner. We
shall see that this dislocation of the activity from the interpersonal dimension of
learning is not what was intended by Papert. But perhaps his vigorous challenge to
the 'controlling' image of traditional educational software was bound to shift
concerns towards stressing the *autonomy* of the learner.

We shall see that the image of the solitary learner sketched in the quotations
earlier has been resisted by teachers in practice. This is certainly the case in early
education, where the usual impression is one of computers being absorbed into the
familiar bustle of primary class life. The main strategy used to achieve this has been
a preference for organising computer activities as group work (Jackson *et al.*, 1986,
1988). However, the 'social' character of effective educational experience is a more
delicate quality than that conveyed by bustle alone. The view to be developed later
in this book is that computers require us to consider more carefully the nature and
scope of 'collaboration' as it may be organised within education and, in particular,
to judge how far the social energy that might be visible in classrooms incorporates
a kind of interaction that has great significance for learning and cognitive development. To pursue this, we must outline a theoretical perspective that puts the social
dimension at the centre of educational experience. This will be taken up in the next
chapter.

CONCLUDING COMMENTS

In the very short space of the past ten years, considerable effort has been invested
in establishing the microcomputer as a significant resource within education. This
effort has been evident within primary, secondary and tertiary sectors. There must
be few educational media that have been promoted with such energy (and funding).
The reasons for this seem to be a mixture of two commitments on the part of
educational politicians and practitioners. First, it is considered important that
children should now encounter powerful new information technologies at school –

where they may become comfortable and confident with the medium before entering a working world where it so pervasive. The second reason for all this effort is a belief that the technology can transform learning and teaching across a variety of existing curriculum areas: it is a very general educational resource.

There is a current of opinion amongst close observers of this scene that the impact so far has been modest. One measure of a shortfall is the poor outcome of training efforts aimed at encouraging teachers to incorporate new technology into their work. Many teachers are slow to gain confidence in making active use of computers. Perhaps there is a (fatal) irony in asking teachers – a profession where self-assurance about what one knows and does is paramount – to incorporate a technology of such patent complexity. Mastering it only at the level of running isolated applications is bound to feel unsatisfactory, especially in the (all too likely) event of unscripted technical problems.

In my own experience, it has always seemed that the educational application of new technology can too often have a 'bolted on' feel of just that kind. Some of the literature reviewed in this chapter lends support to this as a general view of present practice. The educational thinking that lies behind the main categories of application do little to challenge this setting apart of computer activities. If the computer is conceptualised as another kind of tutor, it is highly likely to be put to work independently of any human tutors in the environment – such an economy is the implicit advantage in this conception. However, the other models of computer implementation that have been discussed here invite similar marginalising. In those cases, the problem may arise from the powerful interactivity the medium offers: it is simply too easy for pupils to sustain independent activity.

I am drawing attention to the way in which computer-based learning might readily become decoupled from the mainstream of classroom life. In fact, we may have mixed reactions to this. So, for example, to point out that a setting for learning is effective in sustaining independent activity might be taken to define a quite desirable state of affairs. Yet, I believe that many practitioners will also become uneasy about learning that readily excludes the involvement of others – teachers or peers. Surveys of teachers reacting to the introduction of classroom computers tend to support this (e.g. Bliss *et al.*, 1986; Lichtman, 1979; Woodrow, 1987). Cuban (1986), in particular, traces much of the suspicion among teachers to this concern over the isolating property of computer-based learning. I believe our thinking about this tension between independent and socially organised learning needs to be guided by an overarching theoretical perspective. I shall offer such a framework in the following chapter.

Chapter 2

Human cognition as socially grounded

The deployment of computers in education is a venture not greatly influenced by theories of cognition. One reason for this is the simple fact that psychologists have not made computer-based learning a topic of special empirical interest. Perhaps that is not surprising, given the confusingly multi-faceted nature of the technology. There is nothing uniform about what these instruments 'do' for learners, even though their uniform appearance may suggest that there is. Practising numerical estimations, using a word processor to compose stories, programming the movements of a floor robot, exploring an ecological simulation, the graphic design of a poster: this a very mixed bag of practical uses for a classroom computer, although it is typical of what we can witness happening – even within primary schools.

Some of these learning activities seem commonplace enough (say, estimating); while others appear to be familiar but, on reflection, turn out to be mediated by computers in quite distinctive ways (e.g. word processing a story). Yet others, while related to the established curriculum (say, maths), seem to involve radically novel approaches to its content (e.g. controlling robot movements). It might be thought unlikely that this mixed bag could be easily embraced by singular psychological theories. If there is to be any generative relationship between theory and practice it might seem likely only at the piecemeal level of inspiring particular software in particular curriculum areas. Some such examples have already been mentioned: mathematics learning software has been informed by cognitive psychology (e.g. Resnick and Johnson, 1988; Sleeman, 1987); computer-based reading and writing aids have been informed by ideas from research on metacognition and its development (Salomon, 1988b; Woodruff, Bereiter and Scardamalia, 1982).

These localised influences of psychological theory are certainly welcome. However, can psychology furnish any more overarching theoretical perspective to help us think creatively about the development of this technology in education? I believe that it can. Indeed, to an extent, psychological thinking may already be exerting a concealed influence. I will argue later (in Chapter 3) that certain significant directions taken by current computer-based educational practice can be readily legitimised by psychological 'worldviews' (Agre, 1993) – although such influence is not always explicitly identified. This creates one good reason for discussing certain broad traditions of psychological theorising here. It will help to articulate some of the theories of learning and cognition that form a background against which some recent design and practice has been managed in this area. Another reason for reviewing psychological theory is more forward-looking: to find a credible framework for addressing some of those particular problems associated with computer-based practice that were identified in Chapter 1.

Later (in the next chapter), I shall make a thorough comparison of three psychological perspectives on learning and cognition and consider what they each imply for the effective use of new technology. Two of these perspectives (computational theories of cognition and constructivism) are well developed and well described in other sources. The third (socio-cultural theory) is of more recent influence and still subject to misrepresentation. For this reason (and because it is the approach that I favour), I shall use the present chapter to describe it more fully. I believe it is the perspective that best addresses some of the problems of implementing computer-based learning that I have already identified: particularly those relating to our concern for the social context of educational activity.

In this respect, one issue that theory should help clarify is the reason for believing that education should preserve a strong interpersonal dimension. It is significant that practitioners are worried about new technology on this basis. So, a formal account of learning as a socially grounded achievement would inform any challenge to technological visions of the isolated pupil. Second, it will be valuable to have a theoretical platform for dealing with these concerns in a concrete, practical manner. In short, an integrating theoretical perspective could be a powerful resource to help guide computer-based educational ventures.

Both of these tasks can be addressed by the particular theoretical perspective outlined below. This perspective is the cornerstone for the remaining discussion in this book. It establishes learning as a fundamentally social experience. It encourages the assessment of all new educational resources in terms of their potential for enriching the interpersonal contexts of learning. This view also suggests a framework for thinking about real options whereby this social incorporation might occur – for example, it may help us do this for a resource such as the microcomputer. The theoretical perspective in question is one associated with 'socio-cultural' thinking in psychology. More recently, the term 'cultural psychology' has been used. This is theorising pitched at a fairly grand level: indeed, it is about the very nature of cognition.

The term 'cultural theory' as applied to cognition usually refers to a body of ideas inspired by the Soviet socio-historical movement of the 1930s (notably the work of Vygotsky, Luria and Leont'ev). Lately, that thinking has been enriched by other lines of theorising: particularly from within the disciplines of cognitive science (e.g. Suchman, 1987) and anthropology (e.g. Lave, 1988). The idea of a cultural psychology has been most clearly defined by two groups: one comprises Shweder and his colleagues (Shweder, 1990; Shweder and Sullivan, 1993); the other comprises various researchers associated with the Laboratory of Comparative Human Cognition (Cole, 1987; LCHC, 1983, 1986). Their two agendas do not perfectly match (Jahoda, 1992) but they share a core commitment to the notion of cognition as being profoundly social in nature. Their perspective on educational practice is, accordingly, one that stresses the socially organised nature of the achievement.

In the remainder of the present chapter, I shall concentrate on capturing the flavour of a cultural psychology. First, I present a general outline that stresses the central concept of mediational means; I consider how it relates to cognitive development through the problematic metaphor of 'amplification'. Then I shall identify central ideas flowing from the application of cultural thinking to education. A brief qualifying observation is necessary at this point. My purpose is not to make the following theoretical framework so convincing that an inevitable agenda for the use of computers in education will have to be endorsed by the reader. The point is more to lay the ground for identifying a certain variety of empirical strategy that is now needed. In particular, I shall recommend research that clarifies the manner in which this technology mediates new forms of social interactions among its (educational) users. I believe that the findings of any such research can remain informative whether or not the theory generating it is judged to be persuasive. Where scepticism regarding the underlying theory might become a cause of friction is in relation to how we should best interpret, and thus apply, the results of that research.

A SOCIO-CULTURAL PERSPECTIVE ON COGNITION

Many 'psychological' perspectives on human nature take biological themes as their starting point. Cultural psychology is distinguished by its declared orientation towards the peaks of human achievement, that is the practices and artefacts that constitute culture. Of course, this does not imply a special concern with *high* culture. In fact, a reference to usage in biology is quite helpful in clarifying the sense of this term as intended here.

For biologists, 'culture' is the medium in which living material might be supported. Cultural psychologists orient towards a *medium* for human activity in this broad sense. The medium that supports intelligent human action will comprise artefacts, institutions and rituals that have acquired their current nature during a long historical development. This history will be interestingly different across different communities. The proposal is that any account of individual cognition and learning must incorporate the nature of this culture into its conceptual vocabulary. A conceptual vocabulary for studying cognition should not exclusively refer to structures and processes concealed within the thinker's skull. It should capture and express the thinker's interaction with an environment: that is, their contact with a culture of material and social resources that everywhere supports cognitive activity.

Given such an orientation, we may anticipate that a cultural theory of cognition will have a strong contextualist flavour. It will focus on *situations* for thinking. It will resist suggestions that the variety of intelligent behaviour can be understood in terms of a small number of core, cognitive processes. We may also anticipate that cultural theories of cognition will have a distinctive interest in the fabric of *socially* organised life: for social interaction is surely central to the rich complexity of human culture.

Wertsch opens a recent volume written in this spirit with the following definition. 'The basic goal of the socio-cultural approach to mind is to create an account of human mental processes that recognises the essential relationship between these processes and their cultural, historical and institutional settings' (Wertsch, 1991c, p. 6). In this account, the cognitive attributes of an individual are fundamentally the outcome of engagement with culture. The analysis of cognition must invoke a vocabulary that includes reference to the formats of this engagement – capturing how cultural resources constrain and enable cognitive activity. The approach invites us to see the genesis of mental life within our commerce with the products of a lengthy cultural evolution. Indeed, it is the capacity for actively exploiting this historical legacy that sets apart humankind as a species. Cole comments: 'Human psychological functions differ from the psychological processes of other animals because they are culturally mediated, historically developing and arise from practical activity' (Cole, 1990, p. 91). A central concept in understanding such a perspective is 'mediation', a concept now commonly discussed in relation to the seminal writings of Vygotsky.

The central place of mediational means

Cole's reference to psychological processes in other species echoes a key point within Vygotsky's development of the concept of psychological mediation. If we remember that this account was articulated in the 1920s, the reference towards animal psychology appears quite natural: much psychological theory of this period arose from empirical work on animal behaviour. In fact, in early formulations, Vygotsky seemed particularly concerned to harmonise a cultural view with the prevailing stimulus–response (S–R) psychology (Bakhurst, 1990).

Vygotsky draws a distinction between elementary and higher mental processes. The former define the limits of animal intelligence; they are biologically based and invite the reductionist analysis favoured within S–R psychology. They include involuntary processes of perception, attention, recognition and need. They underpin a basic repertoire of problem-solving behaviour that can be organised in response to the here-and-now of environmental stimuli. On the other hand, higher mental functions include all the voluntary and reflective processes of thinking, remembering and reasoning that we associate with human mental life. They are not reducible to the elementary psychological functions. Historically, they arose because human beings came to turn inward upon their environment – in the sense of acting creatively upon it to effect certain profound changes in its relationship to us. It might be said the S–R relation was thus rendered bi-directional. The resources arising from this creation of human culture are regarded as central to any account of the nature of cognition.

The important sense in which the human subject came to act back upon nature, and thereby change it, is manifest in the creation of *tools*. These are at once outcomes of human activity upon the environment while, at the same time, they serve to organise further and future encounters with it. Through material tools we gain greater control over the physical world. This control arises from the mediating function of these instruments: we act upon the world indirectly, we act 'through' them.

A distinctively human achievement is to have evolved tools realised in symbolic (rather than purely material) form. Vygotsky, thus, distinguishes between 'technical tools' and 'psychological tools'. Historically, it is claimed, varieties of auxiliary stimuli evolved to have special relevance for controlling the *psychological* world: notations, diagrams, verbal signals and so forth. The mediation effected by this class of tools defines the problems that are now in the domain of cognitive psychology. Through these 'signs' (especially linguistic ones) we come to regulate the behaviour of others. We also come to exert voluntary control over our own basic psychological processes, thereby elaborating the activities of remembering, attention and thought. These artefacts of cultural history are preserved and made available to each new generation. Thus, they may serve to support our children's mediated encounters with the social and material environment. Indeed, the taking of measures to ensure this continuity across generations (i.e. instruction) may also be a uniquely human achievement.

Vygotsky's initial formulation of this cultural conception of mind was fairly conservative; it sought to be compatible with orthodox S–R theory. Perhaps the analogy with technical tools was somewhat constraining in this respect. Technical tools often have a neatly circumscribed character; they are visibly self-contained objects (hammers and so forth). The temptation may be to theorise about psychological tools that also happen to have this singular character: icons, maps, verbal instructions and so forth. Such exemplars more readily take up the role of stimuli. Thus, they might be conceptualised as 'intervening stimuli' located between external events and behaviour – either in some associationist S–R psychology or some cognitive theory of human information processing.

Such a simple formulation is apparent in Vygotsky's discussion of mediated memory and the example of the knot-in-a-handkerchief. This folk custom is a vivid example of a discrete mediating sign: it allows organised control of the present by the past (remembering takes place 'through' this device). So a conservative summary of this example might have the knot-sign function as a class of intervening stimulus: supporting an association between some past event and some response that we now make. A more traditional psychological analysis is, thus, preserved.

However, as Bakhurst (1990) has documented, this conception was rejected in Vygotsky's later writing. Vygotsky became dissatisfied with the implication that signs might be evoked in some S–R manner. The far-reaching impact of mediation was not well enough expressed by some catalogue of discrete signs, with their tool-like properties. Mediational means existed in the form of more complex structural relations, these having a more elaborate involvement with behaviour. So Vygotsky became interested in the human capacity for inventing whole symbolic systems, such as are represented in mathematics, logical notations and varieties of natural language. What is significant about engagement with systems such as these is that they place us in a position of constantly *interpreting* the world, rather than responding to it. They leave us experiencing the world in particular ways, reading it in a manner that reflects our own distinctive history of contact with such systems of mediation.

In terms of accounting for cognitive development, Vygotsky's changing theoretical emphasis orients us more to 'interpretative practices'. These practices are embodied in the cultural life of a community: the artefacts, technologies and rituals that it offers. The course of intellectual growth is, therefore, characterised by gaining access to a culture's resources of mediational means – as ways of interpreting experience. In the course of development, children will necessarily appropriate and deploy whatever local resources constitute their own opportunities for participating in socially organised life. They discover the 'designs for living' (Cole, 1990) that have been historically accumulated within their own culture. These are states of the world we are born into and, to use an analogy of Bruner's, it is as if we thereby enter onto a stage where the drama and its context is well established. Our task is to participate in the action and thus to appropriate the mediational devices that can serve to manage exchanges between ourselves and others.

Three themes arising from an emphasis on mediation

Let us relate these comments about the central place of mediation to our interests in learning and instruction (leading us, later, to considerations of new technology). I wish to focus on three particular implications of the approach being sketched here; each of them has attracted some empirical support. The first is a novel definition of cognitive activity in terms of functional systems: a definition that takes 'cognition' to mean more than repertoires of circumscribed and private mental processes. The second implication is the 'situated' nature of cognitive achievements: what is learned is ways of acting in particular situations. The third is the profoundly social nature of cognition. I will briefly summarise what each of these propositions entails before pursuing their educational implications in separate sections below.

The first of these points is concerned with how we define cognition for purposes of analysing development and change. The present cultural approach is often distinguished by claiming it regards cognition as a 'beyond the skin' phenomenon. A cultural description of mental activity will typically incorporate reference to mediational means – resources 'outside' of the person, but resources which will be included in the units of analysis when doing this form of cognitive psychology. Often such mediational means will comprise artefacts that reside 'outside' in the sense of being clearly visible and external to ourselves: the maps, diaries, notebooks and filing systems of intellectual endeavour. Campbell and Olson (1990) propose that such externally supported human intelligence describes the most common and comfortable realisation of the activity 'thinking'. Not that this is what is captured in popular stereotypes of someone in thought: the popular image tends to conjure up a solitary, deeply reflective state typified by Rodin's hunched-up figure. Provocatively, Campbell and Olson suggest that we naturally take steps to avoid this form of 'inwardly mediated' thinking. Yet, even such contemplative states need to be analysed with proper respect for the externally located mediational means that they will involve: the ways of talking and symbolising that are appropriated from the thinker's socio-cultural environment. The solitary thinker's activity is continuous with the external, socially constituted environment in this sense. In summary, this perspective demands that we view cognition in terms of functional systems of activity integrated by mediational means.

The situated nature of cognitive achievements is the second implication of an emphasis on mediation. Learning is viewed in terms of the guided appropriation of mediational means: such change results in control over the substantive interpretative practices that characterise a local culture. Remembering, classifying or thinking are, thus, ways of acting and talking in particular contexts: contexts drawn from the situations of problem-solving provided by that local culture. So, we become rememberers, classifiers and thinkers. This is not the same analysis as one highlighting *general* cognitive resources that underlie and support a transfer to new domains of practice. So, cognitive acquisitions are regarded as initially situated, in this sense of being tied to contexts of learning.

The social nature of cognition is the third implication of the present mediational approach. There are actually two senses in which cognition is being characterised as a social phenomenon. Cognition is socially located because mediational means are created and evolve within socio-cultural history. The various notations, diagrams, signals, languages and so on that make up our current systems of shared signs all embody a history of involvement in human social interaction: their various contemporary forms will surely reflect this past. Indeed, such an historically determined character will serve to constrain the ways in which they may support our present intellectual endeavours. In addition to this, cognition is identified as socially located because these mediational means are commonly encountered in the course of exchanges among people. This is clearly the case in early life: children are not left to re-invent mediational means from scratch. They are confronted with them: this is arranged within the course of their participation in social life. Thus, when researchers in this cultural tradition come to consider problems of learning and cognitive development, they will surely be interested in problem-solving (in the broadest sense) as it gets coordinated within arenas of people acting *together*.

I have introduced three implications of a cultural psychological approach: cognition as functional systems, as situated and as social. These ideas are central to my perspective of how computers could best be deployed within teaching and learning. I shall, therefore, say more about each below – but now stressing their relation to educational practice. At this point, I will not pursue the link between education and cultural conceptions of cognition by developing the case of computer-based learning. Instead, I shall dwell on the more thoroughly researched case of literacy. Literacy is a technology in the sense that it involves deploying a symbol system (the written word) to mediate interactions between ourselves and our material and social environment. So, we may regard computer-based resources as more modest parallels to this well-established mediational means. With this parallel, we may then seek insight from the more extensive studies of literacy already available.

IMPLICATIONS FOR TEACHING AND LEARNING

To capture the force of a mediational analysis of intelligent action, it is popular to cite illustrations where very vivid prosthetic resources are involved. A challenge made by Bateson (1972) has been widely cited to help focus this conception of cognition as something mediated and extending beyond the skin. Bateson asks:

> Suppose I am a blind man, and I use a stick. I go tap, tap, tap. Where do *I* start? Is my mental system bounded at the handle of the stick? Is it bounded by my skin? Does it start halfway up the stick? Does it start at the tip of my stick? (1972, p. 459)

Cole's thoughts on this challenge express its general implications for an analysis of cognition: 'the precise ways in which mind is distributed depend crucially on the tools through which one interacts with the world, which in turn have been shaped by one's cultural past as well as one's current circumstances and goals' (1991, p. 412). Thus, the existence of mediational means invites us to conceptualise mind as something 'distributed' within an environment, rather than as a repertoire of computational processes constrained to exist only within our heads.

It is easy to see how the effects of a powerful computer application (say, a word processor) might be analysed in parallel terms to the tool in Bateson's example. However, understanding how cognition is organised and how learning is supported will involve more difficult analyses than this example might suggest. For one thing, not all mediational means will be so conveniently circumscribed and concrete. For another, teaching and learning cannot be reduced to initiatives for merely making new mediational means available to pupils. It is not as if education was about helping pupils take these resources off some shelf. That is, the nature of their appropriation will depend upon the nature of the contexts in which they are encountered – and on efforts relating to the guided coordination of those contexts. Such claims are elaborated below in three sections. There I consider issues of teaching and learning in respect of the three themes introduced above.

Functional systems and mediation: the case of literacy

My aim in this section is to consider how we may best conceptualise cognitive change as it might occur within the contexts of education. The cultural approach invites us to analyse this by considering how mediational means become incorporated within functional systems of intelligent activity. I shall develop the discussion around the example of literacy, as this is a mediational means that has been most carefully researched. Thanks to the efforts of Cole and Griffin (1980), this example also allows us to explore how the achievements of learning are best conceptualised:

in particular, whether to view them in terms of quantitative processes of cognitive 'amplification' or in the terms favoured here – of qualitative changes in functional systems of cognitive activity.

For the original socio-cultural theorists, spoken language was the most central of early acquisitions – a view in some contrast to that of their contemporary, Piaget, for whom language played no powerfully distinctive role within developmental theory. For theories in the cultural tradition, speech is seen as an organiser of behaviour. Speech is instrumental; it helps us to *do* things in the world, to make things happen. In particular, we learn to affect others through our speech. It is a small step from this insight to suppose that such external means of regulating activity becomes, in some sense, internalised – to become a form of private *self*-regulation.

The concept of internalisation is not without its critics. However, the central feature of this idea remains persuasive: the various problem-solving experiences of reasoning, remembering, attending, classifying and so on are – first of all – *activities*. They are organised within social experience and supported by the resources of speech. Through participation in social life, the developing individual is exposed to a set of interpretative practices that may be appropriated. It is in this sense that we have to learn to 'become' rememberers, planners, classifiers and so on (e.g. Middleton and Edwards, 1990). Participation in organised social activity serves to reveal these powers and possibilities to us. Cognitive achievements arise as the consequence of entry into particular 'communities of practice'. We encounter particular settings where problems get solved according to specialised practices for the deployment of cultural resources: resources of discourse, technology, ritual. By virtue of participation within such communities we become socialised into possible ways of thinking. Such a perspective on cognition (as embodied in practice) is in obvious contrast to the dominant psychological images of, for example, memory or classification as private cognitive mechanisms.

It naturally follows that the deployment of spoken language within the various 'cultural' contexts of growing up – and the study of its particular consequences – has been a topic of special empirical interest to cultural theorists. Speech is the means whereby much gets done around children and it offers for them particular 'ways with words' (Heath, 1983). It is the means whereby problems are publicly defined and acted upon (Wertsch, McNamee, McLane and Budwig, 1980; Wertsch, Minick and Arns, 1984; Wood, Wood and Middleton, 1978). However, there has also been great interest in the developmental significance of the *written* word. Considering literacy as well as speech may help further clarify how mediational means support cognitive development.

Literacy is, evidently, a mediating technology of the kind we have been considering: it enters into our lives to organise interactions between ourselves and our material and social worlds. One vivid perspective on the technology of literacy is furnished by accounts of its development in *historical* time (e.g. Cole, 1991; Goody and Watt, 1968). These accounts make it possible to trace an historical pattern within which literate practices can be shown to have forced transformations of human relations on the societal level. The nature of these historical transformations then offers a seductive analogy for psychological accounts of development within individual lifetimes. Perhaps in growing up, our thinking undergoes comparable transformations as it encounters new mediational means; perhaps such transformations reflect those documented for whole societies during periods when they are gaining access to new technologies such as writing.

Luria (1976) reports an early psychological investigation in this spirit. He studied (during the 1930s) the impact of literacy on traditional communities within post-revolutionary Soviet society. That is, he was able to observe the cognitive impact of access to a radical new mediational means. The sudden drive to develop a literate population offered an opportunity to evaluate the effects (among adults) of exposure to reading and writing as it was organised in the new schools. The inevitably piecemeal nature of the early educational provision permitted meaningful cognitive comparisons between schooled and unschooled groups.

Luria reports apparently dramatic effects of even brief exposure to literacy. These effects were catalogued for intellectual functions in the domains of perception, classification, reasoning, imagining and so on. Briefly, the impact of literacy seemed to be associated with a new capacity to direct thought towards 'the words themselves', a capacity to extricate discursive problems from the immediate context of a conversational exchange: from the context of expectations and interpretations that normally guide human discourse. Formal consideration of words themselves in this way – as the acquisition of literacy requires – seemed to create for newly literate individuals a sensitivity to the hypothetical. Literate individuals become drawn to reflect on problems that might, sometimes, not actually exist outside of the (mere) words used to conjure them up.

Developmental psychologists have been impressed by the idea that access to reading and writing transforms problem-solving in this way: impressed with the idea that writing is a technology with far-reaching cognitive consequences. For example, Donaldson (1978) appeals to this possibility in accounting for her influential work on development of reasoning in childhood. She describes a number of studies revealing ways in which traditional tests of cognitive development underestimate young children's reasoning (Cole, Gay, Glick and Sharp, 1971; Siegel, 1991a, b). She argues that the format of traditional tests is biased towards reasoning that is most familiar within *literate* forms of communication.

For example, in the traditional test for conserving number a child is asked if two lined-up rows of beads each have the same number. One row is then elongated and the same question is asked a second time. Answering that the longer row now has more beads has traditionally been taken to index a structural limitation in childhood reasoning. However, there may be other factors to take into account, including some relating to the pragmatics of this situation. Thus, simply asking the same question twice in such a short period might lead some children to think they are supposed to change their answer. It seems that this can happen: children are 'more logical' when only the second question gets asked (Rose and Blank, 1974). The implication is that children who fail the traditional form of such tests should not be thought to lack cognitive bits in their logical equipment. Their problem may involve some lack of familiarity with the literate form of communication that saturates traditional formats for testing. Children first mobilise a spontaneous form of reasoning that reflects their rich experience of thinking in social contexts, particularly in making sense of other people's actions. Literate forms of problem demand that children over-ride their expectations of what the experimenter might be asking of them, over-ride their beliefs about likely motives and intentions in the situation. Instead, they are expected to prioritise the language that is being used to define a problem. This may often be an unfamiliar attitude for children taking part in psychological tests. To use Donaldson's phrase, children must cultivate 'disembedded' modes of thinking to do well in these tasks. Their thinking must be disembedded from the matrix of expectations and interpretations that the context naturally affords and, instead, submitted to the literal possibilities permitted by the words themselves.

Donaldson is not alone in believing that schooled contact with the mediational means of literacy is central to making this happen. This view has also been championed by Olson and colleagues (e.g. Olson, 1986; Olson and Torrance, 1983). Indeed, in the judgement of this group, much of development in 'intelligence' can best be analysed in terms of variously mastering the literate modes of thinking cultivated in school.

An important question confronts us at this point. The way we deal with it has implications for our present concern to conceptualise the impact of computers – as a further technology that supports access to new mediational means. The question concerns how we should conceptualise the *process* underpinning the impact of new mediational means on individual cognition. The consequences may be clear and dramatic, but by what mechanism are these outcomes achieved? Two kinds of response to this problem are evident in the literature. One is inclined to view the cognitive impact of cultural experience in terms of acquiring and refining tools of thought (a literate mode of thought, for example). This is a more cognitive kind of account, one that toys with the notion of individuals internalising such technologies. The alternative is more practice-oriented and regards the impact of access to new mediational means in terms of a reorganisation of some underlying way of acting in the world. The distinction is slippery but I believe our attitude to it bears upon how we understand the educational impact of new computing technologies with their tool-like properties.

The more cognitive alternative is implicit in Bruner's arresting metaphor of the cognitive 'amplifier' to describe the effect of contact with some mediational means. He comments: 'Man is seen to grow by the process of internalising the ways of acting, imagining, and symbolising that "exist" in his culture, ways that amplify his powers' (Bruner, 1966, p. 320). The parallel is with more familiar technologies that are said to amplify action – hammers, levers, knives and so on – except that the symbolic equivalents are 'internalised' (and then deployed to support continued cognitive development). On this model, cultures might furnish a (varying) supply of basic cognitive resources (amplifiers) in the form of psychological tools and symbol systems. Cultures might thereby extend cognitive capabilities to varying degrees. This collection of mediational means might now include computer-based resources. However, the amplifier parallel may need a little more exploration. Cultures are certainly forthcoming with mediational means, but is the notion of an amplifier the best way of expressing the process of empowerment that follows from accessing them?

The amplifier is a harmless enough metaphor if it merely implies that access to a cultural technology can multiply our intellectual achievements. The products of human activity may indeed be amplified in this sense, and this will be visible in cultures with a rich and varied supply of technologies. If that is all we intend by it, then it is both harmless and not very useful. Cole and Griffin (1980) have analysed the amplification metaphor further and suggest that, often, we do mean more by it. Furthermore, what we mean in addition might deserve careful review. This is of particular interest to us here, as the notion of amplification is widely appealed to in discussions of the cognitive effects of using computers.

The temptation of the amplifier image is to encourage a more-or-less, or quantitative attitude to the impacts associated with new mediational means. Yet what may actually be needed is a model of cognitive processes that emphasises structural rather than quantitative change. This structural analysis would encourage thinking in terms of functional systems of inter-related components rather than singular (amplified) mechanisms. So, in respect of some cognitive function (such as memory), rather than thinking of cultural resources as producing a more powerful mechanism, we would think of a reorganisation effected in the activities that comprise remembering.

Cole and Griffin invite us to capture the controversy here by reference to the following example. Consider *killing* as a functional system of activity: one that hunters engage in for the capture of their prey. The 'killing power' of a hunter can be extended if we supply him with a gun. Thereby, the products of the killing activity are increased. But that amplification only occurs when the tool is in his hand. So, the effect of the weapon is best described in terms of its *reorganising* the activity of killing, not in terms of it extending some underlying and general-purpose killing power. The same analysis can be applied to more culturally familiar activity systems (perhaps with more vivid cognitive contents). Consider, for example, shopping. Setting out to purchase a new supply of goods for the family will be a different kind of activity if we do so equipped with a pen and paper. We thereby exploit the device of a list; it will probably help us do this task more efficiently (more quickly, more thoroughly, etc.). The incorporation of this mediational means into the activity system serves, again, to re-configure the manner in which it is carried out. In this case, the underpinning activity of remembering has been re-mediated.

Cole and Griffin also refer to the example of memory to express their point about amplification. They note that, in a test, a child with a pencil displays a more powerful memory than an undergraduate without one. It might be said that the child's 'memory power' has been extended. The pencil is a sort of amplifier perhaps: the products of remembering are increased through its use. This seems a straightforward claim, but suppose we take the pencil away? Where does this leave the child's memory in relation to the undergraduate? The effect of the pencil is to reorganise things we do in relation to the task of memorising. This task calls upon a functional system, not a dimensionalised cognitive power. Cognitive amplifiers may largely act through reorganising underlying *activities* (such as might be involved in remembering) – not by amplifying cognitive powers in some general-purpose manner that exists as 'residue' when the mediational means are not to hand.

This last point discourages thinking about the impacts of new mediational means in terms of very *general-purpose* changes in ways of thinking. The reorganisations effected by access to cultural resources may be powerful but quite localised, or situated, in their impacts. Both of these points – cognitive development as functional reorganisations and the situated nature of the achievements – are empirically pursued in cross-cultural work by Cole and Scribner (1974).

Cole and Scribner studied literacy and its consequences among the peoples of Liberia. This setting offered a distinctive opportunity for evaluating claims that access to literacy leads to powerful and general cognitive changes. In Liberia, several different forms of written language existed, serving different communities and different cultural purposes. These scripts included Arabic, English and Vai. For some communities the use of a script was principally associated with a particular form of cultural activity – religious recitation, business transaction, schooled instruction, the writing of letters and so on. With literate and non-literate members of these communities, Cole and Scribner conducted a series of tests of a kind familiar to cognitive psychologists: tests concerned with memory, attention, classification and other traditional cognitive functions. They found no evidence that exposure to literacy itself created across-the-board cognitive advantage. Rather, the effect of literacy was more localised. For example, familiarity with the Vai script for purposes of (postal) communication might confer an advantage on tests of referential communication skill.

This conclusion is in tension with that proposed by Luria to account for effects of literacy among the people of Uzbekistan. Cole and Scribner argue against conceptualising the impact of literacy in terms of general and quantitative extensions of cognition – such as might then be labelled more 'rational' or more 'theoretical' modes of thought. Rather, literacy is conceptualised as a technology that restructures the manner in which we carry out certain cognitive activities, such as those to do with recalling, classifying, ordering and communicating. To understand the action of such technologies on development it is then necessary to study 'literate practices'. Writing enters into particular forms of culturally organised activity in distinctive ways to regulate interactions among the participants. The consequence of becoming literate is therefore visible in situations reproducing particular core activities that literate cultures typically provide. So, for example, if a culture's literacy is mainly for supporting letter-writing, then it will most likely promote a certain sort of cognitive reflection; for example, reflection about how to specify meaning and intention under circumstances of limited communicative context. Experience in such situations will have cultivated practices that are then manifest, for example, in formal psychological tests of referential communication.

I have pursued the example of literacy in order to illustrate the general approach that cultural psychology takes towards issues of cognitive change as it is explored in comparative study: historical, cross-cultural or developmental. The analysis stresses how we variously come to think 'through' mediational means. Goody, Luria, Donaldson, Olson and others show how cognition is extended by access to the particular technology of literate forms. Cole and Scribner caution against too readily interpreting such mediation in terms of a general amplification of the way in which we process information. They observe that the mediational role of the written word may be associated with circumscribed literate *practices*. It thereby supports only bounded sets of human activities. (Of course, where these literate practices are those of 'schooled reasoning' then that bounded set will certainly be a highly prized one for many technological societies.) In the terms used earlier: the child becomes socialised into particular traditions of interpretative practice involving reading and writing. Thus, the key to understanding the impact of literacy during development will be to study how the written word enters into children's activity settings, organising those settings in distinctive ways.

I believe that we can also understand the cognitive impact of access to computing technology according to the same agenda being presented here for literacy. This is an important implication of the present discussion. It follows from this discussion that computers might be regarded as entering into certain problem-solving enterprises and achieving their impacts by reorganising or re-mediating the activities involved. In the end, this is an analysis concerned with conceptualising cognitive changes associated with learning through new technology. However, it is not a traditional cognitive analysis. It is one that dwells upon changes to the structure of activity systems that a pupil participates in – rather than changes in a pupil's covert knowledge structures.

Such a view has important implications for how we think about ways of using new technology in support of learning. If the experience of a computer-based cognitive task is conceptualised as acting to effect some abstract, private cognitive structure (cognitive 'tool' or whatever), then the broader *context* of that experience may seem less significant. On the other hand, the present mediational view highlights this context. Pupils should encounter computers as mediational resources incorporated within suitably rich settings of activity; that is, settings with authentic goals and purposes for those pupils, and settings that are explicitly integrated with other experiences of knowing and understanding as they get organised at other times. The point about actively seeking integration is one that I shall return to: it strongly implicates a role for social (teacher) intervention in support of its achievement. The other point – that activity settings should be authentic – is one strongly argued by Brown, Collins and Duguid (1989) in their analysis of learning as a 'situated' achievement. This takes us to the second broad theme to arise from a socio-cultural analysis.

The situated nature of cognition

Within the psychological literature, there are two related contexts within which the term 'situated' gets used to describe cognition. The first entails an orientation towards the *outcomes* of cognitive activity – what is learned. In particular, it concerns a longstanding issue of how far learning in one situation can be expected readily to influence the activities of the learner within other, different situations. This is the issue of transfer of learning. To say that a cognitive achievement is 'situated' is to draw attention to limited possibilities of transfer: the effects of the achievement are constrained to its context of acquisition (at least, in the first instance). Psychologists associated with the socio-cultural tradition are particularly concerned with this issue.

The second sense of 'situated' arises more commonly within cognitive science. In that discipline there has recently emerged a variety of theorising distinguished by its situated perspective on cognition. This perspective has implications for the question of transfer but, first, it concerns definitions of knowledge itself. It is argued that knowledge should not be conceptualised as a catalogue of stored mental representations; instead, knowledge is always created within the circumstances of interacting with the world – in other words, it is situated within these interactions. Here, I shall comment first on the transfer issue as commonly encountered in socio-cultural theorising and then turn to make a few brief remarks about 'situated cognition' as more typically encountered within cognitive science. Claims about the generality of learning made within the former tradition may be made more substantial by theoretical conceptions developed in the latter. Thus, the two perspectives on cognition as situated are closely related.

Three groups of empirical observation have encouraged a view of cognition as tied to particular contexts of acquisition (rather than as general and context-free). The first is research showing that, at a given point in development, children's thinking may manifest logical characteristics in some domains while the same characteristics do not get mobilised in others. Donaldson (1978) summarises some examples of how the quality of children's reasoning can vary according to the format of the problem itself. The second is a comparable tradition of comparative research involving different cultures (e.g. Cole *et al.*, 1971): utilisation of cognitive resources may vary across cultural settings according to local familiarity with the terms of the problem. The third set of relevant empirical observations are laboratory studies that demonstrate how difficult it can be for experimental subjects sponta-neously to transfer strategic thinking from one problem (where it has worked) to a new and related problem (Detterman, 1993).

Together these lead to a particular conception of intelligence or 'expertise'. Shweder (1990, p. 23) summarises this in his outline of cultural psychological principles:

> what seems to differentiate an expert from a novice (chess player, abacus user, medical diagnostician, etc.) is not some greater amount of content-free pure logical or psychological power. What experts possess that neophytes lack is a

greater quantity and quality of domain-specific knowledge of stimulus properties, as well as dedicated mastery of the specialised or parochial 'tools' of a trade.

Vygotsky's stand on this issue was clear; in his words: 'the mind is not a complex network of [general] capabilities, but a set of specific capabilities ... learning ... is the acquisition of many specialised abilities for thinking' (Vygotsky, 1978, p. 83).

Of course this bias towards viewing new acquisitions as being tied to contexts does bring its own problems. The consequences of a strongly situated view of cognitive achievements have been considered by Jahoda (1980). Something like an integrating theory of situations is needed in order to avoid multiplying accounts of achievements restricted to their contexts of acquisition. Moreover, the unavoidable fact remains that things mastered in one domain can be found to serve us well elsewhere: generalisation of understandings is something we feel surely does occur.

I will take up this challenge in a later chapter. I agree with theorists who argue that it is best to start from situations 'and discover the sources of generality in what are initially context-specific achievements' (Cole, 1990, p. 16). However, I shall argue that what is 'in' achievements that affords generalisation is something that is invariably put there by the social environment. In other words, this is an account of learning that views new acquisitions as initially situated, but which recognises the possibilities of transfer. Such a possibility arises through supportive interventions of a socio-cultural nature.

Evidently, this position carries implications for how we organise experiences in educational contexts. It suggests that things could get done and said around computer-based learning (or other settings of mediated learning) that serve to support the transfer of understandings between situations. This is a straightforward sense in which we must come to define a social context for computers deployed in educational settings. It is part of what we might mean by claiming a social context for cognition – although this rather specific argument relating *transfer* to social experience is not the feature most commonly identified within that claim. In the following section I discuss the more traditional version of the claim.

What has been said so far in the present section reflects perspectives typical of socio-cultural theorising. I shall conclude with some remarks inspired by the second theoretical framework in which cognition is currently said to be 'situated'. In this case, the claims that emerge sit comfortably with cultural thinking about cognition, but their history owes more to debates within cognitive science – particularly in relation to the issue of artificial intelligence.

We may begin by declaring what is not controversial. Human cognition implicates an agent with some underlying neural organisation, and it implicates an environment from which sensory stimulation arises and towards which action is directed. The task for cognitive psychology involves attending to the way in which agent and environment interact. The intelligent action that thereby can result, needs to be described and explained within a suitable theoretical vocabulary. Controversy surfaces at this point. Traditionally, the vocabulary preferred by psychologists has invoked a layer of cognitive concepts. These concepts refer to structures that are somehow instantiated in the neural organisation. They arise as a result of interactions with the environment; they serve to direct such interactions. In short, cognition is said to entail stored, mental representations of the world (knowledge), and mental manipulations performed upon those representations (thinking). Intelligent action is thus driven by the output from such an underlying mental life.

All of this relates to the development of educational practice, including what may be attempted with the help of new technology. It is relevant because educational interventions may be conceived and evaluated by reference to this framework of cognitive concepts. So, the issues being identified here will resurface in later chapters; specifically, the implications of this cognitive theorising for practical applications of computers in learning will be discussed in the next chapter. For the moment, I will just note that cognitive theories of the sort sketched above will tend to promote certain ventures at the boundaries of cognitive science and computer science. In particular, the idea of knowledge as stored representations promotes the venture of reproducing such a knowledge 'database' in machine form. This would be an attempt, perhaps, to reproduce human expertise. This cognitive theory might also imply a particular model of human communication: one in which computers could be programmed to transfer data in such a way as to simulate communicative processes. Any such simulation would be of special interest to us here – in so far as it addresses that special form of communication known as 'instruction'.

However, the credibility of these symbolic theories of cognition has been questioned, along with their implications for computer-based education (e.g. Suchman, 1987; Winograd and Flores, 1986). This questioning includes the promotion of an alternative conception. The alternative is sometimes identified as a 'situated' theory of cognition, a term favoured within the cognitive science community. The situated view makes a commitment to the idea that knowledge is created within interaction; knowledge does not exist 'behind' that interaction as mental events that drive it. Thus, the situated approach is successful in developing the cultural theorist's interest in the distributed, mediated nature of cognition. The empirical strategy of the approach is to study cognitive agents in interaction with their environment – the various contexts of material and social resources that mediate action.

This alternative to traditional cognitive theorising is not as subversive as my contrast might imply. Proponents of a situated view are anxious to stress that cognitive modelling remains a useful resource. Clancey (1991) characterises the situation this way. Cognitive psychology has furnished a description of a covert cognitive space. Essentially, this has involved looking at the products of human rational behaviour (language, rituals, strategies etc.), discovering 'patterns' therein and then (here is the suspect move) locating such patterns inside our heads – supposing this mental world comprises a mechanism that drives the rational behaviour. Clancey argues that this approach has been useful; but its value is more to define an agenda – something to be explained – rather than as, itself, an achievement of explanation. 'Pattern descriptions now serve as a specification for how adapted behaviour must appear, rather than the mechanism to be put inside the robot' (1991, p. 111).

If the traditional approaches only go this far, what must be done to construct a more explanatory account of rational behaviour? It is proposed that knowledge must be conceptualised as an activity, rather than as a (stored) property of the individual. *Knowing* (in preference to *knowledge*) is activity always exercised in relation to the situations individuals find themselves in. Knowing is a relationship between the human agent and a material and social framework that defines the momentary circumstances for acting. *Learning* thus becomes an adaptation of the learning person to aspects of such circumstances, as they encounter them. This has implications for what happens in settings that we arrange explicitly to promote learning. What happens to learners in these settings needs to be expressed in terms that capture a dialectic: in terms that include features of the environment as they entered into some interaction that occurred. At later times, when learners might be said to 'remember' things, their achievements would be expressed as the reorganisation of earlier ways of perceiving and acting. New actions, including purely contemplative intelligence (Greeno, Smith and Moore, 1993), are coupled to past learning in this sense – rather than through the mediating intervention of stored symbolic cognitions.

Theorists of this persuasion will experience an affinity with sensory psychologists, such as Gibson, who have specifically considered the integration of perception and action. Such ecological theories address, for example, how we account for an animal's skilful dash through dense terrain. The account would not be in terms of the animal activating some underlying cognitive plan that triggers a complex sequence of action, but in terms of invariant features of the physical environment that 'afford' certain behaviours at the given moment. Greeno *et al.* (1993) have studied human learning with special attention to the manner in which a material environment affords problem-solving actions in this sense. However, the thrust of empirical work influenced by the situated tradition has concentrated on the management of human action within the *social* 'terrain'. Here, the opportunity has been taken to apply techniques from conversation analysis (Goodwin and Heritage, 1990) to situations where discourse is central to the learning or problem-solving under examination (e.g. Roschelle, 1992; Suchman, 1987). This bias towards studying situations where social interaction predominates is typical of theorising influenced by the socio-cultural tradition. It is this theme within that tradition that I turn to next.

The social nature of cognition

As I stressed earlier in this chapter, there are really two senses in which the cultural perspective insists that cognition is fundamentally social in nature. First, it is claimed that all higher mental functions are entrenched in a framework of rituals, conventions, technologies and institutional practices: this framework arose in socio-cultural history. Even the most private of cognitive pursuits will involve us with media and symbol systems that have a social nature in this sense. Moreover, some are unambiguously social by virtue of being encountered through the behaviour of others: particular ways of talking and acting. Second, cognition is social because the *acquisition* of new understandings is made possible through participation in certain kinds of supportive social interactions.

The influential writing of Vygotsky concerns both of these themes (Valsiner and Winegar, 1992). However, the emphasis of Vygotsky's own empirical work (and, largely, that of his followers also) was on the second of them. Thus, many commentators have been led to reflect only upon the social *interactional* basis of cognition. For example, in a sympathetic but fairly critical review, Schaffer (1992) appears to be evaluating present claims regarding the social constitution of cognition. However, the empirical work cited is exclusively concerned with cognitive outcomes arising from experience in joint problem-solving (bearing, therefore, only on 'social' in the second – interactional – sense above). So, a perspective does get usefully reviewed in this exercise but it forms only part of the claim that cognition is socially constituted.

Some cultural psychologists have been at pains to counter too narrow a conception of the 'social' as it relates to cognition; arguing that interaction among people does not exhaust the proper sense of social involvement. Thus, Scribner (1990) suggests that the contemporary emphasis on interpersonal issues has distracted us from investigating socio-cultural mediation in a fuller sense. A comprehensive empirical agenda must embrace the influence of interpersonal interactions ('social' themes) as well as the influence of artefacts, technologies and conventions ('societal' themes, perhaps). In focusing too much on the former only, researchers have neglected to pursue, for example, 'how cultural communities this world over organise activity settings for the "social transfer of cognition" ' (p. 93). Recent literature indicates that cultural theorists are now turning their attention more in the 'societal' direction (e.g. Wertsch, 1991a).

I shall return to such matters in the next chapter, when focusing more closely on computer-based learning in relation to cultural thinking. The topic will arise there because the institutions and practices of formal education do illustrate a societal theme very well. They illustrate organised activity settings of a kind that our culture has indeed fostered – for the particular purposes of promoting the social transfer of knowledge. New technology is an intriguing new component of such settings. However, I shall suggest that when we do consider this societal theme, we are still required to attend to issues of social *interaction*. This is because cognitive change within educational activity settings may depend upon certain kinds of coordination achieved for us by the efforts of other people in these contexts. For this reason, I shall turn next to say a little more about the typical analysis of instructional interaction that is associated with cultural psychology.

That central place of social interaction in cultural theory is most clearly expressed in the form of one key concept – Vygotsky's zone of proximal development (ZPD). It was conceived to deal with two educational issues. The first issue was how one might satisfactorily assess a child's level of understanding in some domain. Thus, it addresses the problem of testing. Second, it deals with what goes on during processes of instruction. Thus, it is about how learning is organised between people.

The relation of the ZPD to issues of testing arises from Vygotsky's attention to the gap existing between 'actual developmental level as determined by individual problem-solving' and 'potential development as determined through problem-solving under adult guidance or in collaboration with more capable peers' (Vygotsky, 1978, p. 86). This leads to an appealing conceptualisation of assessment that focuses on *potential* to learn and on teachability.

The relation of ZPD to issues of instruction arises from what is said about the nature of productive collaboration as it might be best organised with adults or 'more capable peers'. Just how to define effective interpersonal exchanges within this 'zone' has concerned cultural theorists rather more than the complementary question of how it might serve assessment purposes. Some conceptions of interaction within the ZPD will be outlined here, although this is discussed in more detail in Chapter 4.

If we believed that instruction involved only the efficiency of Initiation–Response–Evaluation exchanges (of the kind described in Chapter 1), then the idea of a teaching *machine* would have some credibility. However, this conception of instruction – one focused on the direct transmission and confirmation of information – misses the rich possibilities of social interaction organised between individuals of varying expertise. Truly productive encounters between them will depend on something more subtle than the didactic exchange. Theorists developing the ZPD concept invite us to view instructional exchanges more in terms of collaborations.

A popular metaphor to capture what a collaboration might involve within instructional settings is that of the 'scaffold' (Wood, Bruner and Ross, 1976). To make this work, we assume that the learner is oriented towards a goal (the completed structure, in our metaphor); the goal would not be attainable without external aids and support; the expert's presence serves to ensure such support and thereby creates an occasion of collaboration. Such encounters do not entail simple demonstration or direct explanation: they require more participation on the part of the novice and more sensitivity on the part of the expert. The encounter is a collaborative one requiring jointly coordinated problem-solving. This image of scaffolding is helpful but, as a number of commentators have suggested (e.g. Newman, Griffin and Cole, 1989; Stone and Wertsch, 1984) the metaphor should not be pursued too slavishly. For one thing, its static and rigid connotations fail to suggest a real dynamic to joint activity as it is organised in this zone of interaction.

A critical commentator will rightly seek fuller definition of this dynamic: exactly how does the expert's presence in the zone of interaction serve to create cognitive support? I shall say a little more in Chapter 4 about the detail of what could actually go on between participants in this zone. Suffice it to say here that I believe the active creation of socially shared understandings (between expert and novice) is an important investment within such instructional interactions. Tutorial initiatives will often need to build upon a mutual foundation of that kind. Then, the sense in which such interventions may become useful – have lasting impacts on understanding – might be pursued in terms of a further important concept associated with Vygotsky's account of this zone: the notion of internalisation.

Vygotsky proposes that all cognitive functions are first experienced on the *inter*-mental plane before they exist on the *intra*-mental plane. That is, our private mental reflections arise from experiences that have first been organised in the public forum of social interaction. A much-cited passage from Vygotsky's writing expresses this well:

> *An interpersonal process is transformed into an intrapersonal one.* Every function in the child's cultural development appears twice: first, on the social level, and later, on the individual level; first *between* people (*interpsychological*) and then *inside* the child (*intrapsychological*).... All the higher functions originate as actual relationships between human individuals. (Vygotsky, 1978, p. 57, italics in original)

Thus, we are offered a parallel between the external world of jointly managed problem-solving and the internal world of mental functioning. Cognitive psychology might become the study of an interplay between these two. In Vygotsky's analysis, a process of 'internalisation' is conjectured to allow the social experiences of one to be realised within the privacy of the other. So, Vygotsky's special interest in language arises from his regarding it as the mediational means common to both the inter- and intra-individual world of intelligence.

This account is not without problems. In particular, some critics have complained that the internalisation concept is underspecified. Even so, this renewed emphasis on learning through the dynamics of social interaction has proved immensely influential within contemporary thinking about cognitive development and educational practice. It is not an easy framework to evaluate empirically (Schaffer, 1992). However, the evaluation strategy typically preferred by cognitive researchers – poorly contextualised, short-term studies of outcomes from joint problem-solving – is a strategy not well matched to the scope of the claims. Yet I believe this kind of theorising does fit the experience of practitioners well and ethnographic descriptions of teaching-in-progress. Deploying this conceptual scheme here for concrete discussion of computer-based learning may help to make these claims fully convincing.

CONCLUSION

In this chapter I have outlined one agenda – taken from contemporary psychology – for the analysis of cognition, cognitive development and educational practice. This is the socio-cultural perspective; or that perspective roughly corresponding to what is now termed 'cultural psychology'. I argued that the central concern of this approach was to understand how new mediational means enter into human behaviour in order to re-coordinate it.

Several commitments are entailed by adopting such a theoretical attitude. First, accounts of intelligent action must now go beyond the narrow, mental-process vocabulary of traditional cognitive psychology. Cultural accounts will want to incorporate reference to the role of mediating technologies as they enter into functional systems of behaviour. These mediational means will include structural features of the environment, artefacts, institutionalised relationships, symbol systems and (most powerful of all) 'ways with words'. Second, the appropriation and elaboration of new interpretative practices is a situated achievement: it is not best analysed in terms of the acquisition of generalised cognitive tools or representations. There are still issues of learning transfer and flexibility to be addressed – they are central to our interest in educational practice – but such issues might best be understood in terms of supportive interventions organised by the socio-cultural environment. At least, I shall argue along these lines later. Finally, this cultural approach converges upon a socially grounded conception of cognition. Mediational means may be appropriated during the short spans of individual lifetimes, but they are themselves resources fashioned over very long periods of cultural history. Most important, "their history reflects their lengthy involvement in human affairs and this constrains how we may relate to them now. Cognition is also social in nature because so many of the specific interpretative practices we encounter during development are made available to us within interpersonal communication. It follows that the settings of formal education will be of special interest to socio-cultural theorists. For it is here that practices of communication have become especially crafted: refined and concentrated for the explicit purposes of conveying interpretative practices to others in the culture. The thesis of this book is that such traditions of educational 'collaboration' should be carefully evaluated when we contemplate the incorporation of powerful new information technologies.

There are, of course, other theoretical traditions addressing problems of cognition and cognitive development. There are other traditions, therefore, that might inform the deployment of a new educational technology. Those that are most influential within contemporary psychology tend not to put such strong emphasis upon social processes. By way of acknowledging this, and trying to learn from it, I shall review these alternatives in the following chapter: making some contrasts between the approach outlined here and that associated with two other significant theoretical traditions. I have chosen these two for their central importance in current psychological thinking, but also because they both have been influential in guiding applications of technology to education.

Chapter 3

Theoretical frameworks from psychology compared

In the previous chapter, I outlined a particular theoretical approach to understanding cognition: a 'socio-cultural' approach. I believe it helps clarify psychological issues arising within educational practice. I suggested that this framework could have a particular value for addressing issues relating to the educational use of new technology. However, it is not the only source for such inspiration: other theoretical frameworks in psychology also claim insights into these same practical problems. In the present chapter, two such psychological perspectives that have been attractive to educationalists will be identified and discussed.

The aim of this chapter is partly to bring the socio-cultural view into sharper focus, by contrasting it with two traditions of psychological theorising that are more established and may be more familiar. Each of these presents a distinctive perspective on understanding teaching and learning. Moreover, each has influenced the deployment of technology within education. Evidently, the nature of that particular influence will be of special concern to us here. The first of these theoretical frameworks corresponds to the mainstream of cognitive psychology – I am choosing to label it 'experimental cognitive psychology' to capture a preference regarding methodology that reflects a distinctive worldview. The second is the Piagetian constructivist theory of development, which has been particularly influential within educational and developmental psychology.

THE PERSPECTIVE OF EXPERIMENTAL COGNITIVE PSYCHOLOGY

The term 'cognitive psychology' describes a broad church. Any critical comparisons made here with cultural approaches do not apply wholesale. The modern term 'cognitive science' is hardly more satisfactory as a target: it seems to embrace all sorts of theory – including some very much in tune with the cultural ideas described in the last chapter (e.g. Hutchins, 1991). Nevertheless, I do feel that within all this variety there is a general direction of thought dominating current cognitive psychology – especially where it is preoccupied with the experimental method. Perhaps another phrase that captures well this tradition is 'human information processing'. To some cognitive psychologists this phrase may sound old-fashioned. Their research literature tends now to refer more to 'symbol manipulation'. However, modern cognitive writers slip easily enough into using the 'information processing' vocabulary of the core metaphor (e.g. Vera and Simon, 1993). It still effectively captures the private, computational nature of their approach – and that is the key to any contrast with cultural perspectives.

The idea of defining and studying a mental 'mechanism' dedicated to information processing has enjoyed great appeal among psychologists. With it, intelligence is understood in terms of managing a flow of information from sensory systems, and from representational devices implicated in the 'coding' and 'storage' of experience. Recent advances in information technology itself, have encouraged computation metaphors as a basis for modelling the cognitive 'apparatus' (e.g. McShane, Dockrell and Wells, 1992). The work of Newell and Simon is seminal in defining this agenda. The link with functions performed by computers is easily identified in their writing:

> The theory posits a set of processes or mechanisms that produce the behavior of the thinking human.... The processes posited by the theory presumably exist in the central nervous system; they are internal to the organism.... Our theory posits internal mechanisms of great extent and complexity, and endeavours to make contact between them and visible evidence of problem-solving. (1972, p. 9–10)

It is true that these concepts are under debate given new developments in cognitive science (such as connectionism), but there remains a widely shared focus on a mental, symbol-manipulating apparatus: an apparatus for encoding, symbolising and decoding – the computational mechanism within our heads, if you will. In such a vision, culture and socially organised experience are important, but they are often considerations to be grafted on afterwards. They become the independent variables of research. Their possible relevance to something central, basic and cognitive easily becomes an issue to be explored later, in experiments designed to 'control' such things.

This language of cognitive psychology has intuitive appeal. More so, perhaps, as we have become accustomed to ascribe 'intelligence' to computers themselves – an analogy encouraging a whole language of explanation common to minds and machines. Such a language also offers some sense of assurance to the seductive enterprise of *measuring* intelligence: it seems credible that we might check the fine tuning of this apparatus by administering suitable cognitive *tests*.

So, I am identifying characteristics of modern cognitive psychology that are appealing, but they are in some tension with my preferred cultural approach. The principal conceptual tension relates to defining appropriate units for analysis. Within experimental cognitive psychology this has generally been the individual – a circumscribed mentality typically examined apart from any embedding in socio-historical context. Only recently have some cognitive psychologists considered that intelligent activity may need to be analysed as something achieved through coordination with an external environment of supportive intellectual resources. Hence, recently, there has emerged an attempt to model such coordination in terms of 'distributed artificial intelligence' (e.g. Gasser, 1991). By contrast, within cultural psychology that mentality has always been seen as inherently continuous with an historical, technological and social context. Intelligence involves mediated action and any conceptual vocabulary for studying it must accommodate mediational means. There is also a methodological tension between these approaches. Cognitive psychology has tended to practice a laboratory-based style of science. Psychological processes are abstracted for controlled study: 'context' may be only conceived as a catalogue of variables, any of which might be manipulated in such settings. Cultural psychologists, on the other hand, are uneasy with the controlled experiment (although, admittedly, they may still be seeking a distinctive empirical strategy of their own).

The methods and analytic vocabulary of cognitive psychology have furnished real understandings. Many psychologists influenced by cultural alternatives are certainly happy to admit this (e.g. Greeno and Moore, 1993; Wertsch, 1991b). The approach has allowed progress on at least some sorts of practical concerns. Surely this is so, or it would not still be flourishing? Yet while there may be real progress arising from this cognitive tradition, the reach of its insights may be less than the investment might lead us to expect. In my own view, the mainstream of cognitive psychology remains a tradition of theorising that narrows our perspective on psychological functions. It is particularly constraining when we turn to address the needs felt by educational practitioners: the theory is weak in addressing issues of learning or cognitive *change*. Arguably, this has meant that cognitive psychology has had rather little impact on educational practice (Saljo, 1987), or it has had localised and, sometimes, rather distorting effects. Desforges' (1985) observation is pertinent here: he notes that most influential psychological theories of learning have been formulated with no empirical reference to what happens in classrooms. This is strange, given that classrooms are the places where learning is explicitly organised. In other words, these theories refer largely to conceptualisations of the abstracted human cognitive system. One theme that is neglected in the laboratories within which such theories are generated is the situated, interactional nature of teaching and learning. That social quality of education is of special interest to the cultural approach and underpins the discussion of computer use pursued in this book.

Earlier, I used the case of literacy to illustrate features of a cultural psychological analysis. The same case serves to mark some of the differences between a cultural and a cognitive approach. For cognitive psychology the topic of literacy largely reduces to theories of skilled reading. Conventional 'psychological' accounts of reading are often couched in terms of information decoding and processing mechanisms. The processes referred to by these models tend to dwell on a 'bottom-up' analysis of reading, approaching it as an activity founded on fundamental information-handling skills and to be cultivated through increased understanding of the nature of those skills.

Such empirical work is elegant and persuasive and it does advance our understanding of an extraordinary childhood achievement. Yet it is incomplete. It fails to capture reading as an activity, as an achievement that is located within a framework of culturally determined possibilities. Reading as we actually experience it is carried out for purposes, and the written word enters into and reorganises our interactions with the world in a wide variety of ways. Making it accessible to novices will depend upon some sensitivity to its place within the novice's world. But there is little suggestion within information processing theories that, for example, reading difficulties are approachable in terms of this context (Brown and Campione, 1986); or little characterisation of reading as an activity involving mastery over cultural resources (Heath, 1983); or little implication that we think 'through' the written word – that our modes of reasoning reflect enforced contact with this medium (Olson, 1986; Scribner and Cole, 1981). This is not to say that this broader, cultural view of the achievement does not inform a lot of what is done about developing reading in classrooms. I think that it does. The point is merely that any such insights will rarely have their origins in influences from traditional cognitive psychology.

I believe the limitation of much cognitive psychology resides in an agenda that is too focused and constraining. The approach creates a determination to conceptualise cognition in terms of general symbolic processes (say, relating to attention, memory or reasoning), and to investigate such processes in the environment of laboratories. In these impoverished settings, contexts can be controlled such that properties of cognitive processes can be documented in their abstracted states. This is not to deny the reality of central cognitive processes that might be shared by all members of our species: characteristics arising under common circumstances of biological and cultural heritage. Neither do I wish to deny that it might sometimes be informative to study these in the abstract. However, by itself, this is a very limiting empirical agenda. The richness of intelligent action is not comprehensively expressed in terms of central representational processes. It surely arises as a consequence of the cognitive subject's participation in episodes of interaction, organised within diverse cultural settings. Human agents are ceaselessly coordinating with their environments, so the nature of the environment and a description of this dynamic exchange needs to be embraced within any analysis of intelligent action. Experimental psychology has fared poorly in capturing and understanding this variety – say, in ways that are of significance to educational practitioners.

So, the legacy of contemporary psychological theorising seems to include a strong faith in the possibility of content-free mental processes. Consider a particular case: many psychologists study human *memory* through observation of how their experimental subjects cope with lists of words. The enterprise assumes a cognitive function of memory can be usefully 'purified' in this way – isolated for exploration in parametric studies. Thereby the components of a memory system are abstracted, the assumption being that they are normally obscured from us by the 'noise' inherent in everyday circumstances of remembering. This approach exemplifies the view that refined experimental materials can help segregate and expose certain core mental functions. If, however, one adopts the cultural perspective of recognising that thinking is mediated through artefacts and social practice, then the device of a word-list seems very constraining. To be sure, there are culturally organised situations where such remembering might be valued as a system of activity, but the minor significance of such circumstances bears no relation to the popularity of the word-list device in memory research.

Not only is the specification of context-free cognitive functions an inspiration for psychological research, such an idea also underpins a strand of everyday educational thinking. There is a common-sense view about learning that seems to regard schools as sites for the transmission of general-purpose intellectual skills. Yet this perspective may require critical consideration. Against it, for example, Lave (1988) offers a vigorous critique of schooling, in which she questions a determination to teach cognitive skills as if they could be disembedded from the particular routines in which they are exercised. The tradition of class tests reflects this – situations in which the testee's thinking is deprived of conventional support from material resources or from classmates. The academic examination has evolved as a highly ritualised and condensed ordeal conceived in this spirit.

So, I am characterising an influential mainstream of cognitive psychology as being closely concerned with isolating human information processing capacities; concerned to characterise a private mental space wherein the manipulation of symbols serves to guide action. How would we expect such an analysis of cognition to interpret and influence the place of new technology in education – and how would it differ from a culturally influenced approach? Some observers conclude that the practical contribution of cognitive psychology in this area remains modest (Benyon and Mackay, 1993; Laurillard, 1987). I believe its influence may be visible in very general terms – in terms of a broad theoretical orientation to computer-based practice – but less visible at the level of specific software design.

Yet, a greater influence at just this level might be possible. I have stressed that an information processing analysis has its strengths. The issue is more one of its scope. So, for example, where a significant part of a learner's task is to decode and manipulate some symbolic system (say, in relation to the written word, mathematical conventions, music, etc.), then we might expect a cognitive psychological analysis to be helpful in designing certain kinds of challenging computer-based experiences. Similarly, the considerable volume of research concerned with the acquisition of reading skills might be expected to inspire a certain class of computer-based learning resources. In fact, this does not seem to be happening on any scale.

On the other hand, I believe there has been quite a strong *indirect* influence from the cognitive tradition of psychology. It is indirect because it tends to legitimise (without always being explicitly invoked) certain commonsense conceptions of cognition: in particular, a faith in content-free thinking 'skills'. This, in turn, tends to encourage a certain kind of educational purpose in relation to computer-based learning. At the same time, the approach has diverted attention from the social fabric that is created during learning. This is a context that it seems easy for most researchers to overlook, yet which is of key importance to a cultural perspective. I shall take up this theme in a later section of this chapter, where each approach is considered in relation to its perspective on computers for learning. First, however, the approach of cultural psychology can be usefully contrasted with the second influential movement within cognitive developmental theory: Piagetian constructivism. I shall suggest similar limitations to this approach as a comprehensive perspective on computer-based learning.

THE PERSPECTIVE OF CONSTRUCTIVISM

Educational practice has not only been influenced by theory within *cognitive* psychology. Developmental psychology has also been influential. In fact, it is widely accepted that psychological theory has had its greatest impact on education through the developmental work of Piaget. In this section I shall make a contrast between the Piagetian 'constructivist' approach and the cultural theory discussed earlier. My main concern will be the priority the different theories assign to autonomous discovery versus guided intervention as underpinning the growth of understanding.

Piaget's work offers us a number of ideas regarding educational practice that we now virtually take for granted. From him we derive a strong sense of the distinction between development and learning; in this scheme, what is termed 'development' has an inwardly driven quality and must proceed in advance of formal teaching. Indeed, its progress must underpin any strategy of organised teaching. The course of such development depends upon things the child discovers independently. Moreover, these discoveries emerge from opportunities to act upon the material world and to reflect upon the consequences, conditions and outcomes of such actions.

One feature of Piagetian theory echoes a theme identified above in the discussion of mainstream cognitive psychology: there is a commitment to 'central process' cognitive functions over more situated, context-specific achievements. Piagetian researchers are not so fond of laboratories as cognitive psychologists. However, their research remains vulnerable to the criticism of neglecting context. Their account of childhood reasoning fails to capture the senses in which it is located in a social and cultural setting (Donaldson, 1978). I will not review this issue again but, instead, focus on a further feature of Piagetian thinking that is in tension with cultural perspectives – one that has attracted more conspicuous unease in recent critical commentary, that is the sparse reference to social factors in Piaget's account of development.

It is frequently claimed that Piaget neglected social influences on cognition. There is some injustice in such claims, or at least the more vigorous of them. Piaget did not overlook interpersonal aspects of cognitive development. Indeed, his early treatment of egocentric and sociocentric thinking (Piaget, 1926) might be said to anticipate more contemporary 'social' perspectives on cognition. Nevertheless, it is fair to claim that this concern played no significant role in the bulk of his later theorising about cognitive development. Moreover, although his concern for the social may be real, Piaget has been largely interpreted *as if* his theory did not accommodate interpersonal influences. Thus, for example, computer-based learning materials inspired by Piaget may choose to neglect consideration of the social context of their use; and this is no less significant a trend because it is based on limited interpretations of Piaget rather than an honest appraisal of his ideas.

In contrast, what seems to be best known about Vygotsky and the early socio-cultural theorists is that they promoted a view of development strongly stressing the impact of social events. Moreover, this was not simply a plea for more social psychology – at least, not if that merely implied more attention to 'social variables'. Vygotsky was not advocating a social psychology in the familiar sense of an interpersonal psychology, one that reduces social experience to the consideration of exchanges between individual social actors. His view has us more thoroughly immersed in the social nature of life. Whereas Piagetian and other psychological theory tends to start from the individual and derive accounts of the social, Vygotsky proceeds the other way round. For Vygotsky the social dimension of conscious mental life is fundamental: 'individual consciousness is derivative and secondary' (Vygotsky, 1979, p. 30).

At first encounter, Vygotsky's alternative might seem to have a natural appeal. It prioritises the role of people (parents and teachers, for example) in supporting the child's psychological development. However, highlighting the role of other people may necessitate querying another appealing perspective: one that puts children themselves at the centre of their own development. This is very much a view we associate with Piaget.

The nature of cognitive development in Piaget's scheme of things is attractively captured in the term 'constructivism': children are actively 'constructing' their understanding of the world. Surely we will feel an affinity towards such a view. It offers us (personal) responsibility for our psychological nature; it does not leave us passive victims of social forces. In this spirit, Wood articulates a widely felt caution when warning that we should be wary of attributing to 'the effects of instruction what is properly an achievement of the child' (1989, p. 59). But as Wood's own work elegantly demonstrates, any simple dichotomy of instruction and autonomy is misleading. In a cultural view, the term 'social' is used to help us see beyond those (important) interpersonal activities that characterise direct tutorial instruction. It identifies the fact that any material environment of learning will manifest a structure reflecting some particular socio-cultural history. Pupils learn interpretative practices that have this social grounding. The appropriation of such practices may not be exclusively within the contexts of face-to-face interaction.

One focal point for confronting this tension might be Piaget's compelling account of the active, constructing infant. In *The origins of intelligence* (1953), Piaget directs our attention towards the energy and curiosity of children in their first two years of life. We are reminded of their relentless exploration of the material world, of the energy invested in acting upon it. In contrast, Vygotsky makes persuasive use of the same infant explorations to illustrate his own contrasting view: a view of early cognition as socially-mediated. He highlights within this early period of development the basic process whereby children come to access mediational means. Vygotsky notes that the infant's act of grasping is re-mediated into a cultural tool (the sign of pointing) by virtue of how the social environment reacts to this simple activity. This was a perspective to be widely adopted later in accounts of the social context for language acquisition (e.g. Lock, 1978). Vygotsky's interpretation of such events renders a re-reading of Piaget's careful natural history a curious experience. One becomes sensitive to a strange neglect of the structuring presence of the observer himself. The parent/researcher Piaget locates and manipulates domestic bits and pieces around which the playful observations are made, yet he fails to incorporate an account of that mediation in the final theory.

Perhaps there is something of a projective test entailed in witnessing infant behaviour. One observer might be most impressed by an autonomous and creative exploration, another by the manner in which the infant's environment is structured to afford particular possibilities, and by how the inevitable presence of adults serves to create structure through joint activity. (This same projective quality might apply to our experience of witnessing classroom life.)

In reflecting on theoretical perspectives that help us to think about cognitive development, Goodnow (1990, p. 277) expresses a contemporary judgement on Piaget's vision of the world:

> essentially free-market and benign. All the information is available. You may help yourself and act for yourself. The only limitations are imposed by the nature of your own abilities – the extent to which your schemas or logical structures allow you to take in the information.

This is a characteristically modern view of the Piagetian tradition. It regrets a failure to recognise ways in which the child's environment is culturally structured and, in particular, ways in which socially organised encounters serve to constrain and afford activity in the Piagetian 'free-market' environment.

Yet, there is also a sense in the contemporary literature of wanting to reach some compromise with Piaget. In particular, the powerful motive to act upon the world that is implied within constructivist accounts may be too important to risk losing sight of. We sense this in the writing of some current cultural theorists. So, Scott *et al.* (1992) refer to 'cultural constructivism' and in the Introduction to his book *Culture and cognitive development*, Saxe (1991) is able to cite both Vygotsky and Piaget as working in the constructivist tradition. Finally, the concept of 'co-construction' has found favour recently, apparently to capture a potent mix of social engagement and creative exploration.

I am persuaded that Piaget's constructivism does fail to come to terms with the inherently social nature of cognition. However, I am also wary that a pendulum of opinion may now swing too carelessly towards a version of the 'social' view that is excessively narrow. Moreover, this narrow view cannot thrive as an exclusive alternative to unadorned constructivism. Earlier in this chapter I contrasted a societal with a social interactional interpretation of cognition's social nature. My concern is that only the social interactional interpretation will be recognised and, for this reason, it will be assumed that all learning has to be organised within contexts of face-to-face social exchange. Expressed as a crude theoretical confrontation: the social encounter within Vygotsky's zone of proximal development is taken as the *exclusive* model of learning – in opposition to the reflective abstractions engaged in by Piaget's privately constructing child.

Gelman, Massey and McManus (1991) have recently toyed with such a contrast. They argue that learning may be supported by a great variety of resources. Moreover, they suggest that learners can themselves sometimes be the best judges of what defines a good supporting environment. They may sometimes be more expert in this than the adults (teachers and parents) who will often make these decisions on children's behalf. The argument is illustrated with studies of young children learning from exhibits in a hands-on science museum. One challenging finding is that accompanying adults often did not take opportunities to scaffold their charges' investigations of the learning materials to hand. So cultural theorists should not assume that adults are always obliging in this respect (although they might be within the structured settings that we observe as researchers). Another finding concerned a display dealing with principles of motion: a computer-based demonstration was more effective in helping children abstract the central ideas than was the spontaneous support of accompanying adults. The warning here is that interaction with sympathetic adults is not the exclusive route to understanding – indeed this museum example highlights computers as one alternative medium.

I do not feel that observations of this kind seriously question the need to view cognition and learning as socially mediated. Take a more classroom-based example than the one described above: consider the pupil who independently explores turtle Logo and discovers something about, say, geometry. The learning is not scaffolded in the same sense as the example above perhaps. But the pupil's discovery is located in a classroom on a device that has been configured by programmers and now used according to a schedule that is determined by teachers and administrators. Classrooms, programmers, and teacher-led routines are typical features of these learning circumstances: features that reveal their socially constituted nature. They may be taken for granted as the (mere) backcloth against which learning occurs, but this familiarity should not cause us to miss the profoundly social nature of the educational setting. Moreover, having noted it, we may accept that a pupil's learning need not finally crystallise in the particular context of (tutorial) interaction with another person. In short, how we organise a pupil's concrete experience at the focus of this socially organised world need not always demand the more intimate engagement of face-to-face discourse.

This possibility is explored in an essay by Davidson (1992). He cites the case of Pascal, who independently reinvented much of Euclid's geometry – an interest expressly forbidden by his father. Surely, this illustrates an intellectual achievement that had to be divorced from the tutorial support of face-to-face interaction? But face-to-face exchanges are just one realisation of the 'social' nature of mental life. While, in this sense, aspects of Pascal's achievements are solitary in character, they remain embedded in the social world. The symbol systems that the young Pascal appropriated arose within the conventionalising discourse of mathematicians. Yet

Davidson's example of Pascal is useful. It illustrates the possibility of considerable intellectual achievement sustained outside of social interaction. We are reminded that such solitary analysis is possible; although we may believe that what is involved is more likely to be precipitated within social interaction: 'the inferences needed to construct knowledge do not differ according to whether they are prompted by independently observed or by socially received reasons – although their rate might vary considerably' (1992, p. 28).

Thus, the cultural perspective should not insist that the final path of all new learning is a scaffolded social encounter. Neither should it deny the creative energy that characterises our typically constructivist attitude as individual learners. However, this does not imply that the cultural and the Piagetian constructivist perspectives are easily harmonised. In the end, the cultural view distinctively analyses learning in terms of the social structure of activity – and not in terms of changes within individuals. This suggests a different style and content to any program of empirical research: a cultural approach will be more about the participatory dimension of problem-solving and of the cultural resources that can be mobilised in the process. These two views of 'learning' also imply different points of focus for the design of computer-based support.

What exactly is implied by constructivism for the design of such support? Papert and his colleagues have been the most vigorous group applying this theoretical framework to development of computer environments for learning. Papert's original (1980) clash with the prevailing conception of computer-as-tutor arose from his faith in a pupil's capacity for self-directed discovery – and his mistrust of didactic, teacher-led alternatives. With the Logo microworld, Papert offered a marriage between this new technology and Piaget's discovery-oriented, child-centred perspective on cognitive development. Logo was a tool for the making of discoveries. The child was thereby allowed to control the computer, not the computer the child. In this conception, the technology presents a responsive and versatile environment within which children may extend their discoveries of nature. Recently, Papert and his colleagues have coined the term 'constructionism' (Harel and Papert, 1991) to capture their particular perspective on teaching and learning, one that arises from their experience of developing these ideas in practice.

However, as we have already noted, there has been a growing unease associated with the outcome of applying the constructivist agenda in the form of Logo. Of course, enthusiasts can claim that the overall vision has not been thoroughly implemented and that Logo still remains the only fully developed illustration of what is possible (Papert, 1987). Yet, the record of success associated with this prime example remains disappointing. A response to this might be to cite the worry I am expressing here: the neglect of interpersonal support for the learning. A teacher's participation does not seem to have been written into the detailed design of such activities. Yazdani voices a solution, although it seems to involve only a tinkering with this balance of autonomy and collaboration. He comments: 'This shortcoming may be alleviated by designing course-ware within which such activity is fitted. Here a human teacher holds the pupil's hand when necessary and leaves him free to explore when educationally effective' (Yazdani, 1987, p. 112). Thus, the social dimension of learning is respected – but here only in the modest sense of teachers being loosely coupled to exploratory microworlds.

This hand-holding conception of teaching participation is, so far, still a rather insubstantial middle ground. It is useful to warn against constructivist theorisers putting so much faith in autonomous learning that the social context is neglected. And it is useful to query cultural theorists who might suggest that all learning must be scaffolded through social dialogue. However, if teacher intervention within pupils' computer-based learning is to be one way forward, we need a greater appreciation of the particular forms that it must take. While agreeing with Yazdani (1987, p. 112) that 'three elements are needed – students, teachers and the computational system', his suggestion that teachers are furnishing the 'emotional context' does not take us far enough. Such a 'missing bit' view also is implied within recent work by Lepper and colleagues (Lepper and Chabbay, 1988; Lepper, Wolverton, Mumme and Gurtner, 1993). Their analysis of limitations in computer-based tutoring suggests that what is characteristically missing from such systems is a social capacity. However, they believe that the difficulties of simulation have arisen in respect of particular social skills: those concerned with managing the affective and motivational dimensions of learning. These are awkwardly fractured from a cognitive dimension inherent in the social discourse of instruction (a dimension whose management is thought to be more tractable).

I doubt that constructivist environments of computer-based learning can be made more complete by simply appending human support – as if it were just another resource to call upon. In particular, I question whether the main gap that such interventions would fill is a gap in the 'emotional context' of learning. In the next chapter, I shall consider how the nature of teacher–pupil collaborative interaction typically goes further than this. However, here I have merely been concerned to identify what is entailed by the theoretical orientation of constructivism in general terms. There is much that is valuable in this perspective. Perhaps it is only the advent of computer technology that has associated it with the controversy of displacing human tutoring. I will return to constructivism in the second part of the present chapter, where I shall consider how each of the perspectives I have outlined – cognitive, constructivist and cultural – influence the way in which computers may be used in educational settings.

SYNTHESIS: ARTEFACT AND THEORY

In this chapter, I have been exploring psychological frameworks on cognition and learning. The point has been to find a useful conceptual vocabulary: one that might help systematise our thinking about teaching and learning supported by new technology. I am anxious to prepare to deal with one characteristic of computer-based learning – the ease with which it separates from the interpersonal communication typical of learning from other resources. In Chapter 1, we noted that this dislocation from the social exchange of classrooms worried practitioners.

The point of adopting some distinctive theoretical framework is to help articulate the basis for such concerns. Until recently, practitioners will have found little support within psychology for any commitment they may feel towards regarding learning as a socially organised achievement. Now there is a framework that helps develop this idea. I outlined the framework in Chapter 2 – the socio-cultural approach.

In the present chapter, the cultural approach to cognition has been contrasted with others from the mainstream of psychology. 'Approach' is a carefully chosen word in this context. The contrasts I have been making identify fairly loosely-knit collections of ideas. Others exploring such contrasts have suggested that these approaches might be best characterised as 'worldviews' (Agre, 1993) – rather than 'theories'. Is there a focal point for that collection of ideas comprising the cultural worldview on cognition? One good contender is found in Suchman's characterisation of this framework: 'constructing accounts of relations among people, and between people and the historically and culturally constituted worlds that they inhabit together' (Suchman, 1993, p. 71). She contrasts this with a perspective more typical of mainstream psychology 'dedicated to explicating those processes of perception and reasoning understood traditionally to go on inside the head' (1993, p. 71).

This *social* perspective on cognition is the one which I am most anxious to capture here. In what follows, I shall call upon this perspective, as well as others that have arisen above in reviewing the various worldviews. I shall consider how they each furnish a distinctive approach to the realisation of computer-supported learning. In my own view, the worldview of cultural psychology offers the most promising way forward. However, concrete examples of practice guided by a cultural perspective may make that claim more convincing. Such examples will be elaborated in later chapters. What should be possible first is a general situating of the culturally inspired approach: locating it in relation to other theoretical options. Characterising my preferred framework in this way should create a useful springboard for the themes of collaboration to be explored in the remainder of this book.

The following synthesis will comprise four brief sections. The aim is to reflect on a tension between artefact and theory: between computers-for-learning and psychologies-of-learning. So, first, I shall make some observations about microcomputers as physical objects that get located in classrooms. It will be argued that their material nature invites a certain pattern of use. Then I shall highlight certain central features of cognitive, constructivist and cultural worldviews that interact with this material nature in important ways. In fact, I hope this review will highlight a certain chemistry involving theory and artefact: one that may be underpinning distinctive (and controversial) varieties of educational practice.

Some relevant features of computers as artefacts

One distinctive feature of this technology is its physically self-contained nature. This is significant for determining how it gets used in teaching and learning. It is true that computers can be hooked up to other classroom equipment (say, in support of scientific measurements) but, in general, they naturally function as circumscribed screen-plus-input devices. A consequence of this design is that they are readily positioned in their own classroom locations, perhaps physically set apart from the main arena of educational activity.

This need not be so, but other properties of computers surely encourage this dislocated status. Many programs written for them may strike teachers as explicitly designed to function as stand-alone activities. Suchman (1987) identifies three properties of the technology that indirectly may promote this way of thinking. She notes that computers have reactive, linguistic and opaque properties. They are *reactive* because user actions are typically and immediately met with (non-random) machine reactions. Suchman argues that this encourages the attribution of a sense of purpose – a capability, perhaps, for sustaining self-contained interactions. Then, they are *linguistic* because users employ common language to control them (rather than buttons and levers). Suchman argues that this reinforces talking about our encounters with computers in the same terms as we talk about human interaction. Finally, they are *opaque*. This argument echoes Dennett's (1978) claim that the urge to ascribe intention to human behaviour arises from our inability to see inside each others heads – our mutual opacity. So, similarly, we may ascribe intention and purpose to these opaque machines. The argument also refers to the complex, yet structurally undifferentiated nature of the computer: the fact that functioning is not readily describable in terms of particular, graspable local events. This encourages a reification – we speak of 'its' activity.

In summary, then, this technology has both a self-contained and an interactive quality. So, it may strike practitioners as offering a focal point within a particular classroom niche: one where autonomous and lively activity can be supported. The apparently purposeful, challenging nature of the medium sustains pupils' interest and keeps them busy. They may be seen as productively 'getting on with it'. Conversely, the technology does not seem strongly to invite teacher intervention. This, of course, may be very welcome in the demanding environment of a full classroom.

How may learning in such an environment be interpreted? What happens to pupils when they to go there to learn? Perhaps they retreat to the computer area and occupy themselves until a task is complete. (Educational software will often furnish a comfortable sense of closure – the exercises are done, the pattern is constructed, the treasure is found, and so on.) At the end, what is there to show for this investment? Sometimes there will be visible, maybe tangible, products; but, even then, the *process* whereby this creativity was possible is invariably lost. What was actually done is too often hidden from tutorial support (from teachers and others). It is hidden simply because of the transitory nature of interactions mediated by screen displays. The task may create a conclusion, and by some criterion or other it may be satisfactory; but there will probably be no recoverable record of the pupils' landmarking achievements along the way to their final product. Moreover, as Hoyles comments: 'correct answers may well hide incorrect processes' (1985b, p.

10) – a point noted and well illustrated in relation to computer work by Moore (1993).

I have suggested that the structural properties of this technology naturally promote a rather dislocated pattern of use. This is for two reasons. The technology is materially self-contained, and it is also 'interactive'. Together, these properties serve to sustain circumscribed pupil engagements. This may or may not be seen as a desirable style of working. So what is its relation with psychological theories about good circumstances for learning – are they in harmony, or not? I shall argue below that some of the theoretical themes discussed earlier seem actively to endorse this pattern of use. Others can be made consistent with it. But others caution that we should configure the place of computers-for-learning differently: we should make them more central to the social fabric of educational communities.

The artefact in conjunction with cognitive theories

Cognitive psychological perspectives were outlined earlier in this chapter. At their core is a commitment to explaining intelligent activity in terms of mental information processing. Human knowledge is understood in terms of stored symbols; thinking or reasoning is understood in terms of symbol manipulation. According to Vera and Simon (1993), these symbols are patterns – of some kind; they are organised into symbol structures through sets of relations. Their physical representation in the brain is assumed, but not known; and, for purposes of psychological analysis, not needed to be known. Such theories, long established within psychology are now attracting some criticism. Clancey (1993) has cited numerous commentators who argue that this view of cognition has exercised an unwelcome influence, serving to distort creativity within a variety of human enterprises. Organisational practices within modern economies are cited as one broad example: Winograd and Flores (1986) make such a case in relation to the deployment of new technology in business. We must include among these examples the danger of distorting effects in respect of computers and education. Cognitive theories, in which all intelligent activity is understood in terms of computations in a private mental world, tend to cultivate a particular stance on the psychology of learning. Traditional cognitive theorising does not adequately challenge the organisation of computers into self-contained arrangements – as characterised above. In fact, it may tend to reinforce them. It may offer some endorsement to the dislocation of computer work from a mainstream of socially organised educational practice.

I suggest that this arises through the promotion of two particular ideas. The first concerns the possibility of empowering computers to participate in something like human conversational dialogue. If this is thought possible, then software authors will attempt machine-based reproductions of the dialogues associated with instruction. The second idea concerns conceptions of the outcomes of 'learning': how the symbolising cognitive apparatus gets altered by participation in educational activities. Some characterisations of such outcomes are, again, in harmony with more self-contained modes of arranging computer-based learning. I shall briefly elaborate each of these two cognitive themes in order to clarify their bearing on educational practice.

First, on the conversational potential of this technology: it was noted above that the reactive, linguistic and opaque properties of computers combine to create a sense of interactivity. Such impressions have intrigued cognitive theorists. They have pursued the goal of refining this interactivity to make it appear increasingly intelligent; increasingly reflecting the feel of human communication. Yet, Suchman (1987) questions whether orthodox cognitive approaches are likely to succeed in this aim. She evaluates their agenda in relation to the problem of designing a particular instructional sequence – one that can be incorporated into a piece of office equipment and delivered so as to guide its operation by a novice user. Even this apparently simple task is shown to be very difficult to bring off. Her empirical observations suggest that simulating real open-ended educational discourse will turn out to be a particularly daunting task.

However, Suchman's view – which I find persuasive – is not simply that, in practice, it proves hard to automate instruction sequences. It may be an inherently flawed enterprise. She argues that it is grounded in a mistaken conception of how human communication is managed. This conception is one derived from cognitive theory. It reflects a preoccupation with explanations of behaviour built around plans: resources arising from cognitive computations and supposedly guiding our actions. In cognitive theory, the execution of plans is supposed to explain individual actions. It is also invoked to explain joint activity, particularly communication. In such a model, effective communication is said to depend upon our capacity to read the underlying plans of others. During communication, this mutual interpretative ability allows us to recognise and exploit access to bodies of shared understanding – data to drive our exchanges. Such a computational model may seem to offer the prospect of simulating discourse (say, instructional discourse) within a human-computer interaction. A machine might be programmed to have the same symbolic computing capacity as a human communicator. So it might generate, and recognise in others, plans. It might, thereby, communicate. Yet this is a controversial account of what must be simulated in order to reproduce human discourse. I shall examine the controversy in the following chapter, where the possible instructional capabilities of computers are considered in a little more detail. For present purposes, I only wish to identify this tradition of cognitive theorising as offering authority to the idea of computers 'instructing'. We need not dwell at once on whether this authority is credible when closely analysed. The point is, it forms some part of a climate of beliefs: beliefs that this technology can, at least sometimes, be trusted to conduct the traditionally social task of instruction. Moreover, to some extent, we can leave it to go about doing this.

Faith in the possible simulation of instructional conversation is one product of cognitive psychology that I believe reinforces the social dislocation of classroom computers. The second concerns how we conceptualise the very ingredients of cognition – and, thus, how we conceptualise what gets learned. There is an orthodox cognitivist perspective on this. It may originate in the attraction many cognitive psychologists have towards research on human skilled action (Miller, Galanter and Pribram, 1960). What research on skills tends to encourage is an expression of the computations of mental activity in terms of 'thinking skills'. From there, the metaphor of intelligence as underpinned by a cognitive 'tool-kit' is easily appropriated. This form of analysis is nicely illustrated in a book on computers and learning written from within the cognitive psychological tradition by Underwood and Underwood (1990).

These authors define an approach for using computers in learning whose aim is:

> to provide children with the ability to think. This is achieved by providing them with the basic skills – the cognitive toolkit – and with experiences of the use of different combinations of the components of their toolkit in problem-solving exercises. (1990, p. 29)

I find this acquisition/application distinction difficult to sustain; a different psychological model may be more helpful. The distinction suggests that we offer learners activities that equip them with the basic tools, and then activities that allow them to reach for these tools and apply them (in creative and novel combinations). But where does the break occur: how clearly can learning tasks be identified as being about acquiring new tools versus using them?

It is implied that teachers need to involve computers in 'two broad classes of activity' (Underwood and Underwood, 1990, p. 29) but they turn out to be hard to differentiate. In fact, these authors resist taking the differentiating step that might tempt many practitioners: offer children one class of focused activities (drills) that give dense practice in the underlying skills while, at other times, offer more open-ended problems in which the skills are integrated and applied. This is the very route that such theorising might encourage. However, Underwood and Underwood's own preference is an exclusive promotion of activities in the open-ended category. This is welcome, but hard to derive from a tool-kit model. Their rejection of programs offering intensive skill-centred practice is made on the grounds of their being less motivating (1990, p. 34). Thus, presumably, they are less efficient. However, even the early developers of computer drills identified the very opposite problem as common: students 'trapped' into a sustained use of such activities (see Noble, 1991, Chapter 7). In any case, when under- or over-motivation does not seem a conspicuous problem, why not provide skills practice in a drilled way – rather than tolerate the low density practice inherent in open-ended programs?

The notion of discrete, general-purpose thinking skills may encourage just this kind of reasoning. The analogies driving this theoretical framework are seductive. We do, intuitively, recognise that certain ways of thinking and reasoning seem to have generality: they seem to get mobilised within a variety of particular situations. So this invites reification. 'Tool' is one metaphor that follows. Although there is a mixed bag of metaphors possible: for example, 'skills', 'tools' and 'cognitive health' (Underwood and Underwood, 1990, p. 38). What they share, however, is a focus on cognition as involving core mental processes that are deployed freely across problem-solving domains. Yet do such processes provide the best explanation of the continuity that we sense within our thinking and reasoning? I believe such theorising trades too much on becoming 'equipped' with private, self-contained mental resources. However, what is relevant to the theme of the present chapter is the classroom practice potentially encouraged by such an analysis. The analysis may tempt the cultivation of core tools through efficient but decontextualised activities. It may, then, tempt a belief that when a learner is witnessed to be exercising a particular cognitive tool, so the work of acquisition for that core skill has been achieved. It is available and we merely have to *motivate* its application elsewhere. Computers may seem to furnish circumscribed settings in which the use of a given tool can be precipitated, or suitably honed for application in other settings – a kind of workshop environment. In other words, the availability of the tool is not contextually studied in this analysis. So, it becomes a perspective that may distract attention from overarching social processes in instruction: the very processes, I would suggest, that are implicated in creating such cross-situational continuities of thinking and reasoning that we intuitively recognise do occur.

In summary, cognitive psychology fails to take seriously the social context of computer-based learning. Indirectly, then, it may legitimise a dislocation of classroom computers: a social decoupling already suggested by the material nature of this artefact. I have argued that, first, a cognitivist orientation encourages attempts to develop machine-based instructional dialogue. Evidently, such computer-as-tutor applications separate the technology from a social context: the whole point is to reproduce and replace (human) teacher intervention. Second, cognitive psychology neglects the contextualised nature of learning in favour of the view that what is acquired are general-purpose ways of acting. So, it encourages a 'bottom-up' analysis of mental life: an orientation suggesting a tool-shed of discrete, cognitive resources. Within such a framework, computers might seem attractive and self-contained laboratory environments for a forging of the tools.

The artefact in conjunction with constructivist theory

Cognitivist and constructivist perspectives have plenty of common ground. For one thing, constructivist theories (as epitomised by Piaget's work) share an interest in defining general purpose cognitive structures. For another, they do not favour contextualist analyses of cognition. Thus, some of the worries rehearsed in the previous section apply again in this one. However, there are two aspects of constructivist thinking that I wish to highlight as distinctive to the tradition. They are each very relevant to this problem of integrating computers into a social context of learning. The first concerns a pupil-centred view of learning; the second, again, concerns the application of a certain tool-for-thinking species of metaphor. Neither aspects of the approach are inherently incompatible with the computational orientation of cognitive psychology. Rather, they represent considerations that are simply more central to a constructivist view.

Cognitive psychologists often turn to constructivism when they confront questions of how conditions for learning should be organised. For, unfortunately, their own perspective on the nature of cognition has inspired few rich theories concerned with managing the processes of learning. Theorising tends to focus on the varieties of structuring that must be imposed on to-be-learned material – structuring that will best harmonise with human information processing strategies. For some, this may seem to place the pupil in an unattractively passive posture: a hapless processor of well-packaged knowledge. Cognitive psychologists sensitive to the atmosphere of actual classrooms (cf. Underwood and Underwood, 1990) may turn to constructivist ideas. They may argue for a learning environment that respects the exploratory, creative basis of cognitive change. In such a Piagetian constructivist environment, the learner acts upon the world, and then abstracts understandings from private reflection on the consequences of that action. There is a metaphor within this of the learner as (experimental) scientist. In general terms, psychologists concerned with information processing may relate favourably to this image. Although it is not clear whether learning that is pupil-centred in this sense can be systematised comfortably within their preferred vocabulary of cognitive computations.

The significant point is that this theorising tends to direct attention towards the crafting of environments suitable for such learning-by-discovery: how to define settings where pupils may explore and, thereby, construct new understandings for themselves. Inevitably, at the same time, pupil-centred theorising distracts our attention from the interpersonal dimension of learning: how it is supported by the interventions of other people. In such a climate of theorising, computers may be appropriated to provide just this kind of self-contained, facilitating setting. In a book concerning constructivist computer environments, the following is asserted: 'But education – real education – is not something performed on someone, nor is it something one *gets*; it is something one *does* for oneself' (Falbel, 1991, p. 30).

The idea that it might be a *collaborative* achievement is not an option in this list. Of course, in principle, actual constructivist computer environments might well incorporate opportunities for support at the level of tutorial collaboration. But, in reality, the interactivity of computer-based microworlds can render this support (apparently) less necessary: pupils who get stuck can often experiment their way forward. Indeed, such autonomy may seem very desirable.

There is a second constructivist theme that I believe can seduce us into neglecting the social context of education. It concerns how to define the nature of structural changes associated with learning something. Again, we encounter the tool metaphor, but in a rather different guise. Constructivism dwells upon pupil activity. It encourages the design of environments in which that activity may be creative. So, under this tradition, computers are unlikely to be deployed in their more didactic tutorial mode. Instead, an ideal constructivist computer environment might be one that furnishes the pupil with some generic tool (text processor, spreadsheet, etc.). At other times, the computer might offer rather more specific 'microworlds' for pupils to explore or control: again, we may say they are enjoying a '*tool* to think with'. If a pupil succeeds in effectively controlling such a tool, the designers of these environments obviously seek to characterise what cognitive benefits have resulted.

Sometimes the framework of cognitive psychology, as presented above, might be invoked. It might be said that the computer environment is allowing the exercise or integration of core cognitive skills. But the ambitious designer might wish to identify more far-reaching impacts than refinement-through-meaningful-practice. In such cases, effects on the learner are naturally expressed in terms of cognitive-structural changes. Most straightforwardly, it may be claimed that acquired ways of acting with the computer tool get internalised. This thereby creates cognitive structures to be understood as new private tools of thought. In Salomon's (1988) apposite phrase, we witness IA, or 'artificial intelligence in reverse'. 'reversed', because the intelligence acquired originates in the artefact: the human computer-user internalises computational resources encountered in the course of controlling the technology. For Salomon and others there is, thus, a 'cognitive residue' arising from mastering certain computer tools or controlling certain microworlds.

'Internalisation' is an attractive concept to express such an outcome, although not the only one. One alternative is that proposed for the 'cognitive residue' associated with learning computer programming. It is claimed that programming in Logo is a cognitively 'powerful' experience because it makes concrete for the novice programmer certain strategic processes fundamental to problem-solving (Lawler, 1987). An example might be the mastery of writing 'procedures' – self-contained units of code, the building blocks of a program. Here, it is argued, what mediates the creation of a useful cognitive residue is not 'internalisation'. It is some (more constructivist) process of reflective abstraction – reflection centred about these procedures as products of thought. Through successful programming, learners are empowered to confront and examine a concrete representation of their problem-solving processes.

Such interpretation converges on a view of learning similar to the cognitive psychological theorising outlined above. The key similarity (for present purposes) is that the outcomes of effective computer-based learning experiences are charac-terised in tool-like, domain-general terms. (On the other hand, a difference might be that the cognitivist orientation tends to focus on activities that afford 'practice' from the learner, while the constructivist orientation tends to focus on activities that afford 'reflective abstraction'.) Regarding the similarities of position, I should stress that neither cognitive nor constructivist theorists will necessarily highlight these claims about tools. They will not necessarily foreground the general-purpose character of a given cognitive acquisition – as if it were always a strong empirical claim. It would be fairer to say that such claims emerge from the literature as implications that invariably are easily drawn. This is simply because cognitive and constructivist empirical work on computer-based learning largely ignores the issue of contextual constraints on acquisitions. It proceeds as if what is learned has generality – or takes the form of new cognitive tools.

Both themes discussed in this section probably enjoy a natural appeal and, thereby, may readily underpin classroom practice. First, the notion of pupil-centred learning probably resonates well with prevailing ideology in cultures where indi-vidual agency is highly prized. Second, the notion of acquiring general tools of thought is an attractively straightforward metaphor for intellectual change during development. It fits with our fashioning the classroom to be a general-purpose environment – rather than another particular context where rather particular things get done (Guberman and Greenfield, 1991; Lave, 1988). Again, my conclusion is as in the previous section. An influential tradition of psychological theorising conspires with the material nature of the computer to encourage a certain pattern of use. That pattern of use makes it too easy for computer-based learning to fracture from a mainstream of socially organised educational practice.

The artefact in conjunction with cultural theory

I see the framework of socio-cultural theorising as a check on this fracturing tendency. However, first, note the continuity between cultural and constructivist thinking – the shared commitment to an active learner. Cole and Griffin's remark: 'thinking is always and everywhere the internalisation of the means, modes and contents of the communications activities that exist in the culture into which one is born' (1980, p. 356). This suggests an image of learners actively abstracting order from the world, as a consequence of their participatory encounters within it. However, compared to traditional constructivist thinking, the cultural version pays more attention to an 'order' in the world that specifically arises from social history (artefacts, institutions, technologies, etc.). It also sees processes of social interaction as more important in supporting cognitive change, where traditional constructivism may stress processes of (independent) reflective abstraction. Finally, socio-cultural theorising is less ready to conceptualise general (tool-like) cognitive changes as the outcome of learning encounters.

These points of contrast identify two themes that I wish to highlight. They are each theoretical commitments relevant to guiding the educational use of computers. The discussion of them will involve some consolidation of points that I have already made. The two themes concern: (1) the cultural perspective on conceptualising the cognitive change arising from 'learning' and (2) how this perspective characterises environments that are supportive of learners – environments of education.

The theoretical concepts central to these two themes are, respectively, mediational means and social interaction. In relation to them, the following typically is claimed. Appropriation of mediational means is central to characterising the achievements of learning. Social interaction is crucial to supporting the effort towards such achievements. However, these propositions may sometimes seem tangled. For social interaction can also constitute the actual mediational means to be acquired – as well as being implicated in the process of educational support (on occasions where other, more materially based forms of mediation are being appropriated). Social interaction can constitute interpretative practices that we acquire as new mediational means: such 'ways with words' may mediate new forms of interaction within our environments. We may often analyse participation within social interaction in terms of these outcomes. Yet, at other times (particularly in classrooms) we may wish to analyse social processes in terms of their contribution to the mastery of some other mediational means: in terms of a system of learning support.

Thus, the contemporary cultural literature happens to have much more to say about social interaction than any other theme. Put the other way round, it has so far been distracted from saying very much about other forms of mediation: other technologies and artefacts entering into cognitive activity. For example, in a recent review, Wertsch and Kanner (1992) can fill several pages identifying studies of social interaction within learning. But when they come to summarise empirical work on mediation, their discussion is much shorter. Moreover, their discussion is exclusively about 'ways of talking' as mediational means. This is quite legitimate: language practices are potent examples for any discussion of this topic. However, a focus on language tends to blur the separate consideration of 'social interaction' and 'mediation' – a distinction being made here (and one made by others such as Wertsch and Kanner). This blurring may contribute to the popular impression that cultural theory is only concerned with interpersonal interaction. While, strictly, this may be a false impression, it remains true that there is scant empirical research in the cultural tradition that is about other mediational means than spoken or written language. So, there are few examples of a socio-cultural analysis applied to learning where material artefacts are central to the mediational process (although see Hutchins, 1986, for one relevant analysis). This is particularly disappointing for my present purposes here, as I am anxious to locate such a potential case for analysis – computers – within this cultural framework.

Yet, such an analysis remains viable. It can be applied most naturally to styles of computer-based learning described in Chapter 1 in terms of computer-as-pupil/tool. In what follows, I shall consider the general directions a culturally influenced account of computer-supported learning might take.

First it may be necessary to accept a different unit of analysis from that typical in psychological theorising. In characterising human cognition, psychologists have focused on the individual (and the individual's covert cognitive structures). Cultural approaches suggest attention to 'functional systems': systems of cognitive activity in which individuals are participants – interacting with various mediational means in the interests of achieving some goal. There is a parallel here with physiological systems (a link developed by certain early cultural psychologists (e.g. Luria, 1973), through their practical interest in neuropsychology). For example, when 'respiration' is termed a physiological function – this does not mean it is something with a simple location in some tissue or other (cf. treatments of 'memory' located thus as a psychological function). Respiration is properly termed a 'functional system' because it comprises a variable mechanism organised towards an invariant goal. That is, the constituent activities of a system such as respiration are versatile: they may, for example, permit substitutions or reorganisations in the face of disruption applied to that system. So, we may say the same for a psychological function: disruption of an existing reliable mechanism may allow reorganisation through alternate mediational means.

The case for orienting towards functional systems – rather than individual cognitions – has been more fully argued by Newman *et al.* (1989, Chapter 4). They suggest that efforts to characterise *internal* cognitive representations should be greatly aided by being able to observe their 'external analogues' in functional systems of activity (1989, p. 73). In other words, the intrapsychological plane of mental life is comprehensively related to an interpsychological plane of practical activity, and theorising should explore that dialectic (cf. Hutchins, 1986). An advantage for our present interest is that this perspective can take much more seriously the status of external cognitive supports, such as the various material technologies that enter into problem-solving efforts. We are, thereby, led to ask how computers – as a particular example of interest – might enter into such functional systems as mediational means.

Consider cases from the computer-as-pupil/tool range of possibilities. A pupil's production of geometrical shapes might be analysed as a functional system of activity – typical of those cultivated within classroom life. The resources of Logo-based turtle graphics could then be viewed as new mediational means that are inserted into this system. Logo provides children with a new device for manipulating certain familiar graphic products: generating visual patterns through controlling the execution of various computer commands and procedures. In the course of all this, we say that the manner in which the activity of *doing* geometry is organised gets altered. Our analysis of this achievement turns away from expressing it in terms of changes in underlying cognitive storehouses of knowledge. It turns instead to characterise mediational changes in cognitive *practice*. To take another example, the effects of computer-based word processing on the functional system of children's writing also might be analysed in just this way. Word processing technology re-mediates the activity of producing text. This is reflected in new ways of presenting, composing and communicating ideas in writing. In these examples, what is changed is how we go about being 'mathematicians' or being 'story writers' (or, on other occasions, it might be changes within our efforts to be 'biologists', 'designers' and so forth).

Of course such changes may not always be welcomed. In fact, some criticism of educational technology is grounded in worries about its mediational effects. For example, in Chapter 1, I noted Cuffaro's (1984) concern that access to highly manipulable computer painting and drawing tools will narrow a pupil's experience of graphical representation. The expressive possibilities in becoming a visual artist, it is argued, can be effectively constrained by this new mediational means. Another example would be Johnson's (1991) concern that database programs might reorganise the activity of being an historian, leading it to become dominated by arid data manipulation. Roszak (1986) voices similar concerns over a much wider range of intellectual activities.

More often, the effects of introducing computers into a functional system are greeted favourably. For instance, this is frequently the case for the examples of Logo and word processing. However, both enthusiasm and criticism arise from the fact that re-mediation involves more than creating some expected intellectual product more quickly, or more profusely or more fluently. This narrower sense of 'amplifying' what is achieved may be claimed (Cole and Griffin, 1980). What is more interesting is how the 'prospects' for the learner may have altered. The creation or elaboration of functional systems promises extended resources for new patterns of intellectual involvement – in mathematics, writing or whatever. New mediational means may sometimes narrow such future creative possibilities (as critics can claim) but they may also enrich them. For example, word processing may well make the writer more productive (more words, more quickly, etc.). But it may also have other effects. It may alter the way the system is operated. So, computer-mediated writing may afford new ways of editing text. It may alter the way in which this system relates to, and enters into, other systems of activity. Thus, computer-mediated writing may permit the products to contribute to new patterns of communication with others (e.g. desktop publishing or electronic mail). It may also displace or undermine earlier skills and patterns of exchange.

Raising these possibilities brings us to what I think is a particularly important contribution of cultural theorising to the interpretation of computer-based learning. It concerns how we understand any extended 'reach' that new forms of mediation might create for a given functional system: how the learner is empowered to think more effectively in new situations. Traditional approaches propose that learning involves changes in underlying cognitive structures: these are then brought into play to enrich new activities. The cultural approach sees the extension of a functional system of activity as arising more from organising and directing pressures arising from the socio-cultural environment. More exactly: first, the approach tends to regard new learning as strongly situated or circumscribed within the particular contexts of activity that are arranged for it. Second, it assumes that generalisation and elaboration occur because of various forms of socially organised intervention. Particularly in school, steps are actively taken by others to appropriate newly organised functional systems into other, associated systems of activity. I shall say more about this in the next chapter.

For the moment, this leads us to confront and define the social organisation that does usually characterise educational settings. For the business of encountering new mediational means is claimed to be strongly supported by such social engagements. Recall that mediation was the first of two cultural psychological themes I am highlighting here – the second being a focus on the socially grounded nature of cognition. I will conclude this section by bringing into focus the nature of the social context that pupils currently encounter during schooled learning. The word 'social' applied to this context is intended to identify more than face-to-face exchanges between people. However, I shall suggest that a richer sense of 'social' that is intended still requires such interpersonal exchanges to be prominent – if the societal context of activity is to work effectively as an environment for learning. This key role for social *interaction* is a theme I shall then develop in the next chapter.

As I have stressed in the last chapter, cultural psychology promotes two senses in which cognition and cognitive change are 'socially' grounded. First, learning has a social quality by virtue of its relation to practices of interpersonal exchange – participating in relevant discourse and joint activity. Second, learning is socially grounded in the 'societal' sense: it takes place within an historically defined and socially organised framework of cultural resources – artefacts, rituals, symbol systems and so forth.

The first of these two senses of social context has been more easily grasped, and more widely implicated in educational theorising. It is evidently relevant to my concern that computer-based learning may not be assimilated into the social fabric of learning. It might lead to the suggestion that teachers intervene more in (solitary) pupil–machine learning. This would create more tutorial input – in the social interactional sense. Such solutions encourage more assertive or more carefully contrived episodes of instructional intervention: teachers playing more part in their pupils' explorations. Lepper and Chabay (1988) and Yazdani (1987) toy with possibilities of this general kind. Perhaps they may be appropriate where the form of activity in question is exploratory (computer-as-pupil); although it is less clear how more assertive involvement is created for more closed types of exercise (computer-as-tutor). However, I believe dwelling only on this form of solution will miss the significance of a cultural analysis as implied by the second sense in which learning is viewed as socially grounded – the societal sense.

What does this second sense of cognition's social character imply for the effective incorporation of computers? It requires us to attend to the kind of consideration expressed in a quotation from Scribner (1990) used earlier in this chapter. She encourages us to give more consideration to 'how cultural communities this world over organise activity settings for the "social transfer of cognition"' (p. 93). This invites us to attend more to the social fabric that surrounds and supports the learner – the established traditions and technologies that constitute 'activity settings'.

To observe a school and to declare that the learning therein has a 'socially organised basis' need not suggest that pupils' activities are constantly guided by intimate tutorial contact. They may be a lot of the time, but – particularly where computers have penetrated – what pupils are often doing may have a solitary character. That is, it may not incorporate much face-to-face social interaction. However, schools and other traditional sites for the organisation of learning are socially defined in a more profound sense than this. Thus, schools and their classrooms are structures comprising conventions, technologies, rituals, architecture and other distinctive features that have evolved through our cultural history. This socio-cultural identity therefore influences learning through its structuring of motives, goals, values, priorities, assessment and so forth. It specifies a pattern of relations among domains of knowledge that define a 'curriculum'; it describes social roles and rules for the management of attention; it exercises various links with other community structures, including families; it furnishes various kinds of technologies and resources to support study; it imposes a particular style of cognitive work through the organisation and management of physical space. Of all the human activity we may suggest to be 'socially grounded', learning within the setting of institutionalised schooling must be one of the most vivid examples.

How can the incorporation of computers into education bear upon its 'social' nature in this sense? At one level, the classroom computer is merely another technological intrusion into an environment that is already preoccupied with technologies and their deployment. This invites a cultural line of analysis that dwells upon the social history of their development: revealing how the activity of designers and innovators has imparted to this technology characteristics that afford or constrain how it might now be used (Habermas, 1987; Noble, 1991). However, my purpose in raising this second sense of learning as socially grounded was not to open up the possibility of that particular discussion. My purpose was to make a more straightforward point: namely, that this social fabric of education does evoke a participant structure. There are ways in which people must act in order to coordinate it and, thereby, make it work for pupils. Such a sophisticated socio-cultural system has to be kept knitted together; the system will incorporate roles, responsibilities and expectations that serve to support such integration. Through it, various kinds of continuity and connection may be created that define the overall experience of 'school' or 'learning'. Particular things get done and said to integrate pupils' discrete learning experiences into a richer texture of shared communication and understanding.

One way to put this is to claim that the classroom community will resist the creation of 'vacuums' for learning to occur in; resist the possibility of learning becoming divorced from other past and present understandings achieved in the overall setting. However, it might be hard for the participants to appreciate that this quality of continuity does characterise their enterprise – hard for them to identify the continuity from the familiarity of being inside it, as it were. The significant point is that this consideration of a schooling context returns us to an interest in the organisation of communicative activities. But now these activities arise, not in the form of intimate tutorial guidance (the most accessible sense in which 'learning' is recognised as being about social interaction). Instead, they arise through the demands of sustaining a certain socio-cultural fabric.

Naturally, I am suggesting that this fabric is important. What pupils achieve depends upon schools grounding learning in a socio-cultural context understood in this sense. But I am also suggesting that the way we deploy new technology in classrooms is very relevant to the quality of such a context. So, the tension between computers and the social character of education arises not simply because we have some rigid belief that learning must always be mediated by a human instructor acting in a tutorial relationship to a pupil. There may be a need to preserve comprehensive opportunities for such focused guidance. However, there is also this other, more overarching sense of social interaction that needs consideration. Computer-based activities may encourage a dispersal of learning into discrete and too self-contained experiences. This technology has a capacity for motivating and directing problem-solving activity to be a fairly autonomous experience. There is something attractive in this. But it does serve to moderate some of the preparatory or synthesising interventions that teachers naturally offer.

CONCLUSION

In this chapter, I identified two well-established traditions of psychological theorising: cognitive psychology and constructivism. I sketched their features in a way that I hope allows the character of a third possible perspective (cultural psychology) to be appreciated more clearly. I then considered the relationship of these theories to computer-based learning. My argument has been that there is a certain chemistry involving the material nature of the technology and ideas at the core of orthodox psychological theorising about learning. The product of this chemistry is that computers are all too readily separated from the mainstream of classroom life. Their material properties tend to invite this, and prevailing theories about learning and cognition do not adequately challenge such a trend.

Is there evidence that dislocation from the social context of learning can undermine what pupils achieve? The little direct evidence available tends to point this way. Thus, to some commentators, evaluation studies of learning with certain computer microworlds (such as Logo) are strongly suggestive: they imply that the impacts of learning in these settings are not readily visible outside of the microworlds themselves (e.g. Simon, 1987; Yazdani, 1987). The shortfall of these microworlds in practice is well expressed in reflections from one commentator working inside the cognitive tradition of artificial intelligence (AI):

> AI has not yet been able to translate its successful attempts with microworlds to the real world. There seems to be such a level of increase in complexity of the domain when moving away from the microworlds to the real ones, that most lessons need to be relearned. (Yazdani, 1987, p. 112)

The evidence suggests that the problems are located in poor contact between the pupils' microworld activity and traditional forms of teacher intervention (Pea and Kurland, 1987). These conclusions are fairly compelling – although there is debate as to whether constructivist agendas for educational technology really did intend that computer-based learning should separate from socially organised instruction (Papert, 1987). Whatever the intention, it seems that this dislocation does easily happen. It is also clear that, in their current work, the early innovators now pay much more attention to specifying a supportive social framework (Ennals, 1993; Resnick, 1991; Turkle and Papert, 1991).

My account here of a cultural perspective on learning and cognition should indicate that this approach will have a particular interest in computers as they are applied to education. This is partly because a central concept in the cultural approach is 'mediation'. Cognition is viewed as human activity mediated by the technologies, artefacts and rituals that have emerged within the history of a particular culture. Cognitive change and development, then, involve the appropriation of such mediational means as those represented in new technology. I suggested above that the proper unit of analysis for understanding this cognition was a functional system: coordinated cognitive *activity*, often incorporating forms of external support (as well illustrated by the example of computers). Mediation, as it occurs within functional systems of activity, helps us understand the nature of cognition. What of learning, or cognitive *change*? Here again the cultural perspective should have a special interest in computers. This is because their common pattern of use can conflict with a second key concept in this tradition of theorising: the social basis of cognition.

A concern with mediation was certainly one concept central to the cultural approach of Vygotsky and his contemporaries. But, alone, it would not set the socio-cultural theorists apart as a distinctive movement within psychology. What does set them apart is the combination of their concern for mediation and their commitment to a related claim: the claim that cognition is *socially* constituted. Cultural psychology makes sense of 'learning' by reference to the social structure of activity – rather than by reference to the mental structure of individuals. We are encouraged to analyse learning by paying careful attention to two features of its typical format. First, learners bring established functional systems of cognition to any new situation for learning: we should try to understand their nature. Second, other people (particularly teachers) act in ways that allow these systems to be re-mediated or elaborated. Social interaction, it is claimed, makes possible the extension and transformation of existing cognitive systems. This is a theme to be taken up further in the next chapter.

If cultural theory alerts us to the social texture inherent in educational activity, what is recommended when we sense its disruption – as we might in the face of new technology? Evidently, any answer to this will arise from better understanding of the interpersonal *processes* that normally are active within classrooms. The repair will have to be organised at these points. I shall consider what we understand about these processes in the next chapter, using it to start deriving preferred ways of deploying new technology. A key concept will be that of socially shared cognition or – to employ a term in contemporary favour – 'intersubjectivity'. I shall argue that the opportunities to create and exploit this state underpin much of what is achieved in formal educational settings. We discover it not just in the face-to-face social interactions that constitute 'tutoring' in these settings but also in more extensively mediated forms of social exchange. The significant challenge will be to determine how computers can 'enter into' these practices – rather than sidestep or undermine them.

Chapter 4

Collaborative interactions *with* computers

So far, I have identified some controversies arising from the increasing use of computers to support learning (Chapter 1); and I have identified some traditions of psychological theory that might help us think more clearly about these issues (Chapters 2 and 3). In the present chapter, I shall start to discuss particular configurations whereby computers enter into learning activities, developing the term 'collaboration' as an organising concept. I believe the term is central to the cultural approach in the sense that 'computation' or 'construction' are central to other relevant theoretical traditions in psychology. However, in the end, the term serves as a device to think with. I do not claim there is any widely shared commitment to 'collaboration' as the key concept in socio-cultural thinking.

Each of the remaining chapters in this book concerns social configurations for computer-based learning. In this and the following chapters, I am concerned with the most orthodox of situations: that involving organised asymmetry of expertise (expert and novice; teacher and pupil). I wish to look at very general arrangements for incorporating new technology into the teacher–pupil exchange. I have already claimed that there are some who hope computers might actually *become* the teacher in this interaction. That possibility is the first to be considered: it will be discussed in the present chapter.

In the first section below I raise the prospect of computers simulating social processes in the tutorial sense. It must be decided whether interactions *with* computers can capture the social quality of traditional guided instruction. There is a kind of educational software that is written to do this. We shall find that it is interesting but modest in its 'social' achievements. So, from the user's point of view, computer-based instructional dialogue typically feels limited in its reach. It is brittle and inflexible. I shall apply the framework of cultural psychology to make sense of why this should be so. This will require presenting the cultural analysis of just what does constitute effective instructional dialogue – as it occurs in those interpersonal contexts of teaching and learning that we are familiar with. It will become clear that comprehensive computer-based modelling of such interactions is not a realistic enterprise.

In the course of considering computers and instruction in these ways, one important theoretical concept will surface. That is the concept of 'intersubjectivity' or, briefly, shared understanding that is mutually recognised. I suggest that inter-subjectivity is central to what occurs within instructional communication. The following discussion of how such talk is typically organised will draw attention to one aspect of what instruction involves. However, I will suggest that the cultural approach to cognition has not taken real advantage of the intersubjectivity concept. The approach could mobilise the concept in order to extend its theoretical resources for interpreting the management of learning. My own discussion here will converge on a particular conceptualisation of what the act of instruction involves: a powerful form of collaboration arising when the human capacity for intersubjectivity is explicitly deployed to achieve guidance within arenas of joint activity.

THE SOCIAL INTELLIGENCE OF TUTORING SYSTEMS

One response to the fear that computers will undermine the social quality of education is to argue that such concerns will inevitably evaporate: the present tension will be resolved and the problem will go away. The argument proposes that what we value in the social experience of learning will be preserved: it will merely, in some way, be taken over by the technology. Such visions aim to respect what we wish to retain in the current system – by supposing that it can be simulated and not remain dependent upon the interventions of other people (in particular, teachers). This does not seem likely to happen in the near future but enthusiasts will simply plead for more time. Given a few more technical developments, it is argued, computers will engage in instructional conversations just like the ones pupils already enjoy with human teachers. With varying degrees of confidence, this view is voiced by those working in the tradition I have identified as computer-as-tutor. The idea is to incorporate whatever is important in novice–expert dialogue into the design of computer programs. This is often the sense of 'intelligence' that is appealed to in so-called 'intelligent tutoring systems'.

This approach has its enthusiasts. Appealing to certain recent technical advances, Henderson (1986) comments: 'In effect, we believe that an instructional system comprised of a videodisc player interfaced with a microcomputer should be able to simulate a coach or the master/apprentice relationship quite effectively' (p. 430).

Of course, it is accepted that any such enterprise must be founded on much basic research concerning just what gets done by 'coaches' or 'masters' as they interact with learners. In Lepper and Gurtner's (1989) overview of educational computing, this is identified as one important priority for future research: learning about conventional instructional processes in ways that will help us to model them.

The goal of simulating tutorial exchanges has been pursued for some time by educational software authors. Collins (1977) reports an early and influential explor-ation of the problems. His work includes an intriguing systematisation of the Socratic form of teaching dialogue as gleaned from transcripts of authentic instruc-tion. The aim was to extract principles that might be modelled in an intelligent tutoring system. Yet, fifteen years on, the promise of this analysis, and others like it, does not seem to be visible in any strong tradition of dialogue-based teaching software. In fact, Collins himself appears to have adopted a different approach to the design issues (e.g. Brown, Collins and Duguid, 1989; Collins, 1988) – as it happens, an approach more in tune with cultural psychological ideas.

Moreover, other authors working under the rubric of intelligent tutoring systems have proposed a switch of focus away from the literal simulation of tutorial dialogue. For example, in Chapter 1, I referred to the work of Schank and others on tutoring systems designed to support case-based forms of reasoning: styles of problem-solving that, it is supposed, are more natural for us (e.g. Riesbeck and Schank, 1991). Such systems expose learners to a range of problem 'cases' (typically as simulations) – supposing that solutions to novel problems are naturally made with reference to private accumulations of case-based experience. This is certainly an alternative to traditional intelligent tutoring systems, with their stress on modelling tutorial dialogues. However, it does not challenge the principle of reproducing socially organised instruction. It merely challenges the typical conception of what tutorial interventions attempt to do: in particular, the idea that they equip learners with repertoires of rules of the 'if x then y' variety. In the end, a tutoring system built around theories of case-based reasoning may still fall short as a comprehensive system of instruction. For example, it may turn out that human tutorial intervention is an important feature of how the learner is helped to index and retrieve this case-based knowledge (a form of social support that we may suppose will remain particularly hard to simulate).

For whatever reason, no species of intelligent tutoring system has found a firm place within academic education. This mode of computer-supported learning is found more in situations that we might usually refer to as 'training' – perhaps where circumscribed technical skills are being developed. Thus, military and industrial applications have been well documented. However, evaluation studies tend to indicate that their potential in these settings is also limited (Schlechter, 1986). My discussion in the sections below is, in part, an effort to interpret this lack of success. I argue that many difficulties arise from failing to appreciate the subtle nature of instructional talk. Yet, I do not wish boldly to legislate against simulation of such dialogue – as if it inevitably led to applications of no value. It seems to me that such simulation can be attempted for some portion of what teachers and learners might normally talk about. Indeed, there are examples of interesting and effective applications that appear to achieve this. However, such circumscribed successes provide no basis for predicting the wholesale replacement of traditional tutorial exchange – if that is part of any educational vision. Generally, the possibility of computers reproducing the role of teachers by supporting a genuine interpersonal experience is based on some unlikely suppositions. I shall identify them in the sections below. As other critics have expressed it, the idea supposes 'that the teacher's understanding of both the subject being taught and of the profession of teaching consists in knowing facts and rules...' (Dreyfus and Dreyfus, 1986, p. 132). If such knowledge was all that needed reproducing, then the possibility of programming a computer simulation might be credible. But teaching surely involves more than dealing only in tidy rules – either rules pertaining to domains of knowledge or (interpersonal) rules governing the effective performance of instructional talk.

Dreyfus and Dreyfus (1984) consider the danger of conceptualising learning as the mastery of sets of rules defined for various knowledge domains. I shall not rehearse their persuasive arguments here but focus instead on the other part of what tutoring systems typically aim to simulate: the expertise that is involved in the social act of instruction itself. Early innovators felt able to write papers with such titles as 'The computer that talks like a teacher' (Feurzieg, 1964). But is this extraordinary interpersonal achievement one that might be expressed in the rule-based formats that the programmers of computers demand? I suspect not; and, twenty-five years later, some of the same early innovators are now writing articles on computer-based learning with such words as 'apprentice' and 'practitioner' in their title (Feurzieg, 1988). However, to help decide about these matters, we need to consider the psychological processes that underlie effective instructional exchanges. I shall do this next. I shall then return to consider again the prospects of creating pupil-computer interactions that are supposedly 'social' in character: instructional interactions *with* computers.

CONCEPTIONS OF INSTRUCTIONAL DISCOURSE

In this section I review the analysis of instructional talk that has been emerging within cultural psychological theory. As it happens, this is the theoretical tradition that has devoted most attention to such matters. The discussion returns us to a consideration of Vygotsky's zone of proximal development, a concept introduced in Chapter 2. Cultural psychologists have various formulations of what goes on in effective instructional exchanges: these ideas arise from empirical observations of social events within ZPDs. I believe that their analysis has been helpful in clarifying what is precious within socially organised instruction, although, in the next chapter I shall suggest that the distinctions developed below reflect too great a preoccupation with exchanges that are intense and intimate in nature – one-to-one interactions between experts and novices, teachers and pupils. In the end, a full understanding of the social nature of instruction requires us to inquire beyond such a narrow focus. It requires us to consider a wider range of interpersonal interactions that can arise in classrooms.

Supportive encounters in the ZPD

Internalisation

Consider a child solving a jigsaw puzzle by herself. This simple task demands a variety of strategic problem-solving activities. There are helpful ways for the child to go about arranging pieces (say, right side up, grouping by visual features, picking out corner pieces or pieces with a straight edge). A pattern of attention needs to be organised between the pieces on the table and the picture of the completed puzzle.

The child needs to remember juxtapositions that have already been attempted... and so on.

If the child is young – say of pre-school age – and if the puzzle comprises more than a handful of pieces, we can predict that progress will be limited. Very generally, we will always risk provoking disengagement where a problem-solving task is set just beyond a young child's expertise. Yet, for a good learning experience, the task must be challenging. So, a flexible way must be found to support children in the discovery of solutions to more complex tasks – particularly tasks where trial and error explorations are likely to be inefficient and tedious.

Cultural theories of cognitive development argue that humankind has evolved a solution to this problem, one that involves cultivating forums of joint activity. In particular, we have evolved practices whereby individuals who are expert in some domain will collaborate in distinctive ways with novices and, thereby, communicate their expertise. At their most effective, these are occasions in which experts go beyond simply *showing* the novice what is to be done. These are occasions which are potent because expert and novice join to construct a joint 'cognitive system'. It is useful to think of such a system as having a unitary nature, although it is actually comprised of (at least) two thinking individuals. However, although there may be two people involved, their work need not be partitioned and individually allocated. In an effectively organised ZPD, the novice is assumed to be doing it along with the expert, who may be judiciously steering or prompting. Rather than being driven by showing and explaining, these encounters encourage the novice's full 'participation' in the problem-solving act; they are conducted in the spirit of collaboration.

The management of an encounter like the one described above, one involving children with their mothers solving a jigsaw, has been described by Wertsch, McNamee, McLane and Budwig (1980). Joint activity in this case is shown to take on the quality of a unitary cognitive system. It does this by virtue of how responsibility is distributed for the various strategic activities involved. The adult in this situation will take responsibility for some of those strategic moves that seem to be currently beyond the reach of the child – although with both participants remaining focused on the same goals. At other moments, the adult might do and say things to prompt the mobilisation of a strategy that is within the child's repertoire but not spontaneously elicited by the situation alone.

Encounters of this kind are typical of those that children may experience in the everyday world of solving problems. Tharp and Gallimore (1988, p. 32) cite the example of a parent intervening as a child searches for her shoes. The intervention acts at a level of supporting the cognitive activity of remembering; it creates a cognitive system:

... the father asks several questions ('Did you take them into the kitchen? Did you have them while playing in your room?'). The child has some of the information stored in memory ('not in the kitchen; I think in my room'); the father has an interrogation strategy for organising retrieval of isolated bits of information in order to narrow the possibilities to a reasonable search strategy.

The child does not know how to organise an effective recall strategy; the father knows the strategy, but he does not have the information needed to locate the shoes. Through collaboration, they produce a satisfactory solution.

This is a mundane example from domestic life. Tharp and Gallimore endorse a typically socio-cultural analysis by presuming such exchanges are richly produced within formal instruction. Thereby, the child is able to participate in substantial (but meaningfully complete) problem-solving exercises: tasks that it might be impossible for that child to pursue alone.

This conception of joint activity underpinning instruction is appealing precisely because it seems to describe expert–novice interactions in a wide variety of learning situations. Thus, it refers to classroom exchanges (e.g. Palincsar and Brown, 1984; Tharp and Gallimore, 1988) as well as more everyday and informal joint encounters (Greenfield, 1984; Rogoff, 1990). Further, it offers a basis for characterising variation in instructional success: for example, it may assist the optimising of learning opportunities for groups of people with special educational needs (Wood's research (1989) is an example of this in relation to deaf people). Wood also demonstrates that when tutors instruct in the manner outlined here, children may regard them more warmly (after the teaching sessions) than they regard other tutors who adopt a more directive or didactic strategy.

So, to summarise, it is argued that in this zone of proximal development social interaction may serve to create a unified cognitive system. Then it is supposed that the public nature of constituent moves within this system (the talk and action) can promote a process of internalisation by the novice participant. What is performed in the arena of joint action gets internalised into the private world of the novice's own mental life. Under such circumstances, individual cognitive resources are first experienced on this public plane of collaboration; they are then adopted as private.

It is tempting to suppose that this traffic from inter-to intra-mental functioning simply implicates a process of 'modelling'. This may be part of the story. In a busy zone of proximal development, the learner is exposed to exemplars of strategic problem-solving. Questions are asked, directives are issued, remembering is invoked, summarising classifications are deployed, and so forth. Simply being witness to such activities may sometimes be enough to make new resources available to the onlooker. However, it is widely argued that simply modelling such processes for learners is rarely enough. The possibility of internalisation is claimed to depend upon active participation within such encounters (Wertsch and Bivens, 1992). Rogoff (1990) captures the spirit of this idea by referring to successful tuition within a ZPD in terms of 'guided participation'.

The concept of internalisation has been much appealed to by researchers sympathetic to cultural theorising or – more generally – seeking some socially grounded account of cognitive change. However, I believe that unless the definition of 'internalisation' is made very broad (and, thus, not very useful), this emphasis leads us to neglect other socially distributed processes associated with instructional talk. I shall illustrate these in the following two sections.

Semiotic mediation

There is something accessible and appealing about the internalisation concept as reviewed above. Our private cognition is traced to public events: activities in relation to which we were witnesses or participants. Other theorists have enjoyed similar approval with related formulations: notably, Mead (1934) with a conception of thought as something derived from public discourse – conversation with 'the generalised other'. However, it has proved hard to study this internalisation through a fine-grained analysis: hard to trace convincingly the origins of cognitive change in a manner that Vygotsky characterised as demanding 'microgenetic analysis'.

Perhaps for such reasons, there has emerged a further (complementary) perspective on how we may characterise the formative nature of these (ZPD) social interactions. It is one that less readily suggests the notion of internalisation. Moreover, it suggests 'provocation', rather than the 'assistance' of Tharp and Gallimore's (1988) 'assisted performance'. Indeed, it might be viewed as a more cognitive account in the traditional sense. For, it gives emphasis to the elicitation of private cognitive processes: but processes that are prompted by social participation.

Stone and Wertsch (1984) fix the relevant idea as follows. They draw attention to the manner in which instructional dialogues are often characterised by prolepsis. This term refers to communication in which interpretation of the message requires some grasp of the speaker's presuppositions – understandings which are left unstated. Such messages may be termed underspecified or richly presupposing. Consider a casual example involving parent and child:

C: Where did you put my shoes?
P: Over by the animals.
C: (Pause) Oh... by my Heavy Metal poster, you mean.

The parent's underspecified answer here forces the child to pause and seek reflective clarification. So, the child's participation in this brief exchange effectively prompts a resolving inference regarding the parent's opinion of musicians on a rock band poster. If the child had not 'calculated' the meaning of her parent's answer through this route, then the adult might have gone on to supply more of the context to his reply – although necessarily *after* its original utterance.

Prolepsis illustrates a species of dialogue typically of interest to conversational analysts. Our talk is normally saturated with it. However, in the special cases I am considering here, it is being used in a contrived way: deployed just at the thresholds of mutual understanding. In my parent–child example (and within encounters that will arise in the course of formal instruction), shared understanding that normally supports the comfortable continuity of talk seems to have been violated. The violation causes tension; the tension demands repair, and work gets done by the listener to achieve this.

Note that such instructional devices are quite compatible with the strategic management of problem-solving discussed above under 'internalisation'. The point is that internalisation focuses on the *content* of strategic interventions (e.g. questions that mobilise organised recall). There is room for variation in the way that these strategic interventions are verbally realised. Exploiting prolepsis may serve to make the point of the intervention more vivid for the learner. Thus, Stone (1985) uses an example to illustrate prolepsis that echoes situations discussed in the last section. A teacher gives an instruction in relation to solving a jigsaw puzzle: 'put in the next piece'. Stone comments: 'This directive presupposes an understanding of the task's overarching goal, that is to use the model as a guide for defining the location of the pieces' (p. 135). Perhaps the learner has been verbally prompted to generate this idea (in order to create some options for reacting to what the tutor has just said). In doing so, the learner has participated in a (modest) strategic move appropriate to making progress with this kind of puzzle at this kind of juncture. This reasoning involves a link to Vygotsky's ZPD, for it suggests that dialogues conceived for instructional purposes are particularly rich in such disruptions. Moreover, dealing with the disruptions is a potent experience for the learner.

Rommetveit (1979b) offers a fuller argument for identifying processes of this kind as central to human communication. I have cited an example drawn from speech, but he notes that these processes are frequently invoked in fiction and drama. Members of an audience may realise that they have understood more than actually has been said. The author has taken contextual information for granted, but prompted its recovery within the audience's effort of interpretation. The idea that listeners (and readers) are active in this sense – spontaneously making inferences about discourse and text – is a familiar one to cognitive psychologists (e.g. Bransford, Vye, Adams, and Perfetto, 1989; Sperber and Wilson, 1986). However, the idea that instructional processes might involve the organised mobilisation of such devices is more novel.

In a recent paper, Wertsch and Bivens (1992) pursue Rommetveit's interest in identifying prolepsis as a basic communicative resource. They suggest that the effects noted here for the verbal devices of discourse have parallels within a wider range of communicative media. Specifically, they propose a relation between (proleptic) talk of the kind illustrated above and our experiences with certain expository texts: particularly with that property of text that allows it sometimes to serve as a 'thinking device'. Thus, these authors are considering the manner in which cognitive work is generated within interaction – but from a broader definition of what can constitute an interactional context. For them, it is not restricted to the prototypical ZPD of two or more people in problem-solving discourse. It might embrace interacting with written materials.

Influenced by the semiotician Lotman, they refer to the 'dialogic function' of such thinking devices. This function of text is more provocative towards the reader; it demands the construction of shared meanings. The contrast is with univocal texts: they are more like receptacles and communicate more in the mode of passive transmission. Both texts and talk may be too easily thought of as merely narrowly univocal in this sense. Often they may entail more dynamic communicative properties: devices that allow both the spoken and written word to mediate *inter-*

action – to precipitate new meanings through active engagement. So, a close analysis of instructional texts and instructional discourse may be helpful if it serves to reveal a potential dialogic function.

The dialogic presupposition and exploitation of shared understandings is a necessary basis for human communication. Moreover, this manipulation of shared understanding applies beyond the arena of instructional language. A culture's various communication media offer a whole range of dialogic devices with which individuals may manage their interactions with others. So, prolepsis may well be apparent in the talk of a teacher, but it is also evident in the text of an author, or even the advertising images of a graphic designer.

The case of advertising illustrates well the reach of semiotic mediation as an explanatory concept. A concrete example may be useful. At the time of writing, passengers using Edinburgh station may be intrigued by one large poster among the various promotional hoardings in the station concourse. Three sets of (real) objects are attached to the poster backcloth: a tangle of red trouser braces, a jumbled group of traditional black telephones and an empty gilt picture frame. Underneath is the legally required health warning that implies a tobacco product. I have an idea about what specific product is being advertised. But that idea emerged only after a period of reflection – during which time the product was necessarily drawn into the foreground of my consciousness. Perhaps this is the designer's purpose. There is just enough presupposition to evoke active cognitive work on the images and their associations. The viewer is led to a precipice of understanding and thus some reflective engagement with the product has been achieved. At least, it was achieved in my own case; it might not always be so. The danger with this device, as applied to advertising, is that the 'precipice' may be very different for different consumers. Care is needed in identifying the background knowledge necessary for an image to precipitate successful engagement. The knowledge presupposed by a given image may not be widely shared. To be engaging in the present sense, the image may need to be conceived differently for different consumers.

This problem faced by the advertising designer is usually less keenly felt by the teacher – who, I am suggesting, may sometimes be doing similar things. In most educational contexts, teachers have more privileged access to what their pupils already know. They also have situational access to the focus of a pupil's attention, and to the extent of that pupil's motivation as it stands at the moment of instruction. So, communicative devices of the kind discussed above may be more finely judged. The central point is that in text, in images and in talk, the effective deployment of semiotic mediation entails judicious reference to shared understandings. For it is the successful matching of a message to this existing mutual knowledge that is important. That matching is what allows the message to elicit cognitive work in the reader, the viewer or the listener. These encounters thereby provoke reflective engagement of a kind sought by the agent of communication. Indeed, the broad scope of this idea should warn us that, as described thus far, it can do no more than orient us to a significant phenomenon within communication. Much research must be done to clarify exactly how particular dialogic devices may achieve distinctive effects of this kind. In terms of our present interest in schooled learning, we would want particularly to pursue this in respect of the context and character of talk that is instructional. In summary, then, this conception of 'semiotic mediation' must become a further ingredient of any cultural characterisation of effective instructional dialogue – along with the idea of internalisation.

Appropriation

Appropriation is yet a third concept that cultural theorists have deployed to help think about instructional discourse. It is taken from the work of Leont'ev (1981). Appropriation arises from the sense-making efforts of both teachers and pupils as they engage within the contexts of learning. As such, it has recently been very fully exemplified by Newman, Griffin and Cole (1989) who report an empirical study of teaching in an elementary school. I will take their work as a basis for introducing the concept.

First, Newman *et al*. locate their study of instructional processes within the theoretical framework of the zone of proximal development. They define this conception in familiar enough terms:

> The concept of ZPD was developed within a theory that assumes that higher, distinctively human, psychological functions have socio-cultural origins. The activities that constitute a zone *are* the social origins referred to; when cognitive change occurs not only *what* is carried out among participants, but *how* they carry it out appears again as an independent psychological function that can be attributed to the novice. (1989, p. 61)

Appropriation is included in the 'activities that constitute a zone'. Two common features of instructional strategy are identified by these authors as underpinning it. The first refers to that quality of indeterminacy characterising a great deal of instructional talk – indeed, characterising a great deal of interpersonal social life more generally. The participants may be approaching their interaction from different positions of understanding, but they are temporarily caught up going along with each other – trying to create some stable and common ground. This open nature of such social situations is seen by Newman *et al*. as a positive force: it invites a variety of negotiable options to be pursued within the interaction. It is the very thing that allows the participants' differing starting points to be addressed.

The second feature of such situations that is important arises from the first – from the fact that the participants may not initially understand each other at all well. In this situation, a meeting may nevertheless be achieved if the partners are prepared to appropriate from each others activities: to behave *as if* there were more common ground than, in reality, there is. Encounters of this kind are central to early psychological development. As Vygotsky (1978) comments: 'From the very first days of the child's development his activities acquire a meaning of their own in a system of social behaviour...' (p. 30). The point is that this meaning is often something to be negotiated in a collaborative way. So, Newsom (1978) notes the manner in which the parents of infants will be actively interpretative in their reaction to a child's behaviour. Parents ascribe meaning and intent to a degree that exceeds the child's actual capabilities. There is a compelling tendency towards such creative attribution of meaning and intent. In a sense, the infant's behaviour is thereby 'appropriated' to the purposes and frameworks of the adult. Newman *et al.* suggest this is a common state of affairs between expert and novice in the ZPD; a common characteristic of organised instruction.

The analysis is partly inspired by an earlier account of interactions in a pre-school setting by Gearhart and Newman (1980). These observers were impressed by how teachers would often interpret what a child was doing in a manner that presupposed the teacher's own perspective. The child is scribbling: the teacher asks 'What is it?' Such a question presupposes a planful activity on the part of the child – an interpretation of the activity from the teacher's point of view. In terminology developed in the previous chapter, the pupil comes to this situation with established functional cognitive systems: including, say, one concerned with making scribbled marks. The pupil's progress depends on the prior existence of such systems and upon the interest of other people in elaborating them through appropriation: for example, by their reacting to scribbles as an effort at representational drawing. Finally, the pupil's experience of social communication prompts retrospective sense-making along just such intended lines.

It is this overarching *contextualising* feature of appropriation that distinguishes it from the other two categories of instructional talk discussed above: those were more motivated by assisting strategic control of activity at the moment-by-moment level. Newman *et al.* regard the appropriation process as 'a "stand-in" for the child's self-discovery' (p. 142). This indicates the shift of balance in cultural theorising away from more pupil-focused models of learning characteristic of constructivist perspectives. Now it is assumed that socially organised practices are central to the learning process. However, this is not to undermine the creative dimension of intellectual development. Creativity exists within the appropriating social interactions themselves, and the new functional systems that result do equip the learner for self-discovering opportunities – as might well be the case for the example of drawing.

Modest exchanges of the kind illustrated in this section are widely reproduced within classroom encounters. They depend upon both partners appropriating the activities of the other – acting as if they were all 'somewhere else'. The somewhere else, of course, is generally some approximation to that place where instruction is carefully leading. Newman *et al.* note an intriguing paradox in this process: 'for a lesson to be needed, in say, division, it must be presumed that the children cannot do division; but, for the lesson to work, the presumption is that whatever the children are doing can become a way of doing division!' (1989, p. 64).

SYNTHESIS: INSTRUCTIONAL DISCOURSE AND INTERSUBJECTIVITY

I have sketched here three varieties of instructional talk that have been identified by psychologists of a socio-cultural persuasion. These ways of talking support three possible kinds of instructional influence. First, *internalisation* is associated with the creation of joint problem-solving formats, or cognitive systems. These allow the novice to witness and participate in more advanced strategic cognition on a public, inter-individual plane. Second, prolepsis illustrates a form of *semiotic mediation* available as a conversational device to prompt the novice into private cognitive reflection. Third, *appropriation* is a related device whereby (perhaps over a more extensive section of talk) a collaborator will act 'as if' a partner's intentions and motivations matched their own. This 'strategic fiction' (Newman *et al.*, 1989) allows them each to act as if their partner's behaviour was locatable within their own goal structure, thereby achieving more effective direction and coordination of purposes.

Of course, these distinctions do not exhaust the possibilities for instructional talk. Direct explanation or exchanges that encourage passive modelling may well be adequate to promote learning – although perhaps learning of more modest scope. The point is that talk of the kind identified above comprises what is typically found when local circumstances have been chosen that are most favourable for full concentration on the business of 'teaching' (Edwards and Mercer, 1987). The effects of such talk on pupil achievements is hard to evaluate cleanly (Schaffer, 1992). However, there is empirical evidence that, when variation is studied, the features discussed above are indeed a powerful basis for supporting learning (Freund, 1990; Rogoff, 1990; Smagorinsky and Fly, 1993; Wood, 1988).

Three cultural approaches to systematising instructional talk have been summarised here. Commentators may differ in which they stress. I believe that the three are mutually compatible and that the distinctions are necessary. But it would be valuable to attempt some integration, to show that they share a common conceptual core. I shall explore this possibility in the remainder of the present section; suggesting that integration is possible through an appeal to the peculiarly human capacity for *intersubjectivity*. This is a concept of great topical interest to psychologists; it may identify an inter-individual achievement that is uniquely human (Humphrey, 1976). Particular interest is apparent among developmental psychologists who are concerned to trace its ontogeny (Astington, Harris and Olson, 1988), as well as the consequences of its disturbance (Frith, 1989). A parallel interest is shared by linguists, who are concerned to understand how it is maintained within routine conversation.

The nature of intersubjectivity

I shall use the work of a linguist to introduce the idea here. In a series of influential articles, Rommetveit has discussed intersubjectivity in the course of characterising the management of everyday communication. He expresses it in relation to the interpersonal business of creating shared reference:

> A state of intersubjectivity with respect to some state of affairs 'S' is attained at a given stage of dyadic interaction if and only if some aspect 'A(i)' of 'S' at that stage is brought into focus by one participant and jointly attended to by both of them. (Rommetveit, 1979a, p. 187)

This identifies the concept with a state of mutual understanding and encourages us to regard cognition as something that may be studied as 'socially shared' (see Resnick, Levine and Teasly, 1991, for a cross section of reactions to such an idea). However, Rommetveit's definition is not entirely satisfactory here. It orients us in one particular direction – towards a kind of common object that can be the shared reference point of communication. The object metaphor is slightly mysterious, although useful for some purposes. I shall return to it later in this chapter. What I prefer to stress here are the social psychological processes through which we create and sustain such common objects of attention. Rommetveit implicates them in defining a state of 'perfectly-shared social reality'. Such a state exists at a point of communication: 'if and only if both participants at that stage take it for granted that "S" is "A(i)" and each of them assumes the other to hold that belief' (1979a, p. 187).

This mutual recognition of a partner's understandings is more what I wish to highlight here: the registration by one person that particular mental states (particular beliefs or intentions, etc.) exist within another person. This registration has a recursive character. I may acknowledge that you have certain understandings; you may acknowledge that I have made that acknowledgement, and so forth. Such mutual projection of mental states may be exploited to finely tune the communication between us. As Davidson (1992) puts it: 'Sociality and rationality combine to produce curiosity about what is in others' minds and motivation to formulate a *fit* between one's own thoughts and the thoughts of respected others – in other words, to create intersubjectivity' (p. 31).

This human concern for mutual recognition of mental states offers the basis for integrating our three categories of instructional talk. I believe that each of them depends upon an ability (and inclination) of both teachers and pupils actively to mobilise intersubjectivity. Of course, the 'motivation to formulate a fit' in this spirit may sometimes have to be skilfully provoked and encouraged. In any case, on this analysis what 'instruction' turns out to involve is the skilful deployment and organisation of human intersubjective capabilities.

This claims more than the simple truth that instruction should take into account the current (cumulative) state of a learner's knowledge. Making such a static characterisation of what-is-known is very much the kind of achievement that computer-based tutoring systems might attempt – rather as if knowledge was merely a commodity to be inventoried. The claim for intersubjectivity within instruction refers to efforts that go beyond this. In particular, it identifies a capacity for interpreting mental states that will arise during the dynamic of the tutorial exchange itself. Teachers will need to be good at this, for the investigative activities of their pupils are not always transparent for interpretation – not always predictably strategic. Instead, what pupils are seen to do may often appear uncertain, volatile and improvisatory. Thus, interpreting learners' momentary psychological states can be inherently difficult; and it does need to be sustained 'on-line', in the course of evolving, situated interactions.

Moreover, interpreting a learner's situated intentions, beliefs and motives is only the first part of an effective instructional intervention. For, on the present analysis, the act of instruction that follows such an interpretation is not always some straightforward interjection, some inevitable consequence of the learner's situation as it has been evaluated. Effective instructional support is not always a question of teachers successfully formulating their interpretations of what learners are doing and then delivering efficient, unambiguous direction. Such a formula-derived approach to interventions (optimising them) might be the very strategy adopted by a programmed tutor. Yet, as illustrated above, the most effective interventions may be those that are not optimised in this sense. The best thing for a teacher to say at some chosen moment may not be the thing that is maximally informative. Instead, the remarks that may be most helpful are those that are studiously chosen to be incomplete or otherwise imperfect; chosen because they are provocative of further engagement by the learner. Such cultivated imprecision seems to be exactly what is found by researchers who have closely observed tutorial discourse under ideal conditions. The apparently laudable and precise patterns of feedback, correction, diagnosis and demonstration that ITS designers strive to achieve do not seem to characterise what expert tutors actually do (Lepper et al., 1993).

Human tutors seem to do something slightly different and, I suggest, their resulting achievements depend upon an inherent capacity for intersubjective understanding. So, successful practice must depend upon a motivation to mobilise this human capacity and upon some capacity to deploy it skilfully. Such skill will derive from histories of interacting with learners in various domains of knowledge. It may also derive from a teacher's own experiences, at other times, of being a pupil. The whole process can be said to depend upon the 'projective work of the imagination' (Harris, 1991). At the root of all that might be achieved is a distinctive mutuality: the engaged pupil will complement what the motivated tutor does in the course of some supportive intervention. That is, the pupil is active in recognising and reacting to the tutor's interpretative attitude and efforts.

Each of the three modes of instructional interaction described above may now be examined within this framework. Take the case of interventions in support of cognitive internalisation. A sensitivity (in both partners) to ongoing events will be necessary to create joint activity that captures the interplay of a genuine 'cognitive system'. From the tutor's viewpoint, the demands of the task and the timing of support must be set to generate real collaboration, thereby affording the novice opportunities for internalisation. So, judgement will be exercised by the more expert collaborator; judgement will define the exact points at which strategic intervention would help. Sensitivity to the longer-range history of what the pupil knows may certainly be relevant. But so also will be sensitivity to the task-in-progress: to what the novice has experienced and attempted, to what they know of the task 'at that moment'. At the same time, the pupil must interpret the tutor's interventions as, somehow, being about what they collaboratively are trying to achieve (perhaps resolving feelings that an intervention may not seem in harmony with those shared intentions as they are inferred at the given moment).

A similar analysis applies to the process of semiotic mediation as it occurs within instruction. The underspecified, presupposing talk that characterises prolepsis will work when judged well enough to bring novice partners to a sort of 'precipice' of understanding – where it is possible for the necessary cognitive reflection to be successfully precipitated within them. This is surely embraced by Rommetveit's (1984) remarks on speaking and listening (in the context of defining intersubjectivity): 'encoding and decoding are complementary processes. Encoding contains always a component of anticipatory decoding and decoding takes the form of reconstructing fragments of an intended message' (p. 25).

The teacher's trick here is to encode in a way that enriches the learner's work of decoding – the trick of effective *anticipatory* decoding. Note, again, this is not necessarily a question of being maximally clear and informative: a degree of opaqueness may be what is important in stimulating decoding work that is creative. In sum, there is a distinct sensitivity that must be mobilised during this kind of instructional exchange – a social commitment that lifts the exchange above more didactic forms of instruction to become something more like a 'collaboration'. It is a sensitivity that depends upon mutual recognition of intention, motive, belief and understandings.

Finally, the concept of appropriation clearly indicates the necessity of intersubjective relations within instruction. Appropriation involves a conspiracy: the strategic fiction of a coordinated task is created before the learner actually has an authentic sense of that task. As Newman *et al.* (1989) put it:

> children can learn new goals and ways of doing things when their responses are appropriated into a system of which they were not previously aware. Because the teacher interacts with the child... the child can learn retrospectively what his response means in the system as understood by the teacher. (p. 142)

This detective work evidently presupposes an active curiosity about the intentions and understandings of the other. Discussing the origins of intersubjectivity in infancy, Newsom (1978) appears to be discussing the very same phenomenon of appropriation (although without identifying it as such): 'only because mothers impute meaning to "behaviours" elicited from the infants, is it that these eventually do come to constitute meaningful actions so far as the child is concerned' (p. 37).

So, I am suggesting that the various ideas from cultural psychology regarding instructional dialogue can be usefully synthesised by reference to the notion of intersubjectivity. This may now help us in relation to the topic addressed at the start of this chapter: the viability of reproducing within computer-based learning the traditionally social processes of instruction. By this I mean the ambition to programme a computer to simulate a particular form of dialogue: the potential for talk that bears some resemblance to what learners normally enjoy with their human teachers.

Intersubjectivity and computer-based tutoring

I have been discussing the ways in which intersubjectivity saturates orthodox instructional talk. I believe that this feature of such talk undermines the possibility of comprehensively simulating it on machines. This is not to deny that sometimes we find parallels between achievements inspired by engagement with a computer, and achievements prompted by human tutors. So, sometimes it might be helpful to claim that a computer is acting as a 'scaffold' for a pupil's learning (Hoyles and Noss, 1987). The discussion of semiotic mediation above predicts this possibility: it leads us to expect that the programmed structure of a computer activity could be provocative or supportive of a pupil's constructive efforts during independent learning. Such a computer program could therefore be said to scaffold the learning. However, while such piecemeal (and, perhaps, teacher-orchestrated) impacts are real enough, they are not unique to this particular technology: other structured problem-solving environments may be provocative in a similar fashion. Thus, while such computer-based contributions to the support of learning are important, they do not correspond to the simulation of an authentic instructional intervention.

The hope for such simulation probably springs from a certain way of conceptualising human communication. For example, a pioneer of intelligent tutoring remarks: 'man–computer interaction is basically a communication between two information structures' (Carbonell, 1970, p. 194). The problem is not that this is inherently mistaken – it depends on our particular reading of key terms – but it is a way of framing communication that easily encourages certain other perspectives that do seem wrong. So, it might suggest that the task of a cognitive science is to implement data structures that correspond to the configuration of any given human 'information system'. Then, on this view of things, communication between that person and any other such 'system' (including a computer) might be readily handled by a set of rules governing interaction (rules for information transfer). Clancey has summarised the important theoretical contrast that this implies:

> The view that knowledge is stored suggests that interactions between people are structured and controlled by pre-existing structures stored in the head. The opposing view is that neural and social structures coordinating our behavior come into being during our interactions. (Clancey, 1992, p. 148)

It is intriguing that the information-storage metaphors of the first view are so appealing to us as ways of characterising communication and instruction. Even the most distinguished of cognitive psychologists may feel compelled to capture an exasperation about teaching and learning by deploying this mechanical imagery: 'I find it terribly frustrating, trying to transfer my knowledge and skill to another human head. I'd like to open the lid and stuff the program in' (Simon, 1983, p. 27).

Perhaps our exposure to means of transferring material in the physical world encourages such imagery. Moreover, the movement of data within information technology is readily expressed in the language of 'stuffing it in'. Yet this will not do: the currency of education is different. Knowledge is not so neatly circumscribed as to allow complete and unambiguous stuffing under some human lid. The problem has been discussed at some length in an influential thesis by Suchman (1987). She comments about the meanings we exchange (within any act of verbal communication):

> the communicative significance of a linguistic expression is always dependent upon the circumstances of its use... the significance of an expression always exceeds the meaning of what actually gets said, the interpretation of an expression turns not only on its conventional or definitional meaning nor on that plus some body of presuppositions, but on the unspoken situation of its use. (p. 60)

This 'situated' nature of human communication is fully explored by Suchman. She argues that an action's *inherent* uncertainty requires that we turn from simply explaining it away 'to identifying the resources by which the inevitable uncertainty is managed' (p. 69). A significant claim is that these resources 'are not only cognitive, but interactional' (p. 69). However, just what are these 'interactional' resources that must be mobilised during routine communication?

They are resources that arise from the dyadic, *in situ* character of communication. Suchman includes the prosodic and temporal structures of talk that give it an ensemble quality; also the informal understandings that define specialised rights and agendas within the conversational ritual. However, she also refers to the 'local coherence' or relevance that conversational partners invariably create within the sequential organisation of their talk. Less is said about the mechanisms for controlling this coherence, but I suggest it is only made possible by the 'intersubjective attitude' that has been discussed in this section. Again, in terms of the conceptual vocabulary developed here, Suchman's account of communication is one in which 'interpreting the significance of action is an essentially *collaborative* achievement' (p. 69, my emphasis). In terms of the purposes of education (creating shared knowledge), and the tutorial methods employed (instructional discourse), Davidson (1992) expresses the position we are reaching here: 'different individuals invent similar answers to a given problem. The intersubjective attitude supports this inventive process because it enlivens curiosity about possible discrepancies between one's beliefs and those of others' (p. 34).

My analysis implies that interactions *with* computers cannot reproduce an at-that-moment richness of dialogue that characterises teacher-led instruction. Debating the possibility of such simulation brings into focus a deeply-rooted theoretical difference. On the one hand, we find developments guided by traditional cognitive psychological perspectives: that is, conceptions of knowledge as stored representations, with thinking as involving their manipulation. On the other hand, we find the sobering influence of socio-cultural or situated theories championing an opposing view:

all processes of behaving, including speech, problem-solving, and physical skills, are generated on the spot, not by mechanical application of scripts or rules previously stored in the brain. (Clancey, 1991, p. 110)

In cases that are being increasingly studied, knowledge and the structures of situations are so tightly bound together that it seems best to characterise knowledge as a relation between the knowing agent and the situation, rather than as something that the agent has inside of himself or herself. (Greeno, 1989, p. 313)

My own discussion here has concentrated on the implications of this opposing position for the goal of reproducing instructional discourse. Earlier in this Chapter, I catalogued distinctive features of such talk. These features surely draw our attention towards an imbalance in the interactional resources available to a human pupil and a tutoring computer. Investigating this asymmetry underpins the agenda of situated theories in this area: '[to] locate the limits of that sense-making ability for machines in the limits of their access to relevant social and material resources, and [to] identify the resulting asymmetry as the central problem for human–machine communication' (Suchman, 1993, p. 73).

So, I have stressed that instructional talk seems to be a collaborative, situated achievement: one founded upon human intersubjectivity. My view is that this excludes its comprehensive simulation within tutoring systems. However, the challenge to machine-based tuition runs deeper than this issue of reproducing instructional dialogue. For the underlying theoretical tension I have explored above is also relevant to other assumptions guiding the design of computer-based tutoring.

The ITS designer traditionally has focused on three problems. How to model tutorial dialogue is certainly one. The others concern how to model some domain of knowledge (i.e. what experts know), and how to model what is currently known by a given learner. The idea that either novice or expert knowledge might be captured in this computational form is evidently encouraged by traditional cognitive psychology. So, ITS researchers will express the target of their modelling thus: 'Much of what constitutes domain-specific problem-solving expertise has never been articulated. It resides in the heads of tutors, getting there through experience, abstracted but not necessarily accessible in an articulatable form' (Sleeman and Brown, 1982, p. 9). This characterisation surely exemplifies the influence of certain cognitive psychological theories: theorising of a kind (sceptically) characterised by Winograd and Flores as supposing: 'Knowledge is a storehouse of representations, which can be called upon for use in reasoning and which can be translated into language. Thinking is a process of manipulating representations' (Winograd and Flores, 1986, p. 73).

The alternative to this has thinking as situated activity. Individuals are constantly responding to a dynamic environment: engaged in a dialectic with the material and social world. 'Knowledge' thereby becomes an activity, not a storehouse to be replicated. It is always a creative construction within the here-and-now, guided by past interactions, but shaped by demands of the moment. The situated approach does not thereby deny the possibility of cognitive modelling – the ambitions of creating artificial intelligence. However, the methods appropriate for creating certain circumscribed *artificial* intelligence may not be the same methods appropriate to modelling *human* intelligence itself (Norman, 1991). So, the achievements of AI to date – while often of real practical value – are typically brittle and inflexible. A situated theory predicts limitations within any design enterprise where symbol structures are created to describe functional relations in only a narrow domain. Instead, it encourages modelling of the intelligence manifest in behaviour that is *adaptive* towards the environment: the capacity for responding to circumstances as they arise – simply 'dealing with' the world (Sterling, Beer and Chiel, 1991). If we must strive to construct artificial intelligences, then this might imply starting with such 'open systems' as those required merely to get around physical space: computational insects perhaps (Beer, 1990). Such an alternative perspective, when adopted for intelligent tutoring machines, does not encourage designs-for-learning grounded only in computed databases of knowledge in catalogue form (although such inventories may be a real resource to refer to within a broader learning context). Neither, as was argued above, does it encourage attempting to reproduce the social interactions that constitute instruction. In short, it does not encourage pursuit of comprehensive computer-based tuition.

This more situated view of cognition can claim some converts. Certain early researchers in the ITS tradition recently have altered their approach towards marrying up computers and education. For example, Brown, Collins and Duguid (1989) have sought new inspiration from studying learning within informal settings: out-of-school learning. Some software developers are particularly interested in the conditions of learning from apprenticeship relationships – such as have recently been documented by culturally oriented researchers (e.g. Rogoff, 1991; Rogoff and Lave, 1984). Attention to these *out*-of-school achievements encouraged Brown *et al.* (1989) to pursue a new approach to the deployment of new technology *in* school. Their basic idea is that the versatility of computer-based environments (particularly simulations and microworlds) can offer a rich repertoire of authentic situations in which pupils' thinking can flourish and develop. This approach is guided by the cultural tradition of theorising both because it emphasises access to mediational means, and because it views that access as a situated achievement. These researchers remain concerned to cultivate the abstract modes of thinking that schooling has always pursued, but they challenge any notion that this must be cultivated within relatively context-free tasks. Thus, they promote a strategy whereby the power of new technology can be directed towards furnishing a rich variety of contexts – situations – in which the learner can interact.

Yet, the role of social interactional processes within this so-called 'cognitive apprenticeship' strategy remains neglected. Where it has been addressed, it seems to invite a retreat to former traditions of ITS design that focus on computer-based dialogue. So some researchers in this tradition are now considering how a computer can be programmed to prompt and intervene – but as an apprenticeship master rather than a tutor (Katz and Lesgold, 1993). There may be a place for such initiatives. But the arguments above apply: the social nature of tutorial dialogue will not be reproduced wholesale. Certainly, there should be no implication that such social interactional encounters do not arise within the out-of-school settings of cognitive apprenticeships. It should not be supposed that processes of intersubjectivity are irrelevant to these informal learning arrangements just because there is no 'teaching' going on. Far from it: an untutored achievement such as mastering one's native language may be so very impressive simply because it *is* organised within a rich framework of intersubjectivity (Bernstein, 1981; Bruner, 1983).

CONCLUDING COMMENTS

These various doubts about prospects for replacing the interpersonal basis of learning should not be read as part of another sweeping rejection of computers in education. For one thing, existing ITS programs can remain a useful and proven resource (Anderson, Boyle, Corbett and Lewis, 1990). There is no reason to doubt that they have a valuable niche within in a broader context of instructional support. So, situated theorists themselves may continue to be architects of such systems (e.g. Clancey, 1988). The point is to question whether they represent truly comprehensive alternatives to traditional, socially grounded structures for learning.

More generally, the value of designing sophisticated computer-based learning environments is certainly not in question here. However, we do need to be clear about where the most significant increases in sophistication can be achieved. The cultural analysis of cognition has implications for where the creative effort of design might be best concentrated. Reproducing tutorial dialogue may be an area where some progress can be made but, I suggest, progress will be limited and striving for it may not be the most cost-effective way forward. What, then, is a better way? In trying to respect the social character of educational experience, we should not suppose that creating opportunities for interaction *with* a computer is the only option.

Given the central place of these social processes in instruction and given their subtle nature, I would encourage a move away from design strategies based exclusively upon interacting *with* computers, towards solutions that consider computers as a *context* for social interaction. Our aims then would be different. They would no longer be directed towards displacing instructional interactions. They would be more concerned to establish how computer activities can serve as an *occasion* for classroom discourse: a setting in which certain kinds of potent socially organised experience can be arranged. We would be turning our attention towards the social interactional possibilities that the physical presence of this technology affords.

In the remainder of this book, I wish to review this possibility in respect of various configurations of interaction that the technology may support. The first concerns interactions involving both teachers (experts) and pupils (novices). Possibilities considered in later chapters concern interactions between pupils themselves (novices with novices). In all cases, I will refer back to the central place of intersubjectivity and socially shared understanding as introduced here.

The theme of the next chapter concerns socially based instruction as it might exist in harmony with computer-based activity – rather than being supplanted by it. This harmony entails social interactions occurring *in relation to* computers (rather than, in some contrived sense, *with* them). On such occasions, the exchange between teacher and learner is retained as central to the educational activity. However, it is an exchange that is not governed by computers, but catalysed or mediated by them. The underlying computer-based experience may still involve forms of pupil–machine dialogue. But now the technology becomes a focus for a parallel interaction: joint activity that teacher and pupil organise between themselves. An encounter with the computer is thus assimilated into the broader social fabric of educational activity. This may seem a straightforward arrangement, but I shall argue that attending to what needs to be done (within social interaction) under these common circumstances is easily neglected – given the dis-located style of working that computers naturally encourage.

Chapter 5

Collaborative interactions *in relation to* computers

The form of interaction I shall discuss in this chapter is not the one that first comes to mind as being 'collaborative'. I am not intending to conjure up the image of pupil and teacher engaged together in a sustained interaction around some computer task. Such intimate interaction is a relatively rare luxury in most classrooms. So, teachers and pupils in focused and protracted collaboration at computer-based problems is not my present interest. Instead, I will be concerned here with another sense in which pupils and teachers interact in the presence of computers. This is the more commonplace sense in which pupils are engaged in some activity involving their teachers but where those teachers' contributions are more indirect, or mediated, or deferred. That is, they make only intermittent contact with the task or refer to it on occasions when it is not actually in progress. These are still encounters that are conceived of as supporting pupils' learning. The joint involvement with teachers arises because, to varying degrees, teachers will define, interpret or intervene in what is going on, or in respect of what has previously happened. This is a looser sense of teacher–pupil–task interaction but it is typical of children's normal classroom experience and is properly considered one sense of joint 'interaction' in relation to, or inspired by, some activity.

My plan for the discussion of such circumstances is as follows. In the first section below, I shall describe one experience of my own involving the implementation of a primary school computer activity. The point of this example is to identify certain problems that surface when we focus upon teacher–pupil–task interaction of the kind defined above. This example prompts consideration of just what it is that might be done or said by teachers in support of their pupils' computer-based experiences. I shall suggest that what gets said in the course of such supporting talk is something that matters. Moreover, we should understand more about it. Yet, the analysis of instructional talk that guided our consideration of interacting *with* computers turns out (at first sight) to be less helpful to a consideration of situations where the interaction is *in relation to* them. The crux of the problem is that the processes invoked in theorising about ZPD encounters are too intimate: they assume a degree of person-to-person interaction that may not be so easily promoted in the situations that I wish to consider next. This shortfall prompts a return to theory in the final sections of the chapter: conceptions of instructional discourse are extended to encompass categories of classroom talk that reach beyond the contexts of intimate tutorial exchanges.

Briefly, my argument will be that, through analysing zones of proximal development, cultural psychology has furnished useful insights into the character of instructional interactions. However, this analysis may be too focused upon interactions of the traditional tutorial kind. In practice, much real instructional discourse is, instead, embedded in a more open-ended and communal kind of interaction. Thus it is not as intimate as ZPD conceptions suggest. For example, instructional talk is often concerned with linking the current activity to previous events that the participants have jointly experienced. So it is not simply concerned with supervising the actions that might effectively complete some current problem-solving task – although the jigsaws and puzzles of much ZPD research might encourage this image.

In order to address these senses of instructional interaction among pupils and teachers, I shall refer to a further concept that aims to systematise classroom talk. This is the discourse principle discussed by Edwards and Mercer (1987) and referred to by them as 'common knowledge'. Their work will prove a useful basis for integrating accounts of instructional exchanges that refer to a wide range of classroom circumstances. What I shall suggest is that this framework is one that leads us again to recognise the central importance of intersubjectivity. That conclusion urges upon us the need to locate computer-based learning in a context of interpersonal support.

INTERACTING IN RELATION TO COMPUTERS: AN EXAMPLE

Teachers could be forgiven some irritation with cultural psychology – at least, in so far as it seems to foreground the zone of proximal development as a framework for instruction. That characterisation of instructional talk may not seem in tune with the reality of classroom life. When this zone is realised for empirical purposes it will usually be a rather peaceful place. It will not be densely populated, the participants will tend to be mutually engaged, and the action will be allowed to proceed relatively undisturbed. Most formal education, however, does not permit any abundance of such relaxed encounters. As Tharp and Gallimore (1988) comment in discussing ZPD interactions as *classroom* phenomena: 'conditions in which the teacher can be sufficiently aware of the child's actual, inflight performance, simply are not available in classrooms organised, equipped, and staffed in the typical pattern'. In short, the opportunity for dedicated and focused interaction around a task is something of a luxury. Teacher–pupil ratios militate against such pleasures; pressure to sustain order may also do so. Thus, the model of instructional interaction promoted within cultural theorising may seem too remote from what routinely can be achieved within the realities of classrooms.

There is certainly some discrepancy to be confronted here, but the mismatch is not as dramatic as I have sketched it. There is no reason why devices identified within studies of more intimate tutorial encounters should not be reproduced in the busier context of class instruction, albeit with less intensity. Newman *et al.* (1989) illustrate this in their development of the appropriation concept for ZPD activity: their studies were successfully grounded in whole classroom settings. Nevertheless, if these (ZPD) theoretical concepts are claimed to play a significant role in systematising educational practice, they may need some elaboration – in order quite clearly to include the organisation of discourse under the normal and busy conditions of classroom life. As it happens, I believe the concepts of intersubjectivity and socially shared cognition prove valuable in helping us bridge this gap – one between instruction as it gets modelled for theory building and instruction as it often gets practised in institutionalised settings.

To demonstrate the kind of social encounter that we must consider under the present heading, I have chosen to dwell on an example of the implementation of one (primary school) computer program that I have designed and observed myself. The program is modest in its aims. It is in the drill-and-skill tradition but can claim some of the engaging properties illustrated in the estimation/harpooning example praised by Scott *et al.* (1992) and discussed in Chapter 1. It is therefore likely to hold some appeal within primary school settings. It was conceived in response to discussions with teachers regarding the problem of moving children towards understanding multiplication in relation to repeated addition.

Children have to guess the number of squares making up a snake figure (using the screen pointer to select a number from an array at the top of the screen). The program generates number targets by randomly selecting a value between 2 and X, the value of X increasing after each correct choice. The task is difficult because not only do the numbers get bigger, but the snake is constantly repositioning its starting point and then uncurling again. Such a cycle involves the snake uncurling into each of a sequence of N x M rectangular matrices, where N and M are factors of the current target number, T. Sometimes a number, T, will allow only one such matrix (a prime number: $1 \times T$). For other numbers, there may be several matrices according to the set of its factors. All the possibilities are illustrated for the case of T = 12 in the schematic diagram of Figure 5.1. During the activity itself, they would be displayed successively and not simultaneously as pictured here. The leading square has a face drawn upon it. This cycle of repositioning and unfolding the various factor matrices for a target number, T, continues until the guess is made.

The speed at which these cycles occur can be set in advance but it would be such as to make a simple 1–2–3... counting strategy soon prove too limited. The child has to start finding estimating strategies to keep the game going (a score can be incorporated to motivate this: it is calculated as the sum of correctly guessed targets so far and it is zeroed when the activity is restarted after an incorrect guess). Children of 6 and 7 years old will quite quickly adopt repeated addition strategies to cycles where a single row or column of a matrix can be counted – 4 + 4 + 4 giving 12 for example. However, the achievement of special interest is that whereby they move from generating a solution by repeated addition to the more economical and powerful one based upon multiplication of columns and rows – 3 × 4 giving 12.

This program has been observed in three classes of 7-year-old children (Crook,

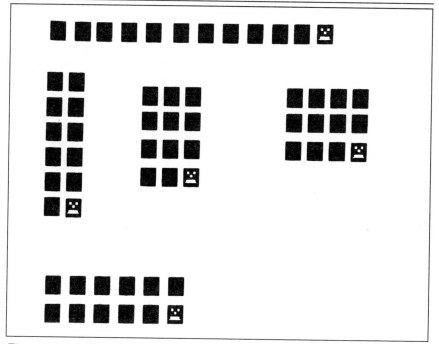

Figure 5.1 Schematic illustration of all configurations that would be displayed (in succession) for the number 12 by the Factor Snake program

1986), all at a stage where they are studying factors and gaining multiplication table knowledge. I would like to extract from these observations two (related) points concerning the use of this program. The first is expressed in Figure 5.2, which illustrates changing performance on the activity with experience: it shows changes in the average highest number that was correctly guessed in successive sessions.

The curves show results for children working singly (S) and working as pairs (P). At two points indicated, all children had a session of the activity alone. The curve appears to have reached a ceiling. Because some of these children were working together, it was possible for the observer to gain more insight into their strategy – as it might sometimes be articulated within their conversations. It was apparent that, for these children, making the move from repeated addition (which works quite well here up to about T = 15) towards multiplication did not occur naturally. This was surprising, because the format of the task seemed well suited to affording that move: repeated trials should serve to highlight the point where an existing strategy tended to break down. Moreover, there was no time pressure forcing hasty and unreflective decisions – the snake keeps moving repetitively until the pupil is ready to make an estimate. There is also little doubt that the children seemed highly motivated to improve on their last effort.

This limit on progress illustrates the first point I wish to make: creating an

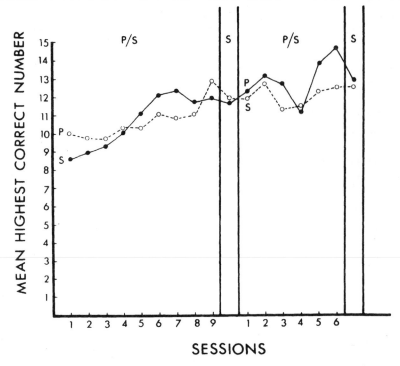

SESSIONS

Figure 5.2 Performance on the number activity for pairs of children (P) and children working alone (S). The two points headed 'S' refer to probe tests where all children worked alone

occasion for extracting some new understanding may not be enough. This is a point that has been most effectively elaborated by Perkins (1985) in relation to classroom activities more generally (but especially those based on computers). He cautions against too easily assuming 'the opportunity does the teaching by itself' (p. 13). The conception of the present program exposes (in myself) a certain naive faith in this principle. On some definitions the activity is a drill. It confronts the pupil with a succession of discrete problems converging on no particular creative endpoint. However, we suppose it might offer more than the chance for sheer practice: the scheduling of the problems and the visual representations used might encourage the pupil to 'stumble' into a firmer conception of multiplication. Unfortunately, it seems they do not.

From some teachers' point of view this might be an attractive program: it is engaging and can be offered without the need of supervision or support. Yet, this independence of operation is both its strength and its weakness. Reluctantly, I concluded that in some classrooms where it was used with enthusiasm it might as well not have been used at all.

This brings us to a second observation about this program. In two of the classrooms, it was deployed intermittently in the computer corner over a period of two school terms. It was judged to offer an agreeable activity for the pupils, one that invited them to use number skills in a playful manner. In the third class, its presence was more conspicuous. On the walls were pictures of matrix-like patterns and bendable snake-like models had been constructed from empty food cartons. In discussing number topics with the class, it was not unusual for the teacher to make use of blackboard illustrations that echoed those in the computer activity. The difficult concept of a prime number was referenced to the children's familiar (and frustrating) problem of making a good guess for those long snakes that only ever uncurled into one straight ($1 \times T$) line. In short, for these children, their experience with this simple computer activity was drawn into the wider context of classroom life. There it was mobilised to support the public discussion of number and to inform various other creative activities.

The children in this class made greater progress on the computer activity itself – although we cannot make too much of this observation as the difference in treatment was not a planned one in an experimental sense. However, it is surely a persuasive idea that such widespread classroom appropriation of the procedure and imagery of a computer activity would make a difference to its impact. So, we should be wary of our faith in the 'opportunity doing the teaching by itself': with computers in particular, this faith may cause us to neglect the effort of integrating the task into the public life of the classroom.

Lest in Chapter 1 I appeared too tolerant of drill-and-skill computer activities, this present discussion identifies my own reservations about computer-as-tutor. It is not that this software is intrinsically suspect on the basis of some common design characteristic, nor that the principle of dense practice in some problem domain must necessarily be avoided. The limitation of this form of computer implementation is that it may cultivate a faith in the self-contained effectiveness of such activity. Of course, this is a species of criticism that might be applied to the support of any classroom activity that is allowed to lose its context. However, it does seem that this possibility might be especially real for the case of activities supported by computers.

I am using this simple example to develop a point of view about computer-supported learning: namely, that it is necessary to incorporate it carefully into the collaborations that characterise organised learning. Moreover, I believe that this is important to get right, because many computer-based resources offer something quite distinctive (and potentially powerful) as educational resources. So, even the very simple activity described above exemplifies the possibility of fashioning a novel experience. It allows a rather distinctive kind of encounter with number: one that is hard to reproduce in other media. The visual representation of number that is achieved is actually no different to that which children may encounter with standard classroom materials (Cuisinere blocks). However, something distinctive is added by the incorporation of simple animation and the opportunity for pupil interaction (number selections and their evaluation). The number matrices move at a pace that invites the discovery and exercise of new strategies for enumeration. This, in turn, will periodically confront the pupil with the need to make informed guesses (to estimate) – something that, traditionally, is hard to cultivate in the early years of mathematical experience.

So, there is often something distinctive and powerful about the experiences that computer-based activities can offer. The present example illustrates this possibility within the most modest of formats. However, it also illustrates another feature of computer use in educational settings, namely, the danger of their dislocation from a main stream of educational discourse (Plomp, Pelgrum and Steerneman 1990). Pupils' enthusiasm during work on computers may easily mislead us into thinking that learning is proceeding in step with engagement. So, in this case, there was a notable discrepancy between some teachers' judgements of what the children were doing (namely that it was a helpful activity with which they were making progress) and the researcher's finding which was that, often, it was of no apparent help at all. The researcher has detailed records of what pupils were actually doing – the trial by trial choices and estimates were captured and stored by the software as part of a research exercise. These records were not so easily extracted by the teacher and the time needed to study them might not be available. Indeed, such feedback is not normally incorporated into the design of commercial software and teachers have, therefore, to rely on more informal glimpses of what is happening with an activity.

This example should illustrate the broader sense of teacher–pupil–task interaction that I am considering in this section. This is not the intimate interaction that might occur in a sustained encounter between a teacher and pupil(s) as the latter worked at a particular computer-based task. Much instructional communication is not so intense as this. It comprises instead the reflection, review and integration that teachers impose upon children's activities; this may be done intermittently as those activities progress, or retrospectively when closure on them has been reached (Edwards and Mercer, 1987).

Such communication is more extended in that it can embrace larger numbers of participants than is typically implied by culturally influenced research on ZPDs. It is more extended in that it may come and go across a longer period of time: the social interaction that organises some particular learning activity in class need not be restricted to the tidy closed session-like encounters that often characterise research modelling of instructional discourse. In our modest concrete example above, the teachers could interact *in relation to* the computer in the more extended sense of their explicitly drawing shared knowledge of a program into the community life of the classroom. The computer activity then becomes (for some classes) a resource that organises discussion intermittently in time and, perhaps, requiring talk that involves large groups or the whole class. Surely, much social interactional work that is done in classrooms is necessarily done at this level – albeit complemented by the more intimate tutorial contacts that psychological commentators are more comfortable with from their research traditions.

My concern in this section has been to illustrate what might be necessary to create an effective teacher–pupil–technology interaction: a social interaction *in relation to* technology. The example suggests the potential of computer-based experiences when they are fully assimilated into this social dynamic of classroom interaction. It also cautions a limitation in what might be achieved when the pupil–technology component of the exchange is isolated from this dynamic. Much more empirical work is necessary to determine the force of this caution. In the absence of such research, I shall take a different approach. This will entail reviewing more general arguments for the potency of classroom discourse: the proper management of computer-based experiences might be inferred from observations of talk organised around *other* kinds of learning activity as it has been documented in research.

MEDIATED TALK BETWEEN TEACHERS AND PUPILS

I shall discuss two perspectives on the mediating role of teacher-organised talk. In each case a form of *continuity* is being created for the participants. First, there is a kind of lateral continuity. This is required in respect of pupil activities that might otherwise be left isolated as practical experiences – where, in reality, they are conceptually related in significant ways. What is addressed here is the problem of achieving transfer of learning: allowing pupil understandings to generalise in important ways to new situations. Second, there is a kind of longitudinal continuity. This might be described as the creation of a kind of narrative state: furnishing a recognised platform for the next set of explorations. It arises in talk which is used to knit together the sequences of disparate actions and observations that constitute some learning exercise. Sometimes, such experiences may have been organised over quite extended periods of classroom time and the integration is a substantial responsibility. This form of continuity may be implicated in transfer also, but it is more implicated in the empowerment of fresh instructional talk.

In the two sections that follow, I shall expand upon both of those senses of the social basis of learning: the creation of both lateral and longitudinal continuities. In doing so, I shall make references to how computers might enter into such communications and, thereby, become effective resources for the support of teacher–pupil interaction. In the first of these sections, I shall consider more closely the grounds for viewing transfer of learning as a socially organised achievement. This identifies the lateral continuity that must be created. In the second, I shall consider longitudinal continuity: the creation of an integrating 'common knowledge' within a learning community.

Creating lateral continuities: transfer of learning

In discussing cultural psychology in the last chapter, we noted that it was a theory that emphasises the situated nature of human understanding. Learning becomes, in Vygotsky's words, 'the acquisition of many specialised abilities for thinking' (1978, p. 83). We also noted a price to be paid for doubting that generalised thinking skills should have a key role in theorising: some other basis is required for explaining how learners manage to transfer their knowledge from one situation to another – for undoubtably they do.

The first thing to be said about transfer is that we may intuitively exaggerate how easily it is achieved: reviews of research into spontaneous transfer suggest it does not readily occur (D'Andrade, 1981; Detterman, 1993; Lave, 1988; Pea, 1988; Perkins and Salomon, 1987; Resnick, 1987). So, we must discover more about what has to be done to make transfer happen. Current accounts of transfer are strongly cognitive, their focus being upon the mediating influence of private, mental structures. A recent example is one proposed by Hatano and Inagaki (1992). They suggest that contextualised knowledge is 'desituated' (i.e. transfers) when the learner synthesises a certain kind of abstract representational device: a mental model of the relevant domain. This synthesis is made possible when learners have enjoyed a particular range of encounters with the domain. But what precipitates such mental modelling? Although a mental model may prove a helpful way for us to conceptualise part of the process, the idea must be complemented by some account of the origins of such models: that is, some account of how children's concrete experiences in a domain are best organised to facilitate the proposed representational synthesis – the supposed basis of the transfer.

Some of what matters may reside in the structure of tasks that are offered to encourage learning (for example, the pace or predictability of action, or the nature of feedback). However, it may be hard to judge whether a highly differentiated and flexible task environment is better described as contributing to a single rich model in the learner – or to the cultivation of a greater variety of situated responses. One more straightforward kind of significant supportive experience comes from the social environment of learning. Understandings may be enriched in the sense proposed by cognitive psychologists (and, thus, transfer more readily) if learners enjoy a certain pattern of tutorial interaction with other people. One pattern might involve pressure to articulate knowledge to others (see Chi, Bossack, Lewis, Reimann and Glaser, 1989, and see also further discussion of peer processes in the following chapter). However, another pattern of potentially useful social relations is closer to the concerns of the present discussion. It arises from the supportive intrusions into our activity that are made by those who are more expert than us: occasions where teachers and other experts act to impose a certain interpretative framework on our actions. This is a proposal more actively pursued by some working in the tradition of cultural theorising.

Rogoff and Gardner (1984) develop this point to help characterise the very earliest learning experiences. They show how adult guidance of participation within infant and pre-school problem-solving can serve to identify for a child links between contexts of novel and familiar problems. The same point is made within the Laboratory of Comparative Human Cognition's discussion of more formal learning settings (LCHC, 1983). They propose that the key to transfer will often lie in how other people (who are more knowledgeable) do and say things that identify the links between contexts (Pea, 1989). Organised environments for learning (say, classrooms) will expose us to an interpretative layer of discourse that is imposed upon our activities – teacher talk. Educational practice involves the provision of distinctive tasks around which this is arranged. Within these tasks, action can be organised and then tutorial interventions serve to indicate for learners the overlap among them. Pea (1988) has elaborated this view and juxtaposed it with traditional psychological theories that suppose transfer is mediated by 'common elements' within the material contexts implicated. Pea argues that such 'sameness' is not intrinsic to things, and detected by us as such; sameness is a socio-cultural concept. It lies within category types the thinker has appropriated in the course of socially organised activity. Expert participants in this activity contribute interventions that serve to achieve this.

This conception of transfer invites more research in which such proposed social processes can be properly exposed and understood. Some movement in this direction is exemplified in the recent studies of Newman, Griffin and Cole (1989): here an attempt is made to analyse the sense in which the 'same task' can be encountered in new situations. Their conclusion is that socially mediated processes are central to how we discover this continuity; in particular, they highlight the significance of teacher-mediated appropriations of pupil activity.

A perspective of this kind may be appealing to practitioners, for it identifies a crucial ingredient of educational experience as being within their hands. It also has a special significance in relation to the use of computers. I have argued above that this is a technology with properties that allow it to be easily dislocated from classroom life. If this happens, then the valuable concrete experiences that computers provide may not be referenced within the discourse that helps mediate transfer. I argued in the last chapter that the nature of computer-based tasks readily *encourages* this marginalisation. How often is this actually the fate of computer activity in classrooms? Probably too often, given that the opportunity for children to use the technology independently is seen as something positive. Some commentators will remark positively on classroom computers because of the opportunity they can provide to release a teacher's time and attention (Clements, 1987; Fraser, Burkhardt, Coupland, Philips, Pimm and Ridgeway, 1988; Lepper and Gurtner, 1989). These observations relate to work in schools; the same approving view of computers is expressed in relation to undergraduate teaching (Hague, 1991). From extensive classroom observation, Eraut and Hoyles (1989) comment: 'assigning pupils to work on computers allows the teacher to attend to the rest of the class in peace, and to give more individual attention to those pupils who are not working on computers'. Yet Eraut has reflected elsewhere (1991b, p. 203) that this is an unfortunate trend: computer work, he argues, needs a great deal of planning in relation to other activities. This is very much my own point. Limited planning of work – and the loss of talk that exploits the continuities and connections thereby created – may undermine the breadth of learning that is supported by computer-based activities.

This possibility gains credibility when we think again of the particular case of Logo projects. The vision of transferable skills arising from Logo work appealed to many practitioners but its realisation has been elusive. There have been some reports of effective transfer (e.g. Clements and Gullo, 1984) but the consensus is that such achievements are not easy (Simon, 1987). Pea and Kurland (1987) have interpreted these difficulties in terms that refer to the social context in which Logo is experienced. They propose that there has been a serious neglect of the role that teachers must play in organising and interpreting the children's activity. They argue that the impact of the Logo experience is correlated with the extent to which there is an external participation of this kind. Others who have reviewed research in this area have endorsed the idea that adult intervention is important (Keller, 1990; Krendl and Lieberman, 1988; Noss and Hoyles, 1992). The history of Logo is one that alerts us to the difficulty with which learning experiences generalise – without social resources to bridge contexts. Logo pioneers may not have denied the relevance of a culture of use but until recently (Harel and Papert, 1991; Papert, 1987) this was never a dominant theme in the promotion of the activity. As Hoyles (1992) notes, this impressive resource typically risks being compartmentalised in at least two senses. Bureaucratically, it risks being bolted onto the curriculum; psychologically, it can become an experience for pupils that is unnaturally separated from a mainstream of classroom-based learning.

Regarding the collaborations of teachers and pupils *in relation to* computers, what has been said so far may be summarised as follows. The technology has characteristics that allow its use to be easily separated from the mainstream of class activity. To some extent, this might be viewed as liberating: a self-contained quality that allows teachers to focus their energies more intently elsewhere. However, we should be wary of this seductive strategy for deploying computers. In the present section, I have identified the role of social interaction in promoting the 'lateral continuity' of schooled achievements: helping the transfer between different situations of practice. The Logo experience reveals that even the most engaging and ingenious computer environment can fail to support pupils' learning. At least, this is what seems to happen for young children when more experienced collaborators (i.e. teachers) are not quite closely involved with the activity.

Moreover, Ryan's (1991) evaluation of a full range of computer-based learning interventions identifies 'teacher pre-training' as the most significant predictor of the outcomes. This must also hint at the central importance of teachers being able to cross-reference computer work with other experiences: such options will not be so readily available to teachers who are not themselves confident with the focal activity.

There is much useful research to be done that clarifies the role of classroom talk in the sense that I have framed it in this section. We must surely accept that social processes have *some* importance in creating continuity between disparate activities. I would submit that they are of central importance to this continuity, in which case computer-based learning is vulnerable to remaining highly context-bound – unless more is done to integrate it into the mainstream of classroom talk. One programme of empirical research that lends further credibility to these conclusions (while not explicitly addressing the same issues) is summarised in the next section. There, I consider the social-discursive creation of more longitudinal continuity. The research described is the work of Edwards and Mercer (1987) who have studied and documented talk in primary school classrooms. They demonstrate the extent to which such settings are indeed saturated with interpretative, sense-imposing teacher talk. However, they frame its significance more in terms of what I am calling longitudinal continuity – rather than the lateral continuity I have discussed here as constituting the achievements of transfer.

Creating longitudinal continuities: common knowledge

Common knowledge, as it will be defined here, is closely tied to the pivotal concept of intersubjectivity. This is the concept that helped us in the last chapter to identify a recurrent theme within cultural accounts of instructional processes: namely, the human capacity for projecting and interpreting mental states in others. In that discussion, I argued that the potency of instructional talk depends upon its exploitation of intersubjective understandings. In what follows, I discuss more of what lies behind this achievement. In particular, I consider how effective instructional communication is facilitated by the prior construction of common ground. For researchers, it is a challenging empirical task to determine how and why we construct such mutual understandings; to determine what makes us curious about uncovering common ground, and motivated to act in ways that exploit its potential. So, just how this is achieved in the special case of instruction is my special concern in the present section.

Outside of educational research, the study of common grounding is often approached through attention to the management of conversations at the moment-to-moment level (Clark and Brennan, 1991; Clark and Schaefer, 1989; Schegloff, 1991). For these researchers, uncovering the nature of a shared context will involve studying something that is done with language as it is used on the fly – talkers creating continuity by reacting to whatever circumstances happen to arise as their interaction unfolds. Extensive participation in routine conversation equips us with resources that make these achievements seem natural and spontaneous (see Forrester, 1992, for a perspective on how children master this during development). However, in the circumstances of teaching, this is only part of what must go on. It is the part that was discussed in the last chapter. The creation of common ground for instructional purposes must be much more of a contrivance: something constructed across sustained and orchestrated patterns of talk. It is something that depends upon a conscious investment of discursive effort; this effort being exercised over extended periods of shared time and space. The consequent achievements only become visible if we research beyond the moment-to-moment level of conversation; if we concentrate on more protracted structures of social exchange.

In the case of instruction, understanding the creation of common ground may require particular attention to the more material context of communication: the special environments within which problem-solving and learning get organised. In other words, structured interaction with material resources may provide participants with important mutual reference points for their common grounding efforts. This may be especially the case where joint problem-solving is located within media with distinctive structural properties – such as computers, perhaps. In any case, to discover more of how mutual understandings are typically created in classrooms, we must look at the patterns of conversation that have been documented to occur within them. I shall turn to this next.

The empirical study of classroom talk is a relatively recent research interest (see Cazden, 1986, for a systematising review). If there has been some neglect of the topic, this might reflect the learning-through-*activity* emphasis of much contemporary educational theory. In commenting on this situation, Edwards (1990) identifies a common attitude that he sees exemplified in the dictums of the (British) Nuffield Maths project: 'I hear and I forget... I see and I remember... I do and I understand.' These are principles offered in a spirit of defining good classroom practice. Edwards regrets the prioritising of the experiential, activity-centred ideal. However, this may not be a fair assessment of what the Nuffield scholars are promoting. Are they implying that the words of teachers are good only for hearing – and then forgetting? That gloss on the Nuffield philosophy may be an exaggeration of orthodox views on talking versus acting. Nevertheless, the orthodoxy may still need examining. There may well be grounds for arguing that educational theory has downplayed (not denied) the significance of things that get 'heard' – teacher talk – in the interests of prioritising the impact of pupils' 'doing'.

Perhaps some prejudices regarding instructional talk arise because of a stark contrast conjured up between 'telling' and 'doing'. In this contrast, talking is framed as something indirect; a substitute for the real thing. The real thing is acting to discover for oneself. Certainly, wherever teaching is being organised, there may be a tension of this kind to be identified and addressed. However, very little routine instructional talk seems to be easily forced into this simple contrast. In reality, such talk gets organised in *relation* to pupil activity – not in contrast with it. Which is not to imply that the reality of classrooms is one of always talking within intimate tutorial dialogue (perhaps in the formats reviewed in Chapter 4). Yet, typically, actual talk may share the contextualisation of those occasions and yet may not need to be analysed in exactly the same terms. Some talk that is not part of an intimate verbal dialogue may still be organised to enter into potent (dialogic) relations with things that pupils are *doing*. Or it may be organised to operate back upon such prior activity. In this manifestation, talk that seems merely 'heard' may still be playing an active part in pupil's constructions of knowledge.

This idea is central to Edwards and Mercer's (1987) discourse analytic work in primary classrooms. Theirs is particularly important research to mention here, for it reinforces our concerns regarding the need for teachers to be *in contact with* pupils and computers. But it also serves further to bridge the gap between the intimate tutorial setting of typical ZPD research and the more diffuse circumstances of classroom teaching.

Edwards and Mercer's approach is distinguished by its concern to characterise classroom talk in terms of its role in defining 'context'. Their approach to this is a timely one. Students of language-in-use have only recently come to terms with the incorporation of context into their analyses (Cazden, 1986). However, in 'contextualising' an utterance, researchers may often appeal only to features of the physical situation in which the talk is organised, or to details of what has very recently been said. Context in this sense is concrete and accessible. Indeed, this is convenient for those researchers who are armed with audio and video recording devices and who may be preoccupied with capturing the here-and-now. Unfortunately, such professional conveniences may distract researchers from considering whether what they capture is what they need; whether what they capture allows them properly to situate the dialogue. The understanding of what gets achieved with talk may require researchers to access contextual information that simply is not included within here-and-now records of this kind.

Specifically, what Edwards and Mercer propose is that we should recognise the context of talk as incorporating *inter-mental* achievements. Context is not just stuff-out-there, directly accessible to all the participants and available for action replay in our research recordings. It incorporates mutual understandings which are inter-mental by virtue of arising from whatever history of joint activity is common to the conversants. If we now seek to understand what guides the momentary formulation of particular utterances, we must do so through attention to this backlog of 'common knowledge'.

The intimate nature of these context-building achievements might seem to make them inaccessible to interpretative research. However, this context of talk need not be private in the sense of being impenetrable to understanding from outside. If it is possible to record conversational strategies for creating and referring to shared understanding, and if those strategies allow some systematisation, then we may make useful progress. An appeal of Edwards and Mercer's formulation is that it focuses on the actual discursive moves involved in creating common knowledge – particularly as such moves might be exercised in more ritualised settings of communication. So, in the setting of a classroom, we might identify the dialogue devices that typically are invoked for this purpose; or we may be able to reveal the ways in which such talk is most effectively interlaced with pupil activity. Those aims are very much the concern of Edwards and Mercer's own empirical work.

In situations such as classrooms, groups of individuals regularly interact over extended periods of time. Their achievements may depend on how effectively a sense of overlapping, compatible understanding is constructed: Edwards and Mercer refer to this in terms of the creation of 'continuity'. Continuity is the inter-mental context that is developing through time. Their own empirical contribution is then twofold. First, they demonstrate the extent to which teachers *are* actively engaged in creating such continuity: talk is relentlessly deployed for that purpose. Second, they illustrate some of the commonly used discourse devices that serve this purpose.

Regarding their first achievement, it is valuable to have documented how much of teacher talk is invested towards the active construction of joint understanding. Edwards and Mercer point out one straightforward reflection of this agenda: their teachers were generally reluctant to admit into class talk too much personal material from pupils' own outside lives. Wertsch (1991a) has also noted how instructional settings generally restrict discourse to experiences that are bounded within them. The image that dominates this research is of teachers actively commenting upon, elaborating and posing questions around what their pupils have experienced as a community. There is certainly plenty of pupil *activity* in these classrooms and that is the feature that the teachers themselves were most anxious to highlight and cultivate. What is easier to miss from within the participant's perspective is how far this activity is filtered through an interpretative and teacher-regulated discourse.

This takes us to Edwards and Mercer's second achievement: cataloguing and evaluating the discourse devices that are put to work in this way. These include techniques of organised recapping that allow the creation of a shared *memory* of what had happened when pupils had done things (Edwards and Middleton, 1986). Also included are techniques of cued elicitation that served to solicit an agreed account of what was currently happening. As an observer, there may be a natural inclination to judge this scene as one in which pupils are merely having their dormant knowledge innocently extracted from them. However, a more coherent account of events stresses that what matters about this talk is the active creation of an agreed, shared understanding of what the community experienced. The teacher is summarising, challenging, questioning and so on, in ways that both check current positions and update the evolving shared context – the backlog of 'common knowledge'. This common knowledge is generative: it becomes the platform for new understandings and new connections to be made. A teacher's contribution towards the progress that can be realised in a classroom depends in an important sense upon being able to exploit this inter-mental creation.

Edwards and Mercer do not use this formulation directly to address transfer of learning, in the way that the issue was discussed above in relation to computer work. However, a distinction they make between ritual and principled knowledge makes contact with the problem of forcing understandings to go beyond the immediate settings of their acquisition. *Principled* understandings are those that do apply widely across settings and lead to greater reflective self-awareness. Edwards and Mercer's analysis highlights discourse practices that may be more likely to cultivate such understanding: this analysis is consistent with the hope that we may make progress on the transfer problem through considering how classroom talk is related to the organisation of pupil's classroom experience.

In short, this is an analysis that both demonstrates the natural penetration of teacher talk into pupil activity and also furnishes a conceptual vocabulary to understand its strategic management. Nevertheless, I feel there are two limitations to this account and they each matter for our interest in educational technology.

First, Edwards and Mercer's inspiration is to conceptualise the context of classroom activity in terms that incorporate the inter-mental achievements of conversation. This challenges our inclination to prioritise the immediate and material setting of action as being what mainly comprises its 'context'. Yet, their shift of emphasis may have led them, in their own research, to swing the other way: effectively neglecting how talk is contextualised within material circumstances.

Thus, they do demonstrate organising principles of teaching talk in relation to the conduct of specific classroom tasks. However, there is little consideration given to how the format of those tasks serves to constrain or facilitate the particulars of the talk that emerges – how the talk is materially situated. So what is documented in the research is not itself contextualised in this spirit. It is one insight to note that the institutionalisation of social relations in the form of schools encourages certain styles of sense-making talk, but that insight needs to be elaborated to capture how particular formats of activity afford particular realisations of this talk. Such a focal orientation to settings themselves is rare within the literature. (One example is evident in the work of Cook-Gumperz and Corsaro, 1977. They have made a clear case for attending to the physical (play) environment as creating or denying discourse possibilities involving children and adults in pre-school.)

I have tried to make this point elsewhere in relation to computers as artefacts within children's social, rather than cognitive, development (Crook, 1992a): suggesting that we could begin more of our analysis from 'things themselves' and consider what kind of social interactions they afford. Here, I am suggesting that the same strategy could apply in our thinking about interactions organised to support learning. The key question might be: what interactions can arise between teachers and learners if they chose to interact around the particular contexts of computer-based activities? I suggest this is a point of entry for empirical work: research that might characterise a social context for computer use incorporating pupils, teachers and computers themselves. This entails defining the possible collaborative interactions of these participants *in relation to* the technology. There is very little organised observation in this tradition; although an example might be one study of secondary mathematics teaching that shows how the presence of computers can create a less teacher-led, more discursive style of class interaction (Ridgeway, Benzie, Burkhardt, Coupland, Field, Fraser and Phillips, 1984). This finding is rather welcome – in view of my second concern regarding Edwards and Mercer's formulation.

This second concern is captured in a critique of the work by Cazden (1990). Edwards and Mercer's account dwells on the teacher-dominated character of classroom talk. In highlighting the frequently directive nature of this talk, it fails to present a sufficiently constructive alternative agenda. Their analysis dwells on identifying limitations in the way discourse is deployed: they are particularly concerned with discursive moves used by teachers to *control* the development of continuity and context; or with teachers' efforts to maintain the 'fiction' of extracting what children already know; or with their management of the dilemma of respecting self-discovery while ensuring the curriculum is 'properly' learned. Edwards (1990) comments about these observations: 'Typically this dialogue turns out to be no simple negotiation between equals but a process that is dominated by teachers' concerns and aims and prior knowledge.' In short, the emerging picture is a somewhat gloomy one. It is thin on examples of what might be considered effective or creative practice.

The implied shortfall concerns how far understandings are 'negotiated' within talk. If Edwards and Mercer's summary picture is persuasive, then one cause for concern will be its demonstration that teacher talk is often reinforcing a model of knowledge that implies a ready-made 'grown-up' version: this is the one to be learned. Teacher discourse is frequently oriented towards creating a common knowledge that reflects an 'official' story. Faced with a perceived obligation of this kind, the challenge teachers may feel is one of working out how the official versions may be discretely precipitated from joint activity. Unfortunately, the interventions that might be necessary to achieve such innocent extractions can sometimes form a poor representation of how knowledge is actually developed and negotiated in investigative contexts outside of the school. So, even work in natural science (which might seem the most straightforward area in which to promote official versions) should enjoy careful discursive management. Steps might be taken to ensure it is experienced as knowledge derived in an atmosphere of conjecture, debate and argument. This version of the *activity* of science was rarely witnessed within the discourse of Edwards and Mercer's classrooms.

We therefore have an account of classroom talk that offers us the useful framework of common knowledge and its creation, but which presents a cautionary view on current practice. Edwards (1990) suggests one way of advancing from this situation. He reiterates Piaget's observations regarding the cognitive developmental possibilities of talk among peers. Because of the equality of status between pupils themselves, pupils working with their peers (rather than their teachers) can create certain richer possibilities. They can create arenas for the precious experiences of motivated argument and reflection. Such situations of collaborative learning might represent better conditions for acquiring the rhetorical skills of knowledge-building than the conditions normally experienced within teacher-dominated talk.

The notion of common knowledge will be an influential one in what follows. I have expressed two limitations to the account arising from Edwards and Mercer's (1987) work. Concern about both of them will inspire empirical work to be described in subsequent chapters. There I shall give more consideration to how the structure of computer tasks constrains or extends the discourse organised in relation to them. I shall also consider the particular issue of peer interaction as it is mediated by computers – hoping that within such arenas we might reveal interactions that allow learning through a more negotiated form of discovery. This respects Edwards' own suggestion for dealing with the more constraining nature of teaching discourse – the tendency for official versions of knowledge to be imposed through such talk.

Common knowledge and intersubjectivity

In the last Chapter, I reviewed some ways in which psychologists have characterised instructional talk, considering whether those perspectives implied it might be simulated by technology. I suggested that the various devices prominent in such talk could be integrated by reference to the concept of intersubjectivity. So, success within an intimate, tutoring style of discourse seems to depend upon the participants cultivating an intersubjective attitude. In the present chapter, the discussion of instructional talk has shifted towards considering a more diffuse version of this activity. Here we have considered exchanges that are not necessarily so closely coordinated with activity-in-progress. They are likely to refer to prior events and experiences. They are often communal in nature: directed towards groups of pupils rather than individuals. I suggest that such talk may also be understood by reference to the concept of intersubjectivity. The point of such a move is to consolidate an argument for firmly associating learning with the deployment of intersubjective attitudes. If this association is granted, then it must limit how far computers can be expected to reproduce the interpersonal dimension of educational practice.

The key to the intersubjective nature of classroom talk (in those formats characterised above) is its natural achievement of common objects for attention: shared resources that the participants understand to be shared, and which can serve as platforms for their further communication. Edwards and Mercer's characterisation of this achievement for classrooms is a novel and useful contribution to our understanding of the discourse of learning. However, their formulation of the common knowledge idea is not entirely new. The technical terminology is borrowed from established work on meaning and human communication (e.g. Lewis, 1969). I shall identify briefly those parallel traditions of theorising that are relevant to my concerns here. This will allow us to acknowledge that the 'level' at which Edwards and Mercer's research is directed remains distinctive: it is a level particularly appropriate to the understanding classroom practice and thus provides a good model for future research.

The conversational analysts Clark and Brennan (1991) capture the spirit of what has been said above about classrooms in their general observation: 'All collective actions are built upon common ground and its accumulation' (p. 127). However, common grounding activity – within instruction or within any form of discourse – is not a unitary phenomenon. It can be said to be managed at more than one 'level', or by the use of more than one set of communicative resources. This notion is well captured within distinctions made by Krauss and Fussell (1991). First, they identify resources that may be available in the form of knowledge about social category memberships. This comprises existing beliefs and expectations about others that are derived from general understandings of relevant social status or social practices (e.g. that which might follow from understanding that someone is 'a New Yorker'). Second, there is a further level of resource; one that arises from the flow of direct, ongoing interaction with a conversant. This is information gathered and exchanged 'on the fly'. Conversational analysts have studied this second level of communicative resource as it is created and discovered within everyday talk (Clark and Schaefer, 1989; Sperber and Wilson, 1986). My own discussion of the management of instructional discourse (Chapter 4) addressed this same phenomena in the particular context of teaching and learning.

The level at which Edwards and Mercer's research is pitched seems somewhere in between those identified above – and is one peculiarly significant to organisational life such as that which arises within classrooms. Their research defines communication that depends on direct experience of social interaction (rather than abstracted social category knowledge). Yet what is being deployed in this communication does extend into a history of the conversants' interaction; that is, it goes beyond the momentary events of the present conversation. In other words, the common knowledge analysis concentrates on a longer-term continuity: a more protracted (but interpersonal) construction of shared understandings. The analysis also helps us to see this process as an achievement motivated and guided by a particular purpose – in this case, the management of learning. Thus, within that important context of education, we may start to identify the particular conversational resources that are available to make communication effective.

Whatever the level research is pitched at, the idea of capturing the control of communication in terms of mobilising intersubjectivity seems appropriate. However, attending to an orchestrated setting like a classroom may alert us to the case for framing communication in terms of a dynamic, interactive achievement. I believe this is more helpful than metaphors that tend to reify what is involved (such as 'common *grounding*' (Clark and Brennan, 1991) or 'an interpsychological cognitive *object*' (Newman *et al.*, 1989), or even 'common knowledge'. Such metaphors tend to reify the achievement. They may even cultivate speculation about programming data structures that might represent these cognitive objects, whereas the real problem for simulation is not one of reproducing some static cognitive entity: it is a problem of capturing the sensitivity, empathy, projection and improvisation that constitutes communicative *interaction*. And that, as has been argued for instruction at the more momentary level of conversation (Chapter 4), is unlikely to be achieved by means of a computer program.

This discussion of common knowledge indicates how human intersubjectivity may be regarded from two perspectives when we consider educational settings. On the one hand, it resides within the prompting, monitoring, intruding talk that makes up instruction-in-progress. On the other hand it resides in talk and action that serve to create that which becomes held in common – and known by the participants to be held in common. How might the impact of access to such resources be optimised? Our answers are likely to be framed in both motivational and cognitive language. Learners must be *motivated* to adopt intersubjective attitudes. This may be a question of cultivating links to their spontaneous goals and priorities as they may be formed elsewhere; it may also involve creating more equable opportunities for them to contribute to (or negotiate) common knowledge. The more *cognitive* dimension to optimising these resources requires us to study carefully the way discourse and activity is coordinated within authentic instruction – as exemplified in some of the socio-cultural empirical work discussed here. In either case, there is a challenge to integrate new technology with these practices, rather than allowing it to be subverted by it. This is a challenge requiring us to attend to the particular manner in which computers can become an activity setting in relation to which common knowledge is effectively negotiated.

SUMMARY COMMENTS ON COMPUTERS AND INSTRUCTIONAL COLLABORATIONS

In this chapter and the previous one, I have considered two senses in which computers might enter into the social fabric of educational activity. In Chapter 4 I evaluated the idea that interaction with a computer might be programmed to reproduce the social character of a face-to-face tutorial dialogue: social interaction *with* computers. This plan seemed too ambitious. We feel this as soon as we reflect on the nature of the human conversation deployed during instruction. Thus, I dwelt upon characterising such instructional talk, arguing that it is grounded in the distinctively human capacity for intersubjectivity – and that teaching involves the organised management of that intersubjectivity.

Such management is partly a question of timely intrusions into learning-in-progress. I invoked Suchman's analysis of 'situated' action to characterise the necessarily improvisatory and versatile nature of this achievement, arguing that it is unlikely to be simulated by computers. However, the management of intersubjectivity entails a further set of discourse resources, these being concerned with the more protracted building of socially shared cognition. Such a proposal arose from arguments developed within the present chapter, where social interactions *in relation to* computers have been discussed. This involved acknowledging that the meaning of some teaching utterance is rarely to be located in, or made manifest through, its simple surface features – as if such meaning were something to be generated by a rule-bound system of the sort that computer programmers would seek to construct. Effective instructional talk will be contextualised. Indeed, its utterances will derive their impact from the skill with which speakers build upon mutually (perhaps laboriously) constructed shared understandings. This richer, inter-mental sense of 'context' as defined for instructional communication is not something to be captured in computer programs. (Perhaps the intellectual work that tutorial language must be made to do in order to create and exploit this context is at the root of what can often make 'teaching' such a peculiarly tiring activity.)

Unfortunately, there are grounds for fearing that computers remain vulnerable to exclusion from this enterprise. I have drawn attention to features of the activities they support that encourage this dislocation from the classroom community. In particular, computers have design features that readily encourage a pattern of use whereby the activity is dissociated from the core of classroom life – and where teachers may less readily engage with what pupils are doing. This is a real problem, given important ethnographic claims that discursive interventions within (other) pupil work are a persistent feature of what teachers normally achieve (Edwards and Mercer, 1987). Such interventions serve the important function of creating continuity of experience. This continuity constitutes a 'common knowledge' that forms the platform for yet more new discourse and new activity. Teacher–pupil collaborations in this sense may be less easily fostered in contexts of computer work.

Because relevant research is scarce, there is still little to be said on the question of how best to integrate teachers, pupils and the particular settings created by

computers. To pursue this theme here would demand rather piecemeal considerations of particular computer-based activities and their potential for incorporation
in class talk. This would make our discussion veer too much in the direction of
curriculum issues of a rather specialist nature. However, I do intend to return to the
themes raised here regarding the pupil–teacher creation of socially shared cognition. The discussion, in a later chapter, will consider how computer-based activities
can offer some *generic* support to such efforts: how the technology can offer an
infrastructure within the classroom that underpins the creation of various useful
continuities, rather than undermines it. This will involve us in considerations of
how communication can be mediated *through* computers rather than simply *with*
them or *in relation to* them. I shall outline a configuration of computers that goes
some way towards avoiding the breakdown of community-based mutual knowledge – as it might otherwise occur in relation to computer work.

First, however, I wish to consider the other important sense in which social
exchange can be organised to involve this resource. This discussion will centre on
classroom 'collaboration' as more traditionally understood. Pupils may be invited
to interact with each other around computers: this technology may support peer-
based collaborative work. In fact, we shall see that the arrangement of peer
interaction *at* computers has attracted considerable practitioner and research interest. Moreover, our discussion of teacher–pupil talk in the framework of common
knowledge did converge on a claim by Edwards (1990) that classroom peer
interaction should be seen as a promising solution to some of the more problematic
aspects of teacher-led discourse. It might prove to be the forum in which the
processes of intellectual discovery and investigation are most naturally modelled
and made accessible to learners.

In the next chapter, I shall first introduce the literature that does exist on this
topic. I shall then review existing theoretical frameworks for making sense of this
literature. My own preference is to emphasise the conceptual vocabulary of intersubjectivity that I have introduced above. In a subsequent chapter, I shall present
some class observations of my own to help develop that theoretical approach.

Chapter 6

Learning within peer collaborations

Early in this book, I noted a contemporary worry that computer-based learning might evolve into a socially isolating experience. I have since argued that the very nature of the technology easily invites activity that can become dislocated from teacher-led communication. Moreover, orthodox perspectives on the psychology of learning may even be encouraging this trend. Yet, when we examine actual classroom practice we find that, in certain significant respects, the computer has facilitated socially organised learning rather than inhibited it. This is an impression that is particularly apparent in settings of early education. It is an impression based upon the prevalence of computer-based *group* work: what is now commonly seen in classrooms is computers used to support learning through peer collaboration.

The reasons for this development may well include an active attempt by teachers to resist the isolating atmosphere of computer use. However, it may also reflect a particular predicament they have faced in the recent period of implementing new educational technology. There has been official concern that computers should penetrate deeply into educational activity, yet the scale of financial commitment barely made this possible. Generally, the solution improvised by schools was to spread the resource thinly through the premises and thereby allow limited access for each pupil. In Britain this strategy is particularly favoured by primary schools. Secondary schools have been more inclined to cluster their machines in customised computer rooms: but this may only have served to increase availability at the expense of concentrating its use within specialist subject groupings – technology classes, for instance. In either case, if pupil opportunities for fair access are to be optimised under these circumstances of scarce resources, then cultivating small group work (rather than pursuing the model of individual 'desktop teachers') may be viewed as the natural solution.

In this chapter, I shall evaluate the state of practice and research relating to the deployment of computers for peer-supported learning. First, I shall review claims that have recently been made for the quality and consequences of such collaborative work. It will be noted that this approach to the management of computer-based activities has attracted some justified enthusiasm. However, I shall argue that the use of computers for peer-based learning deserves richer input from psychological theory. Particularly where younger pupils are involved, we still have only limited insight into what defines an 'effective' collaboration. Rectifying this requires us to develop a suitable conceptual vocabulary for analysing the talk and action that constitutes collaborative work. I shall identify the concepts that are used by researchers to characterise group learning and peer interaction: my argument will be that these concepts turn out to be limited in their reach. In the last section of the chapter, I shall present a perspective on collaborative learning that is consistent with my preferred theoretical orientation: that of a cultural psychology.

In a sense, the chapter converges on a perspective for characterising peer-based learning and suggests that computer-based work is a good vehicle for exploring it. The overall argument can then be elaborated and illustrated through empirical work presented in the chapters that follow. The recurring question beneath this discussion will be: how can new technology serve effectively to resource collaborative arrangements for learning?

STUDIES OF COMPUTER-BASED PEER COLLABORATION

It was implied above that the pace and pattern of introducing computers into schools has served to cultivate a more socially organised style of using them. I mean that logistic problems of optimising access have encouraged their use in group work. However, the prevailing climate of educational practice may, in any case, have been favourable towards such developments. The tradition of small group work is well established in British schools – at least in the primary sector (Dunne and Bennett, 1990; Galton and Williamson, 1992). McMahon (1990) has surveyed a number of educational documents that reveal a strong official endorsement of collaborative structures (although he observes wryly that, while this is encouraged for classwork, pupil *assessment* remains fiercely individual). McMahon goes on to review the potential of new technology for helping to realise the pressure for more group work. In surveying primary practice, Jackson, Fletcher and Messer (1986, 1988) report that most teachers have recognised this and are arranging for small groups of pupils to work together; individual computer work is rare. The situation seems comparable in other countries. For example, Sheingold, Kane and Endreweit (1983) report evaluative reactions from a group of North American teachers adopting computers: these teachers were most impressed with outcomes in the social domain – changes in classroom interaction and in pupil self-esteem.

Thus, before we consider research into peer interaction at computers, we should note that practitioners have identified (independently of such research) a potential for the support of group work. In considering the popularity of computer-based group work, we should therefore be careful not to interpret it *merely* in terms of a pragmatic motive: to make a scarce resource more widely available. Teachers may be intending to pursue more focused educational purposes through their encouragement of such practices.

Often, computer activities have a conspicuously engaging quality relative to other classroom tasks. Where groups of pupils are involved, this engagement is usually characterised by lively conversation. Research reports by practising teachers stress their particular satisfaction with the language sustained during computer work (e.g. Dickinson, 1986; Genishi, McCollum and Strand, 1988; Hill and Browne, 1988; Shooter, Lovering and Bellamy, 1993). This simply complements a long tradition in early education of concern for developing language use. Language is commonly regarded as more than just a means of communication – it is also seen as the point at which meanings get created, and the resource whereby intelligent action itself may be directed. These ideas are very familiar to teachers, particularly through the work of educationalists such as Barnes (1976) and Tough (1977). In so far as computers release this verbal energy from pupils, then they seem to be creating the kind of problem-solving environment that many teachers naturally seek. Nevertheless, further research around this topic is still necessary. We need to see whether these scattered impressions hold up more generally; we need to be more specific about defining effective language use in this context and, finally, we need to determine whether there are additional good reasons for using computers collaboratively.

The release of language in these situations may be one basis for promoting this way of working, for participation in such talk supports cognitive development. Later, I shall return to this argument and examine the more detailed reasons for endorsing it. However, making the case for any kind of collaborative work can, in addition, include a more ideological motive. It may be based upon our intuitions about the ideal intellectual atmosphere for learners to enjoy – simply as participants. So, we may indeed encourage collaborative work because it supports individual cognitive development, or because the world beyond school can reward such skills, but we also might encourage it because we simply believe that joint intellectual activity is a rewarding dimension of human experience. However, in some tension with this, both our psychological theorising and our cultures of educational practice are still strongly oriented to fostering achievements that are clearly those of individuals (hence the solitary circumstances of examinations). So, perhaps for many observers, the most persuasive basis for having children work collaboratively will always tend to be this: it leads to gains in what they can do when we revert later to examining and testing them as *individuals*.

In assessing computers as contexts for joint work we should consider the two issues I have raised. First, do computers support lively group work of the kind we want learners to enjoy? Second, do these encounters allow individual participants to gain at least as much understanding as they would if the same work was individually organised? I will make some remarks on each of these questions in turn.

Quality of peer collaborations at computers

I have noted above that many teachers describe computers as useful catalysts for generating pupil talk. However, the quality of these experiences deserves more systematic documentation. One reason for caution is evident in reports from those teachers who have themselves been especially diligent in documenting the content of talk around computers. Take, for example, a report by Farish (1989). This teacher admitted to being gratified – at first – with what seemed to be happening in her own primary class. The computer seemed to engage her pupils. She then listened more closely to the computer-supported talk: it turned out to be mainly about uninteresting details concerning screen control and keyboard control. In fact, it was less stimulating than talk she recorded in other (non-computer) collaborative settings. So, there is obviously a danger of being misled by a gloss of sheer pupil activity.

Farish's technique for observing was unobtrusive. However, the issue of research methodology defines a further danger associated with many such classroom studies, that is the danger of drawing optimistic conclusions from observations where teachers themselves are very closely involved with the children's activities. For their presence may serve to stimulate more on-task, productive talk than would otherwise be expected. (Of course, professional researchers are also vulnerable to creating this kind of distorting influence.) However, bearing in mind these cautions, there are many favourable reports from all sectors of education concerning the quality of group work when it is organised around computers.

An influential early study is described in Hawkins, Sheingold, Gearhart and Berger (1982). They provide a comprehensive account of a class of 10–11-year-olds making extensive use of Logo: a strong sense of joint purpose was created and a culture of expertise and support evolved. This report may have been influential in defining a model of computer classroom effectiveness towards which many practitioners were subsequently to aspire. However, the study is also a reminder of the difficulty of generalising too freely: the school was private and its access to computers was generous. Moreover, the intervention was done at a time when such technology in early education was still a novelty. Finally, the project was supervised by international experts in the field. Such circumstances are a long way from many teachers' experiences. On the other hand, pupil enthusiasm at least approximating these levels has been replicated in other, less glamorous settings.

Energetic computer-based group work has been most thoroughly documented within the earliest years of education (Dickinson, 1986; Genishi et al., 1988; Hill and Browne, 1988), and in the middle and secondary years (Broderick and Trushell, 1985; Gonzalez-Edfelt, 1991; Hoyles and Sutherland, 1989; Johnson, Johnson and Stanne, 1985; Sheingold, Hawkins and Char, 1984; Trowbridge, 1987; Webb, 1984). There is very little relevant research on this topic that considers further and higher education or work in training communities. However, in all of the school cases, the group work is described as leading to more effective (group) products than the same work organised on an individual study basis. In fact, in a review of cooperative learning and new technology, Watson (1990) fails to find a single claim that the solitary use of classroom computers by individual pupils is a preferable implementation strategy.

This success is not an obvious outcome. Collaborative computer work might have been vulnerable, in particular, to playful distractions or to social dominance. Problems of this kind do seem less serious than has been documented for other collaborative work (Bennett, 1991; Galton, 1990). However, such problems have been reported. So, there has been some research attention to the themes of dominance and gender as troublesome issues in the management of collaborative work at computers.

In relation to gender, Hoyles (1988) has suggested a strong link between this variable and the circumstances of group versus solitary working conditions. In particular, girls may feel more positively towards computer tasks that are organised collaboratively. This invites closer attention to conditions under which mixed and same-sex groups can be compared. Hughes and Greenhough (1989), Siann and Mcleod (1986) and Underwood, McCaffrey and Underwood (1990) all report different outcomes of paired learning experiences for boys and girls – depending on the configuration of the pairings they were party to. Unfortunately, the pattern of these results is not consistent. However, neither were the observed tasks easily comparable. Computer-based tasks are very varied in their nature, and thus they may vary also in the social relations they can support among users. Moreover, these differing findings arise from brief research-oriented interventions carried out in uncertain relation to the mainstream of classroom life. Pupils' attitudes to such activities (and their behaviour within them) may well be unstable under the conditions of such variation. At present, we can only conclude that gender relations are an issue in forming computer work pairs, but suggest that consequences for the quality of the work sustained are variable – depending, at least, upon the nature of the task set.

Regarding dominance, Light and Glachan (1985) report this as a potential problem within pairs in a situation where limited control of the computer was possible. This factor may also interact with gender: (primary school) boys being more likely to take control of an input device when such access is limited (Blaye, Light, Joiner and Sheldon, 1991). Benyon (1993) makes similar observations in relation to boys and girls using Logo and comments that teachers may be oblivious to such details of social interaction, given their necessarily intermittent contact with it. These observations provide a good example of the sense in which computers might be conceptualised in terms of the possibilities for collaboration that are inherent in their design. Here, the thing itself (the existence of only one mouse control device) exerts a significant organising influence on the exchange between the pupils. The outcome in this case being an occasion upon which effective collaboration may be undermined. Elsewhere, Light, Foot and Colbourn (1987) show how this affordance may be modified (a form of dual-key control) and, moreover, that only under those circumstances does collaboration on their task show an advantage for the participants tested later as individuals.

Research of this kind – relating structural features of computer tasks to the social organisations they support – is all too scarce. Numerous studies praise the quality of collaboration associated with computer-based work without identifying how the setting achieves its effect. This is an important relation to clarify, because enthusiasm for computer-based work is increasingly expressed in terms of its collaborative potential. For example, Hoyles and Sutherland (1989) discuss Logo in these terms, suggesting that its real advantage as a classroom resource arises from its capacity to sustain social interaction in a context of mathematical problem-solving. This is a particularly significant observation, as the popular image of Logo has been dominated by the 'tool-to-think-with' theme (Papert, 1980), not the theme of social catalyst. Hoyles, Healey and Sutherland (1991) take these observations a little further by making a structured comparison between computer and non-computer versions of the same (maths) tasks. Their results reinforce the computer's status as an effective setting for pupil discussion. Although, again, it is hard to extract reasons why; they comment: 'evidently the computer somehow draws the attention of the pupils and becomes a focus for discussion' (p. 217). Such observations badly need elaboration.

I shall return to this puzzle of collaborative potency in the next chapter. So far, in relation to pupils interacting together *at* computers, we have reviewed evidence showing that this arrangement can engage them well. This may be satisfying if we believe that skills of discussion and collaboration are valuable, and if we feel that the experience is itself a stimulating one for those taking part. It remains here to make a few remarks regarding the *outcome* of such experiences as judged in terms of later achievements by the participants tested alone.

Outcomes for individuals participating in collaborative computer work

Arranging for a task to be conducted jointly at a computer may well be a good strategy for getting the task completed effectively. Indeed, the overall outcome may be more creative or, by some other criteria, more successful than alternative working arrangements that might have been organised. This may be all we seek. Pupils have had a worthwhile encounter with collaboration; it led to a useful result and the experience will serve them well on other occasions of joint working, both in and out of school. Indeed, it represents to them something of the way a great deal of understanding naturally occurs: that is, it occurs within the contexts of socially coordinated activity. However, teachers may not always make these arrangements only in the interests of creating this kind of authentic experience. In particular, teachers will know that, whatever the social circumstances for making discoveries in the rest of life, schools are places where progress gets assessed in terms of what *individuals* achieve. In short, achievement is often judged in tests (exams) that deny those who take them access to peers as sources of support. We may, therefore, wish to know whether computer-based group work results in gains that show up under this criterion.

Simply because an encounter was effective as a collaboration does not necessarily mean that participating individuals learned more than they would have done if working alone. For example, the task may have been split up among collaborators in ways that denied individuals experience with all its component parts. At once, we sense that there will be no simple generalisation arising from the question posed. Whether collaborative experiences of learning are more effective for individuals – when we test them as individuals – will doubtless depend on the task involved and the management strategy of the participants.

Nevertheless, reviews of this area suggest that gains in individual testing can generally be expected (Dalton, Hannafin and Hooper, 1989; Light and Blaye, 1989; Light and Colbourn, 1987; Rysavy and Sales, 1991; Trowbridge, 1987). This advantage has been reported across a wide range of research environments – although much of the work concerns the 10–13 year age group. In tightly controlled experimental tasks, Light, Foot and Colbourn (1987) and Blaye *et al.* (1991) report individual gains associated with paired work. Hughes and Greenhough (1989) report similar gains for Logo within a small-scale classroom intervention. Johnson, Johnson and Stanne (1986) describe a more extensive classroom comparison of individually, competitively and cooperatively organised computer work in the geography curriculum. Again, significant gains are apparent for the cooperative condition.

One study that found no advantage for group work (and no disadvantage either) makes an interesting peripheral observation. Light, Colbourn and Smith (1987) found no difference in individual 11-year-olds' PROLOG programming achievements when they compared pupils who had been working either singly at a computer, as a pair, or in a group of four. However, videotapes of the experimental sessions revealed that the children working 'alone' had engaged in a good deal of discussion with their neighbours. This subversion of the experimental procedure may have been disheartening to the researchers but it surely bears useful witness to how easily discussion is supported among children mutually engaged in computer work. Researchers with plans in this area might beware that suppressing such inclinations in the interest of experimental design may lead to the creation of unrepresentative models of classroom possibilities. Pupils' spontaneous appeal to peers as resources of support in computer-based problem-solving is a striking tendency, for it stands in contrast with pupils' apparent unwillingness to make use of on-line help facilities that instructional programs themselves often offer (Messer, Jackson and Mohamedali, 1987).

Issues arising from studies of computer-based collaboration

Integrating the above remarks with those made in the previous chapter, there are now grounds for both pessimism and optimism regarding technology's place in any educational culture that prioritises social processes. On the one hand, it has been argued (see Chapter 5) that work with computers is vulnerable to exclusion from the communal discourse that gets organised in classrooms. So, computer activities that easily drift towards the periphery of classroom life may have their impact reduced by this exclusion. This may leave us pessimistic, because such talk is the vehicle whereby teachers can create continuity of experience for pupils. On the other hand, the material reviewed in this chapter indicates that computers may re-enter the social life of classrooms via their support of collaborative work between pupils themselves. This may give cause for optimism among those educationalists who are concerned to locate this teaching technology in some social context.

Of course, any trend towards involving computers in peer collaborations may not, at a stroke, neutralise all our pessimism arising from the easy marginalisation of classroom technology. Work that children do together around this technology may well be lively and productive at the time; yet (just like solitary computer work) it may remain work that is never properly consolidated through incorporation into classroom discourse. In terms of the concerns raised in the last chapter, it may become work that still does not get knitted into the common knowledge of classroom activity.

Those arguments need not be rehearsed again here. Collaborative computer work is as vulnerable as solitary computer work in respect of becoming dislocated from a mainstream of teacher-led talk. Whether or not this is its fate, we may still ask what formats for a collaborative task make the experience as rich as possible for the participants at the time. I believe pursuit of this question brings us back to further considering the concept of intersubjectivity. Earlier, in discussing teachers' creation of shared understandings, I appealed to this concept. I argued that the possibility of creating a shared cognitive context depends upon the participants' mutual appropriation of motives, intentions and understandings. So, teachers must become skilled at saying and doing things that precipitate and exploit such possibilities: they thereby establish resources of common knowledge and can build further upon them. This all reflects a human capacity for intersubjectivity. Here (and in the next chapter), I shall develop an argument claiming that the same capacity should be recognised as central to what takes place within peer interaction – at least, when it is going well.

So, at a very general level, I am concerned to reinforce a useful theoretical link: identifying socio-cognitive processes that are common to both the interactions between teachers and pupils (see Chapter 5) and the interactions between pupils and their peers. Discussion of both arenas of activity can usefully call upon the same theoretical constructs; in particular, the constructs of common knowledge, socially shared cognition and intersubjectivity. All of this may serve, indirectly, to endorse peer interaction as a potentially powerful educational resource.

I am also concerned to explore how computers may be mobilised to become part of such a resource. Yet, given the favourable review of computer-based collaborative work above, what more is there to be done to encourage this? To recap: computers have been discovered by practitioners to create lively forums of joint activity. Close observation suggests that usually – not inevitably – these interactions are productive and lead to (group) products that are superior to whatever may be created by the participants alone. Finally, the individual participants in collaborative learning tend later to perform better on relevant tests of achievement, as compared with peers who learned on their computers in isolation. Surely, the task ahead is merely to investigate the parameters of this advantage – investigating the relative potency of different software, and so forth.

Superficially this may describe the proper research agenda. However, if 'merely' investigating the outcomes of collaborative computer work means doing so in a piecemeal, atheoretical manner, then an opportunity is being lost. Effective investigation of software should converge on accounts that can systematise those specific features of computer-based tasks that afford productive social interaction. However, what do we understand by 'productive' as applied to peer collaborations? We might answer that question solely in relation to the 'products' of individual testing: a productive collaboration is one that leads the individual participants to learn more – as assessed in solitary post-tests. But such pragmatic accounts avoid any concentration on the dynamic of the collaborative act itself. We are left with shopping lists of experimental variables that co-relate task characteristics with collaborative productivity. With this strategy, understanding the processes that mediate the success gets neglected. Instead our research should aim to develop a richer *theory* of collaboratively organised problem-solving. It should allow us to see more clearly why some particular task 'works' as joint activity.

In pursuit of this aim, I shall do a number of things below. First, I shall consider the status of peer interaction within educational practice very generally – with no special emphasis on technology or psychological interpretations. Second, I shall review the most influential accounts of collaborative learning that refer to mediating psychological processes. Third, I shall outline a socio-cultural critique of this contemporary framework. This leads me to formulate an account of learning through peer interaction that stresses the creation of socially shared knowledge. In the next chapter, empirical observations of my own will be deployed to illustrate how computer-based collaborative learning reveals the dynamic of such intersubjectivity.

PEER INTERACTION IN GENERAL EDUCATIONAL CONTEXTS

In Britain, there is little need to make new arguments prioritising group work in classrooms. This style of working is already well established. As far as primary practice is concerned, the principle of such work is often associated with prescriptions contained within the influential Plowden Report on early education (Plowden Report, 1967). This official view is endorsed elsewhere: McMahon (1990) has reviewed policy documents within British education that serve to legitimise and encourage early group work.

The historical basis for an emphasis on group work in classrooms has been discussed by Galton and Williamson (1992). In their view, the origin of this commitment among British teachers had a lot to do with a prior belief in mixed ability classrooms. Such beliefs were, in turn, stimulated by the breakdown of a two-tier secondary education with its associated selection testing at 11. The principle that children would learn effectively in mixed ability settings was widely adopted at this time. Galton and Williamson's point is that active cultivation of group work may not, at first, have been grounded in particular cognitive theory about its benefits.

It seems unlikely that structural changes in the education system were the sole stimulus for fostering group work practices. After all, the idea is surely in some tension with common-sense conceptions of learning. Such conceptions might suppose that learning is properly managed by the official, teacher-dominated talk of lessons (Speier, 1976). Moreover, this common-sense belief in the central role of teachers arises not just because they know more facts about the world. Their greater procedural knowledge must also be of advantage to learners. This is supported by research: for, even in a content-free activity (such as planning a route), there is still an advantage afforded children by collaborating with an adult versus collaborating with a peer (Radzisewska and Rogoff, 1991). In the face of this common sense, it is likely that a contemporary recognition of learning through peer interaction must have arisen partly through influences from educational or psychological theory.

The work of Piaget (perhaps promoted by Plowden) was a likely source of inspiration. Here was an account of cognitive development that lay great stress on the child's capacity for spontaneous, *untutored* discovery. This naturally leads to recognising that circumstance often referred to by the influential educationalist Frank Smith (e.g. Smith, 1981): children are 'learning' all the time, even when not engaged with teachers or other experienced adults. In so far as they are immersed in the peer community of the classroom, that setting will furnish experience of interaction that supports learning also. In fact, given the natural social energy released within children's peer cultures, it seems sensible to mobilise this in the service of educational aims – to regard peers as a positive source of support (Sieber, 1979). This should only require practitioners to evolve some expertise regarding the management of such encounters, working out what sorts of tasks are well suited to joint cognitive activity and what configurations of individuals make the best of the opportunities.

Yet the situation is not so straightforward. There may be a natural social energy to children's early exchanges, but channelling it into the agendas of school learning may prove a more than trivial task. So, despite children's sociability, despite the good sense of incorporating group work and despite the pressure to do so, the reality of how it typically proceeds is somewhat sobering. There have been several substantial observational studies of group work in primary schools. They have been reviewed by Galton (1990; Galton and Williamson, 1992) and by Bennett (1991). The summary picture these reviews present is a disappointing one. There is much investment in creating the material conditions for group work, but there is less evidence that these conditions support productive, on-task joint activity. In other words, the seating has been socialised into collaboration but the pupils have not. Bennett (1991) comments: 'What seems to have happened in practice is that teachers have taken on board the Plowden Report's views on having children work in groups, but have preferred to retain individualisation rather than cooperation in that context' (p. 585).

This conclusion should not imply that teachers have subverted the educational plan by underpinning the surface organisation with an alternative agenda of their own – as if grouping arrangements were then merely cosmetic gestures. It may be that teachers pursue the goal of group work but they enjoy very little guidance on how it is most effectively energised. This point is made in more detail by Perret-Clermont and Schubaeur-Leoni (1981). Or the problem may be different again:

where younger children are concerned, the aim of fostering collaborative practices may simply be too ambitious. This might be so if Kutnick (1983) is right when describing the infant school peer group in his observations as 'largely an ineffectual gathering of pupils greatly dependent on the parents and the teacher' (p. 49).

We already have reason to doubt the generality of this dispiriting observation about young children as collaborators: earlier I cited many reports of such children in lively joint activity with computer tasks. The other suggestion above, that teachers are poorly prepared to manage joint work, may be credible; although one would expect the necessary practical insights soon to emerge through immersion in classroom life – if there are any practical insights to be had. I believe that the gap between expectation and reality for group work has more to do with our failing to characterise the optimal setting for joint problem-solving. We need more sensitivity to the kinds of tasks that are particularly potent in supporting good collaborative interaction. At the moment, the ethnographic literature on classroom group work warns us that such tasks may be scarce and not in widespread use – or that the teacher's job of coordinating them is more demanding than is realised. Although the problem may superficially be one of achieving this fit between tasks and social processes, our limited success in getting it right probably reflects the lack of a persuasive theoretical account of the nature of collaboration itself. Thus the strengthening of such theory will be one useful achievement. It may help us notice the things that are making a difference, or help us actively tease them out.

Naturally, I am going to suggest that a way forward lies in considering computers in relation to this problem. Computers may furnish good settings for meeting the goals of effective small group work. This possibility has already been highlighted above. However, the simple input–outcome nature of that research may be too modest a basis for trying to influence practice. Therefore, my aim now is to make better sense of why computers should be effective in this way. I believe this aim requires us to reflect, first, on the psychological processes active in collaborations that are effective. We may then clarify how computer-based activities manifest properties that are suited to prompting and sustaining those processes. With these goals in view, I turn next to consider developmental research on processes under-lying any peer-based problem-solving exercise.

PSYCHOLOGICAL PROCESSES UNDERLYING CHILDREN'S COLLABORATIVE WORK

There are already some detailed surveys of this topic in the literature (e.g. Azmitia and Perlmutter, 1989; Cazden, 1986; Damon and Phelps, 1989; Forman and Kraker, 1985). Therefore I will not attempt a comprehensive review of all empirical research that relates to the various themes arising. However, I will abstract the important distinctions that characterise understanding in this field, and I will offer pointers to research that supports the main conclusions.

So far, I have been slipping between reference to 'group work' and to 'collabor-ations' fairly freely. However, researchers in this area have adopted informal distinctions that identify more precisely the different kinds of group working that might be arranged. In particular, the distinction is commonly made between interactions that are 'tutorial', 'cooperative' or 'collaborative'. We shall be mainly interested in the last of these, but brief mention of what the other two involve will be useful.

Group work as peer tutoring or as cooperative learning

We might say casually that what characterises interactions in small group work is learning rather than teaching. It is usually a different kind of class experience than any that are managed by a teacher. Yet, peer interactions can be organised to have a tutorial quality. A peer can be assigned to act the role of tutor. This might be arranged simply to free up the 'official' teacher. Peer tutors may indeed be effective because they achieve with their classmates something of what grown-up teachers achieve. But, in addition, the tutoring experience may be educationally valuable because of effects that are advantageous for the tutors themselves. To take the role of teacher may be a useful learning experience. This is a point that arises in a number of research reviews relating to such classroom initiatives (e.g. Topping, 1992).

What is involved in the activity of teaching may include a style of talking that is both specialised and demanding of interpersonal sensitivity. These skills may be cultivated over a long period and are not within the easy grasp of younger children. Yet it might be to the advantage of young children to gain some reflective access to what is involved. In this spirit, Palincsar and Brown (1984) have reported a productive exercise based upon allowing learners to take control of teaching styles of dialogue. However, this format for group work is important but of less interest here: it is not the circumstance under which most small group work is usually managed in classrooms.

Cooperative learning is a more typical arrangement than peer tutoring. It refers to strategies for managing tasks that often implicate a large group working together, or even a whole class. It is common for tasks in this tradition to be partitioned such that different members of a group take responsibility for different components of the task. Johnson and Johnson have reported a number of initiatives that pay close attention to strategies for achieving optimal organisations (e.g. Johnson and Johnson, 1985). Another concern of research in this area is motivational: how to define a structure of rewards that sustains joint activity. Slavin and colleagues have been particularly interested in this problem (e.g. Slavin, 1986).

Nastasi and Clements (1991) have reviewed research in the cooperative learning tradition and highlighted implications for classroom practice. At first sight, such work seems relevant to our interest in assessing computers as vehicles for peer-centred work. It addresses the issue of motivation, something that might prove important to our understanding of effective computer use. However, the analysis is directed at understanding the impact of more overarching aspects of classroom strategy. It is particularly concerned with how reward structures can be defined and negotiated in relation to the outcomes of work. Computers can be fitted into classrooms that pursue cooperative work regimes and there may be good reasons to do so – given the success that has been reported for this method (e.g. Slavin, 1987). However, studies of these regimes do not focus down on the interactions that are supported at the point of actually using the technology. Studies of co-operative classrooms are too coarse-grained to reveal distinctive effects of computers on social interaction. I am more concerned to capture these 'local' conditions of social exchange during peer-based work. The tradition of research that has attended to such matters is normally termed 'collaborative learning' research.

Group work as collaborative learning

The line is thin between cooperative and collaborative learning but one characteristic of research in the 'collaborative' tradition is a greater interest in cognitive processes – as against motivational ones. At least, Slavin (1987) draws the distinction in these terms, arguing that the two research traditions often talk past each other although they are really complementary. Cooperative learning studies help to define a motivational and organisational structure for an overarching program of group work; while collaborative learning studies focus on the cognitive advantages that arise within the more intimate exchanges of working together.

Here I really want to relate to the concerns of both research orientations. On the one hand, computer-based work does have a focused, intense quality and it invites a research technique that examines pupil interactions closely and in relation to aspects of the task. This is the strategy of the cognitively oriented collaborative learning tradition. On the other hand, I believe there *is* a motivational issue to be addressed in relation to work at computers, but it is not one that is easily explored (or even revealed) within the research strategy favoured in studies of cooperative learning. The present discussion will converge on this dilemma.

Part of my present concern is to consolidate the case for making peer collaborations a significant basis for organising computer-based interactions. I have argued that this requires us to look quite closely at the detail of interactions that such activities afford. We may thereby identify the distinctive strengths of computers deployed in this manner. Research on the nature of peer interaction during focused problem-solving has a cognitive emphasis. It identifies a number of processes that might be powerful when released in this social situation: I believe there are three that have been well documented. For shorthand, I shall refer to them as processes relating to (1) articulation, (2) conflict and (3) co-construction.

Articulation

One way in which learners might gain from working closely on a problem with a peer is by being required to make their thinking public and explicit. The learner's opinions, predictions, interpretations and so on will need to be articulated for the benefit of joint activity. These declarations may be a product of problem-solving that inherently supports the learning process. This simple requirement defines a possible value in collaborative work that has been identified by a number of researchers (Chi and Van Lehn, 1991; Hoyles, 1985a; Schunk, 1986). Damon and Phelps (1989) summarise the advantages as follows:

> In order to work productively with their partners, children must publicly recapitulate their own emerging understanding of the task. This, we believe, is a process that strongly facilitates intellectual growth, because it forces the subjects to bring to consciousness the ideas that they are just beginning to grasp intuitively. The responsibility that children feel for communicating well with their peer partners induces them to gain greater conceptual clarity for themselves. (p. 152)

This summary seems to locate the strength of peer work in self-reflective processes arising from the responsibility of justifying and declaring your own ideas to a collaborator. The idea is captured elsewhere in comments made by Bruner on the general role of language in supporting learning:

> It must express stance and counter-stance and in the process leave place for reflection, for metacognition. It is this that permits one to reach higher ground, this process of objectifying in language or image what one has thought and then turning around on it and reconsidering it. (1986, p. 129)

However, there may be a further advantage within situations where ideas are publicly articulated: one that reflects the more interactive (rather than declarative) quality of joint activity. That is, it arises from being witness to your own partner engaging in this articulation of ideas. The advantage here involves something more dynamic in a properly social sense. It may arise in so far as the talk of one participant serves to create for the other exemplars of strategic moves that comprise effective problem-solving.

With this suggestion, a link is made to one interpretation of effective practice in the zone of proximal development. In Chapter 4, the view was presented that some instructional talk worked its effect by virtue of creating a cognitive system. A more expert partner would be particularly suitable for prompting, elaborating and filling in the problem-solving process, thereby allowing the novice to achieve a goal unattainable in a solitary setting. Vygotsky's own account of ZPD configurations referred to novices with 'adult guidance or in collaboration with a more capable peer' (Vygotsky, 1978, p. 86). However, there is no reason why symmetrical peer pairings should not sometimes give rise to a socially defined cognitive system of the same sort: one that is comparable to that traditionally discussed for novices working with more expert partners. As before, the cognitive benefits arising from this would be associated with processes of internalisation. The opportunity to participate in the processes of coordinating a problem-solving strategy creates the conditions for transfer from Vygotsky's inter-mental social plane to his private intra-mental plane.

So, it is being argued that 'simply' articulating ideas is a useful experience for problem solvers and one naturally afforded by socially organised tasks. It is suspected that benefits would arise because of the pressure for reflection that is felt by the individual talking. It is also supposed that making ideas public may allow them to slot into an externally located cognitive system that implicates a partner's contributions also. Participation in such systems may then be internalised. Does empirical work suggest that experiences of this kind carry forward?

There are various classroom observations of group work (particularly involving computers) that draw attention to episodes of publicly declared reasoning (e.g. Hoyles and Sutherland, 1989). However, the impact of such experiences on the participant's problem-solving in subsequent situations (perhaps alone) is harder to demonstrate. A significant obstacle is the difficulty of systematising and quantifying such dialogue so that the relevant correlations might be explored. There are some studies that attempt this on a modest scale. For instance, there are studies of children's interactions that characterise and enumerate discrete problem-solving moves (questions, challenges, requests, etc.) and then relate their occurrence with the participants' subsequent performance on other, related problems. Positive correlations have been reported (e.g. King, 1989; Webb, Ender and Lewis, 1986). The inference is that participation within this kind of problem-solving discourse was indeed a valuable learning experience – perhaps for the reasons implied above. Where there is lots of reasoned discussion there will be benefit that carries forward. Unfortunately, it is in the nature of correlational data that we will be left uncertain as to the precise basis of such performance gains. These studies must encourage us in fostering problem-solving encounters in which thinking gets publicly articulated, but exactly how the benefit of this experience is mediated remains to be demonstrated.

Conflict

There is nothing strongly interactional in the above conceptualisation. The presence of a peer doubtless encourages a pupil to articulate her ideas, but the benefits are not claimed to arise from dialogue – from coordinated *exchanges* with that partner. The second process to be mentioned here, conflict, does arise within such mutual involvement.

In this case, the benefit is supposed to occur in the context of disagreements between peers and their efforts to resolve them. It is a convention of conversation that disagreement should prompt discursive moves of justification and negotiation. So, the cognitive consequences of conflict might be quite productive. This is a claim most closely associated with Piaget. It is a claim at odds with the common belief that Piaget denied the potency of interpersonal experience in cognitive development. What Piaget draws attention to within peer exchanges is the power of argument, or 'the shock of our thought coming into contact with that of others' (Piaget, 1928, p. 204). Piaget supposed that the natural egocentrism of early childhood thinking typically prevented younger children from reflecting on their own thought. However, demands for justification and accountability that will arise within peer disagreements forces them to enter into such reflection. Moreover, as Piaget claimed, simply encountering these differences (during argument) seems adequate to precipitate cognitive restructuring – further processes of negotiating an agreed consensus need not be part of what must occur (Howe, Tolmie and Rodgers, 1990).

Piaget's proposal has led to a significant body of research exploring the conditions under which conflict might effectively induce cognitive change (for reviews see Bell, Grossen and Perret-Clermont, 1985; Doise, 1985; Doise and Mugny, 1984). Much of this work has employed tasks typical of those used within Piagetian tests of cognitive development. Particularly popular with researchers have been the conservation problems: tasks designed for evaluating transition into the concrete operational stage of cognitive development. These have been a natural choice where the aim has been to demonstrate how peer conflict can induce cognitive change – in terms of Piaget's own conception of cognitive structures. However, such brief and circumscribed problem-solving encounters offer a poor representation of interaction as it might occur within sustained classwork. Indeed, Doise (1985) comments on how little communication often takes place in these experimental tasks. However, one study involving a somewhat more elaborate, puzzle-like task (Light and Glachan, 1985) does provide us with a more convincing model for classroom activities. Here it was demonstrated that the degree of conflict arising within a peer pairing was positively correlated with performance later on in the task by individuals acting alone.

Conflict has, therefore, been demonstrated to be a distinctive and productive feature of peer-based problem-solving. But the extensive research attention accorded this feature of peer interaction largely reflects the great interest in cognitive stage transition within Piagetian theory. It is less a reflection of the relative importance or frequency of conflict in classroom group work. There will surely be other characteristics of effective peer-based learning interactions which do not implicate conflict.

Co-construction

A final basis for conceptualising the cognitive benefit of collaborative learning lies in what is termed co-construction. This notion often arises in discussions of peer interaction more influenced by Vygotsky's socio-cultural thinking. There may be some feeling that the Piagetian emphasis on conflict suggests the inevitability of social *tension* within joint problem-solving. We may feel uneasy about this and, indeed, there are examples of research showing that conflict is far from a necessary ingredient of effective group work. For example, Blaye *et al.* (1991) observed children tackling one particular set of problems: in this case, they found no correlation between frequency of children's conflict and the quality of their performance in subsequent individual performance tests.

Thus, some authors have analysed peer-based problem-solving in terms of social processes that do not simply involve adopting declarative attitudes ('articulation' above), neither do they involve more adversarial styles of interaction ('conflict' above). Forman and her colleagues have reported empirical observations that illustrate a co-constructional alternative (e.g. Forman, 1989; Forman and Cazden, 1985; Forman and Kraker, 1985). They dwell in particular on how children may take individual responsibility for complementary cognitive functions while solving a problem. This may be organised within the context of some overall converging discussion about the task. Where Forman and others seem to see joint problem-solving as proceeding well is where the work gets creatively *dispersed*: strategies of sharing responsibility serve to accelerate the participants' joint construction of some worthwhile convergence – a common object of some sort.

Reference to common cognitive objects echoes theoretical concepts introduced in the previous chapter to help discuss classroom discourse managed by teachers. In that context, I dwelt upon activities that assisted the creation of socially shared cognition. The two sets of ideas are certainly in the same spirit of theorising. However, when students of peer interaction identify an object as 'co-constructed', typically that object will be rather narrowly propositional in character. Such objects often turn out to be procedures or hypotheses, or other formalised elements in the structural description of problem-solving. They are discrete ingredients in the sequence of problem-solving moves. Social constructions of this sort are surely valid and useful outcomes of joint activity. However, while I do wish to endorse reference to jointly constructed cognitive objects, I feel that such constructs need to be more richly articulated than those illustrated by the present line of theorising. In particular, they will be more fundamental to the support of problem-solving talk than are the particular conclusions, solutions or predictions that are co-constructed during the course of that talk. Moreover, they may be more hidden from us as observers. I shall return to this point in a section below dedicated to establishing a cultural psychological approach to peer collaboration research.

Summary comments on processes in collaborative work

We set out concerned to justify the further cultivation of peer interaction *at* classroom computers. Research in the 'collaborative learning' tradition proved most relevant to our interests because it studies intimate and focused interactions of the sort necessitated by computer-based work. In reviewing this research, we have encountered a number of ways in which joint work can be cognitively stimulating.

One implication running through this research literature must be stressed. Peer-based work is identified as being more than a mere approximation to some other, more ideal, arrangement for learning – namely, the same interactions involving a more expert (adult) partner. I have already commented that there are persuasive grounds for arranging peer interaction as an experience that is worthwhile in its own right. Children can usefully be offered opportunities to coordinate their problem-solving skills with peers. It is a rewarding and valued achievement to be able to do so effectively. However, it is also argued that such collaborative problem-solving is uniquely suited to the cultivation of certain forms of thinking. That is, there may be varieties of intellectual stimulation arising in work with peers that are less readily furnished within interactions involving more expert adults.

Piaget (1928) makes this point quite strongly in comparing the two kinds of interaction. He argues that the implicit authority characterising children's asymmetrical relations with adults can be counter-productive in some problem-solving situations. It is the symmetry (in authority) of peer-based discussion that most effectively forces useful reflection. It encourages active evaluation of the status of one's own ideas – as legitimate alternatives to those of a partner. The tension arising from two *like* minds coming into conflict prompts resolving argumentation and reflection – rather then deference to authority.

Moreover, a distinctive role in cognitive development for peer interaction need not depend only on argument and conflict (the features of interaction stressed in Piaget's version of this insight). Research suggests further grounds for recognising a selective advantage to problem-solving with peers – advantages, in other words that are not necessarily mediated only by the resolution of disagreements. It is true that the asymmetry of relations with an adult may generally be advantageous in situations of guided participation (such as those discussed in relation to the zone of proximal development). However, this advantage is not inevitable. Kruger and Tomasello (1986) made a formal comparison between children engaged in (moral) reasoning both with peers and with a familiar adult. They showed that the two settings released different contributions from the children. In particular, the asymmetry of the adult encounter seemed to inhibit certain forms of reasoning: certain spontaneous logical operations directed towards a partner's contributions were more likely with peers than adults. Thus, as a forum for 'articulating' (as discussed above) particular kinds of reasoned discourse, peer interactions may offer precious opportunities.

A CULTURAL PERSPECTIVE ON PEER INTERACTION STUDIES

It might be expected that students of peer interaction would be among the most assertive in promoting socio-cultural interpretations of learning. The cultural perspective – as outlined here in Chapter 2 – dwells upon the essentially social nature of instruction and learning. Should not research activity into peer interaction promise some sort of commitment to a truly social characterisation of learning?

It appears that serious commitments of this kind are scarce. Studies of classroom collaboration are a disappointment if we are looking for genuinely radical theoretical perspectives on cognition. Perhaps this testifies to the deeply set nature of our individualistic theorising, but there has been little sign of researchers in this area developing a more socially grounded interpretation of cognitive activity. I shall argue in this section that a truly useful interpretation of research on collaboration requires us to develop a conceptual vocabulary for talking about cognition as a distributed, or shared, achievement.

Let us approach this by considering the way in which claims about the impact of collaboration are derived from research. The predominant orientation towards the issue of peer interaction is to frame questions of the form: 'What is the effect of collaborative learning upon fostering ability x?' Often such questions will be motivated by concern to make recommendations for optimal classroom practice. Sometimes the question will be directed towards evaluating theoretical claims regarding the origins of certain cognitive changes (e.g. that they may originate within social conflicts). In any case, the natural design for a research exercise around this topic can be summarised in the following notation that describes a typical three-stage experiment:

(1) T1 > IND > T2
(2) T1 > PIa > T2
(3) T1 > PIb > T2

In the simplest of research designs, comparisons might be made of events arising in condition (1) vs. condition (2). In each case, subjects are pre-tested (T1) on some problem. The groups differ according to how they are occupied next, during an intervention stage. In condition (1) they work independently at an activity relevant to the problem-solving skill. In condition (2) they engage in some version of peer interaction (PIa) around the same activity. Of special interest will be performance of subjects (working alone again) on a post-test (T2). In the comparison of (1) and (2), there might be post-test advantages associated with participation in condition (2). In this case, it would be claimed that the post-test achievements were facilitated by peer interaction (PIa). Such interaction might lead to more progress than was associated with solitary learning (IND).

Alternatively, in the comparison of (2) and (3), there might emerge distinguishable advantages associated with one of the two arrangements for organising the interaction (PIa or PIb), in which case the research would have made progress towards identifying the particular conditions of interaction that were most favourable for learning in this forum.

Such an interest in pinning down the particular basis of an advantage for collaboration might be pursued in a third kind of design. Without any necessity for pre-testing, very detailed recording of events during peer interactions themselves might be made in order to correlate such measures with individual performance on post-tests. For example, if certain talk within an interacting group was positively correlated with later test performance of the individuals participating in that group, then we might suppose that this kind of talk was a potent factor mediating the advantage of collaboration. We might then take steps to cultivate it.

This all appears suitably elegant and plausible. Moreover, I do not wish to imply that real insights cannot be derived from research designs of this sort. They may well help to specify for teachers some possible consequences of some kinds of classroom arrangements for pupil working. Yet, in terms of developing an underpinning theory, the individualistic orientation of this research strategy needs to be recognised. This orientation may cause us to miss opportunities for re-framing some of these issues and, perhaps, investigating them from new perspectives. My strategy here will be to think further on the way in which we currently conceptualise events associated with 'PI' conditions and 'T2' conditions – as notated in the scheme above.

Interpreting the post-intervention performance

Post-testing (T2) is perhaps the most plausible feature of all in this system and it might seem the most difficult to challenge. Probably we are persuaded of the crucial need for this testing because we are committed to the idea that what matters is how individual pupils function when left on their own – hopefully doing better as a result of our interventions. It would be claimed that, in the end, we must equip pupils for deploying their individual cognitive resources (to 'think independently') in all the situations that this will be required of them. And, of course, life will furnish many such situations; not the least of which will be the formal examinations through which pupils are typically assessed. In fact, our research post-tests may feel very similar to some of those examinations and so our discovery of interventions that optimise performance on such occasions can surely only be of benefit to pupils.

There is one kind of challenge to this reasoning that I do not wish to dwell upon. It notes that intelligence is actually more often exercised in collaborative settings than within solitary reflection. Therefore, it is claimed, what should be of interest to researchers is post-tests of how children perform *collaboratively*. If a post-test demanding unsupported solitary thinking fails to show an advantage of learning through peer interaction, we need not be concerned: why should the one kind of achievement be evident in what is a different arena? I find this challenge relevant but not very comprehensive. It is surely true that educational practice must recognise that much problem-solving does now require the ability to gather and coordinate with others. This may imply that cultivating (and assessing) such capabilities might deserve more attention from research and practice, but it does not imply we should make this an exclusive preoccupation.

Yet I do believe the emphasis on typical post-intervention testing is still problematic and that the problems are made visible to us when a proper cultural orientation is adopted. The cultural analysis of cognition assumes its inherently social nature. But this does not amount to making only a narrow link between cognition and social interaction – a 'social' nature in the face-to-face interpersonal sense. So, situations demanding cognitive competence will be socially situated in that they indeed may require interpersonal negotiations; but they will doubtless also call upon the manipulation of particular artefacts, or the exercise of particular rituals, or the deployment of particular symbol systems – all in the service of particular goals defined within particular social or institutional relationships... and so forth. In short, such occasions of cognitive testing will always require testees to coordinate and deploy a given set of mediational means.

Consider this applied to a concrete case (Howe, Tolmie and Rodgers, 1990). Here certain forms of collaborative discussion around a physics problem of sinking and floating were shown to be a helpful experience for pupils. That is, they facilitated performance in a post-test requiring individuals to make decisions about what will sink and what will float. This is useful: for one thing, it points at possible classroom interventions that might be expected to improve pupil performance on certain sorts of tasks. But exactly what has been shown to have been facilitated in this sense; what has been learned? A lot hinges on our intuitions about the relation between the particular context of the post-test, and contexts typical of other situations in which problems relating to the physics of flotation might arise. The research-based test is just one occasion for such thinking to take place. In this case, it does happen to have an interpersonal dimension that will be relevant: the questioning is managed by a particular individual in a particular relation to the pupils – the experimenter. But the test also involves the manipulation of particular artefacts in a particular problem space (various objects around a water tank); testing that is continuous with a classroom agenda; and all of this, in turn, is embedded in 'schooled' life and values.

Thus, the circumstances of research post-testing (or, indeed, school examinations) seem rather circumscribed from the perspective of a cultural psychology. A number of studies have now demonstrated how the particular circumstances of controlled testing can exert a great influence on how children think in such settings (e.g. Donaldson, 1978; Siegel, 1991a, b). Tests conceived for research purposes typically just characterise one kind of context in which cognitive activity must be organised. They are too easily conceptualised as a convenient instrument for assessing some 'general' cognitive advance that is supposed to have taken place. So, the temptation is to see them as unproblematic evaluations of (private) cognitive resources that are relatively context-independent: the test being just an arbitrary sampling exercise on these resources.

How else can the outcome of experimental interventions be evaluated? One way would be by taking seriously the issue of context: evaluating the range of conditions under which the experiences of an intervention surface to guide action elsewhere. There seems little interest among psychological researchers for developing their work in this direction. I believe this reflects a theoretical prejudice towards isolating relatively context-independent cognitive achievements. This encourages self-contained interventions and self-contained evaluation instruments. When reproduced within classroom practice, it might leave us with pupils who have 'knowledge in pieces' (DiSessa, 1988) rather than truly versatile ways of thinking. So, the authentic circumstances for promoting cognitive development may reside in the knitting together of contextualised experiences – particularly as this may be achieved through the discourse making up a classroom's communal life. This possibility is exemplified in a paper by Edwards (in press), in which he outlines an agenda for analysing conceptual development in terms of children's participation in such discursive practices. This offers an alternative to our preference for always addressing these issues by sampling an inner world of discrete conceptual acquisitions.

The more conventional practice of psychological research is not a *fatal* methodological attitude. In the case of the sinking and floating example, the study remains interesting and the results are compelling. For, often, what gets done by way of testing carries some real face value; it seems to promise achievements in other situations that are not formally evaluated. Yet, a narrowness of reach remains the significant point. It is rarely thought necessary to pursue the question of what has been learned – as if it could be something that was actually bound up with contexts of acquisition or practice, and that such embedding might usefully be documented. It seems very seductive to suppose that a successful post-test confirms that the testee now has some new logical 'bit' in place; or some new cognitive skill has now become available. Such characterisations may reflect the influence upon us of traditional theorising in cognitive psychology. That tradition tends to view the achievements of organised learning as private, contained and relatively context-free: something to be sampled in controlled tests.

Interpreting the joint activity within peer interaction

The same biases of interpretation arise in analyses of events within the peer interactions themselves – as typically organised for experiments. In the notation used above, the intervention stages of PIa and PIb are often characterised in terms that foreground activities of the *individual* participants in the collaboration. The collaboration may be expressed as a sum total of certain sorts of discourse events that were observed. This gives us only limited insight into what is typically happening in these collaborations – and how it may be cognitively significant. I shall follow up this claim in more detail here, giving no further attention to the problems arising from the post-testing of interventions. Generally, I am more concerned with weaknesses in interpreting the collaboration stage of the standard empirical procedure, rather than with weaknesses in interpreting the post-test stage. This is because any prescription for involving computers within collaborative work will need, most of all, to be based upon an adequate account of the interactional processes active during such work.

My plan here is, first, to indicate what it means to claim that typical analyses of collaborations are individualistic, then to speculate as to what a mutualist or more socially grounded alternative analysis would be like.

I believe the orientation to individualistic accounts arises from the tacit influence of two influential concepts from the mainstream of psychological thinking: 'stimulus' and 'skill'. To be more specific, I shall suggest that the potency of a collaboration is typically characterised as some pattern of discrete here-and-now social events (stimuli). These events act upon (and, perhaps, change) the collaborators. This is too limiting a conception. To enrich it, certain recent accounts have made reference to intersubjective achievements that can be mobilised during the joint activity. However, this idea can also be limited in its reach: if such achievements are only framed in terms of social attributes (skills) brought to the situation by the individual collaborators.

Let us consider the influence of 'stimulus' conceptions first. Research that attempts to understand peer-based problem-solving has typically concentrated on the content and organisation of the talk that occurs within it. The common strategy is to classify and enumerate individual utterances made by the participants (e.g. King, 1989; Webb *et al.*, 1986). This allows any such occasion to be summarised as a profile of categorised talk. It may then be found that certain prevalent categories in such a profile are positively correlated with later, post-test performance. I suggest that a very common attitude towards this correlation is one assuming that the talk was effective because it acted as a *stimulus*: it served to prompt some kind of cognitive effect for the collaborating individual. A significant property of an event conceptualised in this manner is that it tends to be taken as having no history or context: it is an event only of the here-and-now.

For example, the Piagetian emphasis on processes of social conflict tends to get elaborated in these terms. Piaget's account is taken to mean that, during collaboration, things that are said by one participant (challenges, denials, assertions, etc.) can serve to precipitate useful cognitive restructuring in that individual's partner. Such talk is, thereby, a 'stimulus' for cognitive change.

As discussed earlier in this chapter, another analysis of collaborative talk stresses the value of simply articulating one's thoughts. In this model, an individual will benefit from entering into a problem-solving situation that prompts participants to make their ideas explicit. Again, the social structure of the encounter facilitates cognitive change in the individual. In this case, we might say that the individual's own talk is the stimulus for change: utterances are elicited by the situation and thereby (may) prompt cognitive restructuring.

My problem with accepting this kind of analysis is its implication that all that collaborators are ever doing is generating a corpus of discrete conversational events. Researchers have then to determine what circumstances of joint activity are potent in influencing the composition of this corpus. They must determine what circumstances facilitate the production of utterances with those properties that post-tests reveal are predictive of a desired performance. Yet what collaborators are actually doing may often go beyond this. What is said by them at any given moment may gain its potency not just from its immediate pragmatic content (assertion, challenge, hypothesis or whatever). A given utterance may be important for its contribution to the construction of a more sustained socially shared framework of interpretation – some form of understanding that is common and that is recognised by the participants as being held in common.

This is a conception that I wish to take up and illustrate in the next chapter. It invites us to view the process of collaborating as involving a discursive achievement: the extended construction of some degree of mutual knowledge. Then, analysis of collaborations in these terms requires us to go beyond the categorisation of individual utterances. Instead, the talk would be approached as discourse: organised and evolving in time. How we understand particular contributions should pay some respect to the context of common understanding that that they are helping create in this way.

Of course, such shared understanding is a species of mental context comparable with that discussed in the last chapter: there it was identified with what teachers typically have to do through their classroom talk. I am anxious to encourage an approach to what happens in peer interactions that learns from this analysis of more instructional forms of conversational interaction. In both cases, the achievement of new understandings rests upon the possibility for adopting an intersubjective attitude (Davidson, 1992).

I believe this has been recognised by some commentators on this topic. However, I am concerned that the insight should not be assimilated to a more traditional form of psychological analysis. This is the reason for my suggesting above that we might be wary of the concept of 'skill' as directing the way in which we thought about intersubjective achievements. I shall conclude this chapter by identifying what this line of tempting thinking involves and how my own reference to intersubjectivity differs from it.

An appeal to intersubjective processes might enter at the point where we consider why effective talk occurs within some collaborating groups and not within others; or why it appears at some stage of childhood development but not earlier. A natural move to make when contemplating such issues is to refer to psychological attributes of the participating individuals themselves. Some notion of differential interactive *skill*, for example, might be cited to account for individual variation in collaborative success or variation associated with the age of participants. Thus, Brownell and Carriger (1991) have analysed events within collaborative encounters from such a developmental point of view. They stress changes within individuals that mediate the impacts of these occasions:

> As they get older, children become better able to comprehend the behavior and intentions of another, as well as better able to affect the other's behavior and to communicate about their own behavior and desires. We are additionally led to conclude, then, that age-related social and cognitive skills contributing to peer collaborations influence what and how children learn from these collaborations. (p. 381)

A similar orientation is apparent in a review by Tomasello, Kruger and Ratner (1993): achievements within collaborative learning are associated with developmental advances in children's 'social-cognitive abilities'. In these interpretations, the success of peer interaction as a setting for learning is linked to skills and competences brought to the collaborative arena by particular individuals, or by children at particular stages of development.

My own view is that it is very helpful to make links of the kind that these commentators are exploring. Thus, students of collaborative learning gain from having their attention drawn to research concerning children's growing interest in the mental life of other people (i.e. children's theories of mind as reviewed in, for example, Astington et al., 1988, or Dunn, 1988). It is helpful to recognise that what children are inclined to do in the situations studied by theory-of-mind research is very relevant to what they do when solving problems with peers. Moreover, it is quite proper to explore age differences and socio-emotional variation as it might bear on the success of collaborative problem-solving. So, we do wish to develop an interesting association between children's varying understanding of mental states in others and their potential for collaborative learning. I am less happy that the way forward is to conceptualise as if it were socio-cognitive skill in this domain. Something is changing among and within individuals, but reifying it in this way may distract us from really understanding the nature of that change. Perhaps this is the very move that is naturally encouraged by theoretical traditions that still keep cognition and social context distinct.

For example, it may be suggested (see Tomasello *et al.*, 1993) that achievements in certain collaborative contexts become possible for 6–7-year-olds because this is the age at which children acquire a certain understanding of mental life in others ('second order mental states', to be precise, see Perner, 1991). A useful correlation is thereby noted. However, such state-like characteristics of individuals tend to carry too much causal responsibility in our explanations, perhaps leaving us too complacent that our account has solved a problem. In the present example, we might ask: what should be explored further now that this link between collaboration and theories of mind has been noticed?

The answer in this case, I suggest, is that we should investigate the social processes whereby children's growing awareness of mental states is mobilised into the particular service of organised problem-solving. The idea here would be that such intersubjectivity emerges at an early age, reflecting something basic to human nature (Trevarthan, 1988). Through participation in cultural activities it is deployed for new purposes of interaction. So, the earliest understandings of other minds may be fostered in very contained, domestic social settings (Dunn, 1988). However, children will then usually come into contact with culturally organised pressures of a powerful kind; for example, pressures that force these new understandings to embrace coordinated activity around schooled kinds of problems: to embrace collaborative learning in fact. So, if intersubjectivity does become a resource to support collaboration, it is because the conventions, rituals, institutions and goals of organised social life arrange that it should do so. This is the phenomenon we need to understand. Teachers and others need to understand how best to mobilise an intersubjective attitude towards the particular purposes of joint problem-solving.

A point that I wish to make here is that our natural focus on individuals (and their social or cognitive attributes) tends to distract us from pursuing research agendas of the kind sketched above. Individualistic accounts furnish one way of talking about our observations. That way tends to deal in a currency of self-contained, central psychological characteristics of individual actors. It is not suggested here that this language is simply wrong and that some definitive experiment might show this. The question is whether these concepts furnish the most productive way of systematising what we have observed.

CONCLUDING COMMENTS

In this chapter, I have reviewed a background of research that concerns collaborative learning. This literature reveals a number of important findings. First, group work is commonplace within the organisation of early education and generally prized throughout formal schooling. Second, ethnographies of actual classroom life indicate that it is hard for young pupils to sustain joint investigative talk within these structures. Third, controlled studies of collaborative problem-solving indicate that pupils often learn more from these socially organised tasks than they do from tasks tackled in solitary working arrangements. Finally, studies correlating collaborative strategies with post-test achievements suggest the importance of a number of interactional variables – particularly, experiences of publicly articulating one's reasoning, experiences of conflict and experiences with the co-construction of problem-solving resources.

I have also reviewed here material suggesting that computers may be one potent setting for the support of collaborative work. This is of special interest, given the findings that such work is not inherently easy to cultivate in classrooms. However, there are also hints that while this technology may sustain interactions that are lively, this does not necessarily mean that they are rich in a cognitive sense. Sheer energy is not all that we may wish to release when organising work in this way. The invitation is to research more closely the dynamic between social exchange and the structure of computer-based tasks. Yet, I have argued that the terms in which collaborative interactions typically have been analysed seem too narrow to provide real insights. It is hard to see that the coding and counting of collaborative utterances is going to shed genuinely new light on our concern for the exact place of computers in all this.

I believe that what is needed is a richer conceptual framework for characterising the psychological processes that are involved. Most research at present is concerned to characterise collaborative interactions in strongly individualistic vocabulary. Collaborations become arenas in which certain classes of event are likely to occur: in particular, certain classes of utterances. Their effects on individual participants are then to to be assessed in subsequent tests. A more socially grounded account is possible and, in particular, there are examples of analyses that have explored the theme of intersubjectivity in relation to collaborative discourse. I am still not satisfied that these are doing the job that is needed. Typically, such accounts set out in the right way. It is supposed that collaborating partners each have capacities to project mental states in the other and that this facilitates their 'co-construction' of problem solutions. However, what is analysed as co-constructed here turns out to be 'social' in only a rather narrow sense. It is the particular solution (hypothesis, prediction or whatever) that the shared problem demanded. The social character of that achievement is judged to reside in the partitioning of task responsibility and the subsequent coordination of individual insights. That is what the co-constructing attitude is said to support. I would like, in what follows, to pursue a further sense to this intersubjectivity.

What else could we mean by socially shared cognition? What other kind of object or outcome could be co-constructed within peer interaction? As hinted above, the position I wish to develop is another view of what must invariably be constructed within collaborative encounters: it is a view influenced by the idea of 'common knowledge' as described in the previous chapter. That was a concept developed to help clarify the nature of collaborations between teachers and pupils. However, it may also refer to socially shared cognition that exists between collaborating peers. I suggest that the success of such encounters will often reside in how effectively the participants co-construct a shared mental context for their problem-solving efforts. So, the cognitive object that gets created will be this common ground. It becomes a point of shared reference and a resource for prompting individual contributions to the problem-solving discourse.

The particular question of concern to us here is how educational technologies mediate in the creation of such socially shared cognition. More particularly, what are the characteristics of computer-based activities that might afford such successful achievements within peer interaction? I shall illustrate some possibilities in the next chapter.

Chapter 7

Collaborative interactions *at* computers

In this chapter, I shall describe certain computer-based interactions that I have observed within primary school classrooms. They all involve circumstances arranged for children to work together *at* this technology. By that, I mean circumstances in which small groups of children (as it happens, usually pairs of children) are organised to work on the same computer-based problem at the same time. As was indicated in the last chapter, such arrangements are typical of current practice within early education. Moreover, psychologists have been quite busy in finding ways to conceptualise the processes that commonly arise within such collaborative problem-solving. Again, discussion in the last chapter dwelt on the various theoretical distinctions that have been applied to learning organised in this way. What, therefore, remains to be done? What can inspire yet more classroom observations of peers working together at computers?

The arguments developed towards the end of the last chapter should suggest answers to these questions. I indicated there that prevailing preferences of theory and method have encouraged a narrow view of what is involved in collaborative learning. I believe the conceptual vocabulary typically used to characterise this form of joint activity requires rethinking – particularly if we are aiming to develop a socially grounded theory of cognition. I would like to check my own efforts at such rethinking against a corpus of material from authentic class-based collaborations. Hence the presentation of such material in this chapter.

However, consolidating a socio-cultural perspective on cognition is only part of my purpose in the present book. I am also concerned with locating new technology as a particular context in which the collaborative nature of learning might get organised. So, towards the end of Chapter 4, I considered what might be the best way to invest research and development effort in the interests of advancing new educational technology: what strategy offers the greatest promise for effectively integrating computers into educational practice? I have since been arguing for a channelling of research effort in one particular direction. That direction leads towards a greater appreciation of how the technology can enter into educational practice to mediate new forms of *collaborative* interactions and, thereby support learning. I am encouraging the question: 'How can new technology *resource* the collaborative nature of education?' So, the empirical material reported in the present chapter will frame computers as a distinctive basis for supporting the particular case of learning within peer interaction. My argument will not be that the technology is qualitatively different from other resources that might be deployed within collaborative work: I shall not argue that it is unique in this respect. However, it does seem to me to have characteristics that are particularly powerful for collaborators, and we should be sensitive to what they are.

In short, there is a reciprocity here that allows what I am describing in this chapter to be viewed from either of two angles. On the one hand, I am suggesting that attention to peer interactions around computers is especially helpful for our efforts at conceptualising the nature of collaboration very generally. On the other hand, I am framing an account of collaborative interactions that has particular implications for how we might best design and deploy computers within classroom life.

My plan for this chapter is as follows. In the first section below, I shall sketch an account of collaborative problem-solving that focuses on the creation of shared understandings and the particular role of discourse in achieving this. I wish to argue that collaborations can be analysed as states of social engagement: occasions upon which some varying amount of effort is directed towards the creation of common ground. Then, in later sections of this chapter, empirical observations of young children working together at various computer-based tasks will be described. These observations will be analysed so as to allow the development of two themes: first, to illustrate that effective collaboration involves a discursive achievement, its analysis must go beyond the traditional technique of counting and cataloguing discrete utterances as they are recorded during peer interactions; second, to argue that accounts of collaboration should recognise that this state of social engagement is, inevitably, situated. It arises within particular contexts of problem-solving and we must seek to understand the constraints and opportunities that the structure of those particular contexts afford.

ON COLLABORATIVE DISCOURSE

The theoretical discussion within this section serves to preface observations of classroom joint activity that follow later. First, I am concerned with sharpening the sense in which we must view collaboration as a discursive achievement growing out of human intersubjective attitudes. The result should be a framework through which some particular observations of collaboration can be viewed.

Collaboration and shared understanding

At the end of the last chapter, I expressed an unease with the scope of concepts currently deployed to explain collaborative interactions. These concepts tend to represent the discourse of collaboration as comprising discrete utterances (or short exchanges) that have circumscribed effects on the cognitions of the individuals concerned: acting rather as 'stimuli' for cognitive change. In this spirit, it might be claimed that a collaborator could experience a cognitive restructuring because of *conflict* stimulated by something that their partner said. Or, it might be claimed that the pressure simply to articulate the logic of one's position stimulates greater reflective self-awareness. Such analyses of collaborative encounters see them as occasions that increase the probability of certain potent events occurring – certain social stimuli that provoke cognitive change in the participants. I do not deny that both experiences of conflict or opportunities to articulate a perspective should be part of our concern when studying collaborations. Yet this framework seems to provide a distorted account of what typically happens on these occasions, as if it misses something else significant that constitutes the experience of joint problem-solving. So, to stress conflict as important seems contrary to how we describe a lot of collaborative experience. It is often harmonious and constructive, not tense or confrontational, while to stress the articulation of ideas seems to make it a more passive, inward-looking experience than it often feels. Moreover, the conceptual focus of both approaches tends to be on the cognitive apparatus of collaborating individuals. So, accounts will refer to metacognitions or to the cognitive structures of individual collaborators; they are less likely to refer to a construction that is inherently interpersonal and that might be best conceptualised in social terms. Yet, this might be an approach that a more socio-cultural orientation should encourage.

In fact, the analysis of collaborative interactions has not been greatly extended by socio-cultural ideas although, as I indicated in the last chapter, the classically socio-cultural concept of 'internalisation' is one idea that has been applied in this context. In his account of the internalising of exchanges within a zone of proximal development, Vygotsky refers tellingly to the 'more capable' peer as a possible partner for internalisation. Again, this seems to distort our casual experience of what collaboration often involves: it creates a constraint we may not always wish to accommodate. Although the internalisation of moves socially produced with an expert may often be a part of what can happen, collaborations are experiences that typically involve quite equitable levels of expertise among the participants. The socio-cultural appeal to processes of internalisation seems to imply that peer interaction must be approached as something less symmetrical: a kind of peer tutoring.

How, then, might a socio-cultural perspective contribute further towards conceptualising the way that peers interact when they solve problems together? This perspective should help define the cognitive gains that arise from collaborating as being gains that are socially constituted. It should help identify a cognitive resource that is firmly located within the dynamic of the social interaction. My suggestion here is that, in part, this might entail recognising the importance of a human capacity for intersubjectivity, and how it allows the possibility of creating structures of shared understanding.

There is certainly something missing from accounts of collaboration that dwell only upon inventories of utterances – coded and categorised for their pragmatic content. What, in particular, is not captured is any sense of participants having used language to construct an achievement of shared knowledge. Typically, analyses of these interactions do not attend to how far collaborators are mutually aware of such common ground, and how they draw upon it as a discursive resource. There is one compelling reason for thinking this is an important way to frame an account of what happens during collaborative relationships: it reflects the way participants in such relationships typically describe their experience when asked. Schrage (1990) has assembled the reflections of a number of eminent collaborators as they discuss the way they work – scientists, journalists, composers and so on. They do not put their emphasis on the potential for productive conflict, or the opportunity to clarify ideas through articulating them publicly. Such notions may be recognised as important products of what goes on, but what successful collaborators are more likely to refer to is the feeling of working towards constructing an object of joint understanding – something that comes to exist between them as a cognitive resource.

I am suggesting that students of educational interactions among peers need to come to grips with this conception. Evidently, it suggests a close link to ideas already reviewed in this book, particularly those ideas concerned with collaborations developed in the course of teacher–learner interactions. It naturally suggests the idea of common knowledge as discussed in Chapter 5. Edwards and Mercer locate this concept at the focal point of instructional activity: 'We can say that the process of education, in so far as it succeeds is largely the establishment of these shared mental "contexts", joint understandings between teacher and children, which enable them to engage together in educational discourse' (1987, p. 69). Yet little has been done to identify the creation of shared mental contexts as an achievement arising within other learning interactions – exchanges other than those that take place between pupils and their teachers. In particular, this idea has barely been considered as a way of analysing the more symmetrical relationships that arise among classroom peers who are engaged in joint problem-solving.

Collaborating and conversing

At present, there is very little analysis of collaborative interaction that adopts this perspective. Only Roschelle and Teasley appear to have worked within a framework of the kind that I am describing here (Roschelle, 1992; Teasley and Roschelle, 1993). They have studied pairs of high-school students working on a computer-based simulation of principles from Newtonian mechanics. Their inclination, like my own, is to characterise what transpires in terms of the partners creating a 'joint problem space'. However, I believe there are several respects in which an analysis of this kind needs to be developed further. One is simple, but is necessary to any approach stressing the situated nature of these events: the process of creating joint problem spaces needs to be understood as something governed by the structure that particular tasks present to collaborators. In other words, these achievements need to be studied with attention to how they are distinctively organised within the constraints of particular contexts for acting. My assumption is that the nature of what is socially constructed will vary in interesting ways that reflect the structure of different problem tasks. I believe that this process is also likely to vary developmentally – reflecting different histories of experience at joint problem-solving. Finally, it is likely to vary in ways that are associated with the overall setting in which joint activity is sustained – the implication of this last point being that we need to respect the ecology within which learners' joint problem-solving is typically organised: in particular, the community structure of classrooms. The observations described later in this chapter represent small steps taken in these directions.

Roschelle and Teasley's work comes closest to the description of collaborations made later in this chapter. Yet I do not wish to apply exactly the same analytic distinctions that they chose for systematising their own observations of collaborative discourse. It is worth elaborating on this difference, as it highlights some important features of the conceptual framework within which this research is located. Teasley and Roschelle (1993) note that conversation is the process whereby their collaborators construct a joint problem space. Thus it may seem natural to borrow from research traditions that are most centrally concerned with the analysis of conversations. Accordingly, Teasley and Roschelle organise their documentation of collaborative talk around the participants' techniques for: (1) introducing and accepting new knowledge, (2) monitoring ongoing activity for divergence of meaning and (3) repairing such divergences. These are distinctions that are commonplace within conversational analysis (Clark and Schaefer, 1989; Schegloff, 1991). However, adopting this analysis raises the question of how we should regard collaboration as a distinct species of human communication – how it is subsumed within that more general category of communication we simply refer to as 'conversation'. This, in turn, raises methodological questions; in particular, whether the distinctions we make in analysing conversational cohesion are adequate to capture the special forms of cohesion that might exist in conversations that are also dubbed 'collaborations'.

It is certainly the case that conversational analysts have always been deeply concerned with the 'grounding' that must go on during talk (Clark and Brennan, 1991; Clark and Schaefer, 1989). This is a concern, like our present one, with shared understanding. Thus one problem that has been studied is how talkers ensure that the demonstrative references they make in their conversation are specified well enough to be understood. This can be managed by relying on conversational grounding. So, if a speaker makes some demonstrative reference but their referent is actually ambiguous, then listeners may cope with this by selecting a referent item on the basis of its 'salience with respect to common ground' (Clark, Schreuder and Buttrick, 1983, p. 296). That is, they select a referent item that is the most striking option; what defines 'striking-ness' is an item's relationship to the intimate context of mutual knowledge that has been constructed between these particular conversants.

More generally, participants in conversation must each do work to establish the mutual belief that what they have said is adequately understood at that moment. So analysts of routine talk have exposed important social-interactive techniques that are deployed to help with this purpose: things that get done to construct the grounding from which a sense of conversational *cohesion* can arise. Now, I have been claiming here that the analysis of collaborations (as a particular kind of interaction) must also concern itself with the dynamics of such shared understanding. This might imply that analysts of conversation will have already done the research that is necessary to clarify how collaborative learning is managed. Or it might imply that at least they already have available exactly the set of conceptual distinctions we need. But although there is a way in which it is appropriate to claim that conversations are occasions that demand collaboration (Clark and Wilkes-Gibbs, 1986), there are also good reasons to respect a common-sense distinction here. Certainly, there is no line that cleanly separates out from 'conversation' a class of interaction that we will invariably label as '*a* collaboration' – a particular kind of conversation. Yet there is undoubtably a contrast to be respected and, because of this, we might suppose that the analysis of collaborations requires additional distinctions to those that we make in analysing routine conversation. I believe this is so and will indicate why, before proceeding to study some particular examples of collaborative talk.

Clark and Wilkes-Gibbs (1986) invoke a *principle of mutual responsibility* to express the sense in which all successful conversations must depend upon collaboration:

> The participants in a conversation try to establish, roughly by the initiation of each new contribution, the mutual belief that the listeners have understood what the speaker meant in the last utterance to a criterion sufficient for current purposes. (p. 33)

They illustrate the exercise of this principle with a corpus of conversational fragments in which speakers and listeners are seen to be comfortably operating rich repertoires of interactive behaviour: speakers' verbal 'presentations' are routinely met with various verbal and non-verbal strategies of 'acceptance' by their listeners. The progress and repair of any conversation is thus made possible through mutual commitment to these collaborative processes. Moreover, the overall structure of such exchanges are said to be managed in ways that minimise joint effort: this amounts to the so-called *principle of least collaborative effort* (Clarke and Wilkes-Gibbs, 1986, p. 26). Speakers will experience pressures to respect the natural pace of conversation, as well as pressures that arise from inherent uncertainty as to their listener's existing knowledge. Such considerations may encourage speakers to limit the effort they invest in making their reference evident (while awaiting confirming feedback). We might say that a capacity for intersubjective understanding allows them to pursue such an optimisation strategy.

Yet, the principle of mutual responsibility, as stated above, invites further research. For example, studies are needed to clarify what boundaries serve to define the notion of a 'contribution' within conversations. This issue has already been explored (Clark and Schaefer, 1989). However, we also need to investigate more of what is meant by claiming a listener has understood something to 'a criterion sufficient for current purposes'. This relates directly to our present interest in collaborative learning. For Clark and Schaefer's phrase reminds us that conversations are indeed conceived for various purposes, and that the particular ways in which mutual responsibility is managed in talk will surely reflect this variety. So, if our 'current purpose' is to have a casual conversation, then the talk may be allowed to weave and turn in ways that indicate we have set this criterion to be quite low. On such occasions, the 'effort' invested in establishing mutual understanding may be limited; we may let uncertainties of reference slip past; we may tolerate inconsistency; we may encourage fluctuations of topic. However, if our 'current purpose' is to *collaborate* – in the narrower, everyday sense of that purpose – then our criterion may be set rather high. What, in particular, we do and say to meet that criterion may be quite distinctive.

Thus, any analysis of collaborative learning or problem-solving will need to go beyond considering only the local management of the conversational exchange. In particular, the issue of 'accepting' a conversational contribution (Clark and Schaefer, 1989) becomes more problematic: it may not simply amount to understanding what the speaker intends, but deciding whether it is an acceptable contribution to a particular common ground that is 'working' in favour of the collaborative purpose. So, our situation in considering peer-based collaborations must be very much like that confronting Edwards and Mercer in their analysis of classroom talk. There also, the participants are motivated by the particular purpose of creating a consensus of understanding. The established framework of distinctions for analysing conversational cohesion will certainly apply – for conversation is surely involved – but that framework will not do the analytic work that we are most interested in getting done. That is, it will offer few pointers to how mutual understanding is actively pursued: how it is refined for the specific purposes of individuals committed to a 'collaborative' enterprise. The joint interest of collaborators in creating a common product, or in reaching a consensus, requires that they make a point of attending to this development of mutual understanding. It must be a more central concern of their conversation. In any event, the context of their effort (the materials and resources, etc.) will doubtless constrain how they may proceed.

Proposed analysis of collaborations

I suggest two distinctive features that should be part of any analysis of interactions that have been termed 'collaborative'. One is an attempt to capture both the form and extent of a heightened *concern* amongst collaborators for the construction of common ground. For, in collaborative interactions, this purpose is brought into the foreground of conversation. Thus, the sense of individuals 'collaborating' (as opposed to 'merely' conversing) will arise the more they explicitly reflect upon the creation of this shared understanding. Analysis of collaborative interactions, therefore, needs to identify the ways in which this patent concern of the participants is managed: an analysis needs to document the explicit investment participants make. In other words, a traditional conversational analysis – dwelling only on local monitoring, divergence and repair – may miss the active investment collaborators make in an organised convergence.

Another feature that I believe should be characteristic of any analysis of collaborations is a sensitivity to how the structure of the underlying shared task affords different opportunities for creating this shared understanding. The social business of creating common ground may be more or less constrained or facilitated in different contexts for interaction. An analysis of what gets done must attend to this dynamic – perhaps, in educational contexts, with a view to invigorating it. An important theme in my analysis here is that shared understanding may be created to a greater or lesser degree, depending on constraints naturally characteristic of different settings for interaction.

This raises the question of how situations may be more or less effective for collaboration. Moreover, allowing the idea that there may be such a variation reminds us that simply putting learners together for the purposes of joint activity may not necessarily be the same as prompting them to collaborate. Curiously, most empirical studies of peer interaction and learning seem to work with just such an operational definition of collaboration. To be sure, they may allow that different occasions can be more or less 'successful', but this judgement is typically derived from quantitative profiles summarising various categories of collaborative action. An occasion that is effective then becomes one that is rich in favoured categories of talk – conflict, hypothesising, challenging or whatever. I am suggesting that we take variation in the quality of interaction (as 'collaboration') more seriously. It may be helpful to regard collaboration as involving a state of social engagement: one that is more or less active on any given occasion. It is not something simply to be taken for granted whenever joint activity is organised; rather, it is a state of affairs to be diagnosed from the partners' detectable commitment to constructing a shared understanding.

In summary, I am arguing that empirical analyses of collaborative learning should, first, focus upon participants' access to a shared understanding, including their explicit concern for elaborating such mutual knowledge. Second, analysis should clarify how particular contexts of problem-solving provide distinctive resources to promote this interactive achievement. I am not concerned with fixing the precise semantics of 'collaboration' and, in particular, do not wish to dictate an exclusive field of use for this term. However, I believe it is helpful to distinguish a state of social engagement that is defined in terms of a striving after shared understanding; and helpful to consider how such striving is effectively resourced.

In what follows, I shall describe observations of primary school children jointly working at each of four computer-based tasks. The interactions were all organised to blend into normal classroom routine and the target activities were selected from among the range of those that were familiar and in use within the schools. I hope that by looking at rather different contexts, some sense of the variety of possible shared understandings will emerge. That is, we shall be able to reflect upon the following processes: how different task environments afford distinctively different kinds of common ground; how such mutual knowledge is negotiated and elaborated (beyond the simple 'repairs' of conversational analysis); and how the resource of common ground is invoked as a platform for the construction of new moves forward.

SOME GENERAL POINTS OF METHOD

The general procedure behind the observations reported below was as follows. Schools were chosen where the use of computers was commonplace and where pupils typically worked at them in pairs or small groups. For the present observations, same-sex pairs of pupils were formed by class teachers and they worked in the normal area where a computer was kept. This was usually a quiet corner of the classroom or a reading area between classes.

Making observations in settings such as these is, I believe, inherently problematic. I am sure that the details of what children say and do on these occasions is highly sensitive to the social context – including the presence and identity of a research observer. For such reasons, clear empirical relationships found in one study may defy replication following seemingly trivial changes to features of the working arrangement observed (Littleton, Light, Joiner, Messer and Barnes, 1992). Indeed, this volatility might discourage any great faith in parametric studies aimed at isolating 'variables' relevant to predicting collaborative performance. Practitioners may find more use for broader characterisations of such performance: these may then be drawn upon to guide the situated judgements that they have to make within specific circumstances of teaching and learning.

However, the particular significance of these considerations here is the practical one of refining an observational method. If, as researchers, we wish to understand the organisation of activity within classrooms, then our intrusions should disrupt the social order of classrooms as little as possible. In the present case, the activities chosen were familiar, being drawn from local resources and curricula; the occasions of observation were those upon which pupils would naturally be working in the manner arranged; the style of observation was discreet although the act of observing was declared, explained and its confidentiality was discussed. All material reported here was drawn from sessions towards the end of school years, during which the researcher would have become a familiar figure. The observer was not himself present during the sessions that were used for research purposes: these were video recorded in an open but unobtrusive manner. Such recording was itself familiar and, with respect to the material discussed here, on only two occasions did pupils make explicit reference to being recorded (in each case, playful comments made during the story-composing activity). The adventure simulation task (Granny's Garden) described below was not video recorded with a camera. In this case, the observer was present in the background making field notes, while the pupils' talk and the screen output signal from their computer were both directed to videotape.

Pupil conversations were transcribed and annotated by reference to video recordings and notes. Where sections of these transcripts are reproduced here, the following conventions of presentation are adopted: the speech is printed towards the left of the page while any contextualising notes are printed towards the right. All cases involve pairs of children and they are arbitrarily identified as 'A' and 'B'. A numeral in front of these letters distinguishes a particular pair – as, say, in the partnership 5A and 5B. The following symbols are used within the discourse:

/	Short but distinct pause
//	Pause of more than 2 seconds
.	Gap of irrelevant talk between two segments
.	
.	
[	Point of overlap between speakers' talk, the overlapping
	utterance being printed directly beneath
?	Question intonation
Italic type	Emphatic speech
s-p-e-l-l	Letters of a word spoken out in turn

TASK 1: ANAGRAM

Six pairs of girls and six pairs of boys aged between 7 and 8 were observed using a program called Anagram. It was selected from a package of basic literacy programs widely distributed to primary schools at the time. Its apparent purpose was to encourage pupils' attention to the structure of simple words by presenting targets of jumbled letters ('anagrams') and offering the opportunity to type the correct word underneath each successive target. The program presents sixteen such problems. A display of the current set of possible words was available at the top of the screen for a pupil to refer to; upon each correct solution, that word was removed from the display. Thus, the activity can be summarised as a recurring sequence of the kind: computer presents target – pupil types response – target removed from display (once correct entry typed).

Given the typical routine of having children work in pairs, what form of joint activity is encouraged by a simple structure such as that described above? I do not wish to become entangled in discussing whether the children observed can be said to have 'collaborated', or not. Exactly what we take this term to refer to should not be prescribed here. However, the simplicity of the present task should help us to make sharper distinctions that may prove broadly helpful for characterising joint activity. So, in describing reactions to this task, I wish to identify a certain range of interactions that an activity such as this seems naturally to afford. Later, I shall be able to contrast such interactions with others that can be observed at computer-based tasks having different characteristics. My view is that a relatively rich, articulated interaction could be sustained by an activity of the general kind described in this section – but that the present structure is not at all effective. We might even worry that the activity it supports can sometimes be counter-productive.

Of the twelve pairs of children observed, only two of these partnerships acted in a way that seemed to invite confident use of the term 'collaborate'. The basis for such an intuitive judgement lies in convergent action and attention: children apparently oriented towards the same thing. Barring only four trials during which minor distractions arose for one member of each partnership, the two pairs I have mentioned reliably attended jointly to the target word, and they also scanned the display of options together. However, the same could be said for most of the other pairs, most of the time. So, sustained attention to the computer screen does not, in itself, set apart the pairs we sense as collaborating more. The single factor that makes a striking difference to the atmosphere apparent within these various pairings is the sense in which the activity is being constructed as a sequence of *turns*. For ten of the pairs, respecting this structure was a significant issue. That is, they maintained a rigid pattern of alternating responsibility for disposing of the current target word.

In three of the pairs there were periodic exchanges in which the partners argued about disruptions of their natural activity sequence. In one case, a brief physical struggle arose. In the example below, one of the girls completes a word that her partner has started (perhaps getting impatient, or thinking her partner has become distracted):

3A: It's my go.   (A moves to take over typing as B
                                                           pauses mid-word, searching for key)
3B: No it's not.
3A: I know where the O is.   (B is now looking for this key)
3B: Got it // that's right.   (B completes last letter of target)
3A: I have another go 'cos you had two
        of my goes.
3B: I haven't.
3A: Yes you did // my go now.
3B: No / you just had a go.
3A: You had two of my goes.
3B: I didn't.
3A: You did.   (A starts typing answer to new tar-
                                                           get)

There are two interpretations of this concern to sustain turn-taking that I wish to confront. The first is the possibility that these pairs are collaborating effectively: they just happen to assign the (trivial) business of keying-in to a structure of turns. The second is the possibility that turn-taking is a strategy to minimise each individual's involvement in a task that might not be very enjoyable. I shall appeal to detail of the interaction to indicate that neither of these interpretations can be readily accepted.

One route towards tackling these questions lies in consideration of what participants do during the periods when it is not their turn. In this, there was some variation. With four of the ten turn-taking pairs, both partners would occasionally call out the correct answer during the other's turn and while the other was still looking for that word. In two further pairs this happened, but only one partner acted this way. Certainly, on the criteria of shared attention we must say that, most of the time, they are focused on the same material: attending to the same target. However, the 'collaborative attitude' of these pairs remains different from that of the two pairs I identified at the outset as working together effectively. With the turn-taking pairs, it does not appear that the alternating structure merely reflects some incidental need to ensure equitable participation in the keying-in (nothing here, or at other times, indicates that this is seen as a particularly interesting thing to do). In other words, these pairs are ensuring they get alternate 'goes'. With these pairs, where one partner declares the answer during the other's control of the keyboard this seems more in a spirit of being assertive, or disruptive – rather than supportive. These contributions may be made from a withdrawn seating posture, and not accompanied with active screen-pointing to identify the item. It is not unusual for the keying-in partner to object to such contributions:

7A:	It's 'like'.	(Identifying the correct answer)
7B:	Alright / I *know*.	(B keys in l-i-k-e)
7A:	My turn.	

By contrast, the two pairs that give a sense of collaborating do not display this tension. They are more likely to be in a similar posture towards the computer. When one of them is keying in a word, if the other verbally recites the letters, then it is in pace with their partner's typing. They are likely to monitor reactions in the other, or talk in the first person plural:

8A:	There's 'come' // shall I put in 'come'?	(A pointing to this word)
8B:	Yes / go on.	

.

.

8B: What happens if we get one wrong?

This is not a kind of harmony that is so apparent in the turn-taking pairs. However, the difference has to be carefully made. This is not a difference based simply upon some pupils enjoying the task and others not. Certainly, if some pupils were not properly engaged, then turn-taking might arise as a way of limiting their enforced participation. In fact, all pairs were quite animated; they seemed to like the exercise and individuals sustained their attention when not taking their own turns. However, in some cases (just the two collaborating pairs), a common pattern of attention organised by this task is complemented by an active effort among the partners at coordination. These efforts are subtle and intermittent (given the simple nature of the task) but, in small ways, they serve to monitor and consolidate a shared understanding. So, a demonstrative gesture may accompany a spoken identification of the correct target – to ensure mutual recognition. Guesses are sometimes put to partners before steps are taken to key them in – to ensure endorsement of the choice. Control of the keyboard is casually managed – because keyboard disputes are typically symptomatic of the 'having of goes' and (in the case of these collaborators) *both* partners are effectively having one extended, coordinated 'go'.

Thus, a small number of pairs convey a sense of collaborating. The talk and action of these partners is more concerned to monitor, update and confirm the topics of a potentially shared understanding. Of course, this is a very modest, undifferentiated task. However, that may make it a good case to reason from. For it is just on the borderline of what naturally might support collaboration. Among an arbitrary population of pairings, it promotes a variety of interactions – and some of those patterns of interacting we may want to say are more 'collaborative' than others. In considering these interactions, I would like to sum up what is taking place in terms of an investment that is, or is not, made in defining mutual objects of attention. The case where there is limited investment of this kind requires us to think about why the effort may be avoided. The case where it does occur requires us to think about characterising what is happening in terms of a certain kind of discursive achievement.

On resisting shared reference

There are three particular observations that are suggested by some children's resistance to adopting a collaborative attitude around this task. First, the interactions clearly remind us that setting up the social arrangements for a collaboration by no means ensures that it will ensue – in the sense of a striving for constructing shared reference. The participants were motivated, they all conversed in a lively manner and the task got completed with good humour. Thus, coordinating the seating and thereby facilitating the talk does not, alone, ensure a coordination of the understandings. Second, these interactions direct our attention to variations in task design. Part of the shortfall in our expectations for joint activity must be traced to structural characteristics of the activity itself. This issue is important to address in relation to computer-based tasks because they are so interactive. Their design may incorporate distinct contingencies involving events presented to users and those users' various inputs in return. In the present case, the rigid pattern of self-contained word problems may be particularly well-matched to the emerging strategy of turn-taking.

However, this response to the contingencies of the program is not inevitable. We have seen in the present case that not all pairs of children adopted it. This variation might be researched in a number of ways – including reference to the history of interaction enjoyed by particular pairs, or to similarities in ability at the underlying task and so on. However, one factor that might be found to moderate whether such contingencies evoke turn-taking strategies or not is the culture of classrooms or schools.

This is my third point suggested by the present observations: the existence of collaboration has to be understood against a background of an institutional culture. This is highlighted by other behaviour in some of these pairs not yet mentioned. In two pairs, one of the partners in each case periodically announced during a 'go' being taken by the other that they knew the current answer. Their reluctance to actually say the word might be taken as reluctance to spoil the other's turn. However, the manner of these intrusions did not suggest this. They were announcements made with a more satisfied tone: as if declaring a certain superiority. The link to institutional life arises if we suppose that this kind of interaction reflects a broader pressure to work independently: to become conscious of one's own understandings as personal achievements.

A related point occurs more forcefully in the interactive style of two further pairs. In these cases, there was an underlying impression that one partner was quicker and more fluent at this task than the other. Indeed, on their own turns, they each reliably found the targets more quickly. In one of these pairs, this more able individual conspicuously sighed and heaved on several of the protracted turns taken by the other, while in the other pair, on several trials the more able partner adopted a distinct (and weary) tutoring tone:

11A: Ummm	(Looking for key 'b')
11B: It's somewhere near the h //.	(Giving a hint)
Don't forget they're capitals.	(Screen letters are lower-case, B assumes A is confused by upper-case keyboard)

Through these examples, I am implying that a pervasive theme within classroom culture may be the idea that, as a pupil, one is generally supposed to solve problems independently. Computer-based joint activities do not necessarily subvert this (although I shall argue later that they have a special *potential* for doing so). The present style of software may even present a task structure that reinforces the idea of competitive and parallel (rather than collaborative) joint activity. In that respect it may be counter-productive: providing a different experience of joint work than that which teachers may be intending to cultivate.

There is a further concealed feature in this kind of task/culture/pairing blend that invites investigation. Where a pattern of discrete problems prompts a turn-taking strategy and where the turn-takers display asymmetry of ability, then the superiority of one individual relative to the other may become visible and potent – to them both. This is not just a product of the sequential organisation of the problems. In addition, these tasks often put a premium on speed of response and they furnish feedback of a clear and evaluative kind. In terms of events reported here, we may only speculate. However, the slower individuals within the asymmetrical pairs described above may have their attention rather explicitly drawn to this discrepancy in ability. Of course, it is true that there are many ways in which such differences are signalled within classroom life. However, the direct and relentless feedback characteristic of these computer activities may prompt a more vivid interpersonal comparison – especially when received in the setting of a close collaboration. Moreover, there is much evidence to suggest that pupils of this age are able and inclined to judge their own intellectual abilities in terms that are relative to their classroom peers (Ruble, 1988). Some activities may furnish particularly striking data that can feed such comparisons.

In the example of this simple language program, we have seen that the nature of the social interactions supported can reflect structural features within the contingencies of the program and can reflect aspects of classroom culture. There is certainly a sense in which we may want to say that – despite comparable levels of animated talk – children may or may not collaborate when we put them together in this way. What it is that is 'resisted' within these turn-dominated interactions is the construction of mutual understanding through shared reference. In the example of Anagram, the potential for working this way is present, but limited. I turn next to summarise what is constructed by those pairs for whom that potential is, in some part, realised – and why it is necessarily 'limited'.

On cultivating shared reference

As I have already remarked, there is a straightforward sense in which all these children have a shared object of attention. They are all attentive to the computer display that presents the problem: they all remain on-task in this sense, even when they do adopt a turn-taking framework of coordination. However, orientation to the same display defines a very limited sense of sharing reference. It may be what leads us to claim that they remain *task*-engaged; it does not provide an adequate basis for claiming that they are *socially* engaged around that task. What is required beyond this joint reference to an external display is a *distribution* of attention across it. In particular, in the case of the simple anagram program, what is required is, first, a process of search (for the target solution) then followed by a process of keying-in the response (itself comprising a sequence of letter searches). Thus the collaborative achievement of shared reference depends upon an active concern for coordination. There must be a concern to coordinate reference with respect to the sequencing of attention and action that the task contingencies invite.

So, in some of these anagram pairs, there is an apparent investment in ensuring mutual recognition and identification of the target word:

8B: It's 'one' isn't it?   (This is the target word)
8A: Yeah / right / o-n-e.

That is, language (and perhaps gesture) is deployed to monitor that both partners are attending to the same task feature at a particular moment. A similar kind of investment may be evident during the point where a chosen word is being typed in:

2A: OK / l // i // k // e.   (Each letter is spoken by A as soon
                                                    as preceding one is typed in by B)

2B: Right // what's this?   (Start of new trial)

This effort towards sustaining shared reference is brought into relief by those turn-taking children who, during their partner's turn, boast that they know the answer but are not going to say it. This is a strategy that certainly reveals a momentarily shared frame of external reference, but it also reveals a (considered) failure to coordinate socially the distribution of attention within that frame. These partners are doing the opposite of 'collaborating' in this sense: they are withholding the communicative contributions that could ensure a fusion of reference at a particular moment – and which might create a platform for subsequent joint action.

This notion of a 'platform' – a shared position from which partners investigate further – is one that I wish to elaborate. In the case of Anagram, the opportunities for collaborators to construct such a resource are very modest. They amount to no more than a possibility of creating a mutuality of reference and attention that can govern the next response in a cycle of action. There is barely any sense in which that mutuality can influence subsequent decisions or can otherwise accumulate to the advantage of the collaborators. If mutuality were to accumulate in the course of joint problem-solving, then it could be characterised as an internal, private object of shared understanding. In the next set of classroom observations, I consider a task that seems particularly rich in its potential for conjuring up this sort of shared object. That task is the requirement for partners to compose a story at a word processor.

TASK 2: COMPOSING A STORY

Computer programs of the kind described above are less popular now than they were at the time my observations were made. Currently, there is more enthusiasm for generic, tool-like software. Text processing, in particular, is an activity that surveys suggest is now widespread within primary education (Becker, 1991). Moreover, the notion that children might use a word processor as a collaborative activity has attracted particular attention. In fact, in Britain, collaborative writing is now a National Curriculum attainment target (DES, 1989a). Practitioner accounts suggest that collaborative text processing works well (e.g. Crawford, 1988), while more formal observational research suggests an advantage for organising joint writing with computers over its organisation with more traditional media (Davies, 1989a, b; Dickenson, 1986).

Children's early exploration of narrative structure is typically a socially or-ganised affair (McNamee, 1979), so it is natural to invite pupils to compose stories as a collaborative task. Moreover, the computer furnishes a setting for them that is well adapted to joint activity. The product of writing is made equally visible to the partners; there is no stigma attached to poor handwriting; any editing that might emerge from discussion can be comfortably executed. In fact, the example is a good illustration of how a technology restructures an activity such as to afford richer possibilities of collaboration (Daiute, 1985). A socio-cultural attitude towards educational research will find the opportunities implied in such a situation espe-cially attractive to study.

Here, I shall report observations of five pairs of 10-year-old children composing a story together at their classroom computer (an Acorn BBC Master, equipped with the word processor 'WordWise'). The procedure was one with which pupils were familiar. Their teacher supplied them with a one-sentence idea which they were required to use as a trigger for their own story. In this case the sentence began: 'The bus driver forced on his brakes, but it was too late...'

The children worked at this task for a single session of around an hour – in the longer cases incorporating a morning break period. Details of this session length, the amount of talk within it, and the length of the stories written are given in Table 7.1. It is clear that there was a lot of talk and that it was fairly evenly distributed within all the pairs: the dominance of the most talkative partner varying across pairs from 57 per cent to 68 per cent. One option for systematising this talk would be to code and categorise the individual utterances. This might generate profiles for each pair describing, for example, how many assertions, questions, challenges, endorsing remarks (and so on) were made within the session. As stated before, I believe this is a style of analysis that has some value but it is not the one that will be adopted here. I am more concerned to capture how far partners are socially 'engaged', in

Table 7.1 Descriptive statistics for stories

Pair	Utterances Pupil A	Pupil B	Session length	Median sentence duration	Median sentence length
1	394	278	50'	2'50"	13
2	406	245	45'	6'30"	21
3	460	278	58'	3'30"	11
4	876	498	81'	4'10"	10
5	679	315	88'	3'20"	10

the sense of being involved with constructing and exploiting shared objects of understanding. This requires examining the talk as coherent discourse – rather than categories of discrete verbal utterances.

How would a shared object of understanding be defined in the context of composing a story? It might be identified with the text the children write: the collection of sentences on their computer screen. This is certainly available as an external, shared point of reference. So it might function rather as the display in the Anagram program described above: an object over which children might choose to coordinate the distribution of their attention. However, the children make surprisingly little explicit reference to this product. In only two pairs was there any re-reading of text further back than the current sentence. And in these cases (two and three examples respectively), this seemed to function only as a loose search for reminders. It was typically read in a quiet, distracted voice (as if awaiting some inspiration) and there was no explicit discussion of the material reviewed in this way. While it may have triggered the next suggestion that a partner made, such suggestions were not discussed with any reference to text that had been read. On the other hand, there was quite frequent re-reading of individual sentences during mid-composition (on average, 38 per cent of sentences got some review of this kind). However, the purpose seemed to be more one of choosing the best syntax, rather than furnishing an occasion for developing content.

Yet the transcripts of these interactions do often convey a strong sense of children focusing on a shared object known to them both. So their discussion seems economical in a way that must be presupposing of particular mutual knowledge. Moreover, as with the Anagram task, there is also an impression of some pairs being more engaged in this way than others. What I believe creates this impression is an underlying variability in how much investment is put into negotiating the narrative detail. In other words, for some pairs, the talk is serving to create a relatively articulated (if implicit) object available for shared reference. This covert object comprises an accumulation of mutual understanding that underpins the sentences selected for the final story.

We may be alerted to the fact that there is such an investment 'behind' the story by looking at particulars in the product itself. Here are a few sentences from the beginning of two of them:

One day in September a coach tour was about to begin on Junction road. It was going to London for three days with the new Zebra coaches...

One day we were taking some old ladies to London. They wanted to see Max Bygraves. In one and a quarter hours they stopped to have some grub. They had a cup of coffee and a glass of wine (very romantic)...

The elements of this story have their own history. Some of it is to be linked with very generally shared cultural experience, while some of it is more intimately linked to local knowledge. 'Junction Road', 'Zebra Coaches', 'Max Bygraves' and 'old ladies going to London' are all highly evocative – that is, they promote distinctive narrative possibilities. Moreover, in these cases at least, such elements have arisen from discursive processes in which their significance is mutually established and agreed. Junction Road is a familiar route near these pupils' school; here are the authors making a commitment to this as one story ingredient and, in doing so, recognising its narrative potential:

1B: You could put / like we were going
along // what road?

1A: Oak Tree Road / Oak*wood* Road //.   (Fictional roads?)
Say we were going along *Junction*
Road.

1B: Junction / yeah.

1A: Go on / make it Junction then the
lollipop lady can fall in.   (Traffic control person)

1B: Alright.

1A: They were going along Junction   (Reciting possible format for B to
Road.   type in)

A similar process is illustrated in the following discussion from another pair. Here they are concerned to establish characterisation within the story. In terms of the way the narrative develops, their discussion and decisions firm up the shared idea of a day trip involving fun-loving old ladies:

5A: Where could we be taking them? //
      To London?
5B: To Scarborough.
5A: I know / think of a really old pop star
      what grannies would like.
5B: I know / Max Bygraves.
5A: Who's he?
5B: That man who's on *Family Fortunes*
      // says he can sing.
5A: What about that man // oh forgot
      what he is called now.
5B: Alvin Stardust.
5A: I know / Russ Abbott // 'cos old
      ladies would like him.
5B: Oh no / he can't sing.
5A: I know but he's funny.
5B: I know // don't put Russ Abbott.   (Privately, has selected earlier By-
                                           graves; this gets typed in)

At later points in the discussion of what to write, it is quite common for the consequences of earlier understandings to work through as, for example, those established in the extract above. They surface as an influence on current planning. For example:

5A: They sang Old King Cole.
5B: We won't want any pop songs / 'cos
  ·   they're old ladies.
5A: I know.
5B: Think of one of Alvin Stardust's   (A sings)
      songs. // What's that called?

In the following extract, an existing, already negotiated context is invoked to support an interpretation of what could happen once the bus had fallen down a deep hole in the road.

1A: Suddenly we heard a scream // the   (Making suggestions for typing)
      Lollipop Lady had fallen down. //
      No / we all looked up.
1B: We wouldn't see anything except the
      roof.

1A: There wouldn't be a roof / it didn't
      cave in on top of us.
1B: Were we on the top deck or the bot-
      tom deck?
1A: The top // but we stuck our head out
      the window and looked up. //
      Right / so we stuck our head out.   (Starts typing)

Characteristically, what gets agreed as the text to input conceals a body of mutual understanding created in the talk preceding this moment of typing ('it didn't cave in on top of us'). While further narrative detail is agreed on the spot, in order to make sense of the current proposal ('Were we on the top deck or the bottom?').

The process of negotiating a shared understanding is made all the more visible by the children's sentence-by-sentence composition. There is very little explicit long-term planning. Each development in the story is worked out at the start of each new sentence – although, as noted above, care is taken to ensure that new developments cohere with what has gone before. There are only a few cases of a new sentence being launched without some advance declaration by the author for their partner to register. (The few exceptions concern Pair 4, one of whom becomes impatient to finish the story in order that he can start something else he is wanting to do.) Exactly what happens at these points of composition reveals something of the collaborative process in each case – as defined in terms of a concern for constructing mutual knowledge.

So far, I have raised the idea of a common object of understanding that is actively created within these pupils' collaborative discourse. I have also illustrated how investment in this process results in the construction of a platform: a position from which further composition might economically proceed. Given this framework, we should next turn to considering how the creation of such a platform is actually managed through structures of talking. I shall explore this theme under three headings below. The first identifies some of the particular discursive strategies employed to refine shared narrative knowledge that is genuinely mutual. Pair 5 are chosen to illustrate this theme as they seem the most strikingly committed to getting this mutuality right. Other pairs illustrate different themes that surface within the constructive process, and these are covered under two further headings below. In particular, I consider the possibility of conflicting goal structures among partners; and also the notion of differential ownership, as this might arise in relation to shared knowledge.

Working to create shared knowledge

Pair 5 displayed the most active investment in negotiating and refining the understandings behind their written narrative. Each sentence was reliably preceded by some exchange that established the next set of options in the story – although further negotiation would also develop once the writing of a sentence had got started. On no occasion did a member of this pair start typing a sentence without declaring what they intended to write. It was also rare for a partner not to react to these proposals: only two of the sixteen sentences written were begun without some verbal exchange around the proposed content – and in each of these cases discussion started shortly after a few words had been typed. In fact, the general impression created by most pairs was one of composing to the following pattern: at each new sentence, one partner would announce an idea; this was either endorsed or discussed until a final form of words was typed. Often this amounted to no more than a phrase, so that a further period of announce-and-discuss would arise in mid-sentence. In either case, it was also common for minor editorial suggestions to be made during the typing of what had been agreed.

The pervasive tendency to declare text before it was typed conveyed an impression of partners recognising the joint nature of the task. However, it is from discussion around those declarations that we get an impression of a richer *collaborative* engagement. For it is there that shared understanding gets defined and is allowed to accumulate. The simplest reaction to a partner's narrative idea is to endorse it – either implicitly by silence (rare), or by some form of explicit agreement. Other reactions become forms of elaboration or challenge. So, the simplest way in which a declared idea for writing becomes elaborated is through what we might term 'associative elaboration'. In such cases, the idea becomes a prompt for a partner to generate a modification by means of some natural semantic association.

5A: We could be taking // it could be a
       school trip / or an old ladies' outing...
5B: Yeah / a grannies' party.
5A: Right // one day ...   (Starts typing this)
.
.
.
5B: They had a cup of coffee
5A: And a glass of water
5B: And a glass of wine // and some wine.   (Writes this)

In the first exchange, a substitution for a proposed idea was generated (grannies' party); in the second, the elaboration took the form of an extension to the original proposal (*and* a glass of water) which is then itself substituted (wine). There is no reasoning invoked to justify the changes, but the associations create a continuity across the partners' contributions. This suggests a concern to converge upon the same object of shared understanding; the acceptance of elaborations serving to sustain the construction of a mutuality.

At other times, contributions were challenged rather than elaborated. However, if partners were still working to sustain shared reference, then we would expect to find these challenges accompanied by commentary that makes some sense of rejecting the idea in question.

5B: Where could we take them to?
5A: I know, Scarborough.
5B: Whitby.
5A: No.
5B: That's too far away for them isn't it.
5A: I know / sunny Spain.
5B: You wouldn't get to Spain on a bus I
     don't think.

The Scarborough/Whitby exchange is an associative elaboration (both towns being seaside resorts in Northern England). Whitby received the stark challenge 'No'. Interestingly, this prompted a self-reviewing response from the original proposer: the rejection was rationalised in terms of the place being 'too far away'. In this way, some possible tension may have been avoided. The next suggestion (possibly frivolous) was also rejected, this time with the listener furnishing a reviewing comment that makes some sense of denying the speaker's suggestion.

Responsibilities for challenging a proposal and then reviewing the basis for a challenge can be the reverse of what is normally expected in argument. In the example below, the challenge came from the author of the proposal ('hang on a minute...') while the reviewing commentary came from the listener who found reasons for persisting with their partner's original idea:

5A: We stopped to have our lunch   (Proposal for text)
5B: And then had a little walk / hang on
     a minute some of the old ladies
     couldn't have a walk / some of them
     would be on wheelchairs.
5A: No 'cos they would be on walking
     wheels.
5B: Walking wheels?
5A: No / like crutches.   (Matter seems to be settled by this)

In a traditional analysis of such talk, 5B's self-challenge ('hang on a minute...') might be coded as an utterance with a particular pragmatic content: perhaps some species of articulating one's own reasoning. Such a coding might then increment 5B's standing (or the standing of the pair) on a researcher's summary statement of their interaction. There is some value in this traditional analysis, but it fails to address how such collaborative talk is effectively occasioned. It fails to reveal how the talk arises from participation in a set of particular circumstances. The talk itself is surely unexceptional: we can be sure children deploy the rhetoric of challenging, reviewing, reflecting and so on, as they argue in the playground. The interesting question concerns how this rhetoric becomes mobilised to support a schooled task – and, moreover, why it becomes vigorously mobilised within some pairs but less so in others. Here I am suggesting that the focus of our approach to such questions should be on the nature of an evolving shared understanding and then on a given partnership's varying commitment to investing in this. The dialogue above illustrates how reasoning (in this case, about narrative) may be motivated by a concern for respecting and contributing to a jointly constructed cognitive object – the context, events and characterisations that lie behind and inspire a written story. So, the same concern motivates my final example of discursive effort clearly visible in these interactions.

Joint thinking of the kind promoted here will often take the form of an exchange in which there is a convergence upon a solution, but not by challenging and re-casting some initial suggestion in the manner illustrated above. In these further cases, the reasoning is more of a 'calculation'. The participants are seeking to refine a suitable status or 'value' for some story ingredient that they are toying with. In the following case, the focus is literally quantitative in this sense:

5B:	So it took two hours.	(Planning to write)
5A:	It didn't because	
	[	
5B:	it took two hours to get *half* way there.	(Thinks A has misunderstood)
5A:	It doesn't because my Nanna lives in London.	
5B:	And how long does it take to get all the way?	
5A:	About five hours / right?	
5B:	So it'll have to be two and a half.	
5A:	But we stopped for half hour lunch.	
5B:	Did you // so that means it was four and a half hours // so that would be two and a quarter hours.	(Writes this value)

5A's contributions here have some force: she has been to London and claims to remember the journey time. More often, these kind of convergences cannot be directed by reference to such external authority. The criteria for decisions will be looser – more what is amusing, or interesting, or consistent with the narrative so far. Of course, in such cases, the argument may well turn on their common access to a shared understanding about that narrative. Such circumstances suggest that joint story-writing is both a good and a poor model system for considering schooled collaborations. It is good because it does involve creating a form of joint understanding that is particularly vivid. For the achievement is continuous with something familiar in more playful experiences – fantasy-making in general. It is a poor model system because conflicts over what should be said next are not so easily resolved. There can often be no legislating reference to some logic inherent in the joint knowledge that has been created: a conflict cannot necessarily be resolved by appealing to some privileged way for developing an existing narrative.

Pair 5 seemed successful as collaborators because they managed effectively the resource of such shared understanding. They freely entered into exchanges that served to enrich the detail of this common knowledge. Moreover, they used the resulting structure as a platform for their joint progress: they appealed to it in order to establish consistency and coherence for their ideas. In particular, this effort was realised in an equable manner. In the next section, I shall refer to dialogue from other pairs where the symmetry of making contributions was not so striking. This raises the issue of partners adopting differing responsibility for creating a structure of shared knowledge.

On owning shared knowledge

Pairs 1 and 3 also engaged in some of the constructive effort illustrated above for Pair 5. They were certainly as talkative and as task-oriented (in neither pair was there any reference to off-task concerns). Moreover, they were as concerned to declare, elaborate, challenge, review and calculate the content of a shared knowledge. Their talk exemplified the general processes that dealt with such things and which were illustrated in the last section. What was more characteristic of these pairs, however, was an asymmetry of responsibility for the content of that common knowledge.

In Pair 3, the first sentences were characterised by give and take of a kind that created for both partners a stake in the narrative:

3A:	We have to name like three important people.	(= central characters)
3B:	There were three *important* people going?	(= special characters?)
3A:	No / not like that / like *main* people.	(Disambiguates)
3B:	Like the bus driver's name // the bus driver was called Alex.	
3A:	No / put like there were three boys / yeah three girls like Vicki, Jean and Shelley.	
3B:	They were going because they won a tickey. [Tickey = local term for ticket]	
3A:	Yea / they could have won a competition.	

Here A is concerned to establish the idea that there are to be three principal characters and, then, who they should be. B's attempt to include the driver is denied in favour of focusing on three children. While B's later idea that these children had won the trip is then accepted. In constructing later sentences, however, B's contributions increasingly follow the fate of the bus driver example above. The extracts below are from sentences 3, 8 and 10 respectively:

3A: It had gone 32 miles when they had
     the first stop.
3B: When the bus broke down.
3A: When they had their first stop.
3B: Yeah.

.
.

.

3B: At a cafe.
3A: No / a restaurant // 'cos they wouldn't
     stop at a cafe they wouldn't all fit in.
.
.

.

3B: What did they eat?
3A: They had ...
3B: Egg.
3A: A three-course meal / including ...
3B: A cup of tea afterwards // not includ-
     ing VAT.
3A: No // including the drink.
3B: Including the drink of cocoa.   (A writes: 'Including the drink with
                                         it')

This final case is typical; all B's specific contributions (egg, tea, VAT, cocoa) fail
to get incorporated. Perhaps the general idea of drinking was hers, but that was
probably already implicit in A's 'meal including...'. For most of the sentences
composed by this pair, B's contributions were either acknowledged and rejected or
re-cast. Although often this might involve some sense-making by A, as in the
second of the three three extracts above.

   The interaction of Pair 1 was similarly asymmetrical, although the dynamic of
their exchange was different. B makes one suggestion early on that is taken up: in
the first sentence she proposed that the characters are on the bus because they are
'going to the pictures'. However, thereafter, although she remained engaged with
the writing and the composition, all the contributions originated from A. This is not
because A re-casts B's ideas (as in Pair 3 above) but because B makes very few
specific suggestions. Instead, she participated by querying all A's input. It is not
clear if this persistence occurs because A never gives ground to negotiate an option,
or whether B has adopted a sceptical attitude for some other reason of her own.

1A: We had already begun to fall down
     the hole.
1B: It wouldn't have been that deep /
     we'd soon hit the bottom.

1A: Not if it landed on a load of things.

.
.
.

1A: When we hit the bottom everyone
      began to panic.
1B: Not everybody would // the driver
      wouldn't.
1A: I would if I was him.

.
.

1A: When she got to the top / she pulled
      the rope down.
1B: This lollipop lady isn't going to do
      all these heroics.
1A: She would.
1B: Probably she'd bring down the food
      and somebody else would do the rest.
1A: No she'd go up and then throw a rope
      down to us / and hold it at the top.
1B: I don't think she'd have enough
      strength / this lollipop lady.

A (amicably) persisted in her suggestions, justifying them by appeal to the variety of possible motives and circumstances that a still-developing narrative can furnish. B also persisted in challenging most of these suggestions. The result is a sense of both partners oriented to shared knowledge but (as with Pair 3) a concern for ownership that leads one partner to take responsibility for most of the final content. In Pair 3, this is accepted harmoniously, while in Pair 1 the situation creates more of a tense atmosphere.

Evidently, for these pairs, there is a perfectly proper sense in which the knowledge base supporting their talk can be said to be 'shared'. It is known to both partners and it thus provides the necessary basis for new narrative ideas that either of them may propose. However, we also see with these pairs how it need not be 'shared' in the sense of co-constructed. While the talk of both partners may address a common object of reference, the form that object comes to take arises from contributions that are more the responsibility of one partner. I cannot pursue empirically the significance of this asymmetry; however, I believe it requires us to consider a feature of pupil collaborations that has been neglected by developmental psychologists. That feature is the *affective* dimension of this joint activity.

There is not enough relevant data to allow reasoning about the emotional tone of the interactions described here so far. For example, it is true that Pair 5 convey an exuberance that might be associated with their equitable investment in creating joint knowledge – an achievement that then can support them in story-telling. However, this observation is merely one of correlation: it is not clear whether effective co-construction is directly arousing in this way, or whether it is a mere correlate of something else that is. On the other hand, the idea surely resonates with our intuitions about successful collaborative thinking. Building a resource of mutually familiar understanding is often an emotionally engaging experience; perhaps because of a certain intimacy that it affords. The achievement allows us to communicate on a topic in a heavily presupposing way – something like what we do when reflecting more privately on the same topic. This observation suggests that *negative* affect could arise within these interactions. In particular, this might occur when collaboration requires that a partner must deploy shared understanding to which they have *not* been allowed to make a fair contribution. This might be the experience of partner B in Pair 1 described above.

In the interactions studied here, there is one further basis for a less than successful construction of shared knowledge. This concerns the motives that participants may have for engaging in the joint activity involved.

On the goals for shared knowledge

In this section I shall briefly refer to the interactions of Pairs 2 and 4. They also made a more modest investment in shared understanding but not for reasons of any asymmetry in the making of contributions. For these pairs, the achievement of mutual narrative understanding seemed a less important goal of the activity. Evidently this is a straightforward way in which collaborations may be less successful: the setting does not motivate the construction of mutual knowledge.

In the case of Pair 2, both partners contributed to the development of a story: that is, the constructions written can be traced about equally to each person's contribution. All of what was written was publicly declared before any typing started. However, these contributions were not refined and enriched within the talk. On only three occasions was there any challenge or elaboration of a proposal. In one case this was to maintain consistency with narrative events that had been established earlier. Much of the talk was about the mechanics of writing the story. Thus, 52 per cent of the dialogue concerned the keyboard, spelling, checking how much had been typed, or reciting words in synchrony with the typing. We cannot claim that these pupils were not engaged with the task (they talked continuously and rarely referred to off-task concerns) and we cannot claim that they did not each make contributions to the overall activity. However, their contributions were not oriented towards the construction of a social resource that might empower the story-telling. It is not reasonable to speculate here as to what their primary goal might have been. It seemed to be more related to the delivery of a product that was too narrowly defined – understood only in terms of being a certain length, grammatically accurate and so on. Thus, the creative possibilities of a collaborative orientation to shared understanding was poorly motivated in this pair.

In Pair 4, the shortfall had more to do with *competing* goal structures among the

participants. During the first half of the session, they developed shared understanding of the story much as Pair 5. However, partner B increasingly presses
contributions that would bring the story to a quicker end. At the start of the extracts
below, A refers to the fact that B is anxious to finish and do something else ('your
animal thing'):

4B: That can be the end // we got out of
      the hole.
4A: No / just because you want to do your
      animal thing.
4B: But what can we put?
4A: We can put we went down caves / we
      left the people in a safe cave.
4B: But we already got them out.

.
.
.

4B: We are not going to put them in caves
      // They are not dozey you know.
4A: No / we are going to put them
           [
4B: They could walk home or jump
           in the bus.
4A: We put them in a safe cave / right?
4B: That's going to make it a funny story.

The dialogue proceeds in the manner illustrated above. The challenges from B entail
alternatives, the effect of which seems to be to make the story come to a speedier
conclusion. Evidently, the prospects for creating a resource of shared knowledge
do depend upon both partners framing the goals of the exercise in similar terms.
Where this has not happened and where there is some incompatibility of the goals
that have been set (as here), then the experience of collaborating may be less
positive.

Summary comments on joint story composition

Compared to the Anagram task discussed earlier, composing a story involves a
more elaborate investment in creating common ground. The task provides a rich
opportunity to achieve some intimacy and scope of shared knowledge. One suggestion has been that this achievement is emotionally gratifying. However, we have
also considered obstacles to satisfactory building of shared knowledge, and they
may generate more negative experiences among the collaborators. For example,
some partners may work to claim greater ownership over the knowledge that is
shared. Others pairs may fail to end up working from a rich common knowledge,
because they differ in their understanding of the purposes driving their joint activity.

In all, the close consideration of these interactions highlights three important points. First, collaboration is clearly seen to involve an active concern for the construction of mutual understandings. The extent to which collaborators are engaged in this has been overlooked in more traditional psychological analyses. Second, the object of shared understanding that can emerge within a collaboration needs to be properly understood. For example, the case for a shared *narrative* understanding can be problematic because partners may have to deal with an uncertainty as to how a new narrative proposal is properly legitimised in reference to the existing structure. Third, there are various obstacles to the construction of shared understanding that is endorsed and respected by both partners. Such obstacles may be inevitable but they may also be more effectively anticipated with suitable attention to task design, task description, the clarification of purposes and, perhaps, social knowledge about the partners themselves.

The present account highlights the importance of collaboration as involving a concern for shared objects for reference. In Anagram, the screen display furnished such an object: an external stimulus that could serve to organise the distribution of partners' attention. In telling a story the shared object becomes something less visible – certainly something beyond the screen display. However, some caution is needed in pursuing an analysis of this sort. It might not be helpful to reify what it is that can get created within a collaborative interaction. It might not be helpful to cast this achievement in terms that inevitably suggest a slightly mysterious sort of 'object', suspended somewhere between the collaborators. Such language may be of some shorthand use – as long as it is not developed in too literal a spirit. It certainly helps keep in mind one important idea: that effective collaborators are able to coordinate the focus of their interest or attention – that they have available a distinctively shared point for reference in their deliberations. Perhaps this is why a metaphor is useful here. It helps us keep in mind some key feature of what we are trying to understand. That feature may offer helpful implications for how we organise research: in this case, towards clarifying the discursive management of joint attention. By the same token, Edwards and Mercer can usefully invoke a variant of their own on the basic metaphor:

> Overt messages, things actually said, are only a small part of the total communication. They are only the tips of icebergs, in which the great hidden mass beneath is essential to the nature of what is openly visible above the waterline. (1987, p. 160)

Perhaps 'icebergs' serve usefully to distract us from only the coding and counting of utterances. The metaphor encourages, instead, the framing of what is said at a particular moment in terms of a more extended discursive effort: a context that is not adequately specified in terms of events visible only at the moment of interaction. This is a helpful evocation.

Referring to 'objects' (including those of Arctic proportions) can, therefore, be productive. However, as observers, our access to what has been achieved remains located in whatever discourse and action we are able to witness. Analysis should not become preoccupied with abstracting from such events some independent cognitive 'object' of social origin. One way in which what is typically achieved during collaboration can be expressed more precisely is by incorporating reference to an essential mutuality. Partner A knows things relevant to the problem at hand and arising from previous collaborative action; A also knows that partner B knows that A knows these things; moreover, B knows that A knows that B knows them also.... and so on. Thus, what they have achieved is based upon the possibility of such intersubjective understanding. However, the achievement is still not an inventory of social actions to be comprehensively reproduced by researchers: talking of cognitive objects here does not take us that much further forward. We may make most progress if, as researchers, we concentrate our attention on how language and action is deployed (1) in the interests of elaborating and refining this common understanding and (2) in ways that take such understanding for granted and, thereby, help focus more precisely what gets done next.

TASK 3: ADVENTURE SOFTWARE

The first task (Anagram) described in this chapter illustrated a rather poor structure for collaboration. The program did not readily offer pupils a resource of mutual knowledge. It provided no opportunity for the *accumulation* of shared experience. If such an achievement was possible at all, it was through orchestrating joint attention towards the modest events that defined a particular anagram problem. However, the cycling pattern of *self-contained* trials provided no strong motive for such coordination and, instead, pupils often adopted an attitude of alternating 'goes'. In contrast, the story-telling of the task discussed above provided a more effective vehicle for this co-construction of understandings. The final achievement in this case is richer, but also more subtle. It is not some stimulus array located between the collaborators. The object of joint attention – the narrative knowledge – is something more private. Fortunately, pre-school children's experience with socio-dramatic play will equip them very well to coordinate their interests towards creating such a resource.

Yet, the familiarity and appeal of narrative formats does not mean that creating shared knowledge around a story is going to be unproblematic. Appropriating story-making to become an activity for the classroom requires the imposition of certain extra demands that might not arise in more playful arenas. In particular, there is a pressure for closure: a pressure on the story-writers to persist towards the production of a single object. Tension may then arise because of a looseness in the authority that any developing narrative can claim over the individual collaborators who are constructing it. So, if their individual contributions diverge, there may be no easy appeal to the *necessity* of a particular narrative route.

There is a popular category of early educational software that seems to exploit some of the potency of narrative understanding, while creating for decision-making a clearer source of authority: one that collaborators might productively refer to in their discussions. Such software uses the metaphor of an 'adventure'. Normally, this involves programming a problem-solving activity to be represented in some narrative format. Thus, pupils follow through a story, becoming participants by responding to various challenges or puzzles that are arranged to occur. Their responses may determine the course of the story, or their own fate within it. The example to be discussed here is the program 'Granny's Garden'. This has been an extremely popular activity within British primary schools (Bleach, 1986) and there are numerous accounts of classroom practice that claim the program can be a good stimulus for collaborative work (e.g. Farish, 1989; Hill and Browne, 1988). Pupils move though a sequence of text and graphics displays by making various keyboard responses. Sometimes these responses will be the answer to puzzles that have been posed in the current display. These puzzles usually involve reasoning or remembering in relation to events or objects in the story. This particular story entails searching for a number of royal children kidnapped and hidden by a wicked witch. The pupils' journey starts in Granny's Garden and goes through four distinct sections with their own motifs and themes. Each section concludes, it is hoped, with the discovery of one of the four missing children – or, where things go wrong, with the witch sending pupils back to the start of that section.

The same pupils who worked on the Anagram task (described earlier) were subjects for the observations made here. Twelve pairs of 7-year-old children used the program on five separate sessions. The final two of these sessions provided material for the analysis reported below. Their speech was preserved on a video recorder along with the corresponding computer screen displays. This talk was transcribed and annotated with material recorded by an observer present in the background of these sessions.

In carrying out such a task collaboratively, what possibilities exist for pupils to create shared knowledge, and how may it then be called upon to support collaborative reasoning? As claimed for the story-writers above, the knowledge that collaborators share within this activity goes beyond their joint access to the transient events portrayed on screen displays at a particular moment. It is knowledge that has accumulated during the course of coordinating activity towards such events, but over some period of time. It is narrative knowledge but, unlike that of the story-*writers*, it is less of the collaborators' own making. Yet, this knowledge is not imposed either: not to be defined merely in terms of the story designed by the programmer. In other words, a particular pair of pupils will know about their own circumscribed experiences of engaging with this story. They will know about particular decisions they themselves made in the narrative sequence; they will know about particular consequences and their reactions to them. Here are two pupils calling upon such shared knowledge:

3A: Where shall we go?   (Of four locations)
3B: The stairs?
3A: No / 'cos the snake, remember.
3B: We've never been in the backroom.   (An untried location)
3A: I know // if there's anything like you

have to pick up / we won't // in case
we get caught.

Certainly, there are constraints to what is understood; they arise from contingencies programmed in the adventure. However, there is also an open-endedness. These pupils have had a *particular* set of encounters with that narrative and, from such experience, they now share distinctive memories and concerns. In the example above, this is reflected in apprehensions they have about snakes appearing, and in projections they make that any objects accidentally encountered might be usefully avoided.

For purposes of appreciating more of where this joint knowledge was constructed, the talk of these pairs was separated according to its relation to the contingencies of the task. Distinct sections of talk were marked on the transcripts and, across the pairs, the mean percentage of the conversational investment at each point was noted. So, on the average, 19 per cent of talk was concerned with input matters (i.e. reading from the screen) and 14 per cent was concerned with output matters (keying-in responses); 6 per cent of talk made very general references to the activity or its execution (i.e. evaluative comments or comments not relevant to the current problem). The remainder were remarks about the current problem or the question currently posed (44 per cent of talk) and, finally, remarks about the outcome or consequences of decisions (17 per cent of talk).

Mutuality was most clearly created within the discourse making up these last two categories. For example, 'outcome' talk is particularly effective in establishing overlapping versions of the events comprising the adventure. There was a great deal of evaluative and emotive reaction in this talk. In the example below, the children are reacting to a character in the story who asks for the children's favourite food and then (invariably, it seems) comments that the food makes him sneeze:

9A: I know why he sneezes at every food
we mention.
9B: Why?
9A: 'Cos he sneezes wherever he is / he
sneezes whatever he's doing or
wherever he is.
9B: What if we put pepper so he really
would sneeze?

Their spontaneous commentary on the narrative serves to increment their joint understanding of events, contexts and characters. This is similarly illustrated in the further examples below:

10A: Here's the Raven coming.
10B: He's flying down to see what we are
up to.
2B: I don't like bees // they sting you.
2A: But this one is our friend.

2B: I know but

   [

2B: but this one is our friend.

4A: Hey // it looks like Brian from the
     Magic Roundabout.

In the above, Pair 10 are watching a bird that crosses their screen and who is introduced early in the adventure as a creature that will help them: the children's talk serves to personalise further their own participation in the story. Pair 2 are reacting to a bee who has appeared with the possible intention of helping them in relation to a particular problem. Again, they seem to be establishing their attitude to this character: locating him in relation to their joint engagement with the story. 4A is forging a particular link to a popular character known to them both through videotapes.

From encountering the narrative events, from developing an interpretative commentary about them, and from a history of deciding about how choices are to be made, these pairs will construct their distinctive version of the narrative. Moreover, it will be mutually understood: each member of a pair can project this understanding into their partner and exploit the mutual knowledge when they come to reason about decisions to be taken at any particular juncture in the adventure. This is very similar to the analysis of story composition offered earlier in this chapter. Except that, here, the format involves pre-established relationships and contingencies in the story and these carry a certain authority in terms of decisions that have to be made. This is particularly felt where children are re-tracing a section of the narrative (perhaps having been returned by the witch to an earlier starting point – by way of penalty). More simply, it will be felt where options for a current decision are constrained by what has most recently been done, and this will have to be jointly recalled:

6A: Where do we go now?

6B: Not the cupboard 'cos we been there   (Acts scared)
     // not some stairs / no way.

6A: Only got three left then // kitchen?

6B: If you want to.   (Not hopeful)

6A: No I think the witch is there // let's
     go upstairs / 'cos we got an apple
     remember.

6B: What will that do / because the
     snake's upstairs.

6A: And we throw the apple at it.

6B: And what will that do? // the witch
     will come won't it?

6A: Yeah.   (Sounds deflated)

If the children are to reason about the problem in the adventure, then part of what must be achieved is an agreement about what has already happened to them. So, as in the example above, the talk will sometimes be deployed in the service of a collective remembering (Middleton and Edwards, 1990). The above example also illustrates how *inferred* aspects of shared memory may inform the reasoning that takes place. Thus, the remark ''cos we got an apple' leaves a lot unstated. Partner A's assumption is that B knows that apples promise a kind of insurance because – from past experience that they have shared and know to have shared – throwing apples at threatening agents can get you out of trouble. (B, however, also recalls that the witch will sometimes appear on these occasions and successfully reminds A of this possibility as being more likely – at this point.)

There is a significant general point within that last example. If we study discourse in order to clarify that shared knowledge is in place and that it is informing the present solution of problems, then we face a curious difficulty. For, where there is a well-developed shared knowledge, an important consequence will be an economy in what does then need to be said. This collaborative achievement allows participants to assume that the context or background to their remarks is known; so they need say less. Thus our difficulty as observers is that this knowledge-building achievement must be traced by us more in terms of what is *not* said. This may be felt as an awkward challenge by researchers whose training encourages them to index the social purposes of talk by coding and counting distinctive kinds of utterances.

As an exercise in building and reasoning from shared knowledge, the adventure game format has a lot to recommend it. The appeal and accessibility of the narrative structure effectively motivates mutual engagement in the task. Moreover, the pre-set nature of the underlying adventure provides an external authority for evaluating the decisions that collaborators make. Under these circumstances, it seems less likely that asymmetries in the working arrangements will arise. The following passage is relevant to these observations. The children are deciding which of a number of foods they should throw, in order to tame a particular dragon:

5A: Oh / try chips.
5B: I don't think we've any chips left.
5A: We should have been counting. // We
      should have a piece of paper.
5B: We can't use chips.
5A: Try them / and see what happens.
5B: Well / it's your fault if we get caught
      you know.

The first person plural references indicate a strong degree of mutual engagement in the activity. Their problem with choosing chips indicates how much decision-making in this kind of activity relies upon fairly straightforward remembering: recalling either what happened on a previous occasion or what they have just done. In this sense, the activity is very limited – the underlying contingencies in the narrative are not programmed to vary between occasions of use. On the other hand, the extract above illustrates how reasoning in this framework can still sometimes be a potent experience: by encountering limits in their capacity to jointly remember events, these children reflect on the value of developing a strategic approach based upon pencil and paper. Finally, the extract illustrates that a fracturing of the collaboration can still occur. Where they are forced into making a sheer guess, the assertive partner faces it being 'your fault if we get caught'.

The Adventure format is recognised in early education as a structure that is engaging and that supports joint work. It illustrates an ingenious transformation of children's playful interest in narrative – borrowing it to support the organised presentation of schooled problems. I have indicated how this format allows pupils to create shared understandings; this can then serve as a resource for the management of joint reference during problem-solving. In the longer run, analyses such as this should contribute to refinements in the design of classroom materials (e.g. educational software) so as to make them more effective for collaborators. I will conclude with two observations relevant to that practical aim. The first concerns how we may go about further clarifying the nature of the joint knowledge arising in activities like Granny's Garden. The second concerns the recurring theme of managing asymmetry in the joint activity.

For any activity of the present kind, it will be important to evaluate the extent to which the potency of shared understandings depends upon their having been co-constructed. For example, it would be possible for two pupils first to use an Adventure program separately. They might then come together and reason in a lively and effective way, based upon inferences about what the other *ought* to know. A collaborator would naturally make assumptions about their partner's knowledge of this program – in the same manner that they would make assumptions about a vast array of worldly experience that a partner might have, some of which might be relevant to the current problem-solving. On the other hand, the dialogue recorded in this study displayed a good deal of more intimate reference. The partners would often refer to what happened last time *they* did something, or they would make idiosyncratic evaluative comments that could never be part of knowledge shared with a new partner. An interesting challenge for research will be to evaluate how important this more intimate sharing of experience is in sustaining an effective collaborative effort. Children working with the same partner across a series of problems may develop more flexible strategies and greater success than children working with a different partner at each occasion (Goldberg and Maccoby, 1965). Others studies suggest that partners can require several sessions to develop an effective problem-solving style (Forman and Cazden, 1985).

My second observation arising from this activity concerns how the structure of the program affords more or less equitable patterns of engagement. Asymmetries of this kind were less evident than in the other tasks described in this chapter. The fact that these were the same children who acted rather uncollaboratively on Anagram reminds us of how important those structural details are for determining the dynamic joint work. However, in seven of these twelve pairs there was a reliable (occurring on every session) asymmetry in the responsibility for reading text from the screen. Moreover, the dominance of screen reading correlated significantly (r = 0.80) with dominance in controlling the keyboard for moving the adventure sequence forward. Subsequent to the collaborative sessions described above, individual children were asked to work through the first part of the activity alone. The median time to move through each frame of the story was recorded and correlated with their dominance when collaborating. This was also significant (r = 0.68), such that the fast individual readers were those who tended to control the display during collaborations. In a very straightforward way, this relationship suggests how computer-based tasks may have structural features that constrain or facilitate certain patterns of joint activity around them. The framework of socio-cultural theorising tends to encourage analysing cognitive practices in terms of these affordances. What is needed is a more lively empirical interest in exploring them.

TASK 4: FACTOR SNAKE

The examples discussed above illustrate how various circumstances of collaboration present their own distinctive possibilities for the creation of shared knowledge. The goals of any given problem-solving task and the contingencies within it will structure a setting in terms of such possibilities. Thereby, they will permit a resource of mutual knowledge to be developed with more or less effectiveness. I am suggesting that the potency of any setting for the support of collaborative learning depends upon its potential in this sense. If partners are able to create a well-articulated object of shared reference, then they will have equipped themselves with a real platform for exploratory discussion. In studying such occasions, the significance of particular instances of rhetorical talk between collaborators needs to be analysed in respect of its relationship to this shared knowledge – and not just enumerated into a profile of utterance categories.

Given our interest here in new educational technology, the relevant questions must now concern how computer-based tasks can be best designed to resource this 'common knowledge-building' enterprise. I will conclude this chapter by reporting on development exercise of my own that was inspired by this concern. My aim was to take an existing program of modest effectiveness and refine it for the specific purpose of better supporting collaborative engagement. The program (Factor Snake) was described in some detail within Chapter 5. In that context, it served to illustrate the limitations of a computer-based experience that was not assimilated into the mainstream of teacher–class collaborative talk. In the present context, I am considering more its limitations in respect of supporting another form of collaborative exchange: that between pupils at the time that they are using the program.

The program could be regarded as an animated version of Dienes Blocks: these are familiar classroom materials for visually representing numbers as rectangular arrangements that illustrate their factor structure. For example, the number 12 could be represented as various matrices – 1×12, 2×6, 3×4, etc. (see Figure 5.1). The Factor Snake program represented a number by continually winding and unwinding (snake-like) a set of small squares: this sequence covered all the possible factor matrices for a given number. The speed of this animation was such as to make it difficult to count more than about seven squares in any given line. Guessing the value of larger numbers therefore depended on attention to the factor structure of a matrix. The pupils thereby executed some arithmetic calculations (e.g. $4 + 4 + 4$ or 3×4).

This program was used periodically across a school year in one particular top infant class (children aged between 6 and 7 years in their third year of schooling). The present observations were made towards the end of that year and involved two groups, each comprising ten pupils. Group 1 used the program in a standard format throughout. Group 2 did also, except on the final three sessions of the year, when these pupils were provided with an extra programmed resource (to be described below). Comparisons reported here between the groups are based upon the very last session of each, during which video recordings were made.

The standard format for the program was as follows. Children had to estimate a succession of values taken by this animated snake: we may call these efforts 'trials'. The set size for possible snake values was incremented on each new trial, thus making the task progressively more difficult. Correct estimates resulted in a screen-based score being increased by the value of the current snake target. Incorrect guesses resulted in feedback and a resetting of the score: target set size was also reset and a new sequence of trials initiated. Estimating involved using a mouse-driven screen pointer to select a number (from a screen bank showing 1–59) corresponding to the current snake target. During the year, the program had been set to deliver target numbers only in rectangular matrix form. For these final sessions, numbers were described by non-rectangular matrices. These, therefore, would be unfamiliar shapes; they demanded calculating a matrix value and adding the 'extra' number of squares appearing as an incomplete bottom row. In summary, children had to deploy their emerging knowledge of factors to make estimates of visually represented numbers that could not always be directly counted.

The extra resource provided for Group 2's final sessions might be called a 'workpad'. In relation to the building of shared knowledge, it was designed to provide an external support for such efforts. It was to be a tool towards which collaborators could direct their attention and action. By placing their pointer on a particular screen icon, a 4 cm square writable area appeared on the display. When the pointer was in this area, clicks on the mouse button caused one small fixed square to be drawn at that point; these squares were the same dimension as those making up the snake (that continued to wind and unwind at all times). Pressing again on a workpad square drawn in this way would erase it. The net effect is illustrated in Figure 7.1: it must be imagined that a pupil is aiming to make a (static) reproduction of one of the factor matrices that constitutes the current snake. Evidently, the construction of this replica requires the children to attend directly to the parameters of the target matrix.

Initial impressions from recording of the interactions suggested a noticeable difference between the groups. This is certainly reflected in the overall amount of

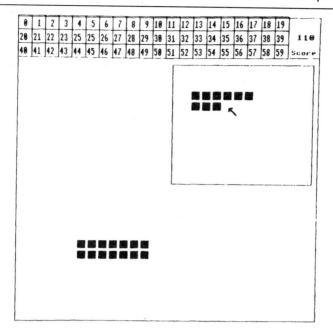

Figure 7.1 Screen display for a pupil in the process of constructing the number 12 using a mouse pointer in the workpad shown towards the top right. Meanwhile the number snake continues to move elsewhere in the screen and is currently completing the 6 × 2 cycle

talking. While Group 1 were quite lively, there was 30 per cent more talk among Group 2 children. However, this difference will not be our main interest: it might be expected, given that the workpad created more involved contingencies for Group 2 to talk more about. What is of greater interest is the effect of this feature on the *distribution* of talk within the pairings. Consideration of this returns us to the issue of turn-taking as discussed for Anagram above.

It might be thought that the structure of this task militated against a turn-taking pattern: if a partner adopting such a strategy gets a wrong estimate on their turn, then the scoring is terminated and the activity is restarted. This is to the disadvantage of both partners. Accordingly, these pupils did not organise their 'goes' on this basis. Instead most of them exchanged control of the mouse (and most of the estimating) as soon as an error had been made (and the score, therefore, reset). Under such a system, it is even in the interests of turn-taking partners *not* to be helpful: for they may want their partners to make an error and, thereby, effect the changeover. In reality, no collaboration was as ruthless as this analysis might imply. Perhaps the passive partner realised that the activity was bound, eventually, to go beyond the ability of the currently active member: goes rarely lasted longer than 5 minutes. In any case seven out of the ten Group 1 pairs showed concern with respecting turns; as did nine out of the ten in Group 2.

However, the atmosphere among Group 2 pairs was more in keeping with what we might expect from 'collaborators'. While there was this pervasive concern to distribute responsibility for controlling the computer, these children's discussion was far less suggestive of a rigid turn-taking regime. This difference between the groups was evaluated by considering more closely the final two runs of estimates made by each pair in each group. Only comments directed towards estimating a current target were considered (teasing 'I know it' kinds of comments were omitted). For each run, a partner's contribution can be expressed as a percentage of this total talk; then the mean of the higher figure taken from each of the two runs is an indication of the overall asymmetry of talking within a typical run of estimates. This was reliably lower for Group 2, indicating a more equitable distribution of constructive talk in the condition where a workpad was made available.

To the casual observer, this difference is visible in the form of a more sustained engagement by Group 2 members with *all* the successive problems they witness. In terms of the concepts of mutual understanding being developed in this chapter, this difference also may be expressed by claiming that Group 2 children had possession of a more potent resource for developing and exploiting shared reference. Talk within this group was typically of the form:

6A: Wait 'till it splits up.
6B: Is it twelve?
6A: Not quite sure.
6B: OK try it in the box.   (Means workpad)
6A: Three fours and a two // three fours
      and a two.
6B: It's fourteen / I think.
6A: Put another four.
6B: Hope this is right.
6A: Josie / just do three fours and a two.
6B: I don't like this.   (Nervous of making the estimate)
6A: We did better than this last time any-
      way.

The pair are using 'the box' to replicate one configuration of the number fourteen. Superficially, the impression is that they are working at it 'together' – certainly, the first person plural references were more typical of Group 2 pairings. In this case, the partners refer to the fact that they 'did better [score] than this last time [sequence of problems]': so they characterise the overall enterprise in a manner of joint responsibility, even though there remains a concern to alternate control of the mouse.

We may say that the workpad has furnished an external point for the fusing of partners' attention and their action. It is evidently a more compelling focal point than, say, the display presented by the program Anagram. This is because the pairs of children are able to manipulate the workpad and discuss interpretations of what happens when they do so. The device certainly serves to support shared reference by effectively coordinating the moment-to-moment actions of responding to the estimating problems. However, it may also support the building of a more subtle form of shared understanding: a mutuality that develops as each particular pair accumulates their own experience in using it. Consider again the fragment of discourse reproduced above. Once transcribed, such talk generally reads as rather sparse. Recurring comments of the form 'three fours and a two' only make real sense when encountered as situated in relation to the screen display. Yet, an interactive workpad may be particularly effective in making concrete and communicable just this kind of sparse representational talk about numbers. The collaborators have access to a (shared) device for supporting talk about structural features of a number. We may suppose that young children's problems in collaborating around the abstractions of mathematics are partly to do with their (normally) *not* having a concrete and shared resource for instantiating the abstract (Turkle and Papert, 1991; Wilenski, 1991). The workpad here serves to support collaboration by offering a concrete, shared reference for the 'manipulation' of numerical abstractions.

CONCLUDING COMMENTS

In introducing this discussion of collaborations *at* computers, I expressed doubts about the strategy that researchers have favoured for analysing such interactions. Analyses based only on coding, categorising and counting utterances fail to do justice to collaborative encounters as states of social engagement. My particular concern in this chapter has been to illustrate an approach to such encounters that would respect this dimension of engagement. In doing so, I have identified structures of shared reference as central to what participants may strive to achieve within joint problem-solving.

The nature of this mutual knowledge may be very different for different kinds of task. Sometimes it may be entirely represented by an external stimulus array (Anagram). In such a case, attention must be distributed across it in a coordinated fashion if there is to be productive collaboration. At other times, it may be expressed in an abstract structure that is largely created within conversation (the narrative of story-writers). We may suppose that all such objects of joint attention will be potent in so far as they readily afford manipulation and exploration by the collaborators. Narrative formats work for this purpose – up to a point – but other abstract joint knowledge may be more volatile. Thus, the trick to successfully supporting much collaborative work in classrooms may involve confronting pupils with abstract material within concrete and manipulable representational formats. Indeed, studies of group work practices in classrooms already hint that this is significant. For example, Bennett (1991) reviews studies that grapple with the correlates of effective group work. He finds that young pupils are selective about when they are reticent. They do not collaborate easily around abstract material such as that encountered in maths work; yet they are quite forthcoming in situations that offer more exploratory possibilities: 'It seems as if, given the opportunity to talk about *action*, the children will take it' (1991, p. 591, my emphasis). Often computers may turn out to be a special resource for creating such opportunities.

As was discussed in Chapter 3, the design of computers (their localised input and output devices) demands a narrow focusing of attention and action. Their interactivity also offers rich possibilities for exploratory manipulation. In particular, the powerful graphic capabilities of new technology can render abstract material manipulable in concrete formats. Emihovich and Miller (1988) have noted the advantage of such representations for integrating talk and activity among pupils and *teachers*. Here, we are considering that the same capabilities can be important in supporting shared reference among pupils themselves – as they collaborate. My own view is that computers can be especially effective in this arena. However, this is not the same as simply noting that computers seem to engage or animate pupils when they use them in their classrooms. The analyses in this chapter highlight an underlying variety in this engagement; the important challenge is to determine when and how the creation of shared understanding is embedded in these lively interactions.

The studies reported here were conceived to explore the dynamics of shared knowledge during collaborative computer work: how collaborators invested in its creation, what form that creation took, and how it could be exploited as a platform for reasoning. Thus, very little of the research has conformed to procedures of *experimentation*. Yet, there is room for experimental work in this area and such research would be welcome. There is a much cited study by Malone (1981) in which a compulsive computer game is dissected to determine which of its components serves to motivate users so effectively. The concern of this study is evidently with the solitary user. But, as reviewed earlier, much educational application of new technology arranges more peer-based practices of working. So, it may be useful to apply Malone's analytic approach to the study of software features relevant to social patterns of use. Thus, we may come to understand more about how structural details of educational software support or constrain the possibility of collaborative work. I am sure such research will have to dwell upon the special potential of this technology for cultivating rich frameworks of shared understanding.

Chapter 8

Collaborative interactions *around* and *through* computers

What is typically suggested by the phrase 'collaborative learning'? Probably the image of individuals gathered together at some materials that they are trying to understand. Naturally, from time to time such individuals may drift into solitary reflection. However, to qualify as a genuinely collaborative interaction, we normally expect there to be an underlying common focus for attention. In the last chapter, I illustrated an approach to analysing such occasions. The analysis highlighted varieties of social coordination that might be achieved at these focal points. It explored the natural concern of collaborators to construct common understandings and shared systems of reference. The analysis also evaluated problem-solving environments in terms of how far they promote or undermine such efforts. Computers may sometimes be effective environments for learning in this sense; sometimes they are not. However, the localised and interactive properties of this technology do suggest that it has a special potential for resourcing the social construction of shared knowledge.

Yet, our spontaneous image of collaborative learning as involving a gathering *at* problem-solving materials may be too narrow. As Landow has put it: 'I suspect that most people's conception of collaborative work takes the form of two or more scientists, songwriters or the like continually conferring as they pursue a project in the same place at the same time' (Landow, 1990, p. 407). This conception is too limiting. In the present chapter, I wish to discuss two broader configurations for the organisation of collaborative interactions. They both entail a reconsideration of what defines a shared problem-solving environment. In particular, I shall discuss circumstances in which collaborations may be dislocated in time – the participants do not need to be co-present. And I shall discuss circumstances in which the participants have less comprehensively overlapping concerns – where the problems that they are each addressing are more loosely coupled. These represent, respectively, central features of interacting 'through' computers and interacting 'around' them.

INTERACTING AROUND COMPUTERS

Of all the educational arrangements whereby new technology might support collaborative activity, this is the one that has attracted least research or commentary. Regretfully, I shall not report new empirical material here that helps to fill this gap. Instead, I shall identify the questions that need to be addressed and argue that they are interesting and worth research investment.

Exactly what belongs under this heading can be approached by reflecting very generally on the material nature of learning environments. For example, Walker-dine (1984) has drawn attention to the typical environment of a primary school classroom. Once one has stepped back from this familiar setting, it becomes possible to see a variety of constraints and supports that are literally built into it. Chairs and desks are oriented into characteristic patterns; walls are decorated with particular material; areas of the room are furnished in ways that afford defined possibilities for acting. In short, the very fabric of the place is designed to manage the business of learning according to distinctive ideas about good practice. It is typical of socio-cultural theorising to dwell upon the manner in which environments serve to mediate cognitive activity. As reviewed in Chapter 2, this theoretical tradition understands cognition in terms of a human subject located in relation to mediational means. In respect of schooling, this approach will consider how local mediational means can resource pupils with particular interpretative practices. Accordingly, one way socio-cultural theory should direct research on new technology is towards investigating options for integrating computers into this 'fabric' of the educational environment.

The present chapter addresses such a concern. This section of the chapter does so in relation to those configurations of computers *around* which social interaction may be organised. In clarifying the idea of such configurations, the above example of the classroom fabric is helpful. It raises a concern for the material setting of collaborative encounters, and it encourages us to think about them very broadly. The example leads us beyond considering only the familiar case of collaborating by intimately working together *at* some location or artefact. For the design of classrooms vividly illustrates the principle that material environments will constrain and facilitate a whole range of social interactions that can occur within them. So, the structure in some particular environment may influence all sorts of collaborative engagements that we may be party to. A sensitivity to such ecological considerations could guide decisions about the optimal deployment of new technology. For it should suggest a constant need to consider how any particular technology (say, computers) is best incorporated into some established material environment (say, a classroom), such that it becomes an effective component within the very fabric of working practice.

As I remarked at the outset, the issue of how to locate computers within the material environment of schools has not been closely studied. In practice, the choices may seem rather restricted. In primary schools there is still too little equipment. So, to ensure equable access and to encourage its use in all aspects of a curriculum, the preference has been to distribute computers evenly across classes. Where some mobility of equipment is possible, this policy may allow creating short-term pockets of extra access, such that a class might enjoy a more intensive period of computer activity. There has been very little attraction to the idea of concentrating computers in circumscribed work areas.

Secondary schools, on the other hand, have been more likely to configure computers into clusters that occupy distinct areas – 'computer rooms' perhaps. Sometimes these are networked and in some schools that network may run through more of the premises (I shall discuss these arrangements further in later sections of this chapter). It is the particular case of grouping together computers to support parallel patterns of working that interests me here. This configuration creates the possibility of what I term 'collaborative interactions *around* computers'.

To a casual observer, these areas can lead classrooms to look more like working environments from the world outside of school. In fact, it is more in relation to social practices in the workplace that these arrangements for new technology have attracted some research attention. Such interest has been partly inspired by new perspectives within the tradition of 'human–computer interaction' (HCI) research. These involve challenging the prevailing concern of HCI researchers to study the solitary user – as if the character of human–computer interaction could be understood independently of the broader cultural setting within which interactions get situated. These new perspectives are well captured in a seminal collection of papers edited by Norman and Draper (1986). This volume includes an essay by Bannon (1986) in which the issue of a computer system's communicative effectiveness is seen to involve consideration of the niche it occupies in a context of existing working practices. So, for example, the familiar problem of users failing to read computer application manuals is understood in terms of tensions with established and preferred modes of acquiring knowledge of this general kind. These, it is argued, are often socially organised: knowledge gets sought and exchanged with other people – on the fly. In many working environments there is a rich but informal pattern of casual communication that supports this. Studies of how new technology is implemented at work tend to stress a need to respect such structures (Huber, 1990; Olson and Lucas, 1982).

Many of us will recognise the force of this description from our own experience of working environments. It is less recognisable as a description of working patterns within classrooms. Sometimes this may be because classrooms impose some prohibition on such communication – identifying it as 'cheating' perhaps. However, sometimes a lack of such communication among students may reflect constraints inherent in the arrangements, materials and goals of working. There may be grounds for thinking that some configuration of computer systems can release a richer exchange in classroom settings. A project reported by Kafai and Harel (1991) raises this possibility.

The work of these researchers concerns the support of collaboration among pupils. However, they distinguish the scope of their own interest in processes of collaboration from that entailed in a more 'conventional' use of the term. The conventional understanding, they argue, will involve two or more individuals working towards a *single* product. In the situations documented by Kafai and Harel, there is a layer of joint activity that is superimposed upon individual work or conventional collaborations. What this amounts to is the existence of an umbrella goal that a whole class will be sharing; the goal is realised by individuals or small groups producing their own distinctive products in relation to that shared goal. In fact, the particular example Kafai and Harel describe is an 'Instructional Software Design Project' (ISDP): thus, the umbrella goal becomes 'to use LogoWriter [an authoring tool] to design a piece of software that teaches about fractions – but each of them also expresses his or her own ideas and produces his or her own project' (1991, p. 87). The style of working then encouraged is one that permits what they term 'Optional Collaboration' (choosing to work alone or with others) and 'Flexible Collaboration' (deciding with whom to work, when and for what purpose).

It is argued that the way in which computers are integrated into the classroom environment serves to make these working practices realistic and successful. In the ISDP project, the computers were organised into circles with a great deal of freedom of movement and obvious opportunities to take in what peers were doing. This arrangement seemed to support what the researchers termed 'collaboration through the air'. This corresponds to something like the patterns of exchange typical of the corridors and coffee rooms of many traditional workplaces. Kafai and Harel describe a number of case studies that identify children gaining from the loosely-knit communication that the setting readily affords.

Valuable though these observations are, I believe that more needs to be done to characterise the social dynamic that is involved. The nature of this alternative collaborative structure is defined above in terms of the existence of an umbrella goal. But this is hardly a distinctive feature: it may also characterise other routine circumstances arranged in conventional classrooms. Children are often working on such shared, overarching goals: they are, as a class, writing project descriptions, making maps and so on. Moreover, the open-plan character of many British schools does encourage some degree of lateral communication within a classroom. So, what must be clarified is how far the possibilities for creative, through-the-air collabor-ation are extended because of the particular properties of working around computers. I think it is likely that computers are a powerful context in this sense. Moreover, the source of their strength may lie in a referential anchoring capability: a capability of the very kind discussed in the last chapter in relation to more conventional collaborations.

This analysis assumes that the constraints on collaborating through the air arise from the 'air' normally being too thinly resourced: there are not usually enough available anchor points at which action and attention can be coordinated. Loose communication can often flourish in workplaces because the collaborators there are frequently drawing upon a richly articulated body of mutual knowledge. This is an inter-mental achievement; it will have developed over a long history of interconnected communications. School work is less likely to be easily grounded in this way. The immediate concerns of school work are less often situated within such intimate and evolving understandings. Instead, schools create problems that are more localised and less easily related to some prevailing and shared set of institutional purposes. However, where school problems are explored in the medium of new technology, then collaborators may be better provided with referential anchors for the development of their shared interests. For they will be pursuing their various goals with overlapping sets of tools; these tools will be visible and manipulable as a common point of reference; their mechanics will provide a sensible vocabulary that a pupil can use confidently with any collaborator who has had experience with the same resources.

In summary, I am not suggesting that configuring computers into classroom clusters is necessarily the ideal way to arrange them. There may be other institutional factors that dictate other possibilities. In particular, there is a valid concern that too rigid a separation of computers into their own rooms serves to identify them with a curiously dislocated and special class of activity (Chandler, 1992). Yet, however such organisational decisions are made they should include some sensitivity to the issue of how different working arrangements can afford different possibilities for collaboration. These possibilities are not confined to the case of small groups working *at* computers, as already discussed here. There is a level of community-based collaboration that can arise where class activities are more loosely coupled. Nevertheless, in both kinds of situations the technology may be serving to support collaboration by providing strong points of shared reference. A similar claim can be developed for the networking of computers – a strategy that is sometimes adopted as an alternative to the clustering discussed here. I shall turn to this strategy next.

INTERACTING THROUGH COMPUTERS: A UNIVERSITY COMMUNITY

The key issue introduced in the last chapter has arisen again. That issue concerns how we may resource the constructing of a shared object of understanding. In many circumstances recognition of this 'object' will arise from a common concern to make progress with some self-contained task (such as writing a story, or scoring high on a number puzzle). The activity takes place, together, at the site of the problem. However, in the configurations to be discussed in this section, the form of a shared understanding may sometimes be less tightly related to some such circumscribed problem. What it is that comes to be held in common – that becomes a source of shared reference – is more a set of broader intellectual practices. So, I shall be partly interested here in how new technology can mediate forms of activity that create *communities* of shared understanding. Understandings that are held in common need not be exclusively relevant to the short-term goals of working together on localised problems. There are circumstances where mutual knowledge provides a general underpinning relevant to a whole range of collaborative encounters: this arises in situations where people are held together in communities that share a common set of concerns – such as might sometimes arise within institutionalised education.

In this section, I intend to sketch the nature of network configurations in general and then consider the particular implications of networking for educational practice.

I shall pursue the educational theme by reporting an example of network-based innovation with which I have a close involvement: an initiative directed at an undergraduate population. This will enable me to make a number of points about collaborative structures mediated *through* computers. Some of these points I shall take up later to consider their significance for practices in the earlier years of education.

The nature and application of distributed computing

For a long time, the popular representation of computer use was that of a user occupied at a self-contained machine. This may still capture well enough the domestic experience of this technology. However, in institutional settings, it is increasingly likely that the user will be occupied at a machine that is less isolated: it is likely to have connections to other computers at other locations. Equipment that is linked together in this fashion is said to be networked. Local area networks (LANs) allow communication within the premises of some workplace. Wide area networking (WAN) involves links with geographically very remote computing systems. The original attraction of such connectivity was to permit a large number of individual computers (network stations) to gain shared access to a central resource of data (a file server). Quite simply, this centralisation offered a saving on the amount of computer hardware required for data storage. It also allowed central administration of those data facilities that members of an organisation might wish to share. However, the design of networks has become more sophisticated in recent years. The model of a central file server passively delivering data to connected stations as they request it is now a fairly primitive conception of networking. The modern concept of 'distributed computing' identifies a more dynamic environment. 'Servers' in such environments can themselves be very powerful. They can take responsibility for some of a user's computational needs – as well as delivering files that might be accessible to the computational resources of that user's own network station. This has led one company active in this area to adopt the commercial slogan: 'The network *is* the computer'. Certainly, at any moment, exactly where the computing is taking place can be well hidden from a typical user of a distributed computing network.

These configurations of computers might have evolved originally to achieve straightforward economies of resource. As such, they might have been seen as merely extending and optimising the computing power available to some community of solitary users. However, it has become clear that these arrangements have significant implications for patterns of coordination among those users themselves. A widely cited example is that of the ARPAnet – a pioneering US defence network, originally conceived to distribute computing power among the research community. It quickly became apparent that this network unexpectedly was supporting a great deal of interpersonal coordination. Researchers were finding their needs for collaborative contacts were being increasingly mediated by a person-to-person connectivity made possible by file transfer over the net. Newell and Sproull (1982) provide an early summary of how research communities appropriated this technology for such purposes.

Network configurations permit two key procedures: the transport of files between users and controlled access to data files held centrally. Network-based collaboration is then made possible by tools and structures that elaborate these core capabilities. Files become objects that a community of users may view, share and transform through the use of these tools – much as they might manipulate resources in the material (non-computed) world of collaborating. More recently, networks have also permitted the direct transmission of voice and video, thereby allowing more vivid communication between remote users, as well as their coordinated exchange and manipulation of data structures.

For our present interests, it is not important (and probably not possible) to establish a rigorous taxonomy of the supporting structures that have been documented for communication within networked environments. However, certain broad distinctions and themes are useful to identify, particularly as they relate to developments within educational settings. One class of widely used resource stresses structures for interpersonal exchange. These more generic tools permit text-based communication on a one-to-one or one-to-many basis. The best-known example is electronic mail (email) which allows a user to compose text messages at a network station. A mailer program can then be instructed to transfer them immediately to the file space of some remote user(s) – who will activate their own mailer to read, reply or forward the material. Increasingly, it is now possible to incorporate sound and visual images into these messages. A variant on this pattern is the electronic bulletin board, whereby material may be posted in a central file space that can be widely read by users within some networked community. This structure has, in turn, been elaborated in the form of so-called 'conferencing programs'. These allow orchestrated discussions by imposing topic structures on text entry (and, sometimes, a moderating mechanism). Users may write their own entries into a free space within this structure: the effect is to create threads of contributions. Participation in these computer conferences may come to resemble the experience of a seminar or workshop interaction.

Other network resources are tailored to supporting interactions with more circumscribed purposes. That is, they may impose greater structure on a group interaction and/or offer more specialist tools for manipulating material of joint interest. Such software is sometimes termed 'groupware' and useful characterisations of the genre can be found elsewhere: particularly, within reviews by Ellis, Gibbs and Rein (1991) and by Johansen (1988). Naturally, the emergence of this software has encouraged associated research enterprises concerned with its impact in organisational settings. Thus, there is now an active community of researchers studying the general phenomenon of computer-mediated communication (Lea, 1992) and the more particular circumstances of 'Computer-supported Cooperative Work' (Bowers and Benford, 1991; Grief, 1988). There is also an active interest in how the culture of organisations can be affected by the penetration of computer-mediated communications (Rice, 1992).

Many of these networking developments have indeed penetrated a variety of workplaces (Collins, 1986; Malone and Rockart, 1991). Commercial contexts, rather than educational ones, now provide the real stimulus for creating new resources. Educationalists can take advantage of these developments, although not all the structures developed for commercial purposes are relevant to the needs of education. For example, in the commercial sector there is much interest in Group Decision Support Systems (Vogel and Nunamaker, 1990), some of which may be fashioned for networked environments. But, framing and converging on 'decisions' is less central to the concerns of educational practice, and tools that help students do this may be of limited application outside specialised problem-solving exercises. So, the network-based structures that have been of most interest in teaching settings are these: first, resources that support interpersonal exchange and debate, particularly email and conferencing. Institutions that service non-residential students who might be widely dispersed have made the most effective use of these tools to support their 'distance education' (Harasim, 1990; Mason and Kaye, 1989). Second, information servers, which are programs offering individual users easy access to database collections of files relevant to some curriculum or organisational structure. These files may be located within some menu-style screen environment and then examined, copied or printed by students. Third, co-authoring tools, which allow two or more users to jointly edit or create documents in an asynchronous manner (Landow, 1990).

Most educational initiatives exploiting these structures have been concentrated in the university sector. I shall briefly review their progress later in this section. First, we might note certain findings that have emerged from more workplace-oriented research: these may provide some pointers regarding what can be expected in educational contexts. A recurring proposition is that network-supported communication is potentially subversive: it can challenge existing procedures that maintain a social order within some organisation. Perhaps for this reason, the implementation of groupware-based practices is not always successful. Thus, in reviewing this mixed progress, Grudin (1990) comments that 'a medium which allows widely separated people to aggregate their needs is, in fact, quite frightening' (p. 181). In general, organisations may be slow to respond to these structural possibilities. Yates (1989) locates innovations of the kind being discussed here in a broader historical context. He notes that few management technologies were ever adopted when they were invented, but only when shifts in management theory made the possible applications more apparent. He comments: 'Real gains await innovative thinking about the underlying managerial issues' (Yates, 1989, p. 275). This may be a common fate for all new media (Winston, 1986). So, by the same token, we may assume that these new technologies of communication will not easily penetrate and transform established practices within the organisations of education: this is already implicit in the historical review of teaching and technology authored by Cuban (1986).

A further recurring claim about communication in networked commercial environments is that the exchanges supported become deregulated or uninhibited

(Hesse, Werner and Altman, 1988; Sproull and Keisler, 1986). It is widely believed that this arises from the lack of social cues that can be conveyed in text-dominated and asynchronous communication. However, some commentators have questioned whether this medium is really so impoverished in terms of its social texture. Lea, O'Shea, Fung and Spears (1992) argue that uninhibited exchanges are quite rare in computer-mediated communication: they may simply be more memorable and visible in this text-based, archival context. Moreover, they accept that interpersonal social cues are necessarily minimal in this medium, but suggest that users make active regulatory use of social identities as given by other kinds of cues – text and format cues that specify affiliations to various social categories. It is uncertain, therefore, how this medium might influence the style of communication in educational settings. However, it is clear that educational settings have traditionally respected hierarchical structures of authority; whether or not these become somewhat flattened by computer-mediated communication will be one outcome of interest.

The most optimistic message to be derived from studies of workplace communication through computers is that it loosens up patterns of exchange within an organisation (Malone and Rockart, 1991); this may support more creative coordinations. However, simply putting network-based structures in place is not enough to ensure that real transformation of communication practices ensues. This has often been observed for the case of email (Carasik and Grantham, 1988; Eveland and Bikson, 1986). We may heed Bannon's warning (1986) that the success of innovation within some setting will depend upon innovators proceeding with a sensitivity to the informal system of rules and procedures that already govern working practices. I shall consider this more closely in the educational context of universities – the teaching institutions where collaboration through computers has been most actively considered.

Computer-mediated communication in undergraduate education

There is much to be worried about regarding the manner in which universities are being encouraged to deploy new technology (e.g. Hague, 1991); however, it is unfortunate that critics (e.g. Robins and Webster, 1985) are led to wholesale rejections of new technology in this sector before its potential for supporting more collaborative opportunities has been fully explored. This is a direction for computer-based innovation that has yet to be properly explored and judged. When the application of computers to university teaching is discussed, it is curious how little attention is given to distributed computing; and curious how slow educational practitioners have been to recognise the relevance of networking to the support of collaborative practices.

For example, in a recent collection of papers summarising IT-based teaching innovation in various UK universities (Gardner and McBride, 1990), there is no mention of networks as a teaching resource. Similarly, Darby (1991) does not include communication infrastructures in his review of future needs, when reflecting on the outcomes and implications of a UK initiative to promote computers in university teaching. Hale (1990) describes an example of a computer-rich teaching department: yet this model does not incorporate communication considerations. Part of the reticence on this matter may arise from not being able to see networks as offering anything more radical than a passive file serving mechanism. For example, Kay's recent review of networks in higher education converges on the recurrent theme of more efficient information delivery: 'pervasively networked computers will soon become a universal library' (Kay, 1991, p. 106). Gardner (1989) may have a similar vision of the 'electronic campus' when he concludes: 'There is at the moment no irrefutable series of arguments which demonstrates that electronic campuses are necessarily better places for staff or students' (1989, p. 348). Unfortunately, it is hard to promote convincing arguments when there are so few model systems to refer to.

As it happens, there is a more active educational interest in network infrastructures in North America. Thus, some campuses there have made considerable investments in distributed computing for teaching: notably, Carnegie-Mellon University (Hansen, 1988) and MIT (Stewart, 1989). Technical and academic strategy within the major US initiatives has been summarised in a review by Issacs (1989). Issacs' review indicates that networks often only service a fairly traditional teaching strategy: they deliver computer-aided learning packages to students at workstations. However, it is also apparent that these computing environments, to some extent, have made possible new and imaginative forms of coordination within their respective communities. Some of these possibilities have been reviewed in more detail by others. In particular, Kiesler and Sproull (1987) have published a volume of essays describing the impact of networking at Carnegie-Mellon. Their commentary suggests that the computing infrastructure is transforming patterns of communication within the campus community.

At first glance, this might seem likely and desirable: electronic mail opens up otherwise sluggish lines of communication, course material can be made widely accessible when and where it is needed, student assignments can be transferred within this medium – and so on. Hiltz (1990) has evaluated four courses intensively run in this way, with most of the communication managed by electronic distance-teaching methods. These 'virtual classrooms' are favourably judged by students who report a greater sense of participation and more access to the course tutors. However, some caution is necessary: the student constituency was self-selected and Hiltz indicates that access to computing resources has to be very good and considerable commitment is required from staff and students to master the new tools. Final grade scores were no better or worse than controls. Other reports of successful classes suggest a similarly mixed picture. Philips and Santoro (1989) describe the experience of running four parallel speech communication classes that made extensive use of electronic mail and bulletin board systems. The system was heavily used, the course ratings high, and the outcomes good. Yet engagement was localised: a third of the class made extensive use of the computing resources while 20 per cent barely used them at all. The mainframe computer system at its core was somewhat cumbersome and this may have made workloads high. Evidently, the usability of systems will be relevant to the progress of these initiatives. Although, in the present case, it is reasonable to suppose that the distribution of course engagement was at least what one would expect from more traditional teaching methods.

These initiatives are slow to spread. Indeed there are numerous commentaries suggesting opposition to developments of this kind. Hiltz and Meinke (1989) indicate that their virtual classroom provoked 'active resistance' from many faculty members. McCreary describes the University of Guelph's longstanding commitment to using computer conferencing and notes that its adoption has not been pervasive. In particular, there is a lack of presence in the system of senior members of the community. Komsky (1991) describes efforts in one university to deploy email for more administrative purposes, commenting: 'Despite a high degree of computer literacy and frequent use of computing for other applications, these faculties have been unwilling to alter their existing communication patterns to include electronic mail' (p. 311). So, where faculty (or students) are not so computer literate, we can presume the resistance will be greater still. Moreover, that obstacle is not easy to anticipate. Stewart (1989) indicates that resistance has been evident even at MIT where 'technical blood flowing through their veins' has not ensured that members of this community would be active computer users.

Of course, all of these cautions are made from within traditional university settings. Where the student constituency is more geographically dispersed, then it is likely that computer-mediated communication will be particularly successful. There is some indication that such success is possible (Harasim, 1990; Mason and Kaye, 1989). The UK Open University is one of the largest and most experienced distance-teaching institutions in higher education. It has reported some success with computer conferencing (Mason, 1989). However, the success was for students taking a technology course and the conferencing resource has yet to spread further into the university's teaching program. Moreover, there are indications that such course-related communication may not always be experienced as a liberating opportunity for equitable student participation. Grint's (1992) report of a small group of users indicates that the resource was not necessarily radical for them in this way. Partly, he argues, the difficulties arise because student participation depends upon a community 'solidarity', and that is not easily created within the medium.

Yet, in terms of our present theme of 'collaboration', this is very much the quality of experience that it is hoped interacting *through* computers can furnish. Here, I am hoping that communicative activities pursued through this technology might create for learners new forms of mutual knowledge. Such achievements could then underpin further collaboratively developed understandings: much as interacting *at* computers and interacting *around* them might. My brief review of developments within the present university community suggests that computer infrastructures do not yet have a significant role in teaching and learning practices. This may reflect a lack of faith and funding from policy makers. It may reflect interfaces to the technology that are still too cumbersome or students who, in any case, are still uncomfortable using computers. It may reflect a failure to achieve critical masses of participation within the community.

There is one further consideration relevant to making such initiatives work; it concerns the institutional level at which network-supported practice is organised. In North American universities, network structures may be generic resources oriented to the campus community as a whole. It is then possible for these resources to be appropriated into particular teaching units where they are adapted to local needs. Thus, the *course* becomes the level for organising interactions through this technology (Barrett and Paradis, 1988; Hiltz and Meinke, 1989; Kinkead, 1987; Landow, 1990; Philips and Santoro, 1989). In Britain, the natural unit of organisation may be the *department*. This is because most administration assumes that individual students have strong affiliations to such an academic body – sometimes, in the case of combined degrees, they may have more than one such affiliation. Evidently, modularisation of courses (currently under way) is likely to loosen these kinds of link. Perhaps this is all the more reason to be contemplating new strategies for sustaining them under such pressure. Many students will continue to pursue study plans that focus on a circumscribed academic subject: yet the options of modular structures may serve to undermine their sense of association with a fixed cohort of peers pursuing a common set of goals. While computer-mediated communications may well be conceived to meet the typically course-focused needs of these students, perhaps they might also help to recover some of the students' sense of involvement in a larger academic community.

I will describe below a case study that is organised at this level. It is unusual in that it represents a consensual effort to create structures for interacting through computers at the level of a whole teaching department. The observations are also interesting, as they cover a period during which all other circumstances of the department were stable. Moreover, this was a lengthy period (five years) and thus conclusions are not subject to the limitations of 'snapshot' research: observers of electronic communications in office settings have cautioned against drawing conclusions from brief accounts relating only to the early period of innovation (Rice, Grant, Schmitz and Torobin, 1990). Space does not permit a full description of this project and – as it is my own department – I will rely, to some extent, on participant observations. However, the exercise should be adequate to make some general points about the problems and possibilities of collaborative structures realised in this network context.

University case study: context and implementation

The observations that follow refer to a medium-size university department teaching psychology students entirely on its own premises. These students come from both arts and science backgrounds. The group of interest here are those combined cohorts of forty or so students who, in any of the years of a three-year course, are registered for an honours degree in psychology. Each such group was recruited into a etworked communication structure during their second year of study; other undergraduates taking various combined degrees involving a component of psychology could also make use of the network resources but they experienced less organised encouragement to do so. The exercise also involved all academic staff, a small technical staff (around seven people) and a postgraduate and research community (around fifteen people at any one time). My remarks here cover a five-year period (1986–1991) where circumstances were notably stable. So the core curriculum and teaching strategy in the department happened not to be altered during this time. Student numbers remained level and the computing infrastructure itself did not change in fundamental ways. Moreover, academic staffing remained constant (nine lecturers) with only one (temporary) appointment changing during this period.

It seemed to the staff in this department that Durham provided an attractive context to explore network-based resources at the departmental level. Even in 1986, Durham enjoyed a well-developed computing infrastructure. This partly arose from the university's involvement in a regional consortium that had taken early steps to promote campus-wide, multi-user services. These were based around the innovative and powerful operating system, MTS. Thus, access to a central service was very widely available: in libraries, in departments, from telephone dial-up services and in student residences. The strongly residential character of Durham (70 per cent of undergraduates live in college-style accommodation) was significant in several respects. It ensured that most undergraduates would have residence-based access to network resources. However, it also defined part of the reason these resources were thought educationally valuable. A strongly residential student community leads students to make their colleges the organising setting for social life. Departmental staff tend to note that this can undermine the ease with which shared academic interest catalyses student relations – and, perhaps, gets explored within them. For example, forty final year psychology students would be evenly dispersed across a dozen residential settings (and some would live in private accommodation). This offers most of them a rich social life, but usually not one that exploits common academic commitments. In 1986, an unannounced poll of the psychology students assembled for final year registration, revealed that, on looking round the room, the average student could only identify by name half a dozen peers from this common academic cohort.

In 1986, this department needed to upgrade computing equipment that supported teaching. The decision was made to invest in thirty new connections into the University network. Terminal access would then be available to all staff and there could be generous facilities in public spaces for students. It should be stressed that these innovations were achieved within the normal budgetary framework for teaching support: I am describing relatively low-technology innovations within the reach of many university departments – should they so choose. However, as is widely appreciated in commercial settings (e.g. Strassman, 1985), the real initial investment is not usually concentrated in hardware provision, but in handling the human issues of introducing a set of new working practices. The present example was not unusual in needing what McCreary (1990) terms a 'diffusion manager' – someone taking responsibility for drawing members of the community into acting within this medium. This was a role that I partly took upon myself and, therefore, I can comment on the implementation process from a close association with it.

Interactive communication media are vulnerable to start-up problems: where there is less than universal participation at the outset, this usually imposes a high cost and lower benefits for those who do take part. Markus (1987) has analysed this paradox and highlighted the problems of creating an early critical mass. Success appears to depend upon a small group of key users making a disproportionate contribution – perhaps making themselves more openly available than would otherwise be the case. In the present example, the teaching staff could be said to have made this gesture in respect of the larger community of students. Of course, these staff themselves have to arrive at their motivation. The present situation may have been unusual in that these particular individuals would be guided by pedagogic commitment and, perhaps, by theoretical curiosity. This might not so easily drive such an initiative in other academic contexts. It might even suggest social science departments as likely innovators in this area (Hiltz and Meinke's (1989) virtual classroom was for sociology students and, at Durham, the one department so far to have reproduced our own strategy is sociology). Yet, the diffusion manager in this case did find it necessary to create network facilities that staff could not otherwise easily enjoy: in particular, easy access to software for statistical analysis as well as central printing facilities that improved on what was locally available. Moreover, key administrators in the department made regular use of electronic mail for management purposes.

Managing the involvement of students was in some respects easier. It was seeded by building a requirement of usage into their coursework. This was not shamelessly manipulative: these students had always been required to learn the use of a statistical analysis program. All the necessary resources for that exercise were located in the same computer environment as the communication facilities under consideration here. They were introduced in parallel early in the students' second year. Also, a potentially prescriptive atmosphere was, in a small way, defused by introducing a number of frivolous resources (Marvin, 1983). These included on-line jokes, a database of student events, and randomly selected humorous items delivered when signing off. Students also benefited by having unrestricted access to a full screen text editor and printing facilities which many of them were able to use for basic word processing. Keyboard skills was a further need that had to be met: typing-tutor programs were made available at workstations and a professional instructor took a voluntary class in the department.

Even after ten years of computers being in schools, it should not be expected that contemporary undergraduates will find learning the basic use of a new system easy or agreeable. A computer attitude scale (Stevenson, 1986) was completed by all these students at the start of each year. This instrument comprised twenty statements requiring endorsements on a five-point scale from 'strongly agree' through 'undecided' to 'strongly disagree'. Figure 8.1 indicates that a similar pattern of responding was reproduced in each generation. If anything, the course-based experience of a networked environment is correlated with a gradual softening of attitudes towards using computers. Yet it is noticeable that there remains a significant unease over using this technology. The survey included supplementary questions probing particular experiences that students felt were associated with negative or positive feelings about using computers. The most commonly cited category of negative experience concerned feelings of being less competent than others or feeling resentment over having had inadequate opportunities to gain expertise during their education. Ironically, the second most commonly cited problem related to bad experiences of being taught about technology in previous contexts.

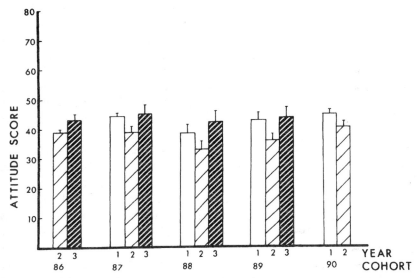

Figure 8.1 Attitude scores taken over five years (1986–1990). The numerals beneath the histogram bars indicate mean scores for pupils in either the first, second or third year of their course. Standard error of mean is shown

There has remained a significant minority of students (around 15 per cent) who seem seriously intimidated by this technology and feel very reluctant to use it regularly. Typically, they have mastered the small number of basic actions that provide them with teaching-related material through this medium (elaborated below). On the other hand, the overall picture of usage suggests a buoyant situation. The use of selected local commands (including signing on to the service) was recorded in a system log file. To ensure anonymity, this data was directed into a Computer Centre account and the identity of particular users hidden – although their status as individual representatives of a particular student or staff cohort was coded. Figure 8.2 summarises the extent of system usage over this period – in terms of average number of weekly log-ons by teaching staff, by second year and by third year students. All teaching staff became and remained active users of the network, so it would be normal for them to log into this system more than once a day. Student use is also active with most students logging-on three or four times a week.

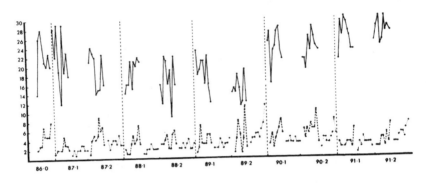

Figure 8.2 Number of system log-ons per week for the first and second terms of six successive academic years. Staff data is presented as solid lines; second and third year students as dotted lines (shown as adjacent for clarity)

There were three kinds of network-based resource relevant to the support of collaborative interactions. I shall define them briefly before saying more about the fate of each in practice. First, electronic mail furnished a tool for interpersonal communication. It also supported communication to groups. Over fifty such group aliases were defined. These mainly related to the various teaching units – seminars and practicals, taught option courses and so forth. Thus, rapid person-to-person and person-to-group communication became possible. Second, an information server was written to collate and distribute documents relevant to teaching, administration and research within the department. A menu-driven interface allowed users to converge on files classified under such headings; they could then view, copy or print this material. Third, such common access to files also allows more interactive structures. The concept of computer conferencing mentioned earlier is a case in point. In the present environment, a program ('Forum') was available that allowed the creation of a conference (for example, it might concern a particular taught course) and then the development of 'topics' (conversational strands) falling under that heading. Users could add their own written contributions to a developing exchange. A simpler program ('Intray') was also written to allow self-defined groups of individuals to share access to a single file. In some ways this resembled an electronic mail program. On running the utility, a user would see a list of files to which they currently had shared access. Any one could be selected through menu-style reference and then edited or printed. When signing on to the network, a message would indicate whether any such shared file had recently been updated.

Observations below on the fate of these resources is based upon three kinds of information. First, some system-level programming allowed usage statistics to be gathered. Second, student reaction was polled at various times through interview and written accounting. Third, staff recounted their experiences informally to myself under periodic questioning as a record of network activity was developed. I shall also draw upon my own experiences as a participant who may have been especially active in promoting network resources for collaborative purposes – arising from a professional interest in their value. The social-psychological distinctions I wish to make do not map cleanly onto the system resources as summarised above. I shall review the experience in terms of varieties of collaborative arrangement – each of which might involve some mix of these tools.

Computer-mediated discourse

Under this heading I am considering how communications *through* computers can support collaborations that stress interpersonal exchanges. So, the resources of interest are those that help to reproduce the opportunities of that discourse typically enjoyed in face-to-face discussion. Evidently, electronic mail is of special interest. It provides an accessible means of communication that can be referred to at times that suit individual users. Computer conferencing provides a further framework for the support of text-based discussion. However, in the present case, conferencing can be dealt with quite quickly: it never proved a resource that could be sustained. Part of the problem may have arisen from a user interface that many people found cumbersome. However, even when thorough preparation had been ensured and where it was formally built into the work of project groups, it did not prove a popular or effective resource.

The experience with electronic mail makes an interesting contrast. There are two important differences to note. One is that using the mailer program was never felt to be as difficult. The other is that electronic mail *was* widely used and widely appreciated. In annual surveys at the end of each academic year, students reliably cited mail as the most engaging network resource. During the first two years of this initiative, the mailer happened to deliver unusual levels of feedback to the senders of messages. Thus, it could be determined, at any given time, who had seen a particular message. When a message was sent to a group, this feedback was listed for all its members. By sampling such group-directed mail that happened to be sent by myself, it became possible to estimate the typical delay between sending an item and it being widely read within some target constituency. I performed such calculations in terms of 'working hours' – assuming a 9 am until 5 pm day – for a message to have been read by at least half the receiving group. During the second year of the project this message half-life was two hours for lecturing staff and ten hours for students. The point I wish to emphasise is that these statistics, along with student feedback on the attractions of email, indicate that the resource was accessible and effective (see also Figure 8.2). We might therefore expect it to be widely used for tutorial exchanges. Indeed, staff nervously expected this. At the outset of this initiative, lecturing staff were invited to write brief declarations of how they expected the use of networking resources to enter into department life (these were kept sealed and only examined very recently). A common concern was that electronic mail would open up a flood of student contact that would be difficult to manage.

In understanding the network-based practices that have actually evolved, there are other background observations that are relevant. These concern the extent to which this community already supported strong traditions of interpersonal colla-boration – in the form of talk between staff and students and talk among students themselves. These traditions were sampled in two ways. First, academic staff kept daily diaries during three one-week periods just before the networking initiative was launched. In these diaries, staff availability and contact with students and colleagues was logged. Second, the extent of student collaboration was assessed with an unannounced survey of how one particular piece of coursework was managed.

Staff diaries summarised the opportunities that students would normally expect for informal advisory contacts – and the extent to which such opportunities were taken. The pattern of statistics was very even across staff. When time allocated to formal teaching, official meetings, and research-related absences are subtracted, an average of 4.7 (range 3 – 6.8) hours per day remained as time during which lecturers were potentially 'available'. Undergraduates claimed a relatively small proportion of this time: 17 per cent of it was absorbed in meetings with other individuals; 12 per cent of it was taken up by undergraduates. This was enjoyed by a daily average of 2.9 students; around half of whom were students being supervised in specialist project work by that member of staff. Moreover, for most staff this number was made up of a significant core of individuals seen quite regularly (usually in relation to their supervised projects). These statistics suggest substantial opportunities for staff–student tutorial contact, but relatively modest uptake. The same picture emerges if we approach the question from a more student-centred perspective.

The student-focused exercise considered the natural history of one substantial piece of coursework required towards the middle of the second year course. This work was associated with fortnightly staff-led seminars, each involving about six students. The work set may have varied between groups but was to be submitted at the same time. At the submission meeting, students completed an anonymous questionnaire concerning the scheduling and support of this piece of work. The assignment needed to be done within a 12–14-day time-frame, but it would have been the only written work required in that period. It was assessed but the mark did not count towards degrees. For present purposes, I only wish to comment on the collaborative relations that might support this work. My point is that a project of this kind was typically a solitary achievement: 72 per cent of the students had no further conversation with their tutor in relation to the assignment, and 62 per cent had no discussion with their peers. Moreover, of those that did, three-quarters commented that these conversations were 'very brief' or 'cursory'. The relative lack of collaborative engagement with peers is supported by a survey of study time allocation carried out within the same class. Students reported only 1 per cent of their study involved discussions with peers, and over 75 per cent of the class claimed no time at all invested in this form of learning. Hounsell's (1987) study of undergraduate practices of essay writing endorses these findings: he also discovers 'no substantive discussion of essay writing amongst peers' (p. 113).

I am dwelling on this background context of working practices because it aids interpreting the subsequent impact of computer-based communication media. In general terms, a description of the present initiative might be helpful in suggesting likely outcomes elsewhere; but only if the present local circumstances are fairly fully articulated for purposes of comparison (not because those circumstances are 'typical'). In this spirit, there is one further dimension of this situation to comment upon. That is, the traditions of communication within this setting as they were interpreted by the students themselves. To get some sense of this, ten final year students were randomly chosen and approached to keep a reflective (but anonymous) record of their learning and interactions across this year. They were encouraged to be alert to attitudes among their peers and incorporate these impressions into an accounting of student experiences as they perceived them. At the outset the terms of reference were fully discussed and organised in relation to a number of open-ended, orienting questions concerning: 'activities' (the processes of study), 'contexts' (the locations and resources for study) and 'people' (relations with staff and peers). The exercise generated ten accounts, each around 2000 words in length.

The features of these accounts that are most relevant to present concerns are those about which there was most unanimity. First, it was widely claimed that the course was engaging and respected. Second, staff were regarded as approachable and the social atmosphere relaxed:

> Generally, staff are pretty accessible: one merely knocks on their door... many members of staff are only too pleased to help out with questions. (Student C)

> Students feel fairly few pressures compared to other students in different departments mainly due to the fact that the staff are fairly accommodating and understanding. (Student E)

Third, although less widely identified, it was remarked that discussion among students was limited. Where this was claimed to occur it was often expressed in terms of students monitoring their peers: to check that they were themselves 'keeping up', or to confirm that others were experiencing similar classes of difficulties and pressures. Some students identified the need for some kind of formal structure that could promote what they perceived as a shortfall:

> While psychology is a fascinating subject, very few students actually sit around amongst themselves and talk about it ... so, people need timetabled tutorials in which to talk about psychology. (Student A)

The lack of communication between psychology students is depressing. Some-how, discussion about the course 'outside of hours' as it were should be encouraged. Perhaps psychology students should only be accepted by certain colleges, thereby creating a hard core of psychologists with increased oppor-tunities for communication. (Student C)

Student perception of the collaborative nature of their learning seems in keeping with the formal sampling of this described earlier. Their reference here to limited study-centred peer interaction is consistent with those observations. However, their sense of an accessible and 'collaborative' staff might seem less consistent. The diaries and student work summaries have suggested that, in reality, a relatively small number of students have tutorial contact with staff outside of formal teaching settings. Of course, there may be no real inconsistency here. Students may detect a receptive teaching culture and yet choose not to take advantage of it by initiating frequent collaborative conversations.

There are good reasons to expect that electronic mail between students and staff might flourish in such a setting. For one thing, email has been widely described as a communication medium that causes users to be less inhibited. This may facilitate exchange in educational contexts where there are perceived status differences. Kiesler, Siegel and McGuire (1984) have noted its effectiveness in this sense with undergraduates. Some commentators (Turner, 1988) have even expressed concern at an excessive loosening of manners that the medium can encourage among university users. However, our own experience has not been one of electronic mail radically altering patterns of communication. This conclusion arises from summary accounts elicited from staff, sampling of individual student mail use, and more detailed participant records of my own.

All teaching staff took part in a lengthy interview one year into the present period. The topics for discussion were circulated in advance, responses were noted during the interview, and summarising accounts of these confirmed or negotiated later. There was universal agreement that the network resources had been a great asset. Several staff commented that they could not remember how they managed previously; others remarked they had not at first appreciated the significance of the initiative and had been surprised at how effective the facilities were. Also, they all agreed that electronic mail was a significant advantage in support of their teaching. However, the reasons cited for this all concerned opportunities for contacting students – delivering course material, inviting meetings, cancelling meetings, calling in missing books and so forth. No staff admitted to participating in anything like tutorial exchanges over this medium. The most widely cited examples of student-to-staff academic queries related to the supervision of individual practical projects. My own detailed records of mail to and from students echo these reports across the five-year period discussed here (and beyond). In every year, mail relating to these final year projects outnumbers all other incoming student mail. Even then, they are relatively scarce: in an average year they amounted to nine messages from a typical yearly group of five project students. Almost all other incoming mail took the form of two-turn exchanges. These arise within the context of some particular academic contract (usually a recently required piece of work): I can only trace six items that are context-free academic inquiries – such as might arise as reactions to a particular lecture or reading.

Thus, the summary picture from staff describes a pattern of communication very similar to that already apparent in their diaries of informal face-to-face student contact. There are relatively few unsolicited queries and much of the communication grows out of more sustained and personalised obligations associated with supervising specialist practical work. Six final year students who kept logs of their own mail confirm this pattern. The student with the largest number of outgoing email items to staff reported twenty-five: most of which were brief administrative matters. All reported more outgoing mail to other students and more incoming mail from staff. A small amount of student-to-student mail (on average around six items in the year) was course-related. However, it is clear that the availability of this medium does not transform or greatly amplify existing patterns of collaborative communication. This is true even in circumstances where the need for greater staff and peer collaboration is acknowledged and even after the following operating conditions have been satisfied: (1) a reasonable period of network institutionalisation has occurred, (2) electronic mail has become familiar, regularly used and appreciated, (3) the freedom to approach staff and peers in this way has been well advertised.

For these reasons, I am inclined to view unstructured use of electronic mail as a rather limited resource for extending the collaborative experience of learning – at least, within the traditional culture of British department-based teaching. Arguably, it is too cumbersome ever to suit tutorial-type dialogue and conceptions of computer-mediated communications in education surely need to look beyond this simple analogy. Only in distance-teaching contexts might this tutorial application make sense. Electronic mail remains useful to coordinate other activities, including scheduling face-to-face meetings. And it *could* be useful for student-driven, two-turn exchanges that might not otherwise occur. That this tends not to happen reflects a need to refashion other aspects of the culture of teaching and learning: electronic mail does not seem, by itself, to create new conditions for empowering such collaboration.

Network structures for joint activity

One enthusiast for computer-mediated communications in education comments: 'Knowledge is not something that is "delivered" to students in this process, but something that emerges from active dialogue among those who seek to understand and apply concepts and techniques' (Hiltz, 1990, p. 135). Many such innovators properly wish to dissociate themselves from 'delivery' models of educational practice, fostering instead opportunities for participation in educational discourse. Yet, it may be optimistic to assume that new arenas of dialogue will naturally open up once the electronic infrastructure and tools are in place. Certain persuasive studies within distance-teaching settings might encourage this belief. However, empowering collaborative practices within more traditional cultures of teaching and learning may require going beyond simply giving access to these new conversational tools. Productive educational dialogue usually depends upon a previous investment: a background of more carefully cultivated social practices. So, in the end, the challenge for developing collaborative interactions *through* computers may be one of re-mediating established practices: using these tools to transform existing forums of socially organised teaching and learning. Once such new structures are discovered, then they may motivate activity within the dialogue-supporting devices we have been discussing above. The purpose of this section is briefly to elaborate this argument.

I will mention two exercises carried out within the context of my own teaching. They each made use of network resources to structure a traditional activity in a more collaborative fashion. Neither depended centrally on the dialogue functions of electronic mail and thus they take us beyond the examples of the preceding section. The first example concerns support for the management of written assignments. The second concerns student-led discussion groups. They illustrate something of what is possible, but they also illustrate an optimistic assumption that new structures can be easily bolted on to existing learning practices.

To introduce the first, I shall return to the exercise described above, in which students were confronted with an inquiry to characterise the natural history of an assignment they had just completed. I commented earlier on the solitary nature of this work. The other striking outcome was poor time management. This might have been anticipated, as student procrastination is a well documented problem (e.g. Silver and Sabini, 1981). The present exercise required a breakdown of the work in terms of time spent on preparatory reading, drafting and final writing; students described how these activities were distributed across the two-week period. Two particular observations are worth highlighting: first, the proportion of time given to preparing plans and drafting was relatively small (around 15 per cent) and, second, most work on the assignment was concentrated in the latter part of the available period. Thus, 65 per cent of the work was done within the last four days and 20 per cent was done within the final twenty-four hours. Only a fifth of the students had given the work any attention at all within the first week of the allotted time. Arguably this is a problem of procrastination rather than lack of commitment. On average, ten hours were spent preparing these essays: this is a fairly generous investment in absolute terms, the problem is that its distribution across the available period is skewed.

I suspect that the underlying pattern of management endorses Hounsell's conclusions from an interview study of essay writing among history and psychology students:

> there was no substantive peer discussion and communication from tutors to students appeared to be largely formal, post hoc, product oriented and limited

in scope. Essay writing thus appeared to be a central assessment activity but a peripheral pedagogical one. (Hounsell, 1987, p. 118)

The situation invites, among other possibilities, more imaginative support from tutors, and support that encourages more effective use of preparatory time. The writing of an assignment might become a collaborative activity, if procedures could be instituted to draw tutors into the writing *process* (rather than their only entering at the end as commentators on the *product*). Evidently this does not happen spontaneously: observations made above on tutor–student contact indicate that students do not seek out such involvement. Neither does technology greatly assist by offering an accessible and legitimate new communication medium (electronic mail). The problem seems to require establishing a recognised (and economical) collaborative practice: some set of procedures whereby joint involvement in the preparing and planning of work becomes possible. This might require the construction of a more accessible object of shared reference than might be naturally achieved within a brief face-to-face (or computer-mediated) tutorial dialogue. Participation in a networked computing environment might make this possible.

My own exploration of this possibility involved two teaching forums. The first was the same assignment-requiring seminar referred to above when discussing student procrastination. Students were asked to produce a first plan for their written assignment during the following week. This could then be developed iteratively within further exchanges, if that seemed useful. The exercise either used electronic mail or the Intray file-sharing program. Perhaps such a procedure could be effected with reference to paper drafts, but its management would be more difficult. Collaborating through the computer network means that the task can be turned around very promptly and editing facilities mean that comments can be effectively interleaved into existing text. This affords something more like a dialogue in relation to the topic under development. Moreover, when the time comes to discuss the finished product (as might occur in a seminar meeting), participants will have a richer understanding of the nature of that product through shared access to its conception.

Such procedures work, up to a point: the medium supports the activity and it does not seem to overstretch a tutor's commitment. Yet the collaboration is hard to precipitate and hard to sustain. Of course, other tutors might do so more skilfully and more successfully. However, I suspect that there is more to the problem than this. Additional effort is required to identify procedures that could be effective: procedures that make sensible contact with existing work practices and, yet, can then act to enrich or extend them. In this case, formalising the development of an essay in successive text drafts was accessible and useful for some students, but unfamiliar and awkward for others. The discrepancy in reaction makes it more difficult to sustain the initiative: for the culture of seminar groups tends to encourage procedures that *all* members can appropriate.

However, the obstacles may be substantial. To consider this, I have implemented the same procedure with different operating circumstances. In particular, I have encouraged computer-mediated dialogue around text plans for a final year assignment that was part of formal degree assessment. Thus this work was important, and because the completed assignments were blind marked and the class was large (thirty-five), there should be limited fear of tutor prejudices carrying over from planning dialogues to influence ultimate assessments. Yet, whenever it has been instituted, this procedure has never attracted more than one or two collaborating engagements. Moreover, passing the responsibility to a postgraduate assistant – who might be less threatening – makes no significant difference.

One of these postgraduates raised this topic during interviews with randomly selected students following completion of their degree. From the transcripts, it became clear that the assignment was taken seriously. It was also regarded positively (coursework assessment for degrees being unusual in the department). Procrastination was frequently cited as a problem: to submit material for discussion close to the deadline was seen as only exposing one's own inefficiency. A further problem was simple lack of exposure to an interaction of this kind. These students were one year further into their undergraduate education than those described above: procedures for collaborative interaction around the development of an assignment were still more unexpected and unfamiliar. Thus, the networked environment does offer a resource for this possibility and, for a small number of people, it can be effective. But, for the majority, more preparatory effort has to be invested in making such structures work. The *collaborative* involvement of tutors and students in ways other than institutionalised discussion forums (seminars) remains unfamiliar.

I will outline a second collaborative structure that is more student-centred and which also suggests a similar conclusion: networks furnish real possibilities for new structures but they may be hard to launch as *widespread* practices. This case case concerns thirty-five or so students taking an optional course in their third year. The class is semi-formal; partly because it incorporates one hour each week when small (self-selected) groups within the class take responsibility for leading a discussion. Encouragement is given for students to exploit these groupings as a basis for creating their own structures of mutual support. This rarely happens. The interviews with graduating students mentioned above confirm this. However, I am aware of two such groupings that did sustain such activity, and that did draw upon collaborative support through the computer infrastructure. These groups enjoyed regular meetings at which a nominated scribe summarised what they had discussed and understood. These were mailed to the tutor (or placed in a shared Intray file) and became the potential target of some further dialogue – either within that file or at other times when the participants (and, perhaps, the tutor) met.

What is notable is that the experience was very potent for those participants. But also, this venture was notable for being unusual: few students easily adopt this manner of collaborating. I have highlighted the examples above to stress two points. First, the computer network does suggest novel structures through which collaborations can be supported: the networked technology furnishes a resource that helps build up productive shared understandings. Second, the promise of such a resource can only be assessed in relation to a background culture of collaborative practices. This is merely to stress that, when deployed within traditional undergraduate settings, the technology is unlikely to function like a magic bullet.

Yet it *can* be subversive in these settings. So, other colleagues in this department recently have reported localised successes in using the computer network to support small group collaborations within their advanced (third year) teaching forums. What seems to help precipitate this are ingredients not included in the relatively unstructured initiatives described above: there may need to be a degree of enforced group responsibility and also a well-specified purpose or goal. Then it is more likely that the shared computer space will emerge to offer a valuable repository for group-based understandings, and it is possible that these can become an authentic part of common knowledge.

Participatory structures

Bruner (1991, p. 3) quotes Nobel prizewinner Harriet Zuckerman as suggesting that the chances of winning the prize increase immeasurably if one has worked in the laboratory of somebody who has done so themselves. With this observation, we are alerted to the significance of cultural contexts for learning. This requires us to think from yet another perspective about the technological resourcing of collaborative structures. In discussing interactions *through* computers, I have touched on possibilities that reproduce some of what happens during interactions together *at* problems. Thus, electronic mail might support the creation of shared understandings through affording approximations to conversational dialogue. I have also discussed possibilities involving more diffuse collaborative structures: in particular, possibilities based upon using a common computer space to maintain (asynchronously) certain documents that can become shared objects of reference. Under the umbrella of 'participatory structures', I wish to introduce the idea that interactions through this technology might be relevant to supporting cultures for learning – in the sense that Bruner (and others) identify them. In this case, more overarching shared frameworks of understanding are generated and accessing these frameworks may help create platforms from which new understandings get collaboratively negotiated.

Theorising in the socio-cultural tradition recently has been influenced by anthropologists who describe informal settings for learning. Lave (1988), in particular, has studied such settings, thereby conceptualising teaching and learning in terms of learners encountering activity within 'communities of practice'. Such social structures, it is argued, relate very broadly to educational agendas: 'Even in cases where a fixed doctrine is transmitted, the ability of a community to reproduce itself through the training process derives not from the doctrine, but from maintenance of certain modes of coparticipation in which it is embedded' (Lave and Wenger, 1991, p. 16). Such a perspective has encouraged interest in apprenticeship relationships. However, Lave cautions that the master–apprentice terminology should not become a disguise for traditional teacher–pupil organisations. Instead, she toys with an alternative vocabulary that dwells more on the fabric of social relations and their role in transforming persons and practices. For example:

> Newcomers develop a changing understanding of practice over time from improvised opportunities to participate peripherally in ongoing activities of the community. Knowledgeable skill is encompassed in the process of assuming an identity as a practitioner, of becoming a full participant, an oldtimer. (Lave, 1991, p. 68)

I believe this vocabulary is helpful for thinking about the conditions of undergraduate learning. The present influence of psychological theory on university education is rather limited (Laurillard, 1987; Saljo, 1987). It sometimes surfaces in a concern to cultivate in students more effective 'study skills'. Yet, research suggests that such skills cannot be abstracted and taught independently of subject content or meaningful contexts (Ramsden, Beswick and Bowden, 1987). A more useful theoretical perspective may be one that considers the nature of students' engagement with the practice of their discipline. This issue concerns the participant structure of learning as it might be created within, say, a university department. Our particular interest here is whether technological resources can contribute to enriching such structures.

What might this involve in the current example of a psychology department? It must involve some kind of exposure to the *doing* of psychology – an encounter with the subject in a context where it is in progress. Fifty years ago, Lewin was stressing that learning is most effective when pursued collaboratively within communities of practice. He argued that watchmakers becoming carpenters involves more than their learning how to use certain tools: it involves coming to swear like carpenters, to walk, eat and see the world from the carpenter's point of view (Lewin and Grabbe, 1945). In an undergraduate context, this might be achieved, in part, by a certain simulation of the discipline's professional routines. It is tempting to demand of students scaled-down versions of professional practices, such as research reports, conference-type presentations, traditions of peer commentary and so forth. Yet, the most potent learning experiences may arise from opportunities to witness the art, values, tricks and vision of practitioners as they actively engage in the subject. Exposure to this culture affords newcomers a chance of 'legitimate peripheral participation' (Lave and Wenger, 1991). It might allow them to approach the status of oldtimers 'through a social process of increasingly centripetal participation, which depends upon legitimate access to ongoing community practice' (Lave, 1991, p. 68).

I believe that considering the management of communication structures within an educational setting will play some small part in transforming it into an accessible 'community of practice'. There are some pointers to be drawn from the undergraduate example that has been discussed in the present section – although, admittedly, they are modest. One network-based resource that relates to this purpose is the information server: the tool that collates and distributes documents relevant to the life of the department. Teaching material is one category of material that dominates this database. At a superficial level, it is valuable to students as a repository of their course-related documents. In the final weeks of the period described here, there was an average of 900 accesses to this database per week. However, the availability of this resource has done more than merely duplicate existing paper-based operations. In particular, it has led some staff to incorporate novel material that would not previously have been in circulation: their own lecture notes for example, or (anonymous, and with approval) examples of previous student approaches to tackling some topic of mutual interest. An incidental effect of this is to create a more vivid bird's-eye view of departmental activity. This is achieved partly because the material is centralised in a format shared by all users and partly because it is topical and detailed in a way that traditional handbook summaries are not.

One feature of usage that became clear from system logs was that users consulted entries that were not relevant to their own course-related study needs (this observation includes staff – some of whom were active in cross-checking the curricula of their peers). It was hoped that this curiosity among student users could be deflected towards aspects of the department's activity less centrally related to the undergraduate syllabus. Thus, the database came to include material relating to research activity, recent publications, the administration of the department, new library and equipment purchases, minutes from staff (and staff–student) committee meetings and so forth.

This exercise in opening up windows onto departmental life is cited, as with several other examples in this case study, to illustrate a principle: namely, that of linking computer-based structures to collaborative purposes. Thus, in the present case there may be a real possibility of drawing individuals towards a closer appreciation of the life of the department, as defined by its core concern with the practice of psychology. However, in reality, these materials peripheral to the official syllabus have attracted very little student attention. Again, the existence of such access does not, of itself, create a new level of engagement with the local culture of the discipline.

Undergraduate network: concluding comments

The departmental case study sketched above illustrates three senses in which collaborations may be supported by interactions *through* computers. They all relate to joint concerns that are relatively dislocated in time and space: collaborators are not co-present in the familiar sense. First, computer networks may facilitate some of the dialogue-based processes that are a traditional part of forming shared understandings: electronic mail is the most accessible tool to help achieve this. Second, access to shared file space may resource the creation of useful objects of shared reference: I have discussed the example of staff and students collaborating on the conception of a traditional assignment, and also the example of a tutor's computer-mediated involvement with the products of student-led discussion groups. Third, collaboration may be resourced more at the level of very loosely coupled shared interests and understandings. This is a matter of electronic media creating for learners a greater sense of awareness of overlapping purposes and a greater sense of participation in a community of practice.

In relation to this final sense of collaborative support, it would be naive to hope that investing in computer networking infrastructures naturally met these needs. It is certainly possible that they could undermine them instead. For example, electronic communication could be deployed to obstruct the circumstances of joint understanding, it could comprehensively displace rich interpersonal communication and render relationships more remote. This has certainly not happened in the quite long experience of the present case study. Yet it is also clear that widespread participation in the present initiative has not had a productively transforming effect on collaborative structures either.

The important lesson of the example may relate to the *potential* of computer-mediated communications when implicated in such transformations. In the present case, I believe it has become clear that much needs to be done in terms of confronting the limited culture of collaboration that students bring to their undergraduate experience. There is also much to be done at the level of facilitating a richer intersubjectivity between the learners in this situation and the tutors with whom an effective collaborative relationship needs to be built. This is true even in a setting that students may rate as relatively successful in this respect. In the following section I make some brief observations regarding related initiatives at much earlier stages of education. The cautionary observations of a sociologist discussing electronic media in schools may serve to link the above discussion and the one that follows:

> the professional optimists confuse community and communication. What they forget or affect to forget is that communication is the expression of a will, of a will to be or live together, which almost invariably pre-exists it. In one sense, it is the community which precedes communication and not the reverse, even if communication may eventually reinforce the community. (Balle, 1991, p. 107)

INTERACTING THROUGH COMPUTERS: A PRIMARY SCHOOL COMMUNITY

Networks may have been slow to penetrate teaching within undergraduate contexts; they have made still less impact on practice in the earlier stages of education. Yet I believe that the forms of collaborative interactions made possible by interacting through this medium also hold promise for younger learners. Again, my discussion will be dominated by personal experience with one particular model system. I shall draw on this to suggest ways in which computer networking may underpin valuable collaborative structures in early education. The discussion in this section will be shorter, as many points generally relevant to this form of activity have been introduced above. Moreover, the case study to be discussed is still in a relatively early stage of development.

In the first section below, I shall review the status of networking structures within early education. Then I shall move on to describe particular possibilities for practice as revealed in one primary school setting. The discussion will focus on collaborations as they might evolve in relation to children's early experience of writing.

Computer networking in early education

Few educational commentators have considered how the networking of computers in schools can support innovative teaching and learning. Handbook reviews rarely mention networking (e.g. Salomon, 1989; Smith, 1989). A significant European conference on information technology and schools gave no serious consideration to network infrastructures (Eraut, 1991a). Where they are considered, it is often in terms of configuring an isolated room to create a more efficient file serving mechanism (Henderson and Maddux, 1988). The schools that do have networks are almost always in the secondary sector and their networking is almost always clustered into a circumscribed space – rather than integral to the school (Wellington, 1987).

Yet, in both primary and secondary settings, there has been an attraction to the broad idea of collaborative interactions *through* this medium. Curiously, it has inspired communication initiatives of a different kind to those pursued in the universities. In schools, interest has started from communication over wider areas – links made outside of the school itself. In universities (as reviewed above), the communication structures have been more at the local level. Thus, in the school system there has been some lively exploration of cross-site communication, but relatively little interest in local structures of computer communication, while in universities, there has been more interest in the local level and virtually no exploration of cross-site links. Universities have been well enough equipped to follow either route, while schools, in choosing to foster remote communications, arguably have chosen the route with more cumbersome technical demands. Their commitment may reflect traditional concerns to challenge the often too-insulated nature of pupils' school experience.

Communicating through computers to other institutions is made possible if a school has a modem. This is a device allowing some computers to be linked to a telephone line and, thereby, to exchange files with a remote site similarly equipped. In practice, the usability of such a link depends upon access to certain software tools that organise and direct such communication. For this reason, early projects often called upon university contacts to mediate the link – thus allowing access to electronic mailers. These more effectively formatted and targeted the files transmitted. More recently, commercial concerns have acted to occupy this mediating role. In Britain, a news company has launched the 'Times Network for Schools': for an annual subscription, this offers electronic mail as well as conferencing and bulletin boards (Wellington, 1987). In North America, AT&T have supported the development of a comparable resource aimed at schools (Riel, 1990).

An early and influential exercise based around cross-site communication was reported by Levin, Riel, Rowe and Boruta (1985). Their rationale was to become widely endorsed by others. They argued that this form of communication created a credible functional environment to support student projects. It created new topics, new audiences, and new purposes for such work. Indeed, some researchers (Cohen and Riel 1989; Riel, 1985) were able to demonstrate that participation in these exercises resulted in improved grade point scores for writing. This seemed to result from an active engagement in the editorial responsibilities that this form of communication afforded.

There have been similar case studies of successes in British schools (e.g. Keep, 1991; Wishart, 1988). Yet, the overall impression is that these initiatives can be hard to promote and hard to sustain. Maddux (1989) cautions the use of telecommunications before careful considerations of cost and whether the same goals could not be achieved more economically in other media. In reviewing a number of such initiatives, Riel and Levin (1990) argue that users do quickly discover the communication medium offers a qualitatively distinct kind of interaction. But they also stress that a coherent need for the exchange must be in place, and that there must be an active commitment by some enthusiastic project manager. In reviewing a number of computer-mediated school twinnings, Turnbull and Beavers (1989) also refer to very careful planning and serious consideration of the real compatibility of interacting communities. Keep (1991) conveys a similar impression of the need for much energy in order to maintain that critical level of exchange that sustains pupil interest. The consensus seems to be that this medium can support valuable activity if it is embedded in a larger framework of cross-site communication and concern. The passing of text messages alone is too decontextualised an experience to sustain serious pupil interest.

In the ten years since this idea of schools communicating through computers was seeded, it is hard to conclude that an active and effective culture of such communication has emerged. There are still only pockets of success. It would be unfortunate if the general principle of such collaborative school-based interactions were judged on this variety of activity alone. From studying the reviews mentioned above and from my own involvement in supporting a primary school to develop such links, I believe the goal of such cross-site communication is worthwhile but it needs to be approached more gradually. The problem is well crystallised by Hawkins, who comments:

> In the educational world of the kindergarten through twelfth grade there is, in most places, a relatively narrow band of activities that these technologies make more efficient. As has been often noted, our classrooms tend to be quite self-contained in terms of interactive relationships and resources. (Hawkins, 1991, p. 161)

Thus, it may be necessary to institute stronger traditions of *local* computer-mediated collaboration before embarking on these more ambitious communication exercises. It may be necessary to establish practices of coordinating with the next classroom, before venturing towards collaborations that span cultures and continents.

At least, this was the thinking behind a primary school networking project established in cooperation with two colleagues, Geoff Alred and Jack Gilliland. In the last three years, I have been considering the kind of software structures that can support novel forms of coordination at the level of a self-contained school site. This, therefore, is a project focused at communicating *through* computers – within the forum of a single community. In the longer term, one of its achievements may be to establish a culture of communication that would be well prepared for further-reaching relationships.

Open-plan computing

I have chosen the phrase in this heading to suggest a link between traditions of social organisation in British primary schools and a particular computer infrastructure to be described below. This configuration for school computers is conceived to create an environment in which innovative communication might flourish – rather as might also be achieved within the physically open-planned layout of many classrooms.

Our configuration of computers entailed installing a low-cost (Acorn Computers) network throughout the premises of a school. Various programs were then written to manage this network and to sustain certain forms of pupil activity within it. The school comprises 7 classes corresponding to the successive years of primary education: from ages 4–5 until 10–11. All classes always have at least one network station and, by negotiation, around five additional machines can be clustered in areas close by any class to promote more dedicated activity. As with the university case study described in the previous section, this is a structure realised at a fairly low-technology level: the aim is to explore what is possible within the resources of a typical school, rather than to demonstrate some state-of-the-art (but inaccessible) model system.

I will summarise the main features of the software environment to convey the possibilities for collaborative interactions through this technology. The network centralises a great many programs that are characteristic of those used in any British primary school. Thus, the widely recognised advantage of networks for simply serving such files to pupil-users is realised in this instance. However, there are four particular programs that are crucial to developing the structure in more educationally distinctive ways. I will describe each of these in turn. First, a menu-driven interface allows pupils to navigate their way through the disc space of the central file server. Teachers may configure menus to be relevant to activities current in their own classes. Moreover, each pupil is allocated their own file space and file space may be associated with short-term collaborative projects. Second, a conventional word processor suitable for primary pupils is available to all users. Third, pupils may nominate files to be incorporated into a database structure that organises them into a system of 'folders'. Folders are associated with particular pupils and also with particular projects and/or classroom communities. Their contents may be examined through suitable movement through the network menu-structure. The route a child might make to enter a new item in her folder is illustrated in Figure 8.3 which shows a schematic sequence of screen displays. Fourth, an electronic mail utility allows pupils to have their own mail box. Text messages may be dispatched within the community and to addresses of outside sites (these are collated and dispatched as an automatic night job).

As in the case of university networks, when we are considering structures for coordination, we might think first of electronic mail. After all, this utility supports communication that is closest to what spontaneously we associate with collaboration. It supports dialogue between individuals. Although this school has still had only modest experience with electronic mail, it is clear that this resource can be engaging and effective. However, it has acted by gluing together other more substantial coordinated activity – rather than being itself the central feature of some collaboration. For example, it has proved a very effective resource in support of a school-wide project for producing a newspaper. Material could be distributed over the network to reach groups working on different aspects of this common concern. Moreover, this mailer (SJ Research's 'Interspan') allows seamless links to outside sites. So, given a meaningful context, such as producing a magazine or newspaper, cross-site electronic mail can be effectively integrated with a well-grounded local project.

However, here I am concerned to highlight less obvious collaborative resources. In particular, the folder structure that was described above. At the moment, much of the material within this system comprises pupils' written work of a fairly traditional kind. Yet, the collation that is achieved – perhaps in conjunction with certain orienting teaching practices – serves to create a stronger social framework for these children's efforts. The most straightforward transforming effect relates to the creation of a strong sense of audience. Surveys indicate that much pupil writing in education is crafted only for the teacher-examiner (Britton, Burgess, Martin, McLeod and Rosen, 1975). Educationalists have recently promoted a new paradigm of writing instruction that puts more stress on the rhetorical nature of literacy (Davies, 1989a, b; DiPardo and Freedman, 1988). The National Writing Project (1989) gives a range of examples of how this can be organised. Yet, in practice, it remains hard to foster a sense of the school as a 'community of writers' (Dunn, 1989). Evidently, the network-based structures I am describing take us some way towards an infrastructure that can support credible audiences in this sense. For example, it may facilitate the kind of exercise described by Somerville (1989) in which older children write stories that become the focus of reading and discussion among younger children in the school.

The existence of a structure to collate and make accessible pupils' work invites other collaborative engagements. One that I believe is poorly exploited within all sectors of education can be expressed in the phrase 'leaving tracks'. Martin (1989) has discussed the general place of furnishing for writers models of practice: these may become resources for reflection and inspiration. This principle can be usefully realised in the present computer structure. In so far as each school class reproduces the aims and efforts of its predecessors, it may be a source of some insight to have

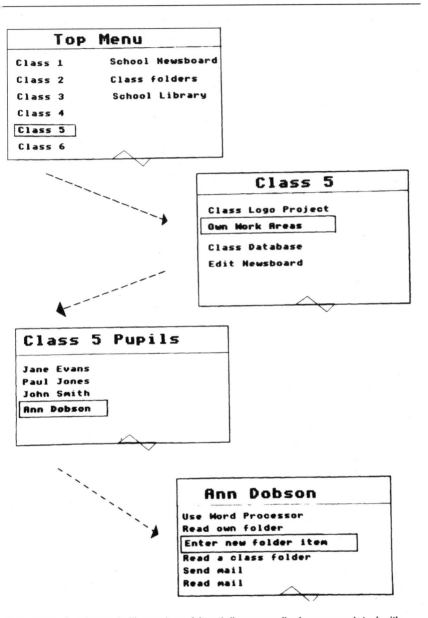

Figure 8.3 A schematic illustration of (partial) screen displays associated with navigating the primary school local network. The sequence shows a pupil making a four-step sequence of selections converging on the operation of entering a new folder item

access to the achievements of previous generations. The network allows a class to leave these kinds of traces behind it. I view this as a 'collaborative' initiative, as it involves a socially organised concern to create and to coordinate around objects of shared understanding.

The principle of leaving tracks applies to individual pupils also. So, pupils in this environment build up a portfolio of work that captures their own development as writers (or scientists, or journalists, etc.) and this portfolio can become a resource for their own reflections on this process (Brown, 1989). Indeed, pupils can be found referring to these folders spontaneously, apart from any encouragement they might encounter to do so in the context of teacher-led activities. There is a link in this to one feature of traditional computer-based learning tools that has been widely discussed in the literature: that is, the capacity of these resources to make visible the *processes* of intellectual construction. Thus, J. S. Brown comments: 'We are missing the real source of power for computer-based tools: the computer can record and represent the process underlying the created product' (Brown, 1985, p. 182). However, this idea is always cited in reference to underlying processes of a private, cognitive kind. It has not been effectively developed at a level that recognises the socially grounded nature of much intellectual construction. In a sense, what the organised, archival character of this network affords is opportunities for such processes of reflection in the social domain.

It is clear that this example of interacting *through* computers involves a resourcing of 'collaboration' in the broadest sense of that term. We may summarise the resulting opportunities as follows. These structures can create circumstances where distinct groups of children can coordinate their efforts across barriers of time and classroom separation. The production of a newspaper is a vivid example of this. The networking can also create structures that allow children's work to reach further into the common knowledge of the school and, thereby, play some part in motivating new achievements. There may also be a deeper sense in which the structure can support such common knowledge: this finds a parallel with the 'participatory structures' discussed for a university community above. It is possible that the coordination and access that networks can create may serve to bring pupils nearer to the socially organised experiences of *being* biologists, or historians, or dramatists, or whatever. This is a point made by other researchers who have witnessed something of what local-level networking might achieve in early education (Newman, 1989, 1990; Ruopp, in press).

CONCLUDING COMMENTS

The examples discussed in this chapter should put into sharper relief the sense in which the concept of 'collaboration' may characterise effective settings for learning. At the heart of this conception are the activities of creating and exploiting structures of common knowledge and shared reference. However, I am stressing that there are various ways in which understandings can be held in common among learners and teachers. Collaborating should not narrowly describe the circumstances of small groups working together in time and place at a focused problem. In the institutional settings of learning, important common knowledge exists as part of the diffuse background to a variety of problem-solving circumstances. The present chapter has discussed ways in which computers may resource learners investing in this broader framework of understandings.

So, in discussing interactions *around* this technology, we encountered circumstances in which a transient learning community – sharing a common working space – might collaborate 'through the air'. Here, clusters of computers furnish focal points at which individuals (or small groups) may concentrate their work; from these points they may drift in and out of lateral communications with others similarly engaged. Moreover, the computer tools they share provide concrete referential anchors that may more effectively support such collaborative talk.

In discussing interactions *through* this technology, the varieties of collaborative structures encountered was still greater. In these cases, the interactions supported may be displaced in both time and space. I argued that to focus on tools for supporting versions of (text-based) conversational exchange was to present too narrow a characterisation of collaborative possibilities in this medium. An accessible shared file space offers more than this: it offers a rich environment for creating objects of shared reference. Particularly when utilised in a framework of organised social practices, this further illustrates how new technology can successfully resource (rather than deny) collaborative possibilities.

It might be argued that many of these examples do not crucially depend upon computers: the relevant collaborations could be supported in other ways, with other technologies. I have two reactions to this argument. The first is that whatever may be *possible*, in practice many of these collaborative structures simply are not being realised in other ways. Thus, for example, there are various means whereby primary pupils' work *could* be collated and made into an accessible and managed resource for their peers and successors but – by and large – it is not treated this way. These shortfalls often do await a technology that simply makes a critical difference to what may realistically be achieved. My second reaction to this argument is somewhat strategic. Actively identifying new technology with collaborative practices serves to deflect attention from certain less agreeable models of computer-supported learning. If we do not wish to see new technology transform the experience of learning into something solitary and dislocated – then we must demonstrate that it has a credible place in a more collaborative framework.

Chapter 9

Afterwords

In this chapter, I shall not attempt a comprehensive review of the various themes that have arisen in what has gone before. I hope that the summary sections associated with each individual chapter achieve this purpose well enough. Instead, I wish to extract a small number of issues that I think recur throughout this book and make some closing remarks in relation to them.

Of course, the book has been concerned with computers and education. But that is a broad topic, and my own interests around it may appear to be rather particular. Certainly, I have not attempted an overview of all the various ways in which computers can now enter into curricula. Their influence has become so far-reaching that such a task would be too ambitious. In fact, some of the educational software employed in my own observations may seem rather modest illustrations of what computers can offer – these examples may not reflect a state-of-the-art by which some enthusiasts might prefer the technology was judged. However, my interest has not been to describe these frontiers; my real starting point has been a concern with the broad character of educational experience. Observations of learners working at computers have furnished a helpful opportunity for developing this interest. In some respects it has been useful that the tasks observed have *not* been too sophisticated. This should not imply that my interest in computer-based activities has been entirely a contrivance. In the end, I believe that this technology does offer a special potential for enhancing the experience of learning. I shall return to stress this point towards the end of this chapter.

Before going further, I should restate and reinforce the perspective on educational practice that I have promoted throughout this book. In Chapter 3, I suggested that many psychologists approach questions of learning equipped with one of two pervasive metaphors: computation or construction. These are broadly associated with, respectively, the academic traditions of cognitive science and of cognitive developmental theory. My own preference has been to foreground a third conception: collaboration. This I derived in Chapter 2 from the socio-cultural theorising inspired by Vygotsky and his contemporaries. For many developmental psychologists, this theorising has been effective in drawing attention to the socially grounded nature of cognition. In part, that has stimulated attention to processes of social interaction, as they relate to cognitive change. Yet, I feel that the empirical orientation towards this topic has been over-attentive to ideas arising from the scaffolding metaphor – as it is often used to describe the interpersonal dimension of instruction. Socio-cultural research could gain from developing a greater concern for the nature and management of intersubjectivity. I have argued that a socially grounded perspective on learning must acknowledge a human capacity for projective understanding of mental states in others. It is this that creates a deep human concern for the formation of socially shared cognition. Finally, I have argued that such a concern is at the core of what is entailed in collaborating.

On the experience of collaborating

I have suggested that psychological research into collaborative learning has made only modest progress. It has been dominated by a preference for analysing collaborative exchanges by coding and counting discrete social acts – usually utterances. There is some value in such categorising systems but they fail to characterise the sustained and discursive nature of many collaborative encounters. First, these encounters have a temporal dimension: they involve partners in a protracted constructive process. Second, they involve a commitment to coordinating action and attention in relation to some focal point existing between collaborators. In fact, these two features of collaborative interactions are related. Often, what it is that is constructed in this protracted fashion is what can become an 'object' of shared knowledge; this then serves to focus or direct the coordinated action.

The important point is that collaboration should be recognised as a state of social engagement that, on any given occasion, is more or less active and more or less effectively resourced. So, collaborators may vary in their concern to create shared understandings; and their circumstances of joint activity may vary in how readily they permit such achievements to be brought off. The challenge is to discover how discourse is mobilised in the service of creating joint reference; to see how what is created gets used as a platform for further exploration; and to see how the material conditions of problem-solving can be more or less friendly towards efforts after this mutuality.

In Chapter 7, I characterised children talking in ways that were variously successful in achieving shared knowledge, and I described computer-based problems that were variously successful in supporting their attempt to do this. Within those accounts, I also suggested that participating individuals might enjoy very different experiences of this collaborative effort. This notion was prompted by recognising that some children could claim a different degree of investment or ownership in the shared knowledge that underpinned the joint activity. However, the same reasoning raises a question about collaborations that are successful in this respect: can they claim a particularly *positive* affective tone? This notion is entertained in Argyle's discussion of cooperation: 'One possibility is that the experience of closely synchronised interaction is intrinsically rewarding, the result of evolutionary pressures favouring cooperation' (Argyle, 1991, p. 10). Unfortunately, Argyle only pursues this idea in relation to bodily synchronisation – such as we might enjoy during dancing. Yet, the pleasure of being 'sychronised' may extend beyond the case of physical coordination. Our own casual experience of being collaborators surely endorses the idea that being in possession of shared knowledge (and being conscious of its mutual nature) can be a positive experience. Perhaps this is all the more so, the greater our awareness of an interpersonal investment lying behind its accumulation: this may impart to the possession of shared knowledge a certain agreeable intimacy. In fact, this affective dimension may touch on something very basic in human nature. Trevarthan comments: 'But only humans have the kind of appetite a one-year-old begins to show for sharing the arbitrary use of tools, places, manners and experiences' (Trevarthan, 1988, p. 55). This appetite we might choose to read as a precocious expression of the motive for shared reference. Furth and Kane's (1992) discussion of the social creation of mental (narrative) objects seems to make a similar point for the pre-school child.

These observations of very early manifestations of collaborative interactions introduce the second of my closing themes.

On becoming collaborative learners

I am stressing the central place of socially shared knowledge in learning; and, thereby, the central place of collaborative relationships within which such knowledge gets constructed. Yet this emphasis may seem in some tension with classroom realities. In particular, ethnographies of classroom life tend to suggest that peer-based collaboration can be very difficult for young children to sustain (see the review in Chapter 6). Moreover, researchers who have discussed with young children their experience of academic collaboration tend to find that many pupils do not regard those experiences very positively (Cullingford, 1991; Galton, 1990). This might raise in our minds a question around which there is a long history of speculation and research (reviewed by Pepitone, 1980): namely, are we basically cooperative or collaborative creatures? Our attitude to this issue may colour our enthusiasm for organising collaborative circumstances for learning.

Certainly, various anthropologists have argued that we have a fundamentally cooperative nature (Hall, 1976; Trivers, 1983). Moreover, the research of developmental psychologists might suggest that there is indeed something basic in ourselves that is relevant to this issue (a 'basic-ness' that may or may not demand reference to evolutionary arguments). I have in mind the basic capacity and motivation to exercise an intersubjectivity. In fact, Trevarthan regards interpersonal motives as 'the primary organisers of mental growth' (1987, p. 178). He describes a developmental course whereby infants first manifest a primary intersubjectivity – they achieve a harmony of affect and emotion with others. Then they move towards a secondary intersubjectivity – they manifest concern to establish with others shared reference towards external objects and circumstances. Moreover, casual observation does suggest that the achievement of this shared reference is a visible source of considerable pleasure for infants.

Other researchers have traced this concern into the pre-school years. Toddlers may be particularly interested in objects that are seen to be within the attentional span of a play partner (Eckerman, Whatley and McGhee, 1979; Eckerman and Stein, 1982; Hay, 1979). Budwig, Strage and Bamberg (1986) report a (rare) longitudinal study of these processes as they transform from parent-dominated encounters to encounters of shared reference with age-mates. They make the point that parents make a distinctive contribution to these encounters. They naturally work hard to create and sustain shared objects of reference and this leads to a peculiarly rich platform from which new learning and exploration can be supported.

On the other hand, Dunn's (1988) research on pre-school sibling relations suggests a sometimes less harmonious atmosphere within playful family arenas. Hay, Caplan, Castle and Stimson (1991) have observed the fracturing of collaborative attitudes among young peers: they argue that maturity does bring a concern with personalised interests, particularly in conditions of jointly acting in relation to scarce resources. Of course, it is not clear that we should regard such developments as symptomatic of some basic human striving for individual gratification – in conflict with collaborative motives. Again, anthropological research is valuable in drawing attention to how changing conditions of living re-direct basic human motives. Graves and Graves (1983) review a rich variety of such changing conditions relevant to the developing sense of self and community. To express it starkly in their terms: new economic and social orders make it less necessary to 'store food in the neighbour's belly' (Graves and Graves, 1983).

It is important to see the technologies and rituals of modern schooling as part of this cultural influence on development. The infant's concern for shared reference in relation to material objects may continue to feature in collaborative situations; they may reliably recur through the remainder of life. But this secondary intersubjectivity must also become elaborated in new ways with the growth of a more symbolically dominated intelligence. Children will explore new forms of mutual knowledge that are more representational in nature. In particular, shared reference may become increasingly located in narrative structures. For during the pre-school years, children will naturally explore a variety of mutual involvements with narrative (Furth and Kane, 1992). Schooling may further mobilise such playful collaborations, but it also puts a new kind of demand on collaborators. They must come to generate shared objects of understanding that are abstract, but which cannot readily take on a narrative format: they must, for example, collaborate about mathematics and language itself. These are the classroom circumstances where joint work is observed to flounder (Bennett, 1991). As the terms of the task become more complex in this way, so the social interaction may be observed to disintegrate into parallel and solitary forms of work (Perlmutter, Behrend, Kuo and Muller, 1989).

On resourcing collaborative encounters

The above remarks imply one way of looking at the problems and possibilities of school-based collaborations. Such a perspective seeks to understand how schooled tasks create special demands upon collaborators. Thus, it would be argued, consideration needs to be given to how these demands can be resourced. The formation of joint understandings is a natural and visible achievement of children functioning in out-of-school contexts: the challenge is to discover how those achievements can be mobilised for realising purposes defined in classrooms.

This is not a traditional psychological orientation to the problem of making collaborative learning happen. More typically, psychologists might approach this problem in terms of a skill model: so it might be suggested that school children could benefit from some form of training in being collaborators (Johnson, Johnson and Roy, 1984). Alternatively, it might be suggested that collaborative learning is assimilated to a developmental sequence – arguing that it can only occur following the stage-like emergence of various cognitive structures (Tomasello *et al.*, 1993). I prefer to start from the insight that children are collaborators from a very young age. Certainly, before they get into schools they are already highly competent at forming shared reference – and highly interested in doing so. What is needed is a greater sensitivity to how continuities can be forged between the successes of collaborating in domestic and playful contexts and the demands for doing so in schools. Of course, pre-school children's capabilities for coordinating activity with others is a particular kind of achievement: it will be dominated by shared reference that is located in material or narrative structures. So perhaps the trick will be to appropriate and extend these achievements into schooled life.

Computers offer considerable promise in this respect. They can furnish flexible representations that may become the objects of joint reference for learners. This capability reflects their interactivity and their sophistication as a general symbol manipulating technology. Theorists who adopt a constructionist (Harel and Papert, 1991) perspective on computers in education dwell on these properties. Such theorists are keen to highlight the capacity of computers to make learning experiences concrete. Yet the orientation of the influential constructionist tradition has been very much towards the needs of self-contained learners. So, in a paper discussing what is understood by making knowledge 'concrete' through computers, Wilensky remarks: 'The constructionist paradigm by encouraging the externalization of knowledge, promotes seeing it as a distinct other with which we can come into meaningful relationship' (Wilensky, 1991, p. 202). In considering the place of computers within collaboration, I have stressed their capability for creating such externalised resources. But the 'meaningful relationships' thereby afforded need not be simply those between the individual learner and some knowledge domain. They may also be relationships held in common with others and creative collaborations may be especially enhanced by that possibility.

In Chapter 7, I described tinkering with a computer program (one that supported early number work) in order that it might furnish such a referential anchor for pupils using it together. This tinkering was successful, in that pupils' activity became increasingly coordinated around this point of shared reference: they collaborated more effectively. Developing technology to be supportive of the collaborative experience of learning is partly about developing such ways of resourcing joint activity *at* the site of some problem. But in other chapters, I have stressed that the collaborative experience extends beyond this familiar paradigm. So it will be important to understand the assimilation of computers into these broader engagements. For one thing, this means being alert to the danger that computer-based activity may fail to get drawn into the community of discourse that characterises organised learning. The collaborative interactions of teachers and pupils need to be organised *in relation to* computers – just as they are to all class-based learning experience (Chapter 5). In addition, there are other senses in which the collaborative experience of learning is organised. In Chapter 8, I considered how communities of learners may collaborate in a more loosely coupled way *around* a resource – collaborating 'through the air'. It will be helpful to understand more of how the technology can be integrated into a learning environment to take best advantage of opportunities for social exchange. Finally, I have discussed (Chapter 8) collaborations that may be experienced *through* this technology.

On the prospects for computers within collaborations

In this book, I have promoted a particular theoretical perspective on how we might best organise teaching and learning. This has involved foregrounding the collaborative experience of being a pupil. It has involved attending to how organised learning invariably is about the construction and deployment of shared understandings. As participants in this endeavour, we may proceed more or less effectively, and we may be resourced to do so more or less imaginatively. My interest in educational technology is very much for its supporting role in this sense. I have tried to review something of the existing social structures of educational practice and to suggest some of the ways that computers may enter into them to support what people are attempting together. This has involved arguments about the *general* way in which technology is deployed: not more focused considerations of the value of particular computer-based applications – tutoring systems, simulations, tools or whatever. My attitude towards any such particular application is very much determined by how effectively it is being incorporated into the participatory structure of learning (including consideration of how readily its design might afford such incorporation).

These concerns are worth rehearsing. There is currently much enthusiasm for educational software exploiting the new multimedia presentation capabilities of microcomputers. Certainly, if this book had attempted to review computers in education in terms of their technical sophistication and creative ingenuity, then it would have been necessary to have discussed these applications at some length. But in terms of the agenda that I have set here, it is not clear that these new developments are especially promising: it is not clear that they are going to resource a socially grounded experience of education as I have been discussing this. Indeed, accounts of new practice based upon, for instance, hypermedia tools, suggest that these are very much tools conceived for isolated learners. Landow's (1990) work is an exception to this. A recent article by Lehrer (1993) is also exceptional in evaluating a hypermedia resource in terms of its relation to the background culture of educational practice into which it is placed. Perhaps it should be hoped that this signals a new research trend among developers of this challenging technology.

Another area of fast technical development is networking tools and connectivity. Yet, as reviewed in Chapter 8, it is not obvious that the potential of networking is being realised in educational practice. Universities may be the best settings in which to show what is possible here. However, the signs that it will offer such a model are not encouraging. For example, the UK government's support for developing computer-based teaching resources in higher education has been quite generous. Yet none of the many individual projects financed so far have focused on communication structures, and very few of them pay any explicit attention to the support of collaborative learning.

I believe the prospects are not particularly encouraging for an IT development strategy that respects the social themes I have been considering. If anything, the climate is drifting towards 'delivery-system' models of computers in education. This allows politically influential commentators to see new electronic media as a technology for 'capturing the world's best brain power' such that it may 'dramatically increase the rate of circulation of intellectual capital' (Hague, 1991). This commodity approach to education is increasingly visible. One recent advertisement for a British university invites potential students to put it 'at the top of their shopping list': this institution's concerns being illustrated by a supermarket basket filled with packages labelled 'ecology', 'genetics', 'modern art' and so on. Some of the arguments developed here in Chapter 3 may help us to see how computers could be effective in supporting such delivery of packaged knowledge.

All new technology in education is inherently vulnerable to deployment in this way. Thus, it is important to remain vigilant to trends as they are developing. My own advocacy of networks (Chapter 8) should probably have been more sensitive to the potential of this infrastructure to support the delivery model of education. For example, there is now a network-based academic journal called the *On-line Journal of Distance Education*. It has many interesting articles on distance-teaching. However, its masthead carries a sobering prediction:

> In the industrial age, we go to school, in the information age, school can come to us. This is the message implicit in the media and movement of distance education.

This message may be part of the vision shared by many innovators and many politicians. There may be good grounds for contemplating more innovative structures of organised education than those that are currently exemplified in Western schooling. But I hope that whatever alternatives evolve they will respect the need for learners to participate within rich communities of understanding: to partake of the collaborative experience of learning.

References

Agre, P.E. (1993) The symbolic worldview: Reply to Vera and Simon. *Cognitive Science*, 17, 61–69.

Anderson, J.R., Boyle, C.F. and Reiser, B.J. (1985) Intelligent tutoring systems. *Science*, 228, 456–462.

Anderson, J.R., Boyle, C.F., Corbett, A. and Lewis, M. (1990) Cognitive modelling and intelligent tutoring. *Artificial Intelligence*, 42, 7–49.

Argyle, M. (1991) *Cooperation*. London: Routledge.

Astington, J.W., Harris, P.L. and Olson, D.R. (1988) *Developing theories of mind*. Cambridge: Cambridge University Press.

Azmitia, M. and Perlmutter, M. (1989) Social influences on children's cognition: State of the art and future directions. In H. Reese (ed.) *Advances in child development and behavior* (Vol. 22). New York: Academic Press.

Baker, C. (1985) The microcomputer and the curriculum. A critique. *Journal of Curriculum Studies*, 17, 449–451.

Bakhurst, D. (1990) Social memory in Soviet thought. In D. Middleton and D. Edwards (eds) *Collective remembering*. London: Sage,

Balle, F. (1991) The information society, schools and the media. In M. Eraut (ed.) *Education and the information society*. London: Cassell.

Bannon, L.J. (1986) Helping users help each other. In D.A. Norman and S. Draper (eds) *User-centred system design*. Hillsdale, NJ: Lawrence Erlbaum Associates.

Barnes, D. (1976) *From communication to curriculum*. Harmondsworth: Penguin.

Barrett, E. and Paradis, J. (1988) Teaching writing in an on-line classroom. *Harvard Educational Review*, 58, 154–171.

Bateson, G. (1972) *Steps to an ecology of mind: A revolutionary approach to man's understanding of himself*. New York: Ballantine.

Becker, H.J. (1991) How computers are used in United States schools: Basic data from the 1989 IEA computers in education survey. *Journal of Educational Computing Research*, 7, 385–406.

Becker, H.J. and Sterling, C.W. (1987) Equity in school computer use; National data and neglected considerations. *Journal of Educational Computing Research*, 3, 289–311.

Beer, R.D. (1990) *Intelligence as adaptive behavior: An experiment in computational neuroethology*. London: Academic Press.

Bell, N., Grossen, M. and Perret-Clermont, A. (1985) Sociocognitive conflict and intellectual growth. In M. Berkowitz (ed.) *Peer conflict and psychological growth*. San Francisco: Jossey-Bass.

Bennett, S.N. (1991) Cooperative learning in classrooms: Processes and outcomes. *Journal of Child Psychology and Psychiatry*, 32, 581–594.

Benyon, J. (1993) Computers, dominant boys and invisible girls. In J. Benyon and H. Mackay (eds) *Computers into classrooms*. London: The Falmer Press.

Benyon, J. and Mackay, H. (1993) More questions than answers. In J. Benyon and H. Mackay (eds) *Computers into classrooms*. London: The Falmer Press.

Bernstein, L.E. (1981) Language as a product of dialogue. *Discourse Processes*, 4, 117–147

Blaye, A., Light, P.H., Joiner, R. and Sheldon, S. (1991) Collaboration as a facilitator of planning and problem solving on a computer-based task. *British Journal of Developmental Psychology*, 9, 471–484.

Bleach, P. (1986) *The use of computers in primary schools*. Reading and Language Information Centre, Reading University.

Bliss, J., Chandra, P. and Cox, M. (1986) The introduction of computers into a school *Computers and Education*, 10, 49–54.

Boden, M. (1977) *Artificial intelligence and natural man*. Brighton: Harvester Press.

Boden, M. (1981) *Minds and mechanisms*. Brighton: Harvester Press.

Bontinck, I. (1986) The impact of electronic media on adolescents, their everyday experience, their learning orientations and leisure time activities. *Communications*, 12, 21–30

Bork, A. (1980) Learning through graphics. In R. Taylor (ed.) *The computer in the school tutor, tool, tutee*. New York: Teachers College Press.

Bork, A. (1991) Is technology-based learning effective? *Contemporary Education*, 63, 6–14

Bowers, C.A. (1988) *The cultural dimension of educational computing*. New York: Teacher College Press.

Bowers, J.M. and Benford, S. (1991) *Studies in computer-supported cooperative work Theory, practice and design*. Amsterdam: Elsevier.

Boyd-Barrett, O. (1990) Schools' computing policy as state-directed innovation. *Educational Studies*, 16, 169–185.

Bracey, G.W. (1988) In-service training: Still anxiety among educators over computers *Electronic Learning*, Nov., 20.

Bransford, J.D., Vye, N.J., Adams, L.T. and Perfetto, G.A. (1989) Learning skills and the acquisition of knowledge. In A. Lesgold and R. Glaser (eds) *Foundations for a psychology of education*. Hillsdale, NJ: Lawrence Erlbaum Associates.

Britton, J., Burgess, A., Martin, N., McLeod, A. and Rosen H. (1975) *The development of writing abilities 11–18*. London: Macmillan Education.

Brod, C. (1984) *Technostress: the human cost of the computer revolution*. Reading, MA Addison-Wesley.

Broderick, C. and Trushell, J. (1985) Problems and processes – Junior School children using wordprocessors to produce an information leaflet. *English in Education*, 19, 2.

Brown, A.L. and Campione, J.C. (1986) Psychological theory and the study of learning disabilities. *American Psychologist*, 14, 1059–1068.

Brown, J.S. (1985) Process versus product: A perspective on tools for communal and informal electronic learning. *Journal of Educational Computing Research*, 1, 179–201

Brown, J.S. and Burton, R.R. (1978) Diagnostic models for procedural bugs in basic mathematical skills. *Cognitive Science*, 2, 155–192.

Brown, J.S., Collins, A. and Duguid, P. (1988) *Situation cognition and the culture of learning*. Report No. 6886. BBN Systems and Technologies Corporation.

Brown, J.S., Collins, A. and Duguid, P. (1989) Situated cognition and the culture of learning *Educational Researcher*, 18, 32–42.

Brown, N. (1989) Profiling in English: The potential for real pupil–teacher collaboration in assessment. In M. Styles (ed.) *Collaboration and writing*. Milton Keynes: Open University Press.

Brownell, C. and Carriger, M.S. (1991) Collaborations among toddler peers: Individual contributions to social context. In L. Resnick, J. Levine and S. Teasley (eds) *Perspective on socially shared cognition*. Washington, DC: American Psychological Association.

Bruner, J.S. (1966) On cognitive growth. In J. Bruner, R. Olver and P. Greenfield (eds *Studies in cultural growth*. New York: Wiley.

Bruner, J.S. (1983) *Child's talk*. Oxford: Oxford University Press.

runer, J.S. (1986) *Actual minds, possible worlds*. London: Harvard University Press.

runer, J.S. (1991) The narrative construction of reality. *Critical Inquiry*, 18, 1–21.

udwig, N., Strage, A. and Bamberg, M. (1986) The construction of joint activities with an age-mate: The transition from caregiver–child to peer play. In J. Cook-Gumperz, W. Corsaro and J. Sreeck (eds) *Children's worlds and children's language*. New York: Walter de Gruyter.

urns, H., Parlett, J.W. and Redfield, C.L. (1991) *Intelligent tutoring systems*. Hillsdale, NJ: Lawrence Erlbaum Associates.

ampbell, R. and Olson, D. (1990) Children's thinking. In R. Grieve and M. Hughes (eds) *Understanding children*. Oxford: Blackwell.

arasik, R. and Grantham, C. (1988) *A case study of computer-supported cooperative work in a dispersed organization*. Proceedings of SIGCHI '88, Association of Computing Machinery.

arbonell, J.R. (1970) AI in CAI: An artificial-intelligence approach to computer-assisted instruction. *IEEE Transactions on Man–Machine Systems*, MMS-11, 190–202.

azden, C.B. (1986) Classroom discourse. In M. Wittrock (ed.) *Handbook of research on teaching*. New York: Macmillan.

azden, C.B. (1990) Achieving knowledge in the classroom. *Contemporary Psychology*, 35, 66.

handler, D. (1992) The purpose of the computer in the classroom. In J. Benyon and H. Mackay (eds) *Technological literacy and the curriculum*. London: The Falmer Press.

hi, M. and Van Lehn, K. (1991) The content of physics self-explanations. *Journal of Learning Sciences*, 1, 69–105.

hi, M., Bossack, M., Lewis, M. W., Reimann, P. and Glaser, R. (1989) Self-explanations: How students study and use examples in learning to solve problems. *Cognitive Science*, 13, 145–182.

hivers, G. (1987) Information technology – girls and education: A cross-cultural review. In M. Davidson and C. Cooper (eds) *Women and information technology*. Chichester: Wiley & Son.

lancey, W.J. (1988) The knowledge engineer as student: Metacognitive bases for asking good questions. In H. Mandl and A. Lesgold (eds) *Learning issues for intelligent tutoring systems*. New York: Springer-Verlag.

lancey, W.J. (1991) Situated cognition: Stepping out of representational flatland. AICOM, *European Journal of Artificial Intelligence*, 4, 109–112.

lancey, W.J. (1992) Representations of knowing: In defence of cognitive apprenticeship. *Journal of Artificial Intelligence in Education*, 3, 139–168.

lancey, W.J. (1993) Situated action: A neuropsychological interpretation. Response to Vera and Simon. *Cognitive Science*, 17, 87–116.

lark, H.H. and Brennan S.E. (1991) Grounding in communication. In L. Resnick, J. Levine and S. Teasley (eds) *Perspectives on socially shared cognition*. Washington, DC: American Psychological Association.

lark, H.H. and Schaefer, E.F. (1989) Contributing to discourse. *Cognitive Science*, 13, 259–294.

lark, H.H. and Wilkes-Gibbs, D. (1986) Referring as a collaborative process. *Cognition*, 22, 1–39.

lark, H.H., Schreuder, R. and Buttrick, S. (1985) Common ground and the understanding of demonstrative reference. *Journal of Verbal Learning and Verbal Behavior*, 22, 245–259.

lements, D. (1987) Computers and young children: A review of research. *Young Children*, 43, 34–44.

lements, D.H. and Gullo, D.F. (1984) Effects of computer programming on young children's cognition. *Journal of Educational Psychology*, 76, 6, 1051–1058.

Cognition and Technology Group at Vanderbilt (1990) Anchored instruction and its rela tionship to situated cognition. *Educational Researcher*, 19, 2–10.

Cohen, M. and Reil, M. (1989) The effect of distant audiences on students' writing. *America Educational Research Journal*, 26, 143–159.

Cole, M. (1987) Cultural psychology: A once and future discipline. In J. Berman (ed *Nebraska symposium on motivation: cross-cultural perspectives*. Lincoln: University c Nebraska Press.

Cole, M. (1990) Cognitive development and formal schooling: The evidence from cross cultural research. In L. Moll (ed.) *Vygotsky and education*. Cambridge: Cambridg University Press.

Cole, M. (1991) Conclusion. In L. Resnick, J. Levine and S. Teasley (eds) *Perspectives o socially shared cognition*. Washington, DC: American Psychological Association.

Cole, M. and Griffin, P. (1980) Cultural amplifiers reconsidered. In D.R. Olson (ed.) *Th social foundations of language and thought*. New York: Norton.

Cole, M. and Scribner, S. (1974) *Culture and thought*. New York: Wiley.

Cole, M., Gay, J., Glick, J.A. and Sharp, D.W. (1971) *The cultural context of learning an thinking*. New York: Basic Books.

Collins, A. (1977) Process in acquiring knowledge. In R. Anderson, R. Spiro and W Montague (eds) *Schooling and the acquisition of knowledge*. Hillsdale, NJ: Lawrenc Erlbaum Associates.

Collins, A. (1988) *Cognitive apprenticeship and instructional technology*. Report No. 689! BBN Systems and Technologies Corporation.

Collins, E.G. (1986) A company without offices. *Harvard Business Review*, 1, 127–136.

Collis, B. (1987) Developments in the use of microcomputers in North American school! To what extent is the teacher's role changing? *International Review of Education*, 3: 331–338.

Cook-Gumperz, J. and Corsaro, W.A. (1977) Social-ecological constraints on children' communicative strategies. *Sociology*, 11, 411–434.

Cox, M., Rhodes, V. and Hall, J. (1988) The use of computer-assisted learning in primar schools: Some factors affecting the uptake. *Computers and Education*, 12, 173–178.

Crawford, R. (1988) Inside classrooms: Word processing and the fourth grade write *Canadian Journal of English Language Arts*, 11, 42–46.

Crook, C.K. (1986) Paired versus individual working on a microcomputer task. Pape presented at the Annual Conference of the BPS Developmental Section, Exeter.

Crook, C.K. (1992a) Cultural artefacts in social development: The case of computers. In F McGurk (ed.) *Childhood social development: Contemporary perspectives*. Hove: Law rence Erlbaum Associates.

Crook, C.K. (1992b) Young children's skill in using a mouse to control a graphical compute interface. *Computers and Education*, 19, 199–207.

Crook, C.K. and Steele, J. (1987) Self-selection of simple computer activities by infa school pupils. *Educational Psychology*, 7, 1, 23–32.

Cuban, L. (1986) *Teachers and machines*. New York: Teachers College Press.

Cuffaro, H.K. (1984) Microcomputers in education: Why is earlier better? *Teachers Colleg Record*, 85, 4, 559–568.

Cullingford, C. (1991) *The inner world of the school: Children's ideas about school* London: Cassell.

Daiute, C. (1985) Issues in using computers to socialize the writing process. *Education Computing and Technology Journal*, 33, 41–50.

Dalbey, J., Tournaire, F. and Linn, M. (1986) Making programming instruction cognitivel demanding: An intervention study. *Journal of Research in Science Teaching*, 23, 427 436.

Dalton, D.W., Hannafin, M.J. and Hooper, W. (1989) The effects of individual versu cooperative computer-assisted instruction on student performance and attitudes. *Educational Technology Research and Development*, 37, 15–24.

Damon, W. and Phelps, E. (1989) Strategic uses of peer learning in children's education. In T. Berndt and G. Ladd (eds) *Peer relationships in child development*. New York: Wiley.

D'Andrade, R. (1981) The cultural part of cognition. *Cognitive Science*, 5, 179–195.

Darby, J. (1991) Computers in teaching: the needs of the 90s. *The CTISS File*, 12, 9–18.

Davidson, P.M. (1992) The role of social interaction in cognitive development: A propaedeutic. In L. Winegar and J. Valsiner (eds) *Children's development within social context. Volume 1: Metatheory and theory*. Hillsdale, NJ: Lawrence Erlbaum Associates.

Davies, G. (1989a) Discovering a need to write: The role of the teacher as collaborator. In M. Styles (ed.) *Collaboration and writing*. Milton Keynes: Open University Press.

Davies, G. (1989b) Writing without a pencil. In M. Styles (ed.) *Collaboration and writing*. Milton Keynes: Open University Press.

Davis, N.E. (1992) Information technology in United Kingdom initial teacher education, 1982–1992. *Journal of Information Technology for Teacher Education*, 1, 7–21.

Dennett, D. (1978) *Brainstorms*. Cambridge, MA: MIT Press.

DES (Department of Education and Science) (1989a) *English in the national curriculum*. London: HMSO.

DES (Department of Education and Science) (1989b) *Survey of Information Technology in Schools*. London: HMSO.

DES (Department of Education and Science) (1991) *Survey of Information Technology in Schools*. London: HMSO.

Desforges, C. (1985) Training for the management of learning in the primary school. In H. Francis (ed.) *Learning to teach: Psychology in teacher training*. Lewes: The Falmer Press.

Detterman, D.K. (1993) The case for the prosecution: Transfer as an epiphenomenon. In D. Detterman and R. Sternberg (eds) *Transfer on trial: Intelligence, cognition and instruction*. Norwood, NJ: Ablex.

Dickinson, D. (1986) Cooperation, collaboration and a computer: Integrating a computer in a first-second grade writing program. *Research in the Teaching of English*, 20, 357–378.

Dillon, D. (1985) The dangers of computers in literacy education: Who's in charge here? In D. Chandler and S. Marcus (eds) *Computers and literacy*. Milton Keynes: Open University Press.

DiPardo, A. and Freedman, S. (1988) Peer response groups in the writing classroom: Theoretic foundations and new directions. *Review of Educational Research*, 58, 119–150.

DiSessa, A. (1988) Knowledge in pieces. In G. Forman and P. Pufall (eds), *Constructivism in the computer age*. Hillsdale, NJ: Lawrence Erlbaum Associates.

Doise, W. (1985) Social regulations in cognitive development. In R. Hinde, A.-N. Perret-Clermont and J. Stevenson-Hinde (eds) *Social relationships and cognitive development*. Oxford: Oxford University Press.

Doise, W. and Mugny, G. (1984) *The social development of the intellect*. Oxford: Pergamon Press.

Donaldson, M. (1978) *Children's minds*. London: Fontana.

Dreyfus, H.L. and Dreyfus, S.E. (1984) Putting computers in their proper place: Analysis versus intuition in the classroom. *Teachers College Record*, 85, 4, 578–601.

Dreyfus, H.L. and Dreyfus, S.E. (1986) *Minds over machines*. Oxford: Blackwell.

Dudley-Marling, C. and Owston, R.D. (1988) Using microcomputers to teach problem solving: A critical review. *Educational Technology*, 28, 27–33.

Dunn, J. (1988) *The beginnings of social understanding*. Oxford: Blackwell.

Dunn, J. (1989) The school as a community of writers. In M. Styles (ed.) *Collaboration and writing*. Milton Keynes: Open University Press.

Dunn, S. and Ridgeway, J. (1991) Computer uses during primary school teacher practice: A survey. *Journal of Computer Assisted Learning*, 7, 7–17.

Dunne, E. and Bennett, N. (1990) *Talking and learning in groups*. London: Macmillan.

Durndell, A. (1991) The persistence of the gender gap in computing. *Computers and Education*, 16, 283–287.

Eckerman, C.O. and Stein, M.R. (1982) The toddler's emerging interactive skills. In K Rubin and H. Ross (eds) *Peer relationships and social skills in childhood*. New York Springer-Verlag.

Eckerman, C.O., Whatly, J.L. and McGhee, L.J. (1979) Approaching and contacting the object another manipulates: A social skill of the 1-year-old. *Developmental Psychology* 15, 585–593.

Edwards, D. (1990) Classroom discourse and classroom knowledge. In C. Rogers and F Kutnick (eds) *The social psychology of the primary school*. London: Routledge.

Edwards, D. and Mercer, N. (1987) *Common knowledge*. London: Methuen.

Edwards, D. and Middleton, D. (1986) Joint remembering: Constructing an account of shared experience. *Discourse Processes*, 9, 423–459.

Ellis, C., Gibbs, S. and Rein, G. (1991) Groupware: Some issues and experiences. *Communications of the ACM*, 34, 38–58.

Emihovich, C. and Miller, G. (1988) Talking to the turtle: A discourse analysis of Logo instruction. *Discourse Processes*, 11, 182–201.

Ennals, R. (1993) Computers and exploratory learning in the classroom. In J. Benyon and H. Mackay (eds) *Computers into classrooms*. London: The Falmer Press.

Eraut, M. (1991a) *Education and the information society*. London: Cassell Education.

Eraut, M. (1991b) The information society – a challenge for education policies? Polic options and implementation strategies. In M. Eraut (ed.) *Education and the information society*. London: Cassell.

Eraut, M. and Hoyles, C. (1989) Groupwork with computers. *Journal of Computer-assisted Learning*, 5, 12–24.

Essa, E.L. (1987) The effect of a computer on pre-school children's activities. *Early Childhood Research Quarterly*, 2, 377–382.

Eveland, J. and Bikson, T. (1986) *Evolving electronic communication networks: An empirical assessment* (Technical Report). Santa Monica, CA: The Rand Cooperation.

Falbel, A. (1991) The computer as convivial tool. In I. Harel and S. Papert (eds) *Constructionism*. Norwood, NJ: Ablex.

Farish, D. (1989) Computer as catalyst. Talk. *Journal of the National Oracy Project*, 2 17–19.

Feldhusen, J. and Szabo, M. (1969) The advent of the educational heart transplant, computer-assisted instruction: A review of the research. *Contemporary Education*, 40 265–274.

Feurzeig, W. (1964) The computer that talks like a teacher. *Journal of Accounting*, 11; 27–28.

Feurzeig, W. (1988) Apprentice tools: Students as practitioners. In R.S. Nickerson and P.F Zodhiates (eds) *Technology in education: Looking towards 2000*. Hillsdale, NJ: Lawrence Erlbaum Associates.

Fife-Shaw, C., Breakwell, G., Lee, T. and Spencer, J. (1986) Patterns of teenage compute usage. *Journal of Computer-assisted Learning*, 2, 152–161.

Forman, E. (1989) The role of peer interaction in the social construction of mathematica knowledge. *International Journal of Educational Research*, 13, 55–69.

Forman, E.A. and Cazden, C.B. (1985) Exploring Vygotskyian perspectives in education The cognitive value of peer interaction. In J. Wertsch (ed.) *Culture, communication an cognition*. Cambridge: Cambridge University Press.

Forman, E.A. and Kraker, M.A. (1985) The social origins of logic: The contributions of Piaget and Vygotsky. In M.W. Berkowitz (ed.) *Peer conflict and psychological growth* (New Directions for Child Development No. 29). San Francisco: Jossey-Bass.

Forrester, M.A. (1992) The development of young children's social-cognitive skills. Hove LEA.

thergill, R. (1984) Teacher training in England, Wales and Northern Ireland. In F. Lovis and E. Tagg (eds) *Informatics and teacher training*. Amsterdam: North Holland.

aser, R., Burkhardt, H., Coupland, J., Philips, R., Pimm, D. and Ridgeway, J. (1988) Learning activities and classroom roles with and without the microcomputer. In A. Jones and P. Scrimshaw (eds) *Computers in education 5–13*. Milton Keynes: Open University Press.

eund, L. (1990) Maternal regulation of children's problem-solving behaviour and its impact on children's performance. *Child Development*, 61, 113–126.

ith, U. (1989) *Autism: Explaining the enigma*. Oxford: Blackwell.

rth, H.G. and Kane, S.R. (1992) Children constructing society: A new perspective on children at play. In H. McGurk (ed.) *Childhood social development: Contemporary perspectives*. Hove: Lawrence Erlbaum Associates.

alton, M. (1990) Grouping and group work. In C. Rogers and P. Kutnick (eds) *The social psychology of the primary school*. London: Routledge.

alton, M. and Williamson, J. (1992) *Group work in the primary classroom*. London: Routledge.

ardner, J. and McBride, F. (eds) (1990) *Computers across the university curriculum*. Computers in Teaching Initiative.

ardner, N. (1989) The electronic campus: The first decade. *Higher Education Quarterly*, 43, 332–350.

asser, L. (1991) Social conceptions of knowledge and action: DAI foundations and open systems semantics. *Artificial Intelligence*, 47, 107–138.

earhart, M. and Newman, D. (1980) Learning to draw a picture: The social context of an individual activity. *Discourse Processes*, 3, 169–184.

elman, R., Massey, C.M. and McManus, M. (1991) Characterising supporting environments for cognitive development: Lessons from children in a museum. In L. Resnick, J. Levine and S. Teasley (eds) *Perspectives on socially shared cognition*. Washington, DC: American Psychological Association.

enishi, C., McCollum, P. and Strand, E. (1988) Research currents: The interactional richness of children's computer use. *Language Arts*, 62, 526–532.

iacquinta, J. and Lane P.A. (1989) Fifty-one families with computers: A study of children's academic uses of microcomputers at home. *Educational Technology Research and Development*, 38, 27–37.

oldberg, M.H. and Maccoby, E.E. (1965) Children's acquisition of skill in performing a group task under 2 conditions of group formation. *Journal of Personality and Social Psychology*, 2, 898–902.

onzalez-Edfelt, N. (1991) Oral interaction and collaboration at the computer: Learning English as a second language with the help of your peers. *Computers in the Schools*, 17, 53–90.

oodnow, J.J. (1990) The socialization of cognition: What's involved? In J. Stigler, R. Shweder and G. Herdt (eds) *Cultural psychology: Essays on comparative human development*. Cambridge: Cambridge University Press.

oodwin, C. and Heritage, J. (1990) Conversation analysis. *Annual Review of Anthropology*, 19, 283–387.

oody, J. and Watt, I.P. (1968) The consequences of literacy. In J. Goody (ed.) *Literacy in traditional societies*. Cambridge: Cambridge University Press.

raves, N.B. and Graves, T.D. (1983) The cultural context of prosocial development: An ecological model. In D. L. Bridgeman (ed.) *The nature of prosocial development*. New York: Academic Press.

reenfield, P. (1984) A theory of the teacher in the learning activities of everyday life. In B. Rogoff and J. Lave (eds) *Everyday cognition*. Cambridge, MA: Harvard University Press.

reeno, J.G. (1989) Situations, mental models, and generative knowledge. In D. Klahr and

K. Kotovsky (eds) *Complex information processing. The impact of Herbert A. Simo* Hillsdale, NJ: Lawrence Erlbaum Associates.

Greeno, J.G. and Moore, J.L. (1993) Situativity and symbols: Response to Vera and Simo *Cognitive Science*, 17, 49–59.

Greeno, J.G., Smith, D.R. and Moore, J.L. (1993) Transfer of situated learning. In J Detterman and R. Sternberg (eds) *Transfer on trial: Intelligence, cognition and instru tion.* Norwood, NJ: Ablex.

Grief, I. (1988) *Computer-supported cooperative work: A book of readings.* San Mateo, C. Morgan Kaufmann.

Grint, K. (1992) Sniffers, lurkers, actor networkers: Computer medicated communicatio as a technical fix. In J. Benyon and H. Mackay (eds) *Technological literacy and t curriculum.* London: The Falmer Press.

Grudin, J. (1990) Groupware and cooperative work: Problems and prospects. In B. Lau (ed.) *The art of human–computer interface design.* Reading, MA: Addison-Wesley.

Guberman, S.R. and Greenfield, P.M. (1991) Learning and transfer in everyday cognitio *Cognitive Development*, 6, 233–260.

Gwyn, R. (1988) Teacher education and change: The first decade of IT. *European Journ of Teacher Education*, 11, 195–205.

Habermas, J. (1987) *The theory of communicative action.* Boston: Beacon Press.

Hague, D. (1991) *Beyond universities.* London: Institute of Economic Affairs.

Hale, D. (1990) Micros for the masses: Undergraduate computing in psychology. In Gardner and F. McBride (eds) *Computers across the university curriculum.* Compute in Teaching Initiative.

Hall, E.T. (1976) *Beyond culture.* New York: Doubleday.

Hansen, W.J. (1988) The Andrew environment for development of educational computin *Computers and Education*, 12, 231–239.

Hanson, M. (1985) The microcomputer revolution: Another attempt at educational refor *Education and Society*, 3, 75–82.

Harasim, L. (1990) *On-line education: Perspectives on a new environment.* New Yor Praeger.

Harel, I. and Papert, J. (1991) *Constructionism.* Norwood, NJ: Ablex.

Harris, P.L. (1991) The work of the imagination. In A. Whitten (ed.) *Natural theories mind.* Cambridge: Cambridge University Press.

Hatano, F. and Inagaki, K. (1992) Disituating cognition through the construction of conce tual knowledge. In P. Light and G. Butterworth (eds) *Context and cognition: Ways learning and knowing.* New York: Harvester-Wheatsheaf.

Hawkins, J. (1991) Technology-mediated communities for learning: Designs and cons quences. *Annals of the American Association for Political and Social Science*, 51 159–174.

Hawkins, J., Sheingold, K., Gearhart, M. and Berger, C. (1982) Microcomputers in schoo Impact on the social life of elementary classrooms. *Journal of Applied Development Psychology*, 3, 361–373.

Hay, D. (1979) Cooperative interactions and sharing between very young children and the parents. *Developmental Psychology*, 15, 647–653.

Hay, D.F., Caplan, M., Castle, J. and Stimson, C.A. (1991) Does sharing become increa ingly 'rational' in the second year of life. *Developmental Psychology*, 27, 987–993.

Heath, S.B. (1983) *Ways with words.* Cambridge: Cambridge University Press.

Henderson, A. and Maddux, C. (1988) Problems and pitfalls of computer networking educational settings. *Educational Technology*, 28, 29–32.

Henderson, R.W. (1986) Self-regulated learning: Implications for the design of instruction media. *Contemporary Educational Psychology*, 11, 405–427.

Hesse, B.W., Werner, C.M. and Altman, I. (1988) Temporal aspects of computer-mediat communication. *Computers in Human Behavior*, 4, 147–165.

Heywood, G. and Norman, P. (1988) Problems of educational innovation: The primary teacher's response to using the computer. *Journal of Computer-assisted Learning*, 4, 34–43.

Hill, A. and Browne, A. (1988) Talk and the microcomputer: An investigation in the infant classroom. *Reading*, 22, 61–69.

Hiltz, S.R. (1990) Evaluating the virtual classroom. In L. Harasim (ed.) *On-line education: Perspectives on a new environment*. New York: Praeger.

Hiltz, S.R. and Meinke, R. (1989) Teaching in a virtual classroom. *Teaching Sociology*, 17, 431–446.

Holden, C. (1989) Computers make slow progress in class. *Science*, 244, 906–909.

Hounsell, D. (1987) Essay writing and the quality of feedback. In J. Richardson, M. Eysenck and D. Piper (eds) *Student learning: Research in education and cognitive psychology*. Milton Keynes: SRHE/Open University Press.

Howe, C., Tolmie, A. and Rodgers, C. (1990) Physics in the primary school: Peer interaction and the understanding of floating and sinking. *European Journal of Psychology of Education*, 5, 459–475.

Hoyles, C. (1985a) What is the point of group discussion in mathematics? *Studies in Mathematics*, 16, 205–214.

Hoyles, C. (1985b) *Culture and computers in the mathematics classroom: An inaugural lecture*. University of London, Institute of Education.

Hoyles, C. (1988) *Girls and computers*. Bedford Way Papers 34. London: Institute of Education.

Hoyles, C. (1992) Computer-based microworlds: A radical vision or a Trojan mouse. Paper presented at ICME 7, University of Laval, Quebec, Canada.

Hoyles, C. and Noss, R. (1987) Children working in a structured Logo environment: From doing to understanding. *Recherches en Didactique des Mathématiques*, 8, 131–174.

Hoyles, C. and Sutherland, R. (1989) *Logo mathematics in the classroom*. London: Routledge.

Hoyles, C., Healy, L. and Sutherland, R. (1991) Patterns of discussion between pupil pairs in computer and non-computer environments. *Journal of Computer-assisted Learning*, 7, 210–226.

Huber, G. (1990) A theory of the effects of advanced information technologies on behavior. *Academy of Management Review*, 15, 47–71.

Hughes, M. and Greenhough, P. (1989) Gender and social interaction in early Logo use. In J. Collins, N. Estes, W. Gattis and D. Walker (eds) *The Sixth International Conference on Technology and Education*, Vol 1. Edinburgh: CEP.

Hughes, M., Brackenridge, A. and Macleod, H. (1987) Children's ideas about computers. In J. Rutkowska and C. Crook (eds) *Computers, cognition and development*. Chichester: Wiley.

Humphrey, N. (1976) The social function of intellect. In P. Bateson and R. Hinde (eds) *Growing points in ethology*. Cambridge: Cambridge University Press.

Hutchins, E. L. (1986) Mediation and automization. *Quarterly Newsletter of the Laboratory of Comparative Human Cognition*, 8, 47–58.

Hutchins, E. L. (1991) The social organization of distributed cognition. In L. Resnick, J. Levine and S. Teasley (eds) *Perspectives on socially shared cognition*. Washington, DC: American Psychological Association.

Illich, I. (1973) *Tools for conviviality*. New York: Harper & Row.

Isaacs, G. (1989) Athena, Andrew and Stanford: A look at implementation and evaluation in three large projects. *Journal of Computer-assisted Learning*, 5, 84–94.

ITTE (1987) *Information Technology in Teacher Education*. Croydon, UK: ITTE Association.

Jackson, A., Fletcher, B. and Messer, D.J. (1986) A survey of microcomputer use and provision in primary schools. *Journal of Computer-assisted Learning*, 2, 45–55.

Jackson, A., Fletcher, B. and Messer, D.J. (1988) Effects of experience on microcomputer use in primary schools: Results of a second survey. *Journal of Computer-assisted Learning*, 4, 214–226.

Jackson, A., Fletcher, B. and Messer, D.J. (1992) When talking doesn't help: An investigation of microcomputer-based group problem solving. *Learning and Instruction*, 2, 185–198.

Jahoda, G. (1980) Theoretical and systematic approaches in cross-cultural psychology. In H. Triandis and W. Lambert (eds) *Handbook of cross-cultural psychology*, Vol. 1. Boston: Allyn & Bacon.

Jahoda, G. (1992) *Crossroads between culture and mind. Continuities and change in theories of human nature*. Brighton: Harvester Press.

Jamison, D., Suppes, P. and Wells, S. (1974) Effectiveness of alternative instructional media. *Review of Educational Research*, 44, 1–67.

Johansen, R. (1988) *Groupware: Computer support for business teams*. New York: Free Press.

Johnson, D. and Johnson, R. (1985) Cooperative learning: One key to computer-assisted learning. *Computing Teacher*, 13, 11–13.

Johnson, D.W., Johnson, R.T. and Roy, P. (1984) *Circles of learning*. Washington, DC: Association for Supervision and Curriculum Development.

Johnson, M. (1991) Computer tools in the history curriculum. In I. Goodson and J. Mangan (eds) *Computers, classrooms and culture*. Occasional Papers, Vol. 2, Ruccus Project, University of Western Ontario.

Johnson, R., Johnson, D. and Stanne, M. (1985) Effects of cooperative, competitive and individualistic goal structures on computer-assisted instruction. *Journal of Educational Psychology*, 77, 668–677.

Johnson, R., Johnson, D. and Stanne, M. (1986) Comparison of computer-assisted cooperative, competitive and individualistic learning. *American Educational Research Journal*, 23, 382–392.

Kafai, Y. and Harel, I. (1991) Learning through design and teaching: Exploring social and collaborative aspects of constructionism. In I. Harel and S. Papert (eds) *Constructionism*. Norwood, NJ: Ablex.

Katz, S. and Lesgold, L. (1993) The role of the tutor in computer-based collaborative learning situations. In S. Lajoie and S. Derry (eds) *Computers as cognitive tools*. Hillsdale, NJ: Lawrence Erlbaum Associates.

Kay, A.C. (1991) Computers, networks and education. *Scientific American*, 100–107.

Keep, R. (1991) *On-line: Electronic mail in the curriculum*. Coventry: National Council for Educational Technology.

Keller, J. (1990) Characteristics of Logo instruction promoting transfer of learning: A research review. *Journal of Research on Computing in Education*, 23, 55–71.

Kidder, T. (1981) The soul of a new machine. Boston: Little Brown.

Kiesler, S. and Sproull, L. (1987) *Computing and change on campus*. Cambridge: Cambridge University Press.

Kiesler, S., Siegel, J. and McGuire, T. (1984) Social psychological aspects of computer-mediated communication. *American Psychologist*, 39, 1123–1134.

King, A. (1989) Verbal interaction and problem solving within computer-assisted cooperative learning groups. *Journal of Educational Computing Research*, 5, 1–15.

Kinkead, J. (1987) Computer conversations: Email and writing instruction. *College Composition and Communication*, 38, 337–341.

Komsky, S.H. (1991) A profile of users of electronic mail in a university. *Management Science*, 4, 310–340.

Krauss, R.M. and Fussell, S.R. (1991) Constructing shared communicative environments. In L. Resnick, J. Levine and S. Teasley (eds) *Perspectives on socially shared cognition*. Washington, DC: American Psychological Association.

Krendl, K.A. and Lieberman, D.A. (1988) Computers and learning: A review of recent research. *Journal of Educational Computing Research*, 4, 367–389.

Kreuger, L.W., Karger, H. and Barwick, K. (1989) A critical look at children and micro-computers: Some phenomenological observations. In J.T. Pardeck and J.W. Murphy (eds) *Microcomputers in early childhood education*. New York: Gordon & Breach.

Kruger, A. and Tomasello, M. (1986) Transactive discussions with peers and adults. *Developmental Psychology*, 22, 681–685.

Kulik, J.A. and Kulik, C.C. (1987) Review of recent research literature on computer-based instruction. *Contemporary Educational Psychology*, 12, 222–230.

Kulik, J., Kulik, C. and Bangert-Drowns, R. (1985) Effectiveness of computer-based education in elementary schools. *Computers in Human Behavior*, 1, 59–74.

Kutnick, P. (1983) *Relating to learning*. London: Unwin.

Landow, G.P. (1990) Hypertext and collaborative work: The example of intermedia. In J. Galegher, R. Kraut and C. Egide (eds) *Intellectual teamwork*. Hillsdale, NJ: Lawrence Erlbaum Associates.

Laurillard, D. (1987) The different forms of learning in psychology and education. In J. Richardson, M. Eysenck and D. Piper (eds) *Student learning: Research in education and cognitive psychology*. Milton Keynes: SRHE/Open University Press.

Laurillard, D. (1992) Learning through collaborative computer simulations. *British Journal of Educational Technology*, 23, 164–171.

Lave, J. (1988) *Cognition in practice: Mind, mathematics and culture in everyday life*. Cambridge: Cambridge University Press.

Lave, J. (1991) Situating learning in communities of practice. In L. Resnick, J. Levine and S. Teasley (eds) *Perspectives on socially shared cognition*. Washington, DC: American Psychological Association.

Lave, J. and Wenger, E. (1991) *Situated learning. Legitimate peripheral participation*. Cambridge: Cambridge University Press.

Lawler, R.W. (1987) Learning environments: Now, then and someday. In R. Lawler and M. Yazdani (eds) *Artificial intelligence and education. 1: Learning environments and tutoring systems*. Norwood, NJ: Ablex.

LCHC (Laboratory of Comparative Human Cognition) (1983) Culture and cognitive development. In W. Kessen (ed.) *Handbook of child psychology*, Vol. 1. New York: Wiley.

LCHC (Laboratory of Comparative Human Cognition) (1986) Contribution of cross-cultural research to education practice. *American Psychologist*, 41, 1049–1058.

LCHC (Laboratory of Comparative Human Cognition) (1989) Kids and computers: A positive vision of the future. *Harvard Educational Review*, 59, 73–86.

Lea, M. (1992) *Contexts of computer-mediated communication*. Hemel Hempstead: Harvester-Wheatsheaf.

Lea, M., O'Shea, T., Fung, P. and Spears, R. (1992) Flaming in computer-mediated communication: Observations, explanations and implications. In M. Lea (ed.) *Contexts of computer-mediated communication*. Hemel Hempstead: Harvester-Wheatsheaf.

Lehrer, R. (1993) Authors of knowledge: Patterns of hypermedia design. In S. Lajoie and S. Derry (eds) *Computers as cognitive tools*. Hillsdale, NJ: Lawrence Erlbaum Associates.

Leont'ev, A.N. (1981) *Problems of the development of mind*. Moscow: Progress Publishers.

Lepper, M.R. and Chabay, R.W. (1988) Socializing the intelligent tutor: Bringing empathy to computer tutors. In H. Mandl and A. Lesgold (eds) *Learning issues for intelligent tutoring systems*. New York: Springer-Verlag.

Lepper, M.R. and Gurtner, J.-L. (1989) Children and computers: Approaching the twenty-first century. *American Psychologist*, 44, 170–178.

Lepper, M.R., Woolverton, M., Mumme, D.L. and Gurtner, J.-L. (1993) Motivational techniques of expert human tutors: Lessons for the design of computer-based tutors. In S. Lajoie and S. Derry (eds) *Computers as cognitive tools*. Hillsdale, NJ: Lawrence Erlbaum Associates.

Levin, J.A., Kim, H. and Riel, M. (1990) Analyzing instructional interactions on electronic message networks. In L. Harasim (ed.) *On-line education: Perspectives on a new environment*. New York: Praeger.

Levin, J.A., Reil, M.M., Rowe, R.D and Boruta, M.J. (1985) Maktuk meets jacuzzi: Computer networks and elementary school writers. 8. In S.W. Freedman (ed.) *The acquisition of written language*. Norwood, NJ: Ablex Publishing Corporation. 160–171.

Levy, S. (1984) *Hackers: Heroes of the computer revolution*. New York: Anchor Press.

Lewin, K. and Grabbe, P. (1945) Conduct, knowledge and the acceptance of new values. *Journal of Social Issues*, 1, 53–64.

Lewis, D.K. (1969) *Convention: A philosophical study*. Cambridge: Harvard University Press.

Lichtman, D. (1979) Survey of educators' attitudes toward computers. *Creative Computing*, January, 48–50.

Light, P.H. and Blaye, A. (1989) Computer-based learning: The social dimension. In H. Foot, M. Morgan and R. Shute (eds) *Children helping children*. Chichester: Wiley.

Light, P.H. and Colbourn, C. (1987) The role of social processes in children's microcomputer use. In W. Kent and R. Lewis (eds) *Computer-assisted learning in the humanities and social sciences*. Oxford: Blackwell.

Light, P. and Glachan, M. (1985) Facilitation of individual problem solving through peer interaction. *Educational Psychology*, 5, 3–4, 217–225.

Light, P.H., Colbourn, C. and Smith, D. (1987) *Peer interaction and logic programming*. London: ESRC Occasional Paper ITE/17/87.

Light, P.H., Foot, T. and Colbourn, C. (1987) Collaborative interactions at the microcomputer keyboard. *Educational Psychology*, 7, 1, 13–21.

Lipinski, J., Nida, R., Shade, D. and Watson, J. (1986) The effects of microcomputers on young children: An examination of free-play choices, sex differences and social interactions. *Journal of Educational Computing Research*, 2, 147–168.

Littleton, K., Light, P.H., Joiner, R., Messer, D. and Barnes, P. (1992) Pairing and gender effects on children's computer-based learning. *European Journal of Psychology of Education*, 8, 311–324.

Lock, A. (1978) *Action, gesture, and symbol*. London: Academic Press.

Luria, A.R. (1973) *The working brain*. Harmondsworth: Penguin.

Luria, A.R. (1976) *Cognitive development. Its cultural and social foundations*. Cambridge, MA: Harvard University Press.

McCormick, R. (1992) Curriculum development and new information technology. *Journal of Information Technology for Teacher Education*, 1, 23–50.

McCreary, E.K. (1990) Three behavioral models for computer-mediated communication. In L. Harasim (ed.) *On-line education: Perspectives on a new environment*. New York: Praeger.

McInerney, W. (1989) Social and organizational effects of educational computing. *Journal of Educational Computing Research*, 5, 487–506.

McMahon, H. (1990) Collaborating with computers. *Journal of Computer-assisted Learning*, 6, 149–167.

McNamee, G. (1979) The social interaction origins of narrative skills. *Quarterly Newsletter of the Laboratory of Comparative Human Cognition*, 1, 63–68.

McShane, J., Dockrell, J. and Wells, A. (1992) Psychology and cognitive science. *The Psychologist*, 5, 252–255.

Maddux, C. (1989) The harmful effects of excessive optimism in educational computing. *Educational Technology*, 29, 23–29.

Malone, T.W. (1981) Towards a theory of intrinsically motivating instruction. *Cognitive Science*, 4, 333–369.

Malone, T.W. and Rockart, J.F. (1991) Computers, networks and the corporation. *Scientific American*, 92–99.

Mandl, H. and Lesgold, A. (1988) *Learning issues for intelligent tutoring systems*. New York: Springer-Verlag.

Mandl, H. and Renkl, A. (1992) A plea for 'more local' theories of cooperative learning. *Learning and Instruction*, 2, 281–285.

Markus, L. (1987) Toward a critical mass theory of interactive media. *Communication Research*, 14, 491–511.

Marsh, M. (1985) The great computer drill and practice put down. *Computer Teacher*, 13, 4–5.

Martin, M. (1989) Children as critics. In M. Styles (ed.) *Collaboration and writing*. Milton Keynes: Open University Press.

Marvin, C. (1983) Telecommunications policy and the pleasure principle. *Telecommunications Policy*, 7, 43–52.

. (1989) An evaluation of CoSy on an Open University course. In R. Mason and A. Kaye (eds) *Mindweave: Communications, computers and distance education*. Oxford: Pergamon Press.

Mason, R. and Kaye, A. (1989) *Mindweave: Communication, computers and distance education*. Oxford: Pergamon Press.

Mead, G.H. (1934) *Mind, self and society*. Chicago: University of Chicago Press.

Mehan, H. (1979) *Learning lessons: Social organization in the classroom*. Cambridge, MA: Harvard University Press.

Meier, S.T. (1985) Computer aversion. *Computers in Human Behaviour*, 1, 171–179.

Messer, D., Jackson, A. and Mohamedali, M. (1987) Influences on computer-based problem solving. *Educational Psychology*, 7, 33–46.

Middleton, D. and Edwards, D. (1990) *Collective remembering*. London: Sage.

Miller, G.A., Galanter, E. and Pribram, K.H. (1960) *Plans and the structure of behavior*. New York: Holt, Rinehart & Winston.

Moore, A. (1993) Siuli's maths lesson: Autonomy or control? In J. Benyon and H. Mackay (eds) *Computers into classrooms*. London: The Falmer Press.

Murphy, J. and Pardeck, J. (1985) The technological world-view and the responsible use of computers in the classroom. *Journal of Education*, 167, 98–108.

Nastasi, B.K. and Clements, D.H. (1991) Research on cooperative learning: Implications for practice. *School Psychology*, 20, 110–131.

Nastasi, B.K. and Clements, D.H. (1992) Social-cognitive behaviours and higher-order thinking in educational computer environments. *Learning and Instruction*, 2, 215–238.

National Writing Project (1989) *Audiences for writing*. Walton: Thomas Nelson.

Newcomb, A. and Brady, J. (1982) Mutuality in boys' friendship relations. *Child Development*, 53, 392–395.

Newell, A. and Simon, H.A. (1972) *Human problem-solving*. Englewood Cliffs, NJ: Prentice-Hall.

Newell, A. and Sproull, R.F. (1982) Computer networks. Prospects for scientists. *Science*, 215, 843–852.

Newman, D. (1989) Opportunities for research on the organizational impact of school computers. *Educational Researcher*, 19, 8–13.

Newman, D. (1990) Cognitive and technical issues in the design of educational computer networking. In L. Harasim (ed.) *On-line education: Perspectives on a new environment*. New York: Praeger.

Newman, D., Griffin, P. and Cole, M. (1989) *The construction zone: Working for cognitive change in school*. Cambridge, MA: Cambridge University Press.

Newsom, J. (1978) Dialogue and development. In A. Lock (ed.) *Action, gesture, and symbol*. London: Academic Press.

Newton, P. and Beck, E. (1993) Computing: An ideal occupation for women? In J. Benyon and H. Mackay (eds) *Computers into classrooms*. London: The Falmer Press.

Niemiec, R. and Walberg, H.J. (1987) Comparative effects of computer-assisted instruction: A synthesis of reviews. *Journal of Educational Computing Research*, 3, 19–37.

Noble, D.D. (1991) *The classroom arsenal: Military research, information technology, and public policy*. London: The Falmer Press.

Norman, D.A. (1986) Cognitive engineering. In D.A. Norman and S. Draper (ed.) *User-centred system design*. Hillsdale, NJ: Lawrence Erlbaum Associates.

Norman, D.A. (1991) Approaches to the study of intelligence. *Artificial Intelligence*, 47, 327–346.

Norman, D.A. and Draper, S. (1986) *User-centred system design*. Hillsdale, NJ: Lawrence Erlbaum Associates.

Noss, R. and Hoyles, C. (1992) Looking back and looking forward. In C. Hoyles and R. Noss (eds) *Learning mathematics and Logo*. Cambridge, MA: MIT Press.

OPCS (Office of Population Censuses and Survey) (1991) *General household survey*, OPCS Monitor SS92/1. London: Office of Population Censuses and Survey.

Olson, C.P. (1988) 'Who computes?' In D. Livingstone (ed.) *Critical pedagogy and cultural power*. South Hadley, MA: Bergin & Garvey.

Olson, D. (1986) Intelligence and literacy: The relationships between intelligence and the techniques of representation and communication. In R. Sternberg (ed.) *Practical intelligence*. Cambridge: Cambridge University Press.

Olson, D.R. and Torrance, N. (1983) Literacy and cognitive development: A conceptual transformation in the early school years. In S. Meadows (ed.), *Issues in childhood cognitive development*. London: Methuen.

Olson, M. and Lucas, H. (1982) The impact of automation on the organization: Some implications for research and practice. *Communications of the ACM*, 25, 838–847

Owen, M. (1992) A teacher-centred model of development in the educational use of computers. *Journal of Information Technology for Teacher Education*. 1, 127–137.

Palincsar, A.S. and Brown, A.L. (1984) Reciprocal teaching of comprehension-fostering and comprehension-monitoring activities. *Cognition and Instruction*, 1, 117–175.

Palumbo, D.B. (1990) Programming language/problem solving research: A review of relevant issues. *Review of Educational Research*, 60, 65–89.

Papert, S. (1980) *Mindstorms*. Brighton: Harvester Press.

Papert, S. (1987) Computer criticism vs. technocratic thinking. *Educational Researcher*, 17, 22–30.

Pea, R.D. (1988) Putting knowledge to use. In R.S. Nickerson and P.P. Zodhiates (eds) *Technology in education: Looking towards 2000*. Hillsdale, NJ: Lawrence Erlbaum Associates.

Pea, R.D. (1989) Socializing the knowledge transfer problem. *International Journal of Education Research*, 11, 639–663.

Pea, R.D. and Kurland, D. (1987) On the cognitive effects of learning computer programming. In R. Pea and K. Sheingold (eds) *Mirrors of the mind: Patterns of experience in educational computing*. Norwood, NJ: Ablex.

Pea, R., Kurland, D. and Hawkins, J. (1987) Logo and the development of thinking skills. In R. Pea and K. Sheingold (eds) *Mirrors of the mind: Patterns of experience in educational computing*. Norwood, NJ: Ablex.

Pepitone, E.A. (1980) *Children in cooperation and competition*. Lexington, MA: Lexington Books.

Perkins, D.N. (1985) The fingertip effect: How information processing technology shapes thinking. *Educational Researcher*, 14, 11–16.

Perkins, D.N. and Salomon, G. (1987) Transfer and teaching thinking. In D. Perkins, J. Lockhead and J. Bishop (eds) *Thinking: The second international conference*. Hillsdale, NJ: Lawrence Erlbaum Associates.

Perlmutter, M., Behrend, S.D., Kuo, F. and Muller, A. (1989) Social influences on children's problem solving. *Developmental Psychology*, 25, 744–754.

Perner, J. (1991) *Understanding the representational mind.* Cambridge, MA: MIT Press.

Perret-Clermont, A.N. and Schubaeur-Leoni, M. (1981) Conflict and cooperation as opportunities for learning. In W. Robinson (ed.) *Communication in development.* London: Academic Press

Philips, G.M. and Santoro, G. (1989) Teaching group discussion via computer-mediated communication. *Communication Education,* 38, 151–161.

Piaget, J. (1926) *The language and thought of the child.* New York: Harcourt Brace Jovanovich.

Piaget, J. (1928) *Judgement and reasoning in the child.* London: Routledge & Kegan Paul.

Piaget, J. (1953) *The origins of intelligence.* London: Routledge & Kegan Paul.

Piaget, J. (1970) Piaget's theory. In P. Mussen (ed.) *Carmichael's manual of child psychology.* New York: Wiley.

Plomp, T. and Pelgrum, W.J. (1991) Introduction of computers in education: State of the art in eight countries. *Computers and Education,* 17, 249–258.

Plomp, T., Pelgrum, W.J. and Steerneman, A.H.M. (1990) Influence of computer use on schools' curriculum: Limited integration. *Computers and Education,* 14, 159–171.

Plowden Report (1967) *Children and their primary schools.* London: Central Advisory Council for Education.

POST (Parliamentary Office of Science and Technology) (1991) *Technologies for teacher. The use of technologies for teacher in learning in primary and secondary schools.* London: POST.

Radzisewska, B. and Rogoff, B. (1991) Children's guided participation in planning imaginary errands with skilled adult or peer partners. *Developmental Psychology,* 27, 381–389.

Ramsden, P., Beswick, D. and Bowden, J. (1987) Learning processes and learning skills. In J. Richardson, M. Eysenck and D. Piper (eds) *Student learning: Research in education and cognitive psychology.* Milton Keynes: SRHE/Open University Press.

Resnick, L.B. (1987) Learning in school and out. *Educational Researcher,* 16, 13–20.

Resnick, L.B. (1991) Shared cognition: Thinking as social practice. In L. Resnick, J. Levine and S. Teasley (eds) *Perspectives on socially shared cognition.* Washington, DC: American Psychological Association.

Resnick, L.B. and Johnson, A. (1988) Intelligent machines for intelligent people: Cognitive theory and the future of computer-assisted learning. In R.S. Nickerson and P.P. Zodhiates (eds) *Technology in education: Looking towards 2000.* Hillsdale, NJ: Lawrence Erlbaum Associates.

Resnick, L.B., Levine J.M. and Teasley, S.D. (1991) *Perspectives on socially shared cognition.* Washington, DC: American Psychological Association.

Rhodes, V. and Cox, M. (1990a) Current practice and policies for using computers in primary schools: Implications for training. Lancaster University: Inter program paper, InTER/15/90.

Rhodes, V. and Cox, M. (1990b) *Time for training.* London: Kings College.

Rice, R.E. (1992) Contexts of research on organizational computer-mediated communication. In M. Lea (ed.) *Contexts of computer-mediated communication.* Hemel Hempstead: Harvester-Wheatsheaf.

Rice, R.E., Grant, A.E., Schmitz, J. and Torobin, J. (1990) Individual and network influences on the adoption and perceived outcomes of electronic messaging. *Social Networks,* 12, 27–55.

Ridgeway, J., Benzie, D., Burkhardt, H., Coupland, J., Field, G., Fraser, R. and Philips, R. (1984) Investigating CAL. *Computer Education,* 8, 85–92.

Riel, M. (1985) The computer chronicles newswire: A functional learning environment for acquiring literacy skills. *Journal of Educational Ccomputing Research,* 13, 317–337.

Riel, M. (1990) A model for integrating computer networking with classroom learning. *Computers in Education,* 14, 1021–1026.

Riel, M. and Levin, J. (1990) Building electronic communities: Success and failure in computer networking. *Instructional Science*, 19, 145–169.

Riesbeck, C.K. and Schank, R.C. (1989) *Inside case-based reasoning*. Hillsdale, NJ: Lawrence Erlbaum Associates.

Riesbeck, C.K. and Schank, R.C. (1991) From training to teaching: Techniques for case-based ITS. In H. Burns, J. Parlett and C. Redfield (eds) *Intelligent tutoring systems*. Hillsdale, NJ: Lawrence Erlbaum Associates.

Robins, K. and Webster, F. (1985) Intellectual self-mutilation. *Universities Quarterly*, 39, 97–104.

Robins, K. and Webster, F. (1987) Dangers of information technology as responsibilities of education. In R. Finnegan, G. Salomon and K. Thompson (eds) *Information technology: Social issues*. London: Hodder & Stoughton.

Rogoff, B. (1990) *Apprenticeship in thinking: Cognitive development in social context*. New York: Oxford University Press.

Rogoff, B. (1991) Social interaction as apprenticeship in thinking: Guided participation in spatial planning. In L. Resnick, J. Levine and S. Teasley (eds) *Perspectives on socially shared cognition*. Washington, DC: American Psychological Association.

Rogoff, B. and Gardner, W. (1984) Adult guidance of cognitive development. In B. Rogoff and J. Lave (eds) *Everyday cognition*. San Francisco: Jossey-Bass.

Rogoff, B. and Lave, J. (1984) *Everyday cognition: Its development in social context*. Cambridge, MA: Harvard University Press.

Rommetveit, R. (1979a) Deep structure of sentences versus message structure. In R. Blakar and R.M. Blakar (eds) *Studies of language, thought and verbal communication*. New York: Academic Press.

Rommetveit, R. (1979b) On the architecture of intersubjectivity. In R. Blakar and R.M. Blakar (eds) *Studies of language, thought and verbal communication*. New York: Academic Press.

Rommetveit, R. (1984) Language acquisition as increasing linguistic structuring of experience and symbolic behavior control. In J.V. Wertsch (ed.) *Culture, communication and cognition: Vygotskyian perspectives*. Cambridge: Cambridge University Press.

Roschelle, J. (1992) Learning by collaborating: Convergent conceptual change. *Journal of the Learning Sciences*, 2, 235–276.

Rose, S.A. and Blank, M. (1974) The potency of context in children's cognition. An illustration through conservation. *Child Development*, 45, 499–502.

Roszak, T. (1986) *The cult of information*. New York: Pantheon.

Ruble, D. (1988) Conflicting goals in self-evaluation information seeking: Developmental and ability level analysis. *Child Development*, 59, 97–106.

Ruopp, R.R. (in press) *Labnet: Towards a community of practice*. Hillsdale, NJ: Lawrence Erlbaum Associates.

Ryan, A.W. (1991) Meta-analysis of achievement effects of microcomputer applications in elementary school. *Educational Administration Quarterly*, 27, 161–184.

Rysavy, S. and Sales, G.C. (1989) Cooperative learning in computer-based instruction. *Educational Technology Research and Development*, 39, 70–79.

Saljo, R. (1987) The educational construction of learning. In J. Richardson, M. Eysenck and D. Piper (eds) *Student learning: Research in education and cognitive psychology*. Milton Keynes: SRHE/Open University Press.

Salomon, G. (1988a) AI in reverse: Computer tools that turn cognitive. *Journal of Educational Computing Research*, 4, 123–139.

Salomon, G. (1988b) From communication to cognition. The internalization of computer tools. Paper presented at American Educational Research Association, New Orleans.

Salomon, G. (1989) Computers in the curriculum. In M. Eraut (ed.) *The international encyclopedia of educational technology*. Oxford: Pergamon Press.

Salomon, G. (1993) On the nature of pedagogic computer tools: The case of the writing partner. In S. Lajoie and S. Derry (eds) *Computers as cognitive tools*. Hillsdale, NJ: Lawrence Erlbaum Associates.

Salomon, G., Perkins, D.N., and Globerson, T. (1991) Partners in cognition: Extending human intelligence with intelligent technologies. *Educational Researcher*, 20, 2–9.

Saxe, G. (1991) *Culture and cognitive development*. Hillsdale, NJ: Lawrence Erlbaum Associates.

Schaffer, H.R. (1992) Joint involvement episodes as context for development. In H. McGurk (ed.) *Childhood social development: Contemporary perspectives*. Hove: Lawrence Erlbaum Associates.

Schank, R.C. (1982) *Dynamic memory: A theory of learning in computers and people*. New York: Cambridge University Press.

Scheglott, E.A. (1991) Conversational analysis and socially shared cognition. In L. Resnick, J. Levine and S. Teasley (eds) *Perspectives on socially shared cognition*. Washington, DC: American Psychological Association.

Schlechter, T.M. (1986) *An examination of the research evidence for computer-based instruction in military training*. Army Research Institute, Government Document No. AD-A174 817.

Schrage, M. (1990) *Shared minds*. New York: Random House.

Schunk, D. (1986) Verbalisation and children's self-regulated learning. *Contemporary Educational Psychology*, 11, 347–369.

Scott, T., Cole, M. and Engel, M. (1992) Computers and education: A cultural constructivist perspective. *Review of Research in Education*, 18, 191–251.

Scribner, S. (1984) Studying working intelligence. In B. Rogoff and J. Lave (eds) *Everyday cognition*. Cambridge, MA: Harvard University Press.

Scribner, S. (1990) Reflections on a model. *Quarterly Newsletter of the Laboratory of Comparative Human Cognition*, 12, 90–94.

Scribner, S. and Cole, M. (1981) *The psychology of literacy*. Cambridge, MA: Harvard University Press.

Self, J. (1985) A perspective on intelligent computer-assisted learning. *Journal of Computer-assisted Learning*, 1, 159–166.

Self, J. (1988) *Artificial intelligence and human learning*. London: Chapman & Hall.

Sheingold, K., Hawkins, J. and Char, C. (1984) 'I'm the thinkist, you're the typist': The interaction of technology and the social life of classrooms. *Journal of Social Issues*, 40, 3, 49–61.

Sheingold, K., Kane, A. and Endreweit, A. (1983) Microcomputer use in schools: Developing a research agenda. *Harvard Educational Review*, 53, 412–432.

Shooter, M., Lovering, P. and Bellamy, S. (1993) Micros in action: Three case studies. In J. Benyon and H. Mackay (eds) *Computers into classrooms*. London: The Falmer Press.

Shotton, M. (1989) *Computer addiction: A study of computer dependency*. London: Taylor & Francis.

Shweder, R.A. (1990) Cultural psychology – what is it? In J. Stigler, R. Shweder and G. Herdt (eds) *Cultural psychology: Essays on comparative human development*. Cambridge: Cambridge University Press.

Shweder, R.A. and Sullivan, W.M. (1993) Cultural psychology: Who needs it? *Annual Review of Psychology*, 44, 497–523.

Sann, G. and Macleod, H. (1986) Computers and children of primary school age: Issues and questions. *British Journal of Educational Technology*, 17, 2, 133–144.

Weber, T. (1979) Classmates as workmates: Informal peer activity in the elementary school. *Anthropology and Education Quarterly*, 10, 207–235.

Segel, M. (1991a) *Knowing children: Experiments in conversation and cognition*. Hove: Lawrence Erlbaum Associates.

Segel, M. (1991b) A clash of conversational worlds: Interpreting cognitive development through communication. In L. Resnick, J. Levine and S. Teasley (eds) *Perspectives on socially shared cognition*. Washington, DC: American Psychological Association.

Silver, M. and Sabini, J. (1981) Procrastinating. *Journal for the Theory of Social Behaviour*, 11, 207–221.

Simon, H.A. (1983) Why should machines learn? In R. Michalski (ed.) *Machine learning: An artificial intelligence approach*. Palo Alto, CA: Tioga.

Simon, T. (1987) Claims for LOGO – what should we believe and why? In J. Rutkowska and C. Crook (eds) *Computers, cognition and development*. Chichester: Wiley.

Simons, G. (1981) *Women in computing*. Manchester: National Computing Centre.

Simons, G. (1985) *Silicon shock: The menace of the computer invasion*. Oxford: Basil Blackwell.

Sinclair, J. McH. and Coulthard, R.M. (1975) *Towards an analysis of discourse: The English used by teachers and pupils*. London: Oxford University Press.

Skinner, B.F. (1984) The shame of American education. *American Psychologist*, 39, 947–954.

Slavin, R. (1986) Cooperative learning; Engineering social psychology in the classroom. In R. Feldman (ed.) *The social psychology of education*. Cambridge: Cambridge University Press.

Slavin, R.E. (1987) Developmental and motivational perspectives on cooperative learning A reconciliation. *Child Development*, 58, 1161–1167.

Sleeman, D. (1987) Cognitive science, AI and developmental psychology. Are there links' Could there be links? In J. Rutkowska and C. Crook (eds) *Computers, cognition and development*. Chichester: Wiley.

Sleeman, D. and Brown, J. (1982) *Intelligent tutoring systems*. New York: Academic Press

Sloan, D. (1984) On raising critical questions about computers in education. *Teacher College Record*, 85, 4, 539–548.

Smagorinsky, P. and Fly, P.K. (1993) The social environment of the classroom: A Vygotskian perspective on small group process. *Communication Education*, 42, 159–171.

Smith, D. (1989) Microcomputers in schools. In M. Eraut (ed.) *The international encyclopedia of educational technology*. Oxford: Pergamon Press.

Smith, F. (1981) Demonstrations, engagement and sensitivity. *Language Arts*, 58, 103–11.

Smith, L. (1989) Changing perspectives in developmental psychology. In C. Desforges (ed Early childhood education*. Edinburgh: Scottish Academic Press.

Somerville, D. (1989) Listening to children's writing. In M. Styles (ed.) *Collaboration ar writing*. Milton Keynes: Open University Press.

Speier, M. (1976) The child as conversationalist: Some cultural contact features of conve sational interactions between adults and children. In M. Hammersley and P. Woods (ed The process of schooling: A sociological reader*. London: Routledge & Kegan Paul.

Sperber, D. and Wilson, D. (1986) *Relevance: Communication and cognition*. Cambridg MA: Harvard University Press.

Sproull, L. and Keisler, S. (1986) Reducing social context cues: Electronic mail in organi ational communication. *Management Science*, 32, 1492–1512.

Sterling, L.S., Beer, R.D. and Chiel, H.J. (1991) Beyond the symbolic paradigm. In P. Fla and R. Meersman (eds) *Future directions in artificial intelligence*. Amsterdam: Elsev Science Publications.

Stevenson, R.S. (1986) An instrument for the measurement of computer attitudes. Unpu lished manuscript, Durham University Psychology Department.

Stewart, J.A. (1989?) How to manage educational computing initiatives – lessons from first five years of project Athena at MIT. In E. Barrett (ed.) *The society of text*. Cambrid; MA: MIT Press.

Stone, A. (1985) Vygotsky's developmental model and the concept of proleptic instructio Some implications for theory and research in the field of learning disabilities. *Resear Communications in Psychology, Psychiatry and Behavior*, 10, 129–152.

Stone, C.A. and Wertsch, J.V. (1984) A social interactional analysis of learning disabilities remediation. *Journal of Learning Disabilities*, 17, 194–199.

Strassman, P.A. (1985) *Information payoff: The transformation of work in the electronic age*. New York: Free Press.

Suchman, L.A. (1987) *Plans and situated actions*. Cambridge: Cambridge University Press.

Suchman, L.A. (1993) Response to Vera and Simon's situated action: A symbolic interpretation. *Cognitive Science*, 17, 71–75.

Suppes, P. (1966) The uses of computers in education. *Scientific American*, 215, 207–220.

Teasley, S.D. and Roschelle, J. (1993) Constructing a joint problem space: The computer as a tool for sharing knowledge. In S. Lajoie and S. Derry (eds) *Computers as cognitive tools*. Hillsdale, NJ: Lawrence Erlbaum Associates.

Tharp, R.G. and Gallimore, R. (1988) *Rousing minds to life*. New York: Cambridge University Press.

The Times (1984) A teacher on every desktop, 10 July, 10.

Tomasello, M., Kruger, A.C. and Ratner, H.H. (1993) Cultural learning. *Brain and Behavioral Sciences*, 16, 495–552.

Topping, K. (1992) Cooperative learning and peer tutoring: An overview. *The Psychologist*, 5, 151–161.

Tough, J. (1977) *The development of meaning*. London: Allen & Unwin

Trevarthan, C. (1987) Sharing makes sense: Intersubjectivity and the making of an infant's meaning. In R. Steele and T. Treadgold (eds) *Language topics: Essays in honour of Michael Halliday*. Amsterdam: John Benjamins.

Trevarthan, C. (1988) Universal cooperative motives: How infants begin to know the language and culture of their parents. In G. Jahoda and M. Lewis (eds) *Acquiring culture: Cross-cultural studies in child development*. Beckenham, Kent: Croom Helm.

Trivers, R. (1983) The evolution of cooperation. In D.L. Bridgeman (ed.) *The nature of prosocial development*. New York: Academic Press.

Trowbridge, D. (1987) An investigation of groups working at the computer. In D. Berger and K. Pezdek (eds), *Applications of cognitive psychology*. Hove: Lawrence Erlbaum Associates.

Turkle, S. (1984) *The second self*. New York: Simon & Schuster.

Turkle, S. and Papert, S. (1991) Epistemological pluralism and the revaluation of the concrete. In I. Harel and S. Papert (eds) *Constructionism*. Norwood, NJ: Ablex.

Turnbull, G. and Beavers, K. (1989) *100 schools network project*. Glasgow: Scottish Council for Educational Technology.

Turner, J. (1988) Email technology has boomed, but manners of its users fall short of perfection. *Chronicle of Higher Education*, 34, 1.

Underwood, G., McCaffrey, M. and Underwood, J. (1990) Gender differences in a cooperative computer based language task. *Educational Research*, 32, 16–21.

Underwood. J.D.M. and Underwood, G. (1990) *Computers and learning*. Oxford: Blackwell.

Valsiner, J. and Winegar, L.T. (1992) Introduction: A cultural-historical context for social 'context'. In L. Winegar and J. Valsiner (eds) *Children's development within social context. Volume 1: Metatheory and theory*. Hillsdale, NJ: Lawrence Erlbaum Associates.

Vera, A.H. and Simon, H.A. (1993) Situated action: A symbolic interpretation. *Cognitive Science*, 17, 7–48.

Vogel, D. and Nunamaker, J. (1990) Design and assessment of a group decision support system. In J. Galegher, R. Kraut and C. Egide (eds) *Intellectual teamwork*. Hillsdale, NJ: Lawrence Erlbaum Associates.

Vygotsky, L.S. (1978) *Mind in society: The development of higher psychological processes*. Cambridge, MA: Harvard University Press. (Original material published in 1930, 1933 and 1935.)

Vygotsky, L.S. (1979) Consciousness as a problem in the psychology of behavior. *Soviet Psychology*, 17, 3–35.

Wagner, D. (1974) The development of short-term and incidental memory. *Child Development*, 45, 389–396.

Walkerdine, V. (1984) Developmental psychology and the child-centred pedagogy: The insertion of Piaget into early education. In J. Henriques, W. Hollway, C. Urwin, C. Venn and V. Walkerdine (eds) *Changing the subject*. London: Methuen.

Watson, J. (1990) Cooperative learning and computers: One way to address student differences. *The Computing Teacher*, 18, 9–15.

Webb, N. (1984) Microcomputer learning in small groups: Cognitive requirements and group processes. *Journal of Educational Psychology*, 76, 1076–1088.

Webb, N., Ender, P. and Lewis, S. (1986) Problem solving strategies and group processes in small groups learning computer programming. *American Educational Research Journal*, 23, 247–261.

Weizenbaum, J. (1976) *Computer power and human reason*. San Francisco: Freeman.

Wellington, J. (1987) Computer study. *The Times Educational Supplement*, 13 March, 46.

Wellington, J. (1990) The impact of IT on the school curriculum: Downwards, sideways, backwards and forwards. *Journal of Curriculum Studies*, 22, 55–76.

Wertsch, J.V. (1991a) A sociocultural approach to socially shared cognition. In L. Resnick, J. Levine and S. Teasley (eds) *Perspectives on socially shared cognition*. Washington, DC: American Psychological Association.

Wertsch, J.V. (1991b) A sociocultural approach to mental action. In M. Carretero, M. Pope, R. Simons, and J. Pozo (eds) *Learning and instruction: European research in international context*, Vol. 3. Oxford: Pergamon Press.

Wertsch, J.V. (1991c) *Voices of the mind*. Cambridge, MA: Harvard University Press.

Wertsch, J.V. and Bivens, J.A. (1992) The social origins of individual mental functioning: Alternatives and perspectives. *Quarterly Newsletter of the Laboratory of Comparative Human Cognition*, 14, 35–44.

Wertsch, J.V. and Kanner, B.G. (1992) A sociocultural approach to intellectual development. In R. Sternberg and C. Berg (eds) *Intellectual development*. Cambridge: Cambridge University Press.

Wertsch, J.V., McNamee, G.D., McLane, J.G. and Budwig, N.A. (1980) The adult–child dyad as a problem solving system. *Child Development*, 51, 1215–1221.

Wertsch, J.V., Minick, N. and Arns, F.J. (1984) The creation of context in joint problem solving action: A cross-cultural study. In J. Lave and B. Rogoff (eds) *Everyday cognition*. Cambridge, MA: Harvard University Press

Wild, P. (1991) The effectiveness of inset in CAL and IT: An evaluation of the work of an advisory teacher. *Computers and Education*, 16, 289–300.

Wilensky, U. (1991) Abstract meditations on the concrete and concrete implications for mathematics education. In I. Harel and S. Papert (eds) *Constructionism*. Norwood, NJ: Ablex.

Winograd, T. and Flores, F. (1986) *Understanding computers and cognition*. Norwood, NJ: Ablex.

Winston, B. (1986) *Misunderstanding media*. London: Routledge & Kegan Paul.

Wishart, E. (1988) Using a TTNS electronic mailbox in a junior class: A case study. *Reading*, 22, 144–151.

Wood, D. (1988) *How children think and learn*. Oxford: Basil Blackwell.

Wood, D. (1989) Social interaction as tutoring. In M. Bornstein and J. Bruner (eds) *Interaction in development*. Hillsdale, NJ: Lawrence Erlbaum Associates.

Wood, D., Bruner, J.S. and Ross, G. (1976) The role of tutoring in problem solving. *Journal of Child Psychology and Child Psychiatry*, 17, 89–100.

Wood, D., Wood, H.A. and Middleton, D.J. (1978) An experimental evaluation of fou face-to-face teaching strategies. *International Journal of Behavioral Development.* 1, 131–147.

Woodrow, J.E.J. (1987) Educators' attitudes and predispositions toward computers. *Journal of Computers in Mathematics and Science Teaching*, 6, 27–37.

Woodruff, E., Bereiter, C. and Scardamalia, M. (1982) On the road to computer-assisted composition. *Journal of Educational Technology Systems*, 10, 133–148.

Yates, J. (1989) *Control through communication: The rise of system in American management.* Baltimore: Johns Hopkins University Press.

Yazdani, M. (1987) Artificial intelligence, powerful ideas and children's learning. In J. Rutkowska and C. Crook (eds) *Computers, cognition and development.* Chichester: Wiley.

Name index

Subject index